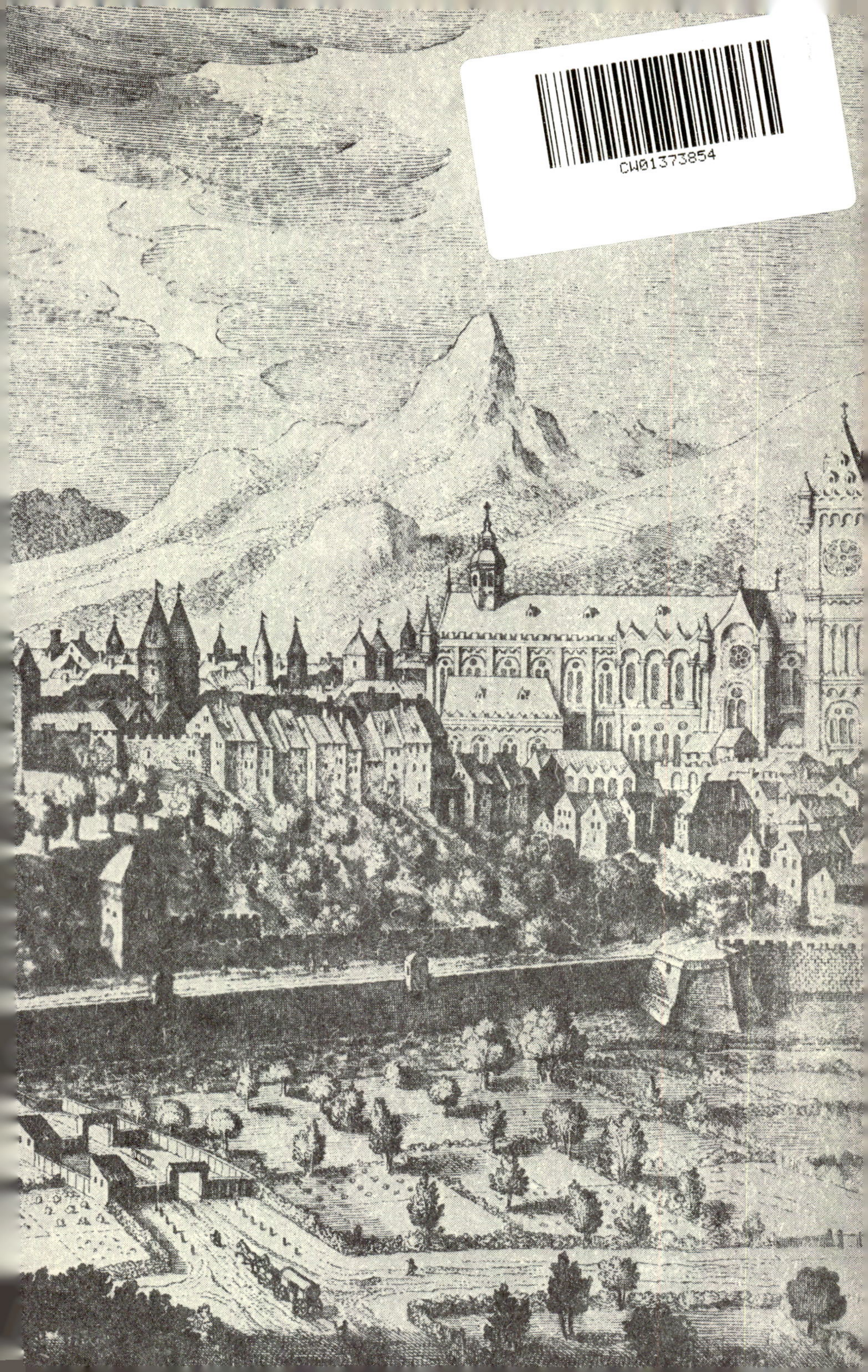

A
GENEVA
SERIES
COMMENTARY

JAMES

A COMMENTARY ON
JAMES

Robert Johnstone, LL.B., D.D.

THE BANNER OF TRUTH TRUST

THE BANNER OF TRUTH TRUST
3 *Murrayfield Road, Edinburgh* EH12 6EL
PO Box 652, *Carlisle, Pennsylvania* 17013, USA

*

First published 1871
*First Banner of Truth Trust edition
reprinted by photo litho* 1977
ISBN 0 85151 257 7

*

*Printed litho in Great Britain
by W & J Mackay Ltd, Chatham
from previous copy*

PREFACE TO THE SECOND EDITION.

These lectures were, in substance, delivered from the pulpit, in the ordinary course of Sabbath ministration. In transcription afterwards such changes were made, by omission, condensation, or expansion, as seemed needful in view of publication. In the study of the Epistle all those expositions of it, both critical and popular, were consulted, from which the author had any reason to believe that help could be obtained.

The basis of the discourses is a careful exegesis. At the same time the author's aim has been not to write a mere commentary on words, but to bring the apostle, with his human sympathies and his divine inspiration, clearly before the reader, as a friendly counsellor, whose statements and appeals have interest and weight for us as well as for the men of his own time. To the exposition of a few passages in the Epistle, which are open to different interpretations, a brief discussion of the construction of the Greek is appended in a footnote.

The first edition contained a translation of the Epistle, embodying such changes on the Authorized Version, with respect to text and rendering, as modern scholarship seemed to require,—accompanied by a considerable body of notes explaining the grounds of the alterations. Since then the Revised Version of the Bible has been issued, and consequently there is no need for reprinting the translation or notes. The omission of these has made it possible to give in the present edition a page less crowded than that of the first, and thus more pleasant to read. The whole work has been subjected to a thorough revision, with the aid of the principal expositions of the Epistle which have been issued since the publication of the first edition. Dean Scott's notes in the *Speaker's Commentary* have been found of especial service.

The question presented itself whether it would not be well, in printing at the beginning of each lecture the portion of the Epistle expounded, to adopt the rendering of the Revised Version. After consideration the author decided not to do this. Admirable from various points of view as the Revision is, still the Authorized Version remains beyond doubt the Bible of the English-speaking world, and there is no convincing evidence that it is likely soon to lose this position. It seems reasonable, therefore, to think that a work like the present will be more useful if the popular version be kept as the basis, and the remarks explanatory of its language, which were originally made in the lectures, be retained.

19 HOPE TERRACE, EDINBURGH,
June 26, 1888.

CONTENTS.

		PAGE
INTRODUCTION,		1
NOTE ON 'THE BRETHREN OF THE LORD,'		12
LECT. I. Joy in Trials,	Chap. i. 1–4,	23
II. Wisdom through Prayer,	,, i. 5–8,	35
III. Rich Poor and Poor Rich,	,, i. 9–12,	47
IV. Genesis of Sin,	,, i. 13–15,	61
V. Good Gifts from God,	,, i. 16, 17,	72
VI. Regeneration,	,, i. 18,	82
VII. Receiving the Ingrafted Word,	,, i. 19–21,	96
VIII. The Spiritual Mirror,	,, i. 22–25,	109
IX. True Religious Service,	,, i. 26, 27,	125
X. Respect of Persons,	,, ii. 1–7,	140
XI. Unity of God's Law,	,, ii. 8–11,	157
XII. Judgement by the Law of Liberty,	,, ii. 12, 13,	168
XIII. Faith without Works,	,, ii. 14–19,	179
XIV. Justifying Faith a Working Faith,	,, ii. 20–26,	193
XV. Responsibility of Teachers,	,, iii. 1, 2,	209
XVI. Power of the Tongue,	,, iii. 3–6,	228
XVII. The Tongue Untameable and Inconsistent,	,, iii. 7–12,	245
XVIII. Earthly Wisdom,	,, iii. 13–16,	257
XIX. Heavenly Wisdom,	,, iii. 17, 18,	268
XX. Origin of Strifes,	,, iv. 1–3,	284
XXI. Worldliness Enmity to God,	,, iv. 4–6,	296
XXII. Submission to God,	,, iv. 7–10,	313

				PAGE
Lect. XXIII.	Evil Speaking and Judging,	Chap.	iv. 11, 12,	326
XXIV.	Vain Confidence regarding the Future,	,,	iv. 13-17,	337
XXV.	Woes of the Wicked Rich,	,,	v. 1-6,	346
XXVI.	Patience through the Blessed Hope,	,,	v. 7, 8,	364
XXVII.	Murmuring against Brethren,	,,	v. 9-11,	376
XXVIII.	Swearing,	,,	v. 12,	389
XXIX.	Prayer and Praise,	,,	v. 13-15,	402
XXX.	Confession and Prayer,	,,	v. 16-18,	417
XXXI.	Error and Conversion,	,,	v. 19, 20,	432

LECTURES
ON THE
EPISTLE OF JAMES.

INTRODUCTION.

THE Epistle of James has from very early times been grouped with the two of Peter, the three of John, and that of Jude, under the name of 'Catholic, or General, Epistles.' This designation has been variously understood; but the ordinary view of the meaning, that these letters are thus named because they are addressed not to particular persons or churches, but to Christians in general, or at least to classes of readers spread over a wide area, is the most natural and satisfactory. The second and third Epistles of John, indeed, are addressed to individuals; but it is easy to understand how these short letters were classed along with the first of the same writer, which is so much longer and more important.

The writer of the letter announces his name at the outset as 'James.' The fact that to the name he appends only the very general description, 'a servant of God and of the Lord Jesus Christ,' shows him to have been one whose prominence in the church was such that his name alone at the head of a document of this kind would, at least for the Jewish Christians to whom he writes, suffice to distinguish him from all others.

The contents of the letter prove him to have had so intimate an acquaintance with the condition of the congregations of Jewish Christians, and presuppose such admitted authority to give them advices and injunctions, that we can scarcely but consider him to have been in all likelihood one who stood in close official relations to them. The *data* seem thus distinctly to indicate that he was either an apostle or, at least, a man almost of apostolic note and influence, who in some way was specially connected with the churches of the circumcision. Now, as we are told in Acts (xii. 2), the Apostle James, the son of Zebedee and brother of John, suffered martyrdom in the year 43 or 44 of our era, which is earlier than the probable date of the Epistle. But we find a James spoken of in Acts and in Paul's writings as for many years the most prominent minister of the church at Jerusalem, and a man of great weight among the Christians generally, particularly the Jewish Christians (Acts xii. 17, xv. 13 foll., xxi. 18; Gal. ii. 9, 12). Everything accordingly points to him as the author of the Epistle, and the all but universal opinion in the church has been that it was written by him.

Whether this James was one of the apostles has been much debated. In the lists of the Twelve there certainly occurs the name of another James besides the son of Zebedee, described always as 'James the son of Alphæus.' But James, the influential minister at Jerusalem and the probable writer of the Epistle, is spoken of in Gal. i. 19 (for to him beyond all reasonable doubt, when we compare that verse with the 9th and 12th verses of the next chapter, the reference is) as 'the Lord's brother,' and is thus identified with the James who in the Gospels (Matt. xiii. 55; Mark vi. 3) is named among the 'brethren' of Jesus. Now is this description compatible with the other, 'the son of Alphæus,' so that both may be held to refer to the same man? An opinion very prevalent in the church has been that the term 'brother' is used in this case loosely for 'a near relative,' and that those described as 'brethren' and 'sisters' of the Lord were the children of Alphæus, and, through father or mother or both, *cousins* of the Saviour. Of late years, however, the whole subject has been very carefully investigated afresh, and the more that it has been studied, the more has doubt grown regarding the soundness of this view. The most probable conclusion from all the *data* seems to be that the 'brethren' and 'sisters' of the Lord were either children of Joseph and Mary, or of Joseph by a former wife.[1] In this case James, 'the brother of the Lord' and the author of the Epistle, must be distinguished from James the son of Alphæus, and was not one of the Twelve Apostles. Paul's words in Gal. i. 18, 19, 'I went up to Jerusalem to see Peter, and abode with him fifteen days; but other of the apostles saw I none, save James the Lord's brother,' seem to include this James among the apostles;[2] and other passages (1 Cor. ix. 5, xv. 7) appear to imply the same. But this does not render it necessary to suppose that he was of the original Twelve. There is reason to think that, besides Paul, who by express appointment of the divine Head of the church was added to the Twelve, some others of the foremost ministers were either by similar though unrecorded

---

[1] For a full discussion of the question, see the Supplementary Note at the close of this Introduction.

[2] Not so decidedly, however, as might at first sight appear; for not unfrequently, both in the New Testament and in classical Greek, εἰ μή loses almost entirely its *exceptive* force for that of a simple *adversative* particle, 'approaching nearly to ἀλλά' (Lightfoot on Gal. i. 7). See Matt. xii. 4; Luke iv. 26, 27; Rev. xxi. 27. The ἕτερον in the first clause favours the exceptive sense; yet the contrast in it may be solely with Peter (ver. 18), and not with James at all. Still, undoubtedly, the simplest and most likely view of the meaning is that James is here called an apostle.

definite appointment recognised as apostles, or at least, according to a somewhat loose use of the name, popularly called apostles. Such was the case with Barnabas certainly (see Acts xiv. 4, 14). The position of James may have been, and probably was, similar. But on any view, whether he was one with 'the son of Alphæus,' and therefore of the Twelve, or an added apostle, or simply one of the foremost men of the primitive church, next to the apostles, it is plain from every reference made to him that he was deemed by all a man of the very highest Christian wisdom, richly endued with the Holy Ghost, and that an official writing from him to the churches would be received as having plenary inspiration and authority.

Of the life of this apostle we know but little. John mentions in his Gospel (vii. 5) that the 'brethren of the Lord' did not believe on Him,—the statement referring to a period less than a year before the crucifixion. No exceptions are stated or suggested, and therefore it is probable that James is included. After the resurrection a special appearance of the Lord was granted to him (1 Cor. xv. 7), and it is not unlikely that from that we are to date his clear apprehension of the Messiahship and divinity of the Brother whom for many years he had lived with and seen so closely, and yet known so little. Regarding the time between the ascension and Pentecost, it is mentioned that the eleven apostles 'continued with one accord in prayer and supplication, with the women, and Mary the mother of Jesus, *and with His brethren*' (Acts i. 14). The next mention of him is in connection with Paul's first visit to Jerusalem after his conversion (Gal. i. 18, 19), about ten years after the ascension of the Lord. The way in which he is spoken of here implies that by this time he was in high repute among the Christians at Jerusalem; and all references to him afterwards clearly indicate that, of all the permanent pastors in the Holy City, he was beyond question the most prominent and influential. Peter, after his deliverance from Herod's prison, said to the friends assembled in the house of Mary the mother of John Mark, 'Go, show these things unto James, and to the brethren' (Acts xii. 17). At the council of the apostles and elders at Jerusalem, to consider the relation of Gentile converts to the Jewish law, it was James who proposed the resolution which was accepted by all,—a resolution well fitted to bring peace to the troubled churches (Acts xv. 13 foll.). And speaking of his visit to Jerusalem at that time, Paul says: 'When James, Cephas, and John, who seemed to be pillars, perceived the grace that was given unto me, they gave to me and Barnabas the right hand of fellowship, that we should go unto the heathen, and they unto the circumcision' (Gal. ii. 9). The last mention we have of him in Scripture is in connection with that visit of Paul to Jerusalem which brought about his imprisonment. James presided at the reception by the brethren of Paul's heart-gladdening report of the progress of the gospel among the Gentiles (Acts xxi. 18, 19). A tradition preserved by the ecclesiastical historian Hegesippus, a Jewish Christian of Palestine, who wrote probably not more than a century after the death of James, tells us that, from his eminent purity of character, and the rigour of his adherence to the Jewish ceremonial system, he was generally known as James the Just, or Righteous,—and this among those Jews who did not believe in the Messiahship of Jesus, as well as among the Christians. These are probably facts, though round them in the statements of Hegesippus we find a considerable accretion of manifest untruth, from the fertile fancies of the descendants of those who had known and loved the great pastor of the church of Jerusalem. Of the death of the apostle we have accounts both by Josephus and Hegesippus; but these do not agree with each other, except to the effect that he met with a violent death through the hatred of some influential Jews who were virulently opposed to Christianity. This statement, put thus generally, can scarcely be doubted; and the martyrdom falls probably within the last seven or eight years before the destruction of Jerusalem, that is, from four to twelve years after James's last appearance in the Acts of the Apostles.

It is clear, then, from everything which we know regarding the character, views, and official position of James, that from none of the apostles could an epistle addressed especially to the Jewish Christians be more naturally looked for, and that a letter to them from him would carry with it the very greatest weight. When we examine the Epistle, we find it in all respects what we should anticipate from such a man. His chief aim is plainly to impress his readers with a conviction that true Christianity is always a great moral power, and will therefore reveal itself through growth in the energies and beauties of holiness. To the Sermon on the Mount, the great exposition of the law of the kingdom of heaven, there is a constant undertone of reference; and, indeed, the whole letter might almost be regarded as a commentary on that Sermon. Conversion, faith, justification, regeneration, the divinity of the Lord Jesus, and the blessed hope of His second coming, are expressly alluded to in the letter; but, on the whole, the specialties of Christian doctrine are little touched upon—less than in any other book of the New Testament. The reasonings of the apostle evidently presuppose in his readers a knowledge of Christian truth; and his great aim is to convince them that this knowledge will not really benefit them, unless godliness of life show that it has been received with welcome by the heart, 'out of which are the issues of life.'

Introduction.

The aspect in which James loved to contemplate Christianity was obviously that of the glorious flower into which the bud of the religion of the Old Economy had opened. Thus it was natural for him to call the gospel system, looked at in its moral relations, 'the law,' 'the perfect law of liberty.' 'His,' says Neander, 'was pre-eminently the standing-point of Jewish piety, as it manifests itself in the forms of the Old Testament. Under this he had been entirely formed, when faith in Jesus as the promised Messiah was superadded: and henceforth he beheld Judaism, in which he had hitherto lived, transfigured. Christianity appears to his mind as true Judaism. The Spirit of Christ glorifies the forms of the Old Testament, and leads them to their true fulfilment. Something would be wanting, had we not James in the New Testament. His standing-point was of peculiar service in bringing over devout Jews to the faith of the gospel. To a Paul, who was elected for the conversion of the Gentile nations, it would have proved a hindrance; to James, in the sphere of action assigned to him among unmixed Jews, in Palestine and Jerusalem especially, it was serviceable.'

In form the Epistle is simple and natural. Being called forth evidently by reports which had reached the apostle regarding serious faults that had shown themselves in many of the Jewish Christian churches—particularly bigotry, bringing with it angry dissensions and vituperations, and worldliness— he passes on by natural transitions from one point to another, exhibiting duty and reproving sin. The style is lively and earnest, and an abundance of apt similitudes proves that the writer had in no small degree the eye and imagination of a poet. In several places, especially paragraphs in the last two chapters, both the sentiments and the diction forcibly remind a reader of utterances of the old Hebrew prophets.[1]

---

[1] The Greek of James approaches nearer to classical purity than perhaps that of any other New Testament writer. Considering how decided a

Considering James's official relations to the church at Jerusalem, it is in every way probable that the Epistle was written in that city. We may suppose it to have been sent in the first instance to the Jewish Christian communities in the neighbouring region of Syria; unless we take the term 'the Dispersion,' employed in the first verse (see Exposition of that verse), to be used in a very wide sense, as including all the Jews not resident in Jerusalem, in which case the letter may have been sent first to some congregation in Judæa or Galilee.

The date cannot be determined so easily or decidedly. It seems, on the whole, most probable that the letter was written before Paul's Epistles, and indeed before the council held at Jerusalem on the relations of Gentile Christians to the Jewish law (A.D. 50). Had it been written after Paul's magnificent arguments on justification by faith were in circulation, it seems likely that, in the observations made, in the second chapter, on justification, we should have found some statement showing clearly to the readers that James was not opposing Paul, but a misapprehension and abuse of the doctrine which Paul held in common with his brethren, and of which he had been honoured to be the great expounder;[1] and had it been written later than the meeting of the council, at a time when almost every Jewish congregation must have included some Gentiles,

Hebrew he was in feeling, this is certainly remarkable. He must have been one of those men whose aptitude for apprehending the delicacies of language is such that, if they speak a foreign tongue at all, they cannot but speak it with elegance.

[1] It may be said that this argument proves nothing, because it might be applied with as much force in the other direction; for if James wrote first, might we not expect Paul to have referred to him somewhere? This is hardly sound, however; for we have no reason to think that the specialties of James's teaching were at all so widely known and discussed as those of Paul's.

the apostle could hardly have avoided touching on the delicate questions connected with the intercourse of Jews and Gentiles. Those 'devout men out of every nation under heaven,' who at the ever-memorable Pentecost received the knowledge of the Messiahship of Jesus, must have carried this blessed knowledge home with them to all parts of the civilised world, and given it to many of their brethren; and thus we cannot doubt that, within a very few years of the ascension of the Lord, there were many Christian churches in 'the Dispersion.' In Damascus, as we know from the history of the Apostle Paul, there were believers before the time of his conversion (about A.D. 37). Those moral defects upon which the Epistle dwells are precisely such as might arise in churches of this class in an extremely short time, being indeed such as were very common in the Jewish synagogues, and thus most likely to show themselves in Christians who had been brought up in Judaism. An argument against the supposition of an early date for the Epistle has been based on some imagined references in it to 1 Peter, and to one or two of Paul's Epistles. But there is no weight in this. The similarities of expression to passages in Paul's writings are merely such as would naturally arise from the fact that from the very beginning the apostolic testimony must of necessity, amid much freedom and variety, have yet, on many cardinal truths, assumed set forms of expression, which were greatly prized and very useful throughout the church—commonplaces of Christian theology. The resemblances between James and 1 Peter are perhaps too close to be accounted for in this way (compare particularly Jas. i. 2, 3 with 1 Pet. i. 6, 7, and Jas. iv. 6–10 with 1 Pet. v. 5–9); but this obviously proves nothing as regards which was the earlier writer. It seems most probable, all things considered, that the Epistle was written before, but not long before, A.D. 50, and that it is the earliest of the books of the New Testament.

The Epistle of James received universal acceptance in the church, as of canonical authority, somewhat later than many other parts of the New Testament. This is easily explained, when we remember the early history of the church, by the jealousy the Gentile Christians would naturally feel in regard to a treatise so distinguished by Jewish colouring, and also by the seeming opposition in which at first sight James's teaching regarding justification stands to that of Paul. A strong argument for the authenticity of the Epistle is found in the fact that it appears in the very early Syriac version of the Bible called the Peshito, from which the Apocalypse and several of the Epistles are excluded, evidently from their not having been as yet fully recognised as canonical. This judgement, coming from the region to which in all probability the Epistle was first sent, and where all the facts regarding it were most likely to be accurately known, is of the highest importance. Luther, as is well known, doubted the authenticity of the Epistle, mainly because of its teaching on the subject of justification; but this ground of hesitation totally disappears on a careful examination of the apostle's meaning. By Calvin, and the Reformers generally, the Epistle was fully received. 'On the whole,' as the case has been well put by Alford, 'on any intelligible principles of canonical reception of early writings, we cannot refuse this Epistle a place in the canon. That that place was given it from the first in some parts of the church; that, in spite of many adverse circumstances, it gradually won that place in other parts; that, when thoroughly considered, it is so consistent with and worthy of his character and standing whose name it bears; that it is marked off by so strong a line of distinction from the writings and epistles which have not attained a place in the canon : all these are considerations which, though they do not in this any more than in other cases amount to demonstration, yet furnish, when combined, a proof hardly to be resisted, that the place where we now find it in the New Testament canon is that which it ought to have, and which God in His providence has guided His church to assign to it.'

SUPPLEMENTARY NOTE

ON 'THE BRETHREN OF THE LORD.'

THE question who 'the brethren of the Lord' were is not without importance in one or two of its bearings; and the student who looks into it finds in it an interest even greater than can exactly be measured by its importance,—an interest due partly to our natural longing to know clearly all that can be known of the home-life of the Saviour, and partly perhaps, as in the case of many other historical problems, to the constancy with which an absolutely certain solution evades us when we seem to be nearest it. It seems desirable, therefore, to treat the matter in a note a little more fully than could conveniently be done in the Introduction.

The *data* in Scripture for forming a judgement on the subject are these :—

1. The language employed in Matt. i. 25 and Luke ii. 7, first clause, naturally suggests, but does not of necessity imply, that Mary bore other children after Jesus.

2. Several times in the Gospels we read of the Lord's 'brothers,' and in two places also of His 'sisters' (Matt. xii. 46, 47, xiii. 55 ; Mark iii. 31, vi. 3 ; Luke viii. 19 ; John ii. 12, vii. 3, 5, 10; also Acts i. 14).

3. In all these passages, except John vii. 3–10, the 'brothers' are spoken of in connection with Mary the mother of Jesus.

4. By John (vii. 5) it is said that the 'brothers' of Jesus

'did not believe on Him.' The remark is made in connection with a conversation which took place between Jesus and them less than a year before the crucifixion.

5. The names of the 'brothers' (probably all, from the manner in which they are brought in) are mentioned by two of the evangelists as 'James and Joses (or Joseph, for the reading varies in Matthew), and Simon and Judas' (Matt. xiii. 55; Mark vi. 3). Of these, two at least came to be prominent teachers, and to occupy an apostolic or semi-apostolic position in the early church, as is shown by Paul's words in 1 Cor. ix. 5. One of these was James, for many years the most prominent of the Christian ministers in Jerusalem, and in all likelihood the author of the Epistle. Paul (Gal. i. 19) expressly calls him 'the Lord's brother.' Another was Judas, or Jude, the writer of the Epistle bearing that name, for he at the beginning of the letter announces himself as 'the brother of James;' and the name of 'James' simply in the early church could point to none but the well-known James 'the Lord's brother.' It has been shown in the Introduction, that supposing this James and this Jude to have been recognised as apostles by the early church, we are not thereby obliged to consider them to have been of the number of the original Twelve.

6. In all the lists of the Twelve Apostles (Matt. x. 3; Mark iii. 18; Luke vi. 15; Acts i. 13) we find one named 'James (the son) of Alphæus.'

7. In Luke's lists, in his Gospel and the Acts (see reff. above), one of the apostles is named 'Judas (the brother) of James.' He is probably the same as the Lebbæus and Thaddæus of the other lists. Whether the supplement should be 'brother' here is very doubtful, and it seems more probable, according to the usage of the language, that 'son' is meant.

Certainly, looking at the forms of expression, particularly in the list in Acts, it appears natural to conclude, that if we rightly render 'James the son of Alphæus,' then we should also render 'Judas the son of James,' for the constructions (which stand very near each other) are absolutely identical. The Revised Version puts 'son' in the text, and 'brother' in the margin. Supposing the sense to be that Judas was the son of James, we have no means of identifying that James.

8. In John xix. 25 it is said that 'there stood by the cross of Jesus His mother, and His mother's sister, Mary the wife of Cleophas' (more exactly 'Clopas'), 'and Mary Magdalene.' Now this may intimate that Mary the wife (some have thought 'daughter' the right supplement) of Clopas was a sister of Mary the Lord's mother. The sentence is ambiguous, however. It may speak not of three women, but of four, the names or designations being grouped in pairs; thus, 'His mother and His mother's sister, Mary the wife of Clopas and Mary Magdalene.' This construction is exactly similar to that in the list of the apostles as given by Matthew (x. 2–4). There seems much probability that the words should be taken in this way; for, though not impossible, it is certainly extremely unlikely that two sisters should both have borne the same name. The old Syriac version, the Peshito, inserts a conjunction, in order to show distinctly that the translator understood four persons to be spoken of: 'His mother, and His mother's sister, *and* Mary the wife of Clopas, and Mary Magdalene.' It is possible that this insertion represents some tradition on the subject.

9. Among the names of the loving women who beheld the crucifixion and visited the grave, we read of a Mary who is called 'the mother of James and Joses' (Matt. xxvii. 56), 'the mother of James the Little (for such is the exact rendering)

and Joses' (Mark xv. 40), 'the mother of James' (Mark xvi. 1 ; Luke xxiv. 10), 'the mother of Joses' (Mark xv. 47), 'the other Mary,' as distinguished from Mary Magdalene (Matt. xxviii. 1). The James here referred to may have been 'the son of Alphæus.' The fact that in two of these passages the name of 'Joses' is added to that of 'James,' and that in one of them the mother is described by her relation to 'Joses' alone, seems to show that whilst this James was a man well known in the church, yet his brother was equally or almost equally so. This renders it likely that he was not the 'James the Lord's brother,' whose name, in the age when the Gospels were published, took rank with that of Peter, and John, and Paul.

10. In John xix. 26, 27, it is related that Jesus, on the cross, seeing His mother and John standing near, said to Mary, 'Woman, behold thy son,' and to John, 'Behold thy mother,' and that John 'from that hour took her unto his own home.' Is this conduct of Jesus and of John compatible with the supposition that at the time Mary had sons and daughters? This question is discussed near the end of this note.

11. In the 1st chapter of Acts, Luke, in his list of the apostles, names 'James the son of Alphæus.' In the 12th chapter he mentions the martyrdom of the other Apostle James, the son of Zebedee. In the 15th chapter he introduces, evidently as a man of prominence, one whom he calls simply 'James.' Is it not natural to suppose that by this James he means the son of Alphæus, of whom he had spoken in the 1st chapter? Had we no other information to guide our judgement, such would certainly be the natural conclusion ; but if we suppose another James to have been so distinguished at the time when the book of Acts was published, that the

mere name would at once suggest him to all readers, the case is altered.

12. To these Scripture statements falls to be added, as among the *data* for a judgement on the matter, the conjecture that Alphæus and Clopas are different forms of the same Aramaic name. This is not impossible; but from the fact that in the Syriac versions, made by men who, we can hardly but suppose, must have known well about Aramaic names and their renderings, different forms are employed for Alphæus and Clopas, it seems probable that they are distinct.

Among the factors in the formation of opinion on this subject, has entered in illegitimately, but most influentially, besides the Scripture *data*, aversion to the thought that Mary the mother of Jesus bore any other children. Springing up at a very early period, as ascetic notions regarding marriage gained strength, this feeling grew so potent and wide-spread, that Mary's perpetual virginity became throughout Christendom a most cherished article of belief. Even among Protestants, to whom the Mariolatry and asceticism of the Church of Rome are utterly offensive, this feeling exercises considerable power, and over certain temperaments probably always will. But it finds no support in Scripture, either in the language of respect uniformly employed regarding marriage, or in what is said specially of the wedded life of Joseph and Mary (see *datum* 1 above).

The most prevalent opinion on the subject before us has been, that Alphæus, supposed to be the same as Clopas (12), was the husband of a sister of Mary the mother of Jesus, who was also named Mary (8, 9); that their children, who were thus cousins of Jesus, were from some cause associated unusually closely with their aunt, Mary the Lord's mother; that by a loose use of the term they were commonly known as 'the brothers of the Lord;' and that at least two of them, James and Jude (7), were in the number of the Twelve Apostles. To this theory the strong objection lies at the very outset, that, as has been conclusively shown by Bp. Lightfoot (in a Dissertation in his *Commentary on Galatians*), it was wholly unknown in the church till near the end of the fourth century, when it was put forth by Jerome, avowedly to remove all doubt regarding the perpetual virginity of Mary. Had it been well founded, tradition would scarcely have left it altogether unmentioned. In itself, the theory involves very doubtful assumptions,— that Alphæus and Clopas were one (12), and that 'Mary the mother of James and Joses' (9) was a sister of the mother of Jesus (8). Again, supposing those called 'the brothers of the Lord' to have been really His cousins, it is inexplicable that, their mother being alive, they should always, when spoken of under the name 'the brothers of the Lord,' be associated with Mary the mother of Jesus, and never with their own mother. Further, supposing two, or even only one, of these 'brothers' to have been in the number of the Twelve, it appears very strange that John makes his statement regarding unbelief (4) without mentioning any exceptions. The unquestionable fact that the Epistle of James has a considerable number of echoes of the Sermon on the Mount, has been appealed to as proving that James, at least, must have been a disciple of Jesus during His public ministry, and not improbably one of the Twelve. The argument is insufficient. He may have heard the Sermon, and been deeply impressed by its ethical teaching, and yet not have allowed himself to believe in the Messiahship or divine commission of Jesus, so as to become a disciple in the deepest sense. Or, conceivably, his acquaintance with the Sermon may have been obtained not from hearing it but from a record. No part of our Lord's teaching was likely to be earlier written down by His followers, and in free circulation, than the great Discourse on the Law of the Kingdom. Finally, the employment of the words 'brother' and 'sister,' when intended obviously to express a definite family relationship (not loosely for 'fellow-Christian' or the like), in any other than the strict sense, is wholly contrary to New Testament usage, and finds very inadequate support in the Old Testament. Lot is called a 'brother' of Abraham, and Jacob of Laban, they being really nephews; but the word is not used of any more distant connection. The suggestion made by some advocates of the cousin theory, that, Alphæus having died, Joseph may have adopted his children, accounts in a measure for the use of the words 'brothers' and 'sisters;' but it does not at all obviate the other objections, and it is totally unsupported by any hint in Scripture or tradition. On the whole, it is difficult to resist the impression that this theory would never have arisen, and would never have found such acceptance as it has, but for the influence of feeling and dogma. The fact that, by rejecting this view, we are left with two families in each of which are a James and a Joses (5, 9), and perhaps (7) also a Jude, need cause no difficulty, for these were very common Jewish names; and if the two sets of brothers were cousins to each other, their having the same names is all the more easily understood.

That those called 'the Lord's brothers' were children of Joseph by a former wife, appears to have been the view generally entertained in the church before the time of Jerome. By some, Tertullian and others, they were considered to have been children of Joseph and Mary. The weight in favour of the former of these opinions, which would otherwise belong to the fact that it was the prevailing one in those early times, when we might suppose some authentic tradition on the point to have still existed, is very greatly diminished by the consideration that, almost from the very first age, the sentimental and dogmatic influence already spoken of was to some extent in operation. Either of these views satisfies many of the requirements of a candid exegesis; and it is not easy to choose with much decision between them. In support of the opinion that those named the 'brothers' and 'sisters' of Jesus were such by a real physical relationship (as children of Mary), these arguments present themselves—that this accords with what Matt. i. 25 and Luke ii. 7 naturally imply (1), and that it accounts perfectly for the closeness of their association with Mary, as described in the various statements made regarding them in the Gospels. Moreover, on the view that they were children of Joseph by a former wife, these 'brothers' must have been, at the time when our Lord was engaged in His public ministry, considerably over thirty years of age, the eldest probably not much under forty. But the statements made regarding them in the Gospels appear naturally to imply that they were still unmarried, and residing with Mary. Now, considering how early the Jews usually married, and that at least two of these 'brothers' did actually marry (see 1 Cor. ix. 5), the supposition that they were so old at the time of the incidents recorded by the evangelists appears unlikely. Further, the genealogies of the Lord given by Matthew (ch. i.) and Luke (ch. iii.) both, in form at least, show our Lord's connection with David through *Joseph*, His reputed father, thus proving Him to be, according to the ordinary principles of Jewish law, the heir to David's throne. The argument on the genealogies seems to imply that there was no older son in Joseph's family. It is true that at the very outset, in the case of Solomon, it was made clear that the succession to David was not necessarily to be according to primogeniture; yet, when a genealogical argument is employed in such a matter, without any note regarding exceptional arrangements, we naturally think, beyond question, of primogeniture. Now, on the view that these 'brothers' were sons of Joseph by a former wife, the Lord Jesus was obviously not the eldest in His reputed father's family.[1]

The only serious difficulty, as it appears to me, affecting the view that they were children of Mary as well as Joseph, is found in the fact that on the cross Jesus entrusted His mother to John, that he might care for her as her son (10). Bp. Lightfoot thinks that, against the opinion that Mary at the time had four sons living, besides daughters, these statements tell with 'fatal effect,' whilst he regards them as 'powerless' against the view that these were merely Joseph's children, which accordingly he adopts. 'Is it conceivable,' he says, 'that our Lord would thus have snapped asunder the most sacred ties of natural affection? The difficulty is not met by the fact that her own sons were still unbelievers. This fact would scarcely have been allowed to override the paramount duties of filial piety. But even when so explained, what does this hypothesis require us to believe? Though within a few days a special appearance is vouchsafed to one of these brethren, who is destined to rule the mother church of Jerusalem, and though all alike are converted to the faith of Christ, yet she, their mother, living in the same city, and joining with them in a common worship (Acts i. 14), is consigned to the care of a stranger, of whose house she becomes henceforth the inmate.' Dr. Eadie, on the other hand

---

[1] From the conduct of these 'brothers' as described in Mark iii. 21, 31, or the tone of their language as recorded in John vii. 3, 4, no decided conclusion can be drawn whether they were older or younger than the Saviour.

(*Commentary on Galatians*, note on i. 19), says: 'The objection has never appeared to us to be of very great force; for we know nothing of the circumstances of the brothers, and there may have been personal and domestic reasons why they could not receive the beloved charge. They might not, for a variety of reasons, be able to give Mary such a home as John could provide for her. As we cannot tell, it is useless to argue. We are wholly ignorant also of their peculiar temperament, and their want or their possession of those elements of character which would fit them to tend their aged and widowed parent. Especially do we know, however, that up to a recent period they were unbelievers in her divine First-born; and though He who did not forget His mother in His dying moments foreknew all that was to happen, still their unbelief might disqualify them for giving her the comfort and spiritual nursing which she required to heal the wounds inflicted by that "sword" which was piercing her heart, as she contemplated the shame and agony of the adored Sufferer on the cross. Every attention was needed for His mother at that very moment; and He seized that very moment to commend her to John, who had been to Him more than a brother, and would on that account be to her more than a son. John was standing by, and so was His mother; so that perhaps his ministrations to her had already commenced.' To me the difficulty appears greater than it seems to have done to Dr. Eadie; and whilst the argument exhibited in the latter part of the quotation given above would have great force, supposing that John had taken Mary home with him only for a few days or weeks, it seems hardly to have much weight if, according to the natural force of the words employed by the evangelist, and the uniform testimony of early tradition, we believe him to have displayed towards her a filial care till her death. But as regards the view espoused by Dr. Lightfoot, these same facts appear to be not so utterly 'powerless' in the way of presenting an objection as he assumes. Considering the closeness of the association of the 'brothers' with Mary, and, according to all appearance, the thoroughly affectionate nature of their relations, it seems strange, even on the supposition of their being only her step-children (not so strange, certainly, as if we deem them her own, but still strange), that the Lord should have given her to another. John may have been her nephew,—a comparison of John xix. 25 (interpreted as speaking of four women) with the lists given by Matthew and Mark of the women who witnessed the crucifixion, suggesting that perhaps Salome, the wife of Zebedee, was the unnamed sister of Mary. Still the bequest to him seems strange. But it was obviously understood and acquiesced in unhesitatingly by all parties concerned; and in all likelihood, as Dr. Eadie says in the beginning of the passage quoted above, its explanation was found in some circumstance or combination of circumstances connected with the position of the 'brothers,' which we cannot now determine. The necessity of our falling back on this supposition holds, as it seems to me, whether we deem them to have been children of Mary, or only step-children. The mode in which 'Mary, the mother of Jesus, and His brothers,' are spoken of in connection with each other in Acts i. 14, makes it not altogether improbable that the whole family were still together, residing with John.

On the whole, it appears to me that the theory which regards 'the Lord's brothers' as His cousins is utterly untenable, and that, whilst the views that they were children of Joseph by a former wife, and that they were children of Joseph and Mary, are both defensible, yet the balance of probability is in favour of the latter.

I.

JOY IN TRIALS.

'James, a servant of God and of the Lord Jesus Christ, to the twelve tribes which are scattered abroad, greeting. 2 My brethren, count it all joy when ye fall into divers temptations: 3 Knowing this, that the trying of your faith worketh patience. 4 But let patience have her perfect work, that ye may be perfect and entire, wanting nothing.'—
JAMES i. 1–4.

THE Epistle begins, like most of the apostolic letters, and indeed like the letters of the ancients generally, with an announcement of the name of the writer, and of that of the persons addressed. After giving his name, he describes himself, you observe, as '*a servant of God.*' The holiest of men is no more than this. Of Messiah the Prince, Jehovah says 'Behold My Servant.' God graciously gives His people many titles of honour: He calls us 'kings and priests,' 'children, and, if children, then heirs;' but the spirit of 'a servant,' simple willingness to obey Him, underlies all such relations. Whatever else we may be, we are servants.

'*And of the Lord Jesus Christ.*' In gospel times, all true acceptable service to *God* must have in the heart of him who renders it this conjunction. Only as we see the claims of Jesus to be our Master and King, and discern God's character as revealed in Him, can we sincerely serve God. 'When the Comforter is come,' said Jesus to His disciples, 'He will convince the world of *sin*' (that is, of refusal to be servants of

God), '*because they believe not on Me.*' In Christ God has been made flesh, and has dwelt among us, full of the grace, and the truth, and the holy beauty of heaven. God is thus in Christ brought very close to us all, and the whole mass of sin in our natures, every sinful affection and energy, will necessarily show itself in antagonism to Him. Rejection of Christ, then, is plainly for gospel hearers the grand manifestation of sin. So the test of character for us, brethren,—the test whether all that may seem beautiful in our life springs from love to God and consequent hatred of sin, or from mere earthly influences, —the criterion by which 'he that *serveth God*' is to be discriminated from 'him that *serveth Him not*,'—is our belief or unbelief in Jesus. 'This is God's commandment,' writes the Apostle John emphatically (as if he would say, 'the commandment in which is gathered up the statement of all duty'), 'that we should believe on the name of His Son Jesus Christ.' All this scriptural teaching, you observe, assumes the divinity of the Lord Jesus, losing all pertinence and force on any other view; and the testimony given in support of that vital doctrine by such a conjunction of names as we have in the verse before us, must be recognised by every candid reader. No mind unwarped by sinful prejudice can fail to see, that to associate the name of any, the highest conceivable, mere created being with that of God the Father in the way in which James here associates that of Jesus, would be a glaring insult to the divine majesty.

Some have thought that the description, 'a *servant* of Jesus Christ,' proves the James who wrote the Epistle not to have been an apostle. The argument is not sufficient, seeing that an apostle, when writing to persons whom he knew to be already well acquainted with his position in the church, and ready, therefore, to receive his instructions with due reverence and confidence, might, instead of giving prominence to the peculiar dignity of the apostleship, prefer to designate himself by some more general term, thus coming nearer to his readers, classing himself with them or with their office-bearers. So John, you remember, in the beginning of his second and third Epistles, calls himself 'the elder.' It is interesting, however, supposing James to have been a *brother* of the Lord according to the flesh, to see how entirely he sinks the earthly relationship. He understood the Saviour's 'Yea, rather blessed are they that hear the word of God and keep it.'

'*To the twelve tribes which are scattered abroad.*' The body of Israelites that returned to Palestine from the Captivity consisted mainly of members of the tribes of Judah and Benjamin. The ten tribes which formed the kingdom of Israel, as distinguished from that of Judah, had been carried away to the east at a much earlier period than the others; and thus, when the permission to return came, these tribes, in which for many generations the *religious* tie connecting them with Canaan had been very weak, had settled down firmly among the heathen, with whom, no doubt, they gradually became completely intermixed. Pious persons from these ten tribes, however, associated themselves with the colony that returned, or with the portion of Judah and Benjamin that continued in Babylonia but clung to the faith of their fathers. There still remained, therefore, a body of worshippers of Jehovah which might truly be called 'the twelve tribes of Israel;' and in all likelihood this name, so full of interesting memories for devout and patriotic Jews, was in not unfrequent use. Paul, you may remember, employs it in his speech before Agrippa, speaking of the hope of Messiah cherished by 'our twelve tribes' (Acts xxvi. 7). To the words 'the twelve tribes' James adds, '*which are scattered abroad,*' more exactly, 'which are in the Dispersion.'

'The Dispersion' was a name in common use among the Jews for the condition in which, since the Captivity, great numbers of their race had been, or sometimes, naturally, for those who were in that condition. Not merely did a great number, as we have seen, remain in Babylonia; but of the descendants of those who returned to Palestine, multitudes were led, for commercial and other reasons, to emigrate to various countries, so that in course of time Jews were to be found in almost all parts of the Roman Empire. This state of things, then, or those who were in it, had the name of 'The Dispersion.' John tells us that on one occasion, when Jesus said to His enemies, 'Ye shall seek Me, and shall not find Me,' they said among themselves, 'Whither will He go, that we shall not find Him? Will He go unto the dispersed (or, more exactly, the Dispersion) among the Gentiles?' (vii. 35). James's Epistle, then, is addressed to the Jews of the Dispersion, the Jews living out of Palestine.[1] The whole tenor of the letter shows that it was written to the *Christians* among these Jews. This limitation is found in the address, however, only when it is read in connection with the designation which the writer has given of himself. 'To the Jews of the Dispersion,—all of

[1] The mystical sense which some have attached to the words, 'the twelve tribes in the Dispersion,' supposing them not specially to designate Jews, but Christians generally as the spiritual Israel, living in this world as strangers and pilgrims, is untenable. The likelihood that the principal terms in the address of a letter are not used figuratively is so great, that very strong arguments are needed to counterbalance this probability. In 1 Peter, where also the name 'The Dispersion' is found in the superscription, such arguments do present themselves,—there being nothing in the letter which appears more suited for Jewish than for Gentile Christians, and some things which seem more suited for Gentiles than for Jews. But in James the addition of the words 'the twelve tribes' makes the likelihood of a reference to the literal Israel very much greater than in Peter,—and with this reference the whole tone of the Epistle accords in the fullest measure.

them for whom the words of *a servant of the Lord Jesus Christ* have interest and value,'—such, no doubt, substantially is the meaning. The breadth of the form of address was fitted to proclaim that to *all* Israel, professedly 'waiting for the consolation' of their nation, the voice of 'a servant of Messiah' *ought* to be welcome; and at the same time to remind the believing Jews—often, no doubt, charged by their unbelieving countrymen with being renegade Israelites, recreant to the religion of their fathers—that they were the true 'children of Abraham,' having accepted God's way of fulfilling His promises with like simple faith as Abraham had shown in accepting the promises themselves.

Having announced his name and intimated to whom he writes, the apostle closes his preliminary words by the formula of salutation customary in the letters of the Greeks: '*Greeting.*' The chief captain who had apprehended Paul begins his letter to Felix in this way: 'Claudius Lysias to the most excellent governor Felix, greeting' (Acts xxiii. 26). It is an interesting fact, one of those little manifestly undesigned coincidences which are often so important in the way of evidence, that the only other *apostolic* document, besides this Epistle, in which this particular form of salutation occurs, is the circular letter issued by the apostles and elders assembled at Jerusalem, which embodied James's proposal, and therefore in all likelihood was drawn up by him (Acts xv. 23).[1]

The apostle proceeds now to his letter itself. His great object in writing it was evidently to impress on his readers the fact that Christianity is not a *faith* merely, but, through the power of faith, a *life;* and, in connection with this, to point out to them some special dangers, and reprove them for some

---

[1] The same form of salutation is *mentioned* by John (2nd Ep. 10, 11), but only incidentally.

special and already notorious defects. Many of them, it appears, were at the time exposed to persecution of one kind or another. With the subject of trouble, therefore, as prominently occupying their thoughts, and being of very great importance in its bearings on religious life, James naturally begins. The particular form of his commencement is perhaps suggested by the salutation that he has just given, which in the original is the verbal form of the word in the 2nd verse rendered 'joy.' We find not unfrequently in this Epistle the *form* of the connection between sentences or paragraphs determined by words, whilst a close connection of thought is generally obvious also. 'James to his readers wishes joy.' 'But how is it possible that we should have joy, environed with troubles as we now are?' This would be a very natural thought in the minds of the readers. To this the apostle responds:

'*My brethren, count it all joy when ye fall into divers temptations.*' The word '*temptations,*' meaning, according to its derivation, 'trials,' has, like the Greek word which it represents, a considerable breadth of signification. It is often used in the New Testament for troubles of any kind, these being looked at as 'tests' of character. Thus Jesus said to the apostles, 'Ye are they that have continued with me in my temptations' (Luke xxii. 28). Paul, in his address to the elders of Ephesus, said: 'Ye know after what manner I have been with you, serving the Lord with all humility of mind, and with many tears and temptations, which befell me by the lying in wait of the Jews' (Acts xx. 18, 19). Peter speaks of his readers as being 'in heaviness through manifold temptations' (1 Pet. 1. 6). '*Joy*' is plainly used here for 'a ground of joy;' and '*all joy*' means 'nothing but joy,' 'pure joy,' or, more loosely, 'the highest joy:' as when Peter says, 'Servants, be subject to your masters with *all fear*' (1 Pet. ii. 18), or Jude speaks of his having given '*all diligence* to write of the common salvation' (Jude 3).

The apostle's injunction, then, is that his readers should 'count it a ground of pure joy when they fell into divers troubles.' To the worldly man this is an utter paradox; but Christians understand it. It is not meant that we are to look on afflictions, considered simply by themselves, as a ground of joy. This is impossible; it is opposed to the very constitution of our nature. Now Christianity, as you know, proves its divine origin, its having the same Author as man himself, by its adaptation in every respect to our deepest nature, its opposing itself nowhere to the nature which God gave us, but only to the perversities which have been introduced by sin. The Bible, therefore, does not require that we should count pain, looked at simply in itself, as a good thing, a source of joy. According to the Epistle to the Hebrews, 'no chastening for the present seemeth to be joyous, but grievous.' The persecuted Christians to whom Peter wrote, were 'for a season in heaviness through manifold temptations,' and he does not reprove them for it. The Lord Himself, in suffering, said: 'My soul is exceeding sorrowful;' 'Father, if it be possible, let this cup pass from Me.' Christians would be glad if the ends of affliction could be gained otherwise; but seeing that, according to God's infinite wisdom, this bitter medicine is needed to conquer the disease of sin, we are enabled by His grace to accept it meekly and thankfully, and, amid the natural suffering, to have, according to the measure of our faith, composure of spirit, or even great joy, in contemplating the blessed results of tribulation. In the degree in which we are enabled by the Spirit to apprehend the truth that nothing but love sends the troubles that come on God's children, will our feeling under them be one of 'nothing but joy.' That the precept of the Holy Ghost here given through James *can* be obeyed, was shown in the first days of the Christian Church, by such cases as those of the apostles, who 'rejoiced that they were counted worthy to suffer shame for Christ's name,' and of the Hebrew believers, who 'took joyfully the spoiling of their goods;' and has, no doubt, been illustrated in the experience of many children of God in all ages. ' *Divers*,' of many different kinds, are the afflictions which God sends,—varied discipline, according to the varied requirements of different persons, or of the different sides of character in the same person; but however numerous, and diversified, and severe, and long-continued, troubles may be, our Almighty Father can give strength to 'count them all joy.'

Observe, however, that the precept, and the promise of needed grace which is involved in it, as in all God's precepts, have reference to troubles which we '*fall into*.' Trials are not to be sought for or rushed into: on the contrary, all lawful means suggested by experience or thought are to be brought into action to avert or mitigate them. Asceticism, or a perverse ambition for martyrdom in any form, has indeed, as the Apostle Paul says, 'a show of wisdom in will worship, and humility, and neglecting of the body;' but it is wholly alien from the spirit of Scripture. What joy may be felt amid such self-induced 'temptations,' will be a joy of foolish arrogance, not that true happiness springing from holy trust and hope, which those may and through divine help will feel, who have quietly waited for the discipline of the Lord, and in His providence 'fall into' troubles.

The apostle proceeds in the 3rd verse to give the reason why believers should 'count it all joy when they fall into divers temptations;' which is, that the testing of our faith, effected through affliction, is intended by God, and therefore eminently fitted, to strengthen our spiritual life, and in particular to ripen the sweet grace of patience and constancy.

'*Knowing this, that the trying of your faith worketh patience.*' Affliction is a '*trying of our faith.*' This was evidently a commonplace of oral apostolic teaching, for the expression occurs in the very same form in 1 Peter (i. 7). The heart of man, brethren, 'is deceitful above all things,' and even the Christian knows very little of himself. Affliction lets down a blazing torch for him into the depths of his own nature, and he sees many things which he little expected to see. He finds his faith weak where he thought it strong, his views dim where he thought them clear, his pride strong and stubborn where he thought it broken; and he cries to his Father for a fuller sanctification. Thus afflictions of every kind are 'trials,' testing and revealing agencies. Through them, to give knowledge to the believer, the Master, Himself all-knowing, tries him as gold and silver are tried by fire.

Thus the 'trying of our faith *worketh patience;*' that is, it elaborates in the soul constancy in the faith and hope of Christ. The meaning of the original word, as you will gather from this explanation, is somewhat wider than that of our 'patience:' it denotes 'perseverance' in confidence and love and devotion to God in Christ. James assumes that there *is* faith, real living faith, though it may be feeble. Where there is but an empty profession, or a mere dreamy sentiment, unbased on firm and intelligent convictions of truth, the fire of trouble will burn it up. When the sun is risen with its burning heat, the grain on the stony ground, having no root, withers away. Satan turns to evil what God had adapted for good, so that the trial worketh impatience rather than patience. But where there is true faith, affliction naturally leads to deeper thought than under other circumstances on sin and its deserts, and thus frees the heart from the control of self-righteousness. The sense of weakness leads to earnest wrestling with God in prayer; and experience of the sustaining grace thus obtained strengthens and exhilarates hope with regard to the time to come. The impression made by affliction of the perishable nature of mere earthly delights, draws the thoughts forth to that blessedness which God has in store for them that love Him; and the troubles of the present time are felt to be immeasurably outweighed by the 'exceeding and eternal weight of glory.' Thus through the trial of our faith is wrought 'patience,'—a humble but firm determination to cling more than ever to the God who sent the troubles in Fatherly love, who sustains us in the midst of them, who will give glory and unmingled felicity by and by.

'*Knowing*' the spiritual helpfulness of afflictions, then, we should 'count them all joy.' And plainly our measure of success in the discharge of this most difficult duty will depend on the clearness and fulness with which we 'know' their usefulness. Here, as everywhere in religion, it is by an intelligent apprehension of God's will that we become strong; it is 'the truth' which 'makes us free.'

The apostle continues: '*But let patience have her perfect work*.' Sore trouble is hard to bear unrepiningly, very hard to bear, as James here enjoins, joyously. Satan and the depravity of our hearts are always lying in wait, ready to make us murmur and break away from trust in God. Even the meekness of Moses and the patience of Job did not bear up under all temptations. These holy men 'spake unadvisedly with their lips.' In the case of many of those to whom James wrote, where the trials spoken of were no doubt persecutions for religion, there was very serious danger of their apostatizing altogether from Christ. 'If you are to profit by your sufferings, then,' he says, 'and not to incur tremendous loss, let your endurance, your constancy in love and trust even amid adversities, have a perfect work. It is doing a great work: it is refining and ennobling your whole nature; it is building up a stately temple of holy character to the glory of God; it is the instrument employed by God to "keep you unto salvation." Oh, let it put the copestone on the temple; let it have its work *perfect*, for "he that endureth *to the end* shall be saved," and he only.'

'*That ye may be perfect and entire, wanting nothing.*' The term 'perfect' is sometimes applied in the New Testament to the ultimate holiness and blessedness of the saints in heaven. But it is frequently employed also in speaking of Christians in this life. Thus used, it has sometimes reference to our state of acceptance with God, as one of complete justification: thus, for example, Jesus 'by one offering hath *perfected* for ever them that are sanctified.' In other instances, of frequent occurrence, the word describes a 'maturity,' a ripeness and richness of knowledge and character, such as might be supposed to mark the full-grown man, as contrasted with the babe in Christ. The naturalness and obviousness of this sense for those among whom the apostolic writings were first circulated will be evident, when I mention to you that the same Greek word here rendered 'perfect' is often employed to designate simply a full-grown man. Thus, in Hebrews, 'Strong meat belongeth to *them that are of full age*' (v. 14); and in 1 Corinthians, 'In malice be ye children, but in understanding be *men*' (xiv. 20). That in this use of the word, 'mature in character,' complete freedom from defect is not intended, is strikingly shown by Paul's words in Philippians, 'Let us therefore, *as many as be perfect*, be thus minded' (iii. 15), immediately after he has said, obviously with reference to *absolute* holiness, 'not as though I had already attained, either were already *perfect*.'

Through their approximate perfection, their ripeness of character and manliness of Christian judgement, such Christians see all the more clearly, and feel all the more deeply, the measure of still remaining defect, and press towards the mark of absolute perfection. Our apostle's injunction, then, is, that in time of trouble we should 'let patience have her perfect work, that we may be mature Christians;' and probably the precise force of 'perfect' is explained by the '*entire*' which follows, and further illustrated, as if to bring the importance of this point with special vividness before us, by '*wanting nothing.*' All of us, my brethren, in religion as in intellectual culture, are in danger of being one-sided. Yielding to natural temperament, we are apt, whilst cultivating certain departments of Christian thought and activity, to neglect others. The believer of a contemplative disposition, for instance, may shrink from taking his proper share of exertion in the church's work; whilst another Christian, strenuous in labour, may forget to some extent that the tree of piety can bring forth fruit to perfection only when watered with the dews of the Spirit through prayer and quiet communion. Thus the new man has deformities, his growth being inharmonious, without fitting proportion of parts. God's varied discipline is designed to produce a perfectly balanced completeness of character. Now there are some elements of holy character which can be acquired only in trouble. The beautiful graces of resignation and sympathy cannot grow but in a soil through which has passed the ploughshare of affliction, and which has been watered by the rain of tears. Therefore it is that God 'scourgeth every son whom He receiveth,' and 'every branch in the true vine that beareth fruit, He purgeth it, that it may bring forth more fruit.' Let constancy under trial, then, dear brethren, 'have her work perfect, that ye may be perfect and entire, wanting nothing.'

II.

WISDOM THROUGH PRAYER.

'If any of you lack wisdom, let him ask of God, that giveth to all men liberally, and upbraideth not; and it shall be given him. 6 But let him ask in faith, nothing wavering: for he that wavereth is like a wave of the sea, driven with the wind and tossed. 7 For let not that man think that he shall receive anything of the Lord. 8 A double-minded man is unstable in all his ways.'—JAMES i. 5-8.

AT this point the thought naturally occurs to the mind of a reader of the Epistle: 'I am sadly wanting in power to exhibit this grace of patience; I am unable to discern clearly or to keep my heart steadily fixed on those truths which are fitted to maintain holy peace within it, but lose myself in a crowd of conflicting thoughts and feelings.' This thought is taken up and responded to by the apostle: the *form* of the connection here again, according to what I have already mentioned to be a characteristic of James's style, being determined by a word, the word 'wanting,' or, as it might— and indeed, to show the connection, should—have been rendered, 'lacking,' in the last clause of the 4th verse. With obvious reference to this word, he goes on:

'*If* (strictly, *But if*) *any of you lack wisdom, let him ask of God.*' Wisdom, in the Bible sense of the word, is the grandest and rarest of the acquisitions possible to man. Knowledge, to a certain extent, is common and easy; but to know and to be wise are by no means the same thing. Knowledge is a most efficient handmaid to, but a most inefficient substitute for, that queenly regulative discretion which sees and selects worthy ends, and the best means of attaining them. This is wisdom.

> ' Knowledge and wisdom, far from being one,
> Have ofttimes no connection. Knowledge dwells
> In heads replete with thoughts of other men;
> Wisdom in minds attentive to their own.
> Knowledge, a rude unprofitable mass,
> The mere materials with which wisdom builds,—
> Till smoothed, and squared, and fitted to its place,
> Does but encumber whom it seems to enrich.
> Knowledge is proud that he has learned so much;
> Wisdom is humble that he knows no more.'

It is evident that if ' the chief end of man is to glorify God and to enjoy Him for ever,' then wisdom in the highest sense is simply another name for religion; and indeed that, looking at the matter from the point of view which an immortal creature ought to take, there is no real wisdom at all where religion is wanting. Suppose the owner of a factory for the making of some delicate and expensive fabric were to bestow great attention on certain departments of the manufacture, and exhibit much ingenuity in devising improvements on the machinery and processes connected with these departments, but neglected other branches, and above all, gave little heed to the grand purpose of the whole, so that he produced unsatisfactory and unsaleable material,—none of us would say that this was a *wise* man of business. An actual case of the kind is not very common, for the interests of this world keep men from such outrageous folly; but, alas, it is by no means rare to see a man of much worldly sagacity heedless of the great ends of his being,—diligent in the twisting of a certain thread, or the preparation of a certain dye, for the web of life, whilst yet the web itself, looked at in the light of the Lord, is worthless. True wisdom lies in the subjection of all our capacities and energies and affections to the control of high moral principle, and the consequent faithful application of them to noble moral uses; and 'the fear of God is the beginning—the foundation —of this wisdom.' 'Happy,' says he whom we designate emphatically 'the wise man,' 'is the man that findeth wisdom, and the man that getteth understanding: for the merchandise of it is better than the merchandise of silver, and the gain thereof than fine gold. She is more precious than rubies: and all the things thou canst desire are not to be compared unto her. Length of days is in her right hand, and in her left hand riches and honour. Her ways are ways of pleasantness, and all her paths are peace. She is a tree of life to them that lay hold upon her; and happy is every one that retaineth her.'

It is clear from the context that the reference of James in the passage before us is specially to the wisdom needed in times of trouble, in order to obtain spiritual improvement from God's discipline, and 'let patience have her work perfect.' Wisdom for this is the highest of all, and the most difficult of attainment. Active performance of God's will is easier than patient endurance of His will,—to do well not so hard as to bear well. The apostle's '*if*,' in 'if any man lack wisdom,' does not imply doubt. All men do, and in this world always will, 'lack wisdom;' and there are few clearer evidences that a man's lack is very grievous than his supposing he has none. The 'if' seems to have reference rather to the occurrence of circumstances in the experience of the apostle's readers calling for the exercise of this kind of wisdom, and thus bringing out their sense of want, and is therefore almost equivalent to 'whenever.' We are all apt to think ourselves wise, until circumstances arise which test the wisdom. Young people, say from seventeen to five-and-twenty years of age, have often much stronger impressions of their ability to journey safely and successfully through life, than, if they come to real knowledge of themselves, they ever have afterwards, when they have had experience of the difficulties of life. So also, probably, many Christians believe that they are able to endure affliction well, till they fall into it. Those of us who have personally undergone sore trials, or have with attention and thoughtfulness witnessed the trials of others, know well what an overwhelming sense of weakness and ignorance comes over the heart at first, and what a deep impression is made of the needfulness of special wisdom to guide and sustain. And where the Christian is subjected to long-continued trial, a sense of the necessity of constant supplies of wisdom from above, if patience is to have her work perfect, grows stronger day by day.

'*Let him ask of God,—and it shall be given him.*' This is plainly an echo of our Lord's words in the Sermon on the Mount, 'Ask, and it shall be given you,'—one proof among many afforded by this Epistle of the profound impression which that divine exposition of the law of the kingdom had made on the mind of James.

It was a touching acknowledgement of one of the wisest and best among the ancient heathen, 'I know nothing certainly, except that I know nothing.' He felt that he 'lacked wisdom.' But whither could he turn to obtain it? Men around could not help him, for they were merely less sensible of their ignorance. The living God was unknown to him,—groped after indeed dimly and wistfully, 'if haply he might find Him,' but not seen to be a Friend, a Father, with whom His children may hold communion, and 'ask' of Him. We know this; and, indeed, the familiarity of the truth, as a commonplace of Christianity, obscures to us the grandeur of the thought that the Infinite One, the 'King eternal, immortal, and invisible,' is willing to hold fellowship with His creatures,—that He listens to the cry of the contrite heart,—that, having by our sins earned the 'outer darkness,' we may yet 'ask' heavenly light, true 'wisdom,' from the 'Father of lights,' the 'only wise God.'

'*And it shall be given him.*' As certainly as He is Himself the 'only wise God,' the only Fountain of wisdom, will He make streams of that wisdom refresh and fertilize the souls of those who ask Him. As certainly as He gave us our souls, with all their faculties and their capacities of wisdom, so certainly, in answer to prayer, will He guide to the apprehension by our souls of all needed truth, and to a realizing sense of its power to sustain and comfort under every form of trial. Prayer obtains this true wisdom,—prayer only, prayer always. As believers grow in prayerfulness, then, they grow in wisdom; and no less certainly, as they grow in wisdom, they grow in prayerfulness.

'*That giveth to all men liberally, and upbraideth not.*' The apostle in these words exhibits the abundant ground of encouragement which we have to pray. In the original, the position of the participle rendered 'that giveth,' sets *giving* forth in a peculiarly graphic way as a grand characteristic of God. 'God *is* love;' and this—His nature—reveals itself to us, His creatures, in *giving*. He is 'the giving God.' We see this everywhere, alike in providence and in grace. 'He *giveth* to all life, and breath, and all things.' 'He *gave* His only-begotten Son, that whosoever believeth in Him should not perish, but have everlasting life;' and having 'delivered Him up for us all, how shall He not, with Him, also freely *give* us all things?' The first of these quotations illustrates the truth that, in the widest sense, God 'giveth *to all*.' 'The eyes *of all* wait upon Thee, and Thou *givest* them their meat in due season.' 'He maketh His sun to rise on the evil and on the good, and sendeth rain on the just and on the unjust.' But whilst this is true, and whilst a great encouragement to prayer is found in the universal beneficence of God, yet, in the connection in which '*all*' stands in the passage before us, it seems most natural to take it in a limited sense—'all who ask Him, all petitioners.' 'Pray for wisdom,' says the apostle, 'for God answers every true prayer; and it is in accordance with the principles of His economy of grace to bestow His richest gifts on those who *ask* them.' 'The righteous cry, and the Lord heareth.' 'He will regard the prayer of the destitute,' and 'fulfil the desire of them that fear Him.'

And to all sincere petitioners He 'giveth *liberally*,'—with unstinted hand, with glorious munificence. Jacob asks for 'bread to eat and raiment to put on,' and God makes him 'two bands.' Solomon prays for 'an understanding heart,' and God says unto him, 'Because thou hast asked this thing, and hast not asked for thyself long life, neither hast asked riches for thyself, nor hast asked the life of thine enemies, but hast asked for thyself understanding to discern judgement; behold, I have done according to thy words: lo, I have given thee a wise and an understanding heart; so that there was none like thee before thee, neither after thee shall any arise like unto thee. And I have also given thee that which thou hast not asked, both riches and honour; so that there shall not be any among the kings like unto thee all thy days.' The prodigal thinks of the position of 'an hired servant,' and his Father says, 'Bring forth the best robe, and put it on him; and put a ring on his hand, and shoes on his feet.' Sweet and beautiful, however, as this word 'liberally' is, the apostle's own word is something even more comprehensive and encouraging. It is the adverbial form of the term employed in Rom. xii. 8, 'He that giveth, let him do it *with simplicity;*' and in Eph. vi. 5, 'Servants, be obedient to them that are your masters according to the flesh, *in singleness* of your heart.' The exact meaning here, therefore, is that God gives 'with simplicity,' 'with singleness of spirit.' He does not, as men often do, give and yet in effect not give, neutralizing the gift by an unkind manner, or by subsequent ungenerous exactions. His kindness in giving does not, as so often with men, 'fold in' upon another motive of a selfish nature. It is without any duplicity, with singleness of aim to bless the recipient, to reveal the love of His own nature for the happiness of His creatures.

'*And upbraideth not*' is pretty nearly an expansion, in a negative form, for the sake of clearness and emphasis, of the thought already given in 'liberally,' 'with simplicity;' just as in the previous verse we had 'entire' explained by 'wanting nothing.' We may easily weary human benefactors. Those who have often shown us kindness are apt to feel continuing it a burden.; and even if they do continue it, there is much chance of our hearing painful references to the frequency and largeness of our applications, and reproaches for the little profitable use to which we have turned their former generosity. Under these circumstances, a suppliant may well feel hesitation and fear in entering the house even of one whom he has good cause to acknowledge as a friend. But God, in His giving, 'upbraideth not.' He makes no mention of our past folly and abuse of His kindness. The beginning of the new life exhibits the character of the whole : the Father runs and falls on the neck of His penitent petitioning prodigal, and 'loadeth him with benefits.' He never tells us that we have come to Him too often, or have asked too much; nay, He always employs His past kindness as an argument to induce us, through trust in His love, to ask for more and greater blessings. 'I am the Lord thy God,' He says, 'which brought thee out of the land of Egypt;—open thy mouth wide, and I will fill it.' And such *is* the confidence of His people. On mercies past they build up a sure hope of new and more wondrous mercies to come. 'The Lord that delivered me out of the paw of the lion, and out of the paw of the bear, He will deliver me out of the hand of this Philistine.' 'The Lord hath been mindful of us; He will bless us.'

Considering all these things, then, my brethren,—considering the constancy and magnitude of His past mercies, and the unweariedness and tenderness of His grace,—surely 'if any man lack wisdom,' it becomes Him to 'ask of God' with humble boldness and lively hope.

'*But let him ask in faith, nothing wavering.*' Without faith there can be no true prayer. Manifestly, 'he that cometh to God must believe that He is, and that He is a Rewarder of them that diligently seek Him.' Outward form of service there may be, but there can be no real approach of the soul to God, no 'asking of God' by the heart for any blessing, unless we have faith in His existence, His pardoning mercy, and His willingness to hear prayer, conjoined with a deep conviction of our need of His help. And faith must, in breadth of apprehension, be proportioned to the fulness of revelation given. For gospel hearers, therefore, the only acceptable prayer is that offered in simple dependence on the mediation of the Lord Jesus. The words rendered in the present passage '*nothing wavering*' occur also in Acts x. 20, where they are translated 'doubting nothing.' 'Arise,' said the Holy Spirit to Peter, when Cornelius's messengers were at the gate, 'and get thee down, and go with them, *doubting nothing*, for I have sent them.' This passage illustrates the meaning here:[1]

---

[1] As here used, διακρίνεσθαι means 'to be at variance or issue with oneself.' Its force in various applications will be seen by referring to Matt. xxi. 21; Rom. iv. 20, xiv. 23. In the first and last of these passages it is

' Let him ask in faith, doubting nothing in regard to his need of heavenly help, or to God's willingness to grant help; let all arrogant trust in any fancied wisdom of his own be laid aside, and let him entertain a childlike, unhesitating conviction that God can and will supply his need in the way which will best promote the suppliant's good and His own glory.'

'*For he that wavereth is like a wave of the sea, driven with the wind and tossed.*' 'For the doubter is as unsteady and aimless, as untrustworthy with regard to gaining any end which needs determined perseverance in a certain course, as a billow on the sea, driven hither and thither by every shift of wind.' He who *wrestles* with God,—who, like the importunate widow, is determined 'not to faint' in entreaty,—this man 'as a prince has power with God.' 'The fervent—energetic—prayer of a righteous man availeth much.' But what can be expected to result from the poor, weak, nerveless prayer of a doubter? God would have our supplication to be, not like the wind-driven surge, but like the strong current of a rapid river, sweeping away obstacles, bearing steadily onward to throw itself into the ocean of the divine grace.

rendered both in the Authorized and Revised Versions by 'doubt.' In the other passage the Authorized Version has 'stagger,' for which the Revisers substitute 'waver.' In the places where James employs it, 'waver' of the Authorized Version (following Tyndale, who, however, so rendering it in the first clause of this verse, oddly enough substitutes 'doubt' in the second) is perhaps the best word; for it is not so much to the intellectual 'doubt' that the apostle directs attention as to that instability of the affections and conduct, that moral 'swaying to and fro,' which really originates the doubt, and is again intensified by it. Now this thought could hardly be more exactly brought out than by 'waver.' Huther remarks excellently, that ' whilst $\pi i\sigma\tau\iota\varsigma$ says Yes, and $\dot{\alpha}\pi\iota\sigma\tau\acute{\iota}\alpha$ No, $\delta\iota\alpha\varkappa\rho\acute{\iota}\nu\varepsilon\sigma\theta\alpha\iota$ is the co-existence of Yes and No, with the No preponderant, and thus it leads to $\dot{\alpha}\pi\iota\sigma\tau\acute{\iota}\alpha$.' It springs from a dominant unwillingness to lean absolutely on the divine strength, and must therefore be distinguished from weak but real faith, and from those doubts and fears to which the man of strongest faith is subject at times, but which the energy of his faith conquers.

'*For let not that man think that he shall receive anything of the Lord.*'[1] This '*for*' is co-ordinate with that in the previous verse, introducing a second reason why the petitioner should ask 'in faith, nothing wavering.' The first reason, which we have just considered, was that a wavering or doubting suppliant exhibits a worthless, aimless instability of character; the second, bringing out explicitly what is suggested by the first, is, that such a person has no reason to expect an answer to his prayers. When we present a request on a matter of importance to a fellow-creature, particularly one much higher in rank than ourselves, common respect requires that we should have well-defined views on the subject in hand, that we should not drift this way and that, but know what we want, and that he to whom we apply can give it to us. Is it reasonable, then,—is it other than grievous folly and sin,—to bring 'wavering' into the audience-chamber of the King of kings? To God belongs all the glory of man's salvation; and, consistently with the principles of His moral administration, He can save only those whose hearts consent that to Him all the glory shall belong. He 'resisteth the proud, but giveth grace unto the humble.' He says, 'Woe unto you that are rich, for ye have received your consolation;' but 'He satisfieth the longing soul, and filleth the hungry soul with goodness.' Now a man who prays—or thinks he prays—yet in heart doubts through all his devotion, has still a proud, self-asserting spirit; his hesitation springs from unwillingness to believe and to

---

[1] Looking at the connection of this verse with the 5th, we naturally regard God the Father as meant by 'the Lord;' and this is James's usual application of the name. In the other epistles, 'the Lord' generally designates Christ. James's use of the word, so common in the Old Testament, accords exactly with the peculiar type of his piety; and when he applies it to Christ (as in i. 1, ii. 1, v. 7, 8), the ascription in it of Deity is all the more distinct.

confess that he is strong only when he receives of God's strength, and wise only as he draws from the fountain of God's wisdom. He will not cast himself wholly on the divine help. But God will have no half honour; therefore 'let not that man think that he shall receive anything of the Lord.'

'*A double-minded man is unstable in all his ways.*' The word 'is,' as you will see from its being printed in our Bibles in Italic type, is a supplement of the translators. Some supplement of the kind is perhaps needful in English; but, according to the connection of the sentence with what precedes, it should rather stand at the beginning, thus: 'He is a double-minded man, unstable in all his ways.'[1] This is a further description, terse and pointed, of the doubting suppliant's real character. Observe that the man is not exactly a hypocrite. He is a man of divided heart, or who seems almost to have two souls,—one disposed to lean on himself and to seek wisdom and strength and satisfaction in the world, the other disposed to look to God, and seek help and happiness from Him. How vivid a picture it is! Is there not reason to fear that it represents with sad exactness the spiritual state of many in the Christian church? Such a person, the apostle adds, is '*unstable in all his ways.*' An inconsistency of life results necessarily from the dissension of spirit, the divided heart. The man, 'halting between two opinions,' would fain conjoin the service of God and of mammon, would fain 'fear the Lord' and at the same time 'serve his own gods.' Hesitation, inconsistency, varying purpose and effort, exhibit themselves therefore everywhere

---

[1] The clause may be construed in more than one way; but at all events δίψυχος, both as importing into the discussion a new and striking thought, and as being a rare word, perhaps coined by James, appears to belong to the predicate rather than to the subject.

in his life. In his business pursuits and in his pleasures there must often be changefulness and manifest indecision, resulting from perplexities and difficulties which to the *mere* worldling—the man of no religious feeling—are altogether strange; and, on the other hand, in religious services and Christian work of every kind, his fitfulness and want of thoroughness betray the divided heart. A poor, miserable, ignoble character this, brethren,—a character which is utterly incompatible with the enjoyment of true peace through God's favour and fellowship. 'Let not that man think that he shall receive anything of the Lord.'

III.

RICH POOR AND POOR RICH.

'Let the brother of low degree rejoice in that he is exalted; 10 But the rich, in that he is made low: because as the flower of the grass he shall pass away. 11 For the sun is no sooner risen with a burning heat, but it withereth the grass, and the flower thereof falleth, and the grace of the fashion of it perisheth: so also shall the rich man fade away in his ways. 12 Blessed is the man that endureth temptation: for when he is tried, he shall receive the crown of life which the Lord hath promised to them that love Him.'—JAMES i. 9–12.

THE connection of this paragraph appears to be mainly with the exhortation of the 2nd verse, on which all that has come between is dependent; with a reference, however, also to the statement made in the 8th. 'Have joy, I say, in tribulations; and the true way to avoid that double-mindedness and instability which would prevent such joy is to keep the eye much directed to those aspects of our spiritual condition that are specially fitted to counteract the misleading tendencies of outward circumstances.' Such, as it seems to me, is substantially the force of the present passage, and its relation to the preceding.

'(*But*) *let the brother of low degree rejoice in that he is exalted.*' '*The brother*' means simply 'the Christian.' 'The brethren' and 'the saints' were the usual terms employed by believers in the first age to designate members of the church. The name 'Christians,' which, as we are told in the Acts of the

Apostles, originated at Antioch, apparently about eight or nine years after our Lord's ascension, was given in all likelihood by the heathen, and only gradually came to be accepted and exulted in by believers themselves.

How sweet a term 'brother' is! Were its force universally understood and felt throughout the church of Christ, what a loud and emphatic reiteration would thus everywhere and continually be given, such as even the inattentive world could not but hear, of Heaven's testimony regarding the objects of Messiah's reign: 'Glory to God in the highest, and on earth peace, good-will towards men!' Sin has filled the world with dissensions and hatreds. Its essence being selfishness, self-glorification, and self-enjoyment, its constant tendency is to disintegrate society—to make men, as far as regards affection, isolated units, looking always on their own things, and not on the things of others, except with the eye of envy and greed. Thus, as we all know, even among persons whom God in His providence has linked most closely—parents, brothers, sisters—coldness, or even bitter alienation, often enters in. What influence can neutralize this tendency to mutual repulsion, and establish among men peace, and love, and happiness? The growth of international commerce, the diffusion of sound principles of trade, judicious legislation on matters where there is a conflict or supposed conflict between the interests of different sections of a community,—these and other things of similar influence may do somewhat to diminish active hostility, or even increase kindliness, between nations, or classes in a nation; but no power can deeply and lastingly counteract the alienating energy of sin, and make men feel and act towards each other as 'brethren'—whom 'God hath made of one blood'—except vital Christianity. 'One is your Master (your Teacher),' said Jesus, 'even Christ, and all ye are brethren;' or, as He stated the same principle on another occasion, 'Have salt in yourselves, and have peace one with another.' The truth taught to humble, candid souls by the One Master is the only salt which (like Elisha's cruse at Jericho), when thrown into the bitter fountain of a heart—of a world—full of hatred, can change it into a spring of the living waters of love, fitted to give health and pleasure, to diffuse fertility and beauty. 'Of His own will the Father of lights begat us with the word of truth;' and believers, being thus all children of the same God, necessarily, in the measure of the clearness and liveliness of their faith, feel themselves to be 'brethren' of each other; and as 'God is love,' His image in His children will be recognised mainly in a character full of love, filial love to Him, brotherly love to all fellow-Christians, compassionate love to the world. My friends, let us think out the questions suggested to our consciences by this scriptural name for a Christian—'brother.' If believers generally fully understood and acted out the truth that the church is a brotherhood, how immeasurably would her power be increased, alike to give happiness to her own members, and to prevail with the unconverted to enter in and share her joy! How legible and persuasive an epistle of Christ would she then be, telling everywhere that 'God is love,' and that the gospel is fitted to make men, in heart and life, like God! It is when the church shall be 'fair as the moon' with holy beauties, the beauties of love, that she shall be 'terrible as an army with banners' to Satan and his hosts,—then, not till then.

'*Of low degree.*' Then, as now, there were many poor Christians. Among the Jews who embraced Christianity there was a special cause of poverty, in the intense bigotry of their unbelieving countrymen, through which, in all probability, many were in one way or another deprived of their former means of earning a livelihood, simply because they called the hated Nazarene their Lord. It is evident from various statements in the New Testament, that in the apostolic age distress prevailed very widely among the Christian Jews in Palestine,—largely, no doubt, from the cause I have mentioned; and it is reasonable to suppose that to some extent the same cause acted among those 'in the Dispersion.' Poverty, therefore, was often most evidently a form of suffering persecution for conscience' sake; as in our own day it often is, for example, among Jews or Hindoos who become Christians. Whatever the immediate cause of his humble worldly position might be, however, you will observe that the Christian 'of low degree' is, none the less for his low degree, a 'brother' in the apostle's view. A truth this,—and the apostle's prominent exhibition of it here,—well fitted to comfort these poor Christians: their poverty was no barrier to their sharing fully in the privileges of God's family. It is a truth important to be borne in mind by others. The application in the church of mere worldly standards and estimates of men is altogether alien from the spirit of brotherhood. If one professing Christian entertain for another anything like a feeling of disregard, dislike, contempt, simply because that other is poor, lacks education, is destitute of some of those graces of manner which men obtain through intercourse with polished society, this proves his heart to be, to a very large extent, uncontrolled by Christian truth. Our Master, the Lord from heaven, was a working carpenter; and the disciple who 'leaned on His bosom' was not one of the believing 'honourable counsellors,' but a poor fisherman.

The poor brother is enjoined by the apostle to '*rejoice in that he is exalted.*' The original word rendered '*rejoice*' is a very strong one, commonly translated elsewhere 'glory' or 'boast.' Thus the paradox of grace is exhibited in the most striking form. Amid the depressing influences of poverty, the Christian is to keep his eye fixed on his *real* dignity, and glory in it. His present low position is merely in external things, and consequently temporary, and is appointed him because his heavenly Father sees poverty to be needful for the good of his soul; his dignity belongs to the man himself, considered apart from surroundings, and is thus unending, like himself. The various representations given in Scripture of the relation of believers to God, and of the blessings connected with that relation, are most graciously adapted to cheer under all aspects of the 'low degree.' Many of those to whom James wrote were no doubt slaves: these are told that they are 'the Lord's freedmen.' If the carnal eye looked upon these poor believers as 'the filth of the world and the offscouring of all things,' faith could see in them Jehovah's 'jewels.' However lowly their birth was reputed here, they were 'sons of God;' however intense their penury here, they had 'the true riches,' laid up in a treasure-house 'where no thief could break through or steal.' They might have to hunger often for the food of the body, but they had in abundance 'bread of life,' which would sustain them for ever. They were obliged to associate with, and were themselves ranked among, the despised of the world; but they could with confidence look forward to a 'crown of glory,' to the fellowship of angels, to the beatific vision of God, and close, uninterrupted communion with Him. Their very tribulations were to the eye of faith an evidence of their dignity, for they were *Fatherly* chastisements; and in so far as they suffered on account of religion, they were companions of Jesus in His sufferings, and might take home to their hearts the sweet assurance that they should 'also reign with Him.'

The precise connection of what follows with the preceding is somewhat doubtful. Perhaps the *general* idea of 'trial' or 'temptation' (any thing or state that tests, wealth as well as poverty) had entered the apostle's mind before he gave the injunction of ver. 9, which we have just been examining. Or —and, as it seems to me, this is more probable—the important precept for the rich may have been suggested to him, as obviously it most naturally might, by the mention of the poor, and is thus a digression from the main line of remark, to which he returns at the 12th verse.

'*But the rich, in that he is made low.*' It is clear, from the general tone of the writings of the apostles, that there were very few wealthy men in the primitive church. Few had energy to face the current of public feeling in the upper classes of society, which then ran strongly against the profession of Christianity, as in all ages it has run strongly against earnest, active, living Christianity. Still there were some in the church here and there, like Nicodemus and Joseph of Arimathæa. It was 'hard,' then as now, but not impossible, 'for a rich man to enter into the kingdom of God.' Timothy received from Paul a charge for some members of the church who were 'rich in this world.' Now, obviously, the special spiritual danger of wealthy Christians—the danger, therefore, on which the charge of Paul just mentioned bears—is, that they may 'trust in uncertain riches.' The 'deceitfulness of riches' is such that, through the falsehoods which the unwise possessors of wealth are induced to believe with regard to its power, they lamentably often neglect the great salvation, and throw away their souls. The more their beneficent God 'loadeth them with His benefits,' the less, in many cases, they think of Him or desire to serve Him. Our apostle's direction, accordingly, to those Christian brethren to whom God has given wealth, is to look not on what the world deems their exaltation, but on the humbling of heart which, through the gracious dealings of the

Divine Spirit with them, they have received. Set high through God's providence in earthly station, they had spiritually, if they were true Christians, been made low in their own eyes through convictions of sin and unworthiness. 'Cherish this contrite heart,' says the apostle; 'live much in the contemplation of those aspects of truth which are fitted to drive away high thoughts of self, and rejoice in that infinite mercy which has led you to see that by nature you are wretched, and miserable, and poor, and blind, and naked. Seek not happiness in luxury and splendour; put off all pride of spirit; remember that before God you must appear as you *are*, not as you *seem*; put on, therefore, as the elect of God, humbleness of mind; be clothed with humility, for God resisteth the proud, but giveth grace to the humble. In the Spirit's testimony to your growing humility you may rejoice; for he that exalteth himself shall be abased, but he that humbleth himself shall be exalted.' Such appears to be the force of the apostle's injunction.

The respective duties, then, in the contrasted cases, are these: 'Let the brother who outwardly is in a low position rejoice that God has made him high in real dignity, and let the wealthy brother rejoice that God has made him low in spirit;' or, expressing it more pointedly by availing ourselves of the fact that 'humble,' the usual rendering in our version of the original word here translated 'low,' has very nearly the same latitude of reference as that original word, denoting sometimes outward circumstances and sometimes feeling,— 'Let the brother who is humble in position rejoice in that he is exalted, and the rich in that he is humbled.'

The extreme spiritual danger of the rich man leads the apostle to speak of this a little further, illustrating the folly of cherishing confidence or pride in mere external grandeur by a beautiful comparison showing its perishableness. For an immortal being like man, it is surely utterly irrational to place supreme trust and take supreme delight in any pleasure or possession which is not, like himself, imperishable. A wealthy worldling, feeling this in the depths of his soul, is sometimes almost led, through the deceitfulness of his riches, to dream that they are an imperishable possession. A very long life of luxury and splendour at least, he supposes, is surely before him, the end of which he will try not to think of; and he trusts, too, that in a sense he will live to all generations,— his name and his glory enduring in a line of rich and honoured children. 'Their inward thought is that their houses shall continue for ever, and their dwelling-places to all generations : they call their lands after their own names.' 'Soul, thou hast much goods laid up for many years; take thine ease, eat, drink, and be merry.' O the folly and the madness! 'Thou fool, this night thy soul shall be required of thee.' 'Like sheep they are laid in the grave; death shall feed on them; and their beauty shall consume in the grave from their dwelling.' 'Let the Christian brother who is rich, then,' says the apostle, 'delight in the grace which has made him poor in spirit, and not in his external greatness; *because as the flower of the grass he shall pass away. For the sun is no sooner risen with a burning heat, but it withereth the grass, and the flower thereof falleth, and the grace of the fashion of it perisheth: so also shall the rich man fade away in his ways.*' The term rendered here '*burning heat*' is often used for a hot, desolating wind which blows over parts of Western Asia from the deserts of the east and south, and which is known as the sirocco. It was this that the Lord sent upon Jonah, after the gourd had withered; and it is to it that David refers in the words, 'As for man, his days are as grass : as a flower of the field, so he flourisheth; for the wind passeth over it, and it is gone; and the place thereof shall know it no more.' In the passage before us, then, the apostle appears to conjoin the sun and this wind as agents of destruction; thus: 'The sun is no sooner risen *along with* the burning wind.'

The figure which we have here is common in Scripture to set forth the brevity and uncertainty of life; and the words of James are but a variation of a well-known passage in Isaiah: 'The voice said, Cry. And he said, What shall I cry? All flesh is grass, and all the goodliness thereof is as the flower of the field: the grass withereth, the flower fadeth, because the Spirit of the Lord bloweth upon it: surely the people is grass. The grass withereth, the flower fadeth: but the word of our God shall stand for ever' (Isa. xl. 6-8). The image is one which very naturally suggests itself to a thoughtful, observant, imaginative Eastern. He walks forth into the fields at early morn, whilst the dew-drops are still smiling up to the dawn, and he sees all around a rich carpet of long and verdant grass, among which many beautiful wild flowers delight the eye. Wandering again in the cool of the evening to the same field, he finds that the intense heat of the sun and the blast of the scorching sirocco have desolated the beauty of the morning,— the grass withered, the flowers faded and dead. Even so is it, he thinks, with human life,—now gay, and beautiful, and happy; but 'the Spirit of the Lord—the hot wind of Jehovah's judgements—bloweth upon it,' and it withers away: for 'surely the people is grass.' In the passage before us a special application of the figure is made to the rich man, he and his splendours being represented by the '*flower* of the grass.' So in Peter (1st Ep. i. 24): 'All flesh is as grass, and all the *glory* of man as the *flower* of grass.' As amid the monotony of green the gay wild flowers, by the richness and variety of their hues, attract the eye, so riches and rank give prominence to their possessors among the crowd of mankind. But the 'flower of the grass' fadeth with the grass: so the honoured and the mean pass alike to the grave. The rich and the poor meet together there. As to-day a pauper is carried from his garret to the churchyard, so to-morrow he who but a few days ago was the envied enjoyer of wealth and luxury may be borne forth from his halls and pleasure-grounds, and 'the place that once knew him know him no more.' As the flower withers, so also shall the rich man fade away,—and this '*in his ways*'—in the very midst of his activities, his purposes to 'pull down his barns and build greater,' his busy pursuit of pleasure, and power, and greater riches. How immeasurable, then, is the folly of setting the heart on mere outward splendour, of seeking to be clothed with the garments of mere earthly glory, since these must all perish, and those who had no other raiment must stand naked in the presence of God!

Before passing from this part of the paragraph, it is proper to mention that some interpreters consider the rich man spoken of in the 10th verse not to be a professing Christian at all; it being supposed that, whilst there were wealthy men in the church here and there, yet these were so very few that the mere word 'rich' would at once suggest a member of the persecuting class. According to the most recent form of this view, from the injunction of the 9th verse, 'Let the poor Christian rejoice,' is to be taken for the next clause simply an assertion of fact, thus: 'But the rich (man, not 'brother'—the wealthy worldling) *rejoices* in his humiliation,' in that wealth and splendour which, as God sees the matter, are degrading to him. As the Apostle Paul puts it, 'their glory is in their shame.' The figure which follows, of the perishing flower, will then illustrate wherein this humiliation or degradation lies.

The mere possession of riches is not in itself a sinful thing, a humiliation or source of shame; on the contrary, wealth is a 'talent,' to be faithfully 'occupied' for the Master: but to seek supreme happiness in perishable riches, and that transitory splendour which riches can supply,—this for an immortal soul, for a nature made to enjoy God's favour and fellowship, is a humiliation, a debasement passing all description. 'The rich worldling glories in what, *as gloried in*, is a shame to him.' The meaning thus given to the passage is in itself important, and suits the context well; for you will see how fitted a statement like this was to keep the poor persecuted believers (the only class whom, according to this interpretation, the apostle addresses throughout the paragraph) in a right frame of heart, when they were tempted to be 'double-minded' and 'unstable' through envy of their rich persecutors. The parallelism of the two clauses also is on this view very exact: the poor Christian should rejoice in his real though not seeming greatness, while the rich enemy of God rejoices in his real though not seeming debasement. The only serious objection to this view of the meaning—an objection, however, so serious, as it appears to me, as to be fatal—lies in the unnaturalness of the supplements, the generic 'man' instead of the special 'brother,' and the assertion 'rejoices' for the injunction 'Let—rejoice.' The translation of the clause (the first half of the 10th verse) in our Authorized Version represents the original exactly; so that even the mere English reader, reading the 9th verse and that clause together, can judge for himself of this unnaturalness.

The 12th verse gives the spirit of the whole passage from the beginning of the chapter, and sends home its teaching with power to the hearts of thoughtful readers, setting before them the glory and felicity which through God's grace await those who 'hold the beginning of their confidence stedfast unto the end.' In '*Blessed is the man that endureth temptation*' we have not a simple repetition of the doctrine of the 2nd verse: an explanation of that seeming paradox is introduced. It is not, 'Blessed is the man that *is exposed to* temptation,' but 'that *endureth*'—'bears with patience'—'displays constancy under trial.' 'Behold,' says our apostle elsewhere, 'we count them happy which endure.' The wicked man *suffers;* he does not '*endure,*' in the Scripture use of the word. It is only when 'patience has her work perfect' that the blessing comes. Only those who have a spirit made willing to bear right on to the end what God sends—and this not through efforts after a heartless and unnatural Stoicism, but in childlike submission to the divine will—are 'blessed,' 'happy,' sustained in holy peace and filled with bright hope, under His chastenings.

The truth, or at least one truth, which inspires this blessedness is exhibited by the apostle in the words that follow: '*For when he is tried, he shall receive the crown of life.*' The meaning of the words translated '*when he is tried*' is 'being approved, found to stand the trial.' The word here rendered 'tried' has 'approved' as its representative in every other place of the New Testament where it occurs; and 'tried' is obviously intended by our translators to have the same meaning, as when we speak of a 'tried friend,' or when we read in Isaiah (xxviii. 16), 'Behold, I lay in Zion for a foundation a tried stone.' In James's words there is probably an allusion to the testing of metals for their purity in a furnace,—the figure fully exhibited elsewhere: 'The Messenger of the covenant is like a refiner's fire: and He shall sit as a refiner and purifier of silver: and He shall purify the sons of Levi, and purge them as gold and silver, that they may offer unto the Lord an offering in righteousness' (Mal. iii. 2, 3). The man who stands the test shall '*receive the crown of life.*' His time on earth may be full of sadness; he may walk much in the valley of the shadow of death, and may even be called on to prove himself faithful unto a martyr's death; but yonder there await him the blessedness and glory of the heavenly life, which is 'a crown' of princely dignity,—for 'they which receive abundance of grace and of the gift of righteousness, shall *reign in life* by Jesus Christ.' With Paul this is 'a crown of righteousness,' with Peter 'a crown of glory,' with Isaiah 'a crown of glory and a diadem of beauty,' and with the Saviour Himself, as here, 'a crown of life.' Oh, brethren, how sustaining is the prospect which the apostle opens to us here! With a 'crown of life' before him, will not the enlightened and prayerful Christian be cheered and upheld, even if he be called on to be, like the apostle of the Gentiles, 'in deaths oft'? [1]

[1] On the 'crown of life' Archbishop Trench has some interesting remarks in his *Commentary on the Epistles to the Seven Churches* (with immediate reference to the occurrence of the expression in Rev. ii. 10). 'Is this crown,' he asks, 'the *diadem* of royalty, or the *garland* of victory? I believe, the former. It is quite true that στέφανος is seldom used in this sense,—much oftener διάδημα; yet the "*golden* crowns" (στέφανοι) of Rev. iv. 4 can only be royal crowns (compare v. 10). Στέφανος, too, is the word all the evangelists employ of the "crown of thorns," evidently a caricature of royalty. Did we indeed meet these words, "a crown of life," in the Epistles of St. Paul, we should be justified in saying that, in all probability, the wreath or garland of the victors in the games, the "crown" in this sense, was intended. Paul was familiar with the Greek games, and freely drew his imagery from them, not fearing to contemplate the faithful under the aspect of runners and wrestlers. His universal—Hellenic as well as Jewish—education exempted him from any scruples upon this point. Not so, however, the Christians of Palestine. These Greek games were strange to them, or only not strange as they were the objects of their deepest abhorrence,—as witness the tumults and troubles which accompanied the first introduction of them by Herod the Great at Jerusalem, recorded at length by Josephus.ᵃ Tertullian's point of view, who styles them *superstitiosa certamina Græcarum et religionum et voluptatum*, would very much have been theirs.'

The argument is obviously equally valid, at least, for James as for Revelation.

This crown '*the Lord hath promised to them that love Him.*' Scripture is full of the promise; and simply on this promise rests the believer's hope. When he looks at his own deserts, he can see no crown before him—nothing but darkness and curse; but, 'walking in the light of the Lord,' he can see a reward of grace in the hand of a loving Father, who has promised, and 'cannot lie.' 'Hath He said, and shall He not do it? Hath He spoken, and shall He not make it good?' This reward is set before '*them that love Him,*' that is, before all the truly pious, for love to God is the essence of piety. Wherever it is present, there is spiritual life; and wherever it is absent, how complete soever may be the decorum of moral conduct and outward religious observance, there is spiritual death. Looking back, you will observe the light cast by this clause of the verse on the 'endureth' of the first. In the apostle's view, they that 'endure' and they that 'love God' are obviously the same class. Any measure of 'endurance,' even though nominally in God's cause, yet without 'love,' is valueless before Him. 'Though I give my body to be burned, and have not love, it profiteth me nothing.' And where true love to God exists, awakened by a sense of God's amazing love to us, it will bear, through His sustaining grace, the severest strain. 'Love endureth *all things.*'

IV.

GENESIS OF SIN.

'Let no man say, when he is tempted, I am tempted of God : for God cannot be tempted with evil, neither tempteth He any man ; 14 But every man is tempted, when he is drawn away of his own lust, and enticed. 15 Then, when lust hath conceived, it bringeth forth sin ; and sin, when it is finished, bringeth forth death.'—JAMES i. 13-15.

THE apostle has closed his first paragraph by declaring the 'blessedness' of 'the man that endureth temptation,' seeing that there awaits him the 'crown of life, which the Lord hath promised to them that love Him.' But many of his readers, he knew, were sensible that they had not 'endured' under trial, but had failed to show persistent and unconquerable love to God. Some of them, perhaps, had under persecution all but apostatized. Some among 'the brethren of low degree' were conscious that they had not rejoiced in their spiritual exaltation, but had murmured at their outward humiliation. Some of 'the rich brethren' were sensible that they had forgotten the transitory, unsatisfying nature of worldly wealth, and too largely placed trust and sought joy there, instead of exulting 'that they were made low.' Many, no doubt, in all classes of society, had yielded to the seductive influences of the licentious heathenism around. To all such the apostle says, in the section on which we now enter, 'Lay the blame of your sin where it is due—on yourselves.' A conviction of personal responsibility and personal guilt must always be the first stage in the passage to true peace. The first part of the mission of the Divine Comforter is 'to convince the world of *sin*.'

'*Let no man say, when he is tempted, I am tempted of God: for God cannot be tempted with evil, neither tempteth He any man.*' You feel here that we pass at once to the bad sense of 'tempt,' that in which the word is commonly employed. Hitherto in the Epistle it has imported 'trial' or 'testing' in the most general way. Here it denotes trial with a malevolent aim, a desire to bring into sin through the test. The sudden transition without explanation to this other use—a transition in English corresponding exactly to what is seen in the original —is somewhat remarkable.

Of the reason given in the second part of the verse—'*for God cannot be tempted*[1] *with evil, neither*[2] *tempteth He any man*'—the force seems to be as follows:—'A tempter to sin must be himself sinful, open to the seductions of evil. Now God cannot thus be tempted. His absolute blessedness, His infinite holiness, remove Him wholly from liability to temptation; and as thus, from His very nature, He cannot be tempted to sin, so, from His very nature, He cannot tempt to sin.' I may observe, in passing, that this representation of God, simple and obvious as it appears to us, is yet due wholly to revelation. The gods of heathen imagination are always conceived both

---

[1] The natural meaning of ἀπείραστος, in the connection in which it stands here, is beyond doubt, as it seems to me, 'untempted' or 'untemptable;' and the αὐτός expressed in the following clause, implying an antithesis, supports this view of the meaning, which accordingly is held by the majority of commentators. De Wette and some other expositors take the word in its more usual sense, 'unversed in.'

[2] The δέ after πειράζει marks a contrast to the 'temptableness' which in the previous clause has been denied of God, or, more exactly, to a thought naturally connecting itself with that: 'Now if God were temptable, it would be conceivable that in some circumstances He might tempt,—*but*.'

as liable to temptation to moral evil, and as themselves tempters. The conception of their character comes from man's wicked heart, and the stream cannot rise higher than its source.

'*Let no man say, when he is tempted, I am tempted of God.*' Under the consciousness of sin and the terror of punishment, we are all prone to cast blame away from ourselves—generally either on other men or on Satan. In the singularly interesting and instructive narrative given us in Scripture of the first sin, which was in all essential respects the type of all sins, we find this feature exhibited very distinctly. When challenged by God, 'Hast thou eaten of the tree whereof I commanded thee that thou shouldst not eat?' Adam answers, 'The woman whom Thou gavest to be with me, she gave me of the tree, and I did eat.' Eve, in her turn, says, 'The serpent beguiled me, and I did eat.' Every descendant of this fallen pair, save that 'Seed of the woman' who 'bruised the serpent's head,' has said, or thought, with regard to himself the same things. But subtle as wicked men may be, subtle and powerful and earnest in all evil as wicked angels undoubtedly are, neither men nor devils can *compel* us to sin. We are free to refuse the evil and choose the good; and it is our welcoming the temptation, our choosing the evil instead of the good, which constitutes sin. In the charge laid against Satan and evil men, however, there may be a proportion of truth: the serpent did tempt Eve, and Eve did tempt Adam. But there is another mode of evading personal responsibility which is wholly baseless, which is indeed utter and awful blasphemy,—devolving the blame of our sin upon God. Certain false systems of philosophy (the fatalistic and pantheistic) avow this doctrine in one form or another; and the semi-atheistic materialism, so lamentably popular among our men of science at present, has a teaching practically the same, making sin exactly analogous to bodily disease. By some expositors, the apostle has been supposed to refer in the passage before us to such views, as professed by some among his readers. This is altogether improbable, I think, since it is difficult to see how, under any circumstances, persons holding and avowing such convictions could number themselves among Christians, or, at all events, what could lead them to do so in an age of persecution. In the words he employs, James may perhaps glance slightly at such philosophical theories, as fitted to exercise to some extent an injurious influence even on those who might seem to be placed by their religious belief in a totally different sphere of thought; but he refers immediately and mainly, no doubt, to foolish and wicked thoughts which are apt to rise at times in the minds of all, even of persons whose general views appear most opposed to them.

The thought which he rebukes will occur in various forms. Thus: 'God has ordained all that comes to pass: He has therefore ordained that I should yield to the temptation under which I have now fallen.' Now, everything connected with the nature and doings of the infinite God has, and must have, aspects of profoundest mystery for man. Thus it is so, of course, with His decrees. But regarding them, these things at least are plainly revealed in Scripture, and to be held fast as fundamental truths on the subject: that God, who 'is of purer eyes than to behold iniquity,' is in no sense or measure the author of sin, and that His decrees do no violence to man's own will. 'The secret things belong unto the Lord our God; but those things which are revealed belong unto us and to our children,'—and nothing is more plainly revealed than this, that God hates sin with a perfect hatred, and that all the influences He exerts on man's spirit are for the overthrow of sin. For purposes of infinite wisdom and love, towards the understanding of which glorified saints will grow throughout eternity, God permits in His universe the existence of moral evil; but it is utterly abhorrent to Him; and whencesoever it springs, in no sense or degree does it spring from Him. And with God's eternal providence co-exists entire moral freedom, and, by consequence, the fullest responsibility on the part of man.

Another common form of the blasphemous thought against which the apostle warns us is: 'I have been driven to sin by the circumstances in which God has placed me.' If a poor man becomes dishonest, he blames his poverty. The drunkard blames the associates among whom he was thrown, and by whom he has been led on from the pleasant social glass to utter debasement. So in innumerable other cases. Looking back again to the first sin, you find this there: 'The man said, The woman *whom Thou gavest to be with me*, she gave me of the tree, and I did eat.' You observe the implied reproach on God; the intended force of the 'whom Thou gavest to be with me' clearly being, 'Hadst Thou not given me the woman, had I been left as I was at first, I should not have sinned.' Similar is the spirit of the rich man's petition to Abraham in the parable: 'I pray thee, therefore, father, that thou wouldest send him to my father's house: for I have five brethren; that he may testify unto them, lest they also come into this place of torment.' There is here an attempt at self-justification. He would suggest that he has been in circumstances of insufficient religious light and influence, and that to these was due his life of self-indulgence, and his coming to the place of torment. The answer of the patriarch may be regarded as conveying God's response to all accusations of this kind: 'If they hear not Moses and the prophets, neither will they be persuaded though one rose from the dead.' These words say in substance: 'The Divine King is not "an austere man," or one who "reaps where He has not sown;" He will make all allowances for circumstances, and never exact more than is reasonable. If He calls on men, then, to live lives of holy obedience, and holds them responsible, He has at the same time given ample light; He has spoken in many ways clearly and impressively of their danger; and if they sin, it is not because of their circumstances, but because they will not hear.'

A third form of the charge brought against God, and the only other which I shall mention, is one that occurs probably not unfrequently to the minds of persons who plunge into gross sensual indulgence: 'I am constitutionally of a very ardent temperament; my passions are strong: therefore it is that I live riotously: I cannot help it; I am made so.' Hear poor Burns addressing God thus:

> 'Thou know'st that Thou hast formed me
> With passions wild and strong;
> And listening to their witching voice
> Has often led me wrong.'

In another place, too, he makes the muse of his country address the poet himself thus:

> 'I saw thy pulse's maddening play
> Wild send thee pleasure's devious way,
> Misled by fancy's meteor ray,
> By passion driven:
> But yet the light that led astray
> Was light from heaven.'[1]

---

[1] These passages from Burns have been quoted also by Dr. Wardlaw, who comments on them with his characteristic earnestness and sound judgement.

This has been well answered by another Burns, also a true poet :[1]

> 'It could not be ; no light from heaven
> Has ever led astray :
> Its constant stars to guide are given,
> And never to betray.
>
> 'When passion drives to wild excess,
> And folly wakes to shame,
> It cannot make the madness less
> To cast on heaven the blame.
>
> 'The light that seemed to shine on high,
> And led thee on to sin,
> Was but reflected to thine eye
> From passion's fire within.
>
> 'O spurn the guilty thought away!
> Eternity will tell,
> That every light that led astray
> Was light that shone from hell.'

All such fancies as we have now been considering, all attempts of every kind to throw off from ourselves responsibility for our sins, are delusions of the devil to draw us to destruction. By nothing in our constitution, by nothing in the circumstances in which God's providence has placed us, or the influences which He permits to act upon us, are we laid under a necessity of sinning. Reason has been given to us, — and truth revealed to guide the reason, — to hold the passions under control, and to derive for the service of God helps, not hindrances, from circumstances of every kind. We may, if we would, shun sin; and we sin, simply because we choose to sin. 'This is the condemnation, that light is come into the world, and men loved darkness rather than light, because their deeds were evil.' 'Ye will not come to Me, that ye might have life.'

In the words which follow, the apostle proceeds to set forth

[1] The late Rev. James D. Burns of Hampstead.

the real spring of sin. '*But every man is tempted, when he is drawn away of his own lust, and enticed. Then, when lust hath conceived, it bringeth forth sin.*' The word '*lust*' here, as commonly in Scripture, is not to be taken in the narrow sense in which we now generally use it, but denotes 'sinful desire' of every kind, desire for any pleasure, or supposed pleasure, which in nature or degree is opposed to the will of God,—be it from wealth, ease, revenge, bodily gratification, or any other source. What God has placed around us for our enjoyment is in itself not evil, but good,—if we would *use* it, and not *abuse*. 'The corruption that is in the world' is there, the Apostle Peter tells us, 'through lust:' which John, classifying its forms, describes as 'the lust of the flesh,' 'the lust of the eyes,' and 'the pride of life,'—exemplified, all of them, at the very first appearance of sin on the earth. 'And when the woman saw that the tree was *good for food*, and that it was *pleasant to the eyes*, and a tree *to be desired to make one wise*, she took of the fruit thereof, and did eat.'

Observe the distinctness and emphasis with which the apostle brings out *personal* responsibility: '*Every*' (rather 'each') 'man is tempted when he is drawn away of *his own* lust.' This is as if he said: 'Be under no delusion, brethren, on this matter of surpassing moment. To think of God as the author of sin is blasphemy: devils and wicked men can do you moral harm only by your consenting to let the evil into your hearts: with *yourselves* rests the blame. And you cannot cover your responsibility with abstract principles regarding human nature; you cannot hide yourselves among the crowd of a fallen race; *each individual* among you is tempted, and that by *his own* lust.'

This Epistle is throughout practical, and the apostle introduces doctrinal statements or discussions only in so far as they bear immediately upon the conduct of life. Here, accordingly, we have no investigation of the moral character of desires themselves, or of the origin of their depravity. In these matters his readers might easily lose themselves in a cloud of metaphysics, and miss the point of conviction to which he wishes to bring them. He assumes the existence of a depraved nature (which, according to the view of the divine character that has been given in the previous verse, could not have derived its depravity from God); and then, taking from the experience of each of his readers any clear, decided breach of the divine law, such as the conscience of every one would readily suggest, he proceeds to show how that sin arose,—and this with singularly graphic force. The sinful desire within us (some affection of the 'carnal mind,' which 'is enmity against God') is represented as a wicked woman, who by meretricious wiles strives to entrap the *will*, which is in fact man himself, morally considered. She '*draws him away*' from the contemplation of true pleasures and noble aims, and '*entices*' him to give himself wholly up to her. For a time, it may be, he resists, thinking of God, of grace, of judgement, of hell, remembering perhaps a mother's prayers or a father's dying counsels. Still she plies her arts, and at last he yields,—the *will* consents to the wicked *wish*,—prompting becomes purpose, desire determination; and the fruit of the unhallowed union of Will and Lust is clear, well-defined, actual Sin. 'Every man is tempted, when he is drawn away of his own lust, and enticed. Then, when lust hath conceived, it bringeth forth sin.' How vivid and powerful this representation is, my brethren! How distinctly does the experience of all of us—our memory of the genesis of our sins—attest the truthfulness of the picture![1]

'*And sin, when it is finished, bringeth forth death.*' 'Lust,'

[1] 'Primo occurrit menti simplex cogitatio, deinde fortis imaginatio, postea delectatio et motus pravus et assensio.'—*De Imit. Chr.* i. 13. 5.

we have seen, 'bringeth forth sin;' but 'the end is not yet.' The wretched line of posterity does not close here: sin, too, has its offspring; for *'when it is finished'*—when it has run its natural course—it *'bringeth forth death.'*[1] The working of sin does not end with the angry speech, the lie, the act of dishonesty or sensual indulgence. It hardens, darkens, debases the nature, renders the heart opener than before to all evil influences, and less open to all good; and, unless the divine mercy in Jesus Christ intervene, will certainly at last yield as its result death, in the most comprehensive and awful sense of that word. From the nature of things, death, in the great Bible use of the term—blight and desolation over the whole man, spirit, and soul, and body,—is the consequence of sin. Sin renders intercourse with God, who is the Fountain of life, impossible. It consists in the exercise of feelings which in their own nature are utterly inconsistent with true happiness; and it increases constantly in strength, in malignity, in power to destroy the peace of the soul. Besides, looked at apart from these essential tendencies of sin, the relation which it bears to conscience and to the justice of God renders the connection between it and death—between iniquity and misery—indissoluble. Death is 'the *wages* of sin,' due to it in justice. Under the righteous administration of the affairs of the universe by God, there is the same obligation in justice that sin should be followed by death, as that a labourer should receive the recompense he has been promised and has worked for. Sin *is* spiritual death, and every act of sin intensifies the spiritual deadness; to sin, and sin alone, is due that awful and

---

[1] In the original, the fact that the words for 'lust' and 'sin' are both *feminine* contributes to the verisimilitude of the figurative representation. The reader will recall, in connection with this passage, the familiar lines of Milton, *Par. Lost*, ii. 747-800, which are evidently based on James's words.

mysterious change which severs soul from body, and which we commonly call death; and when sin is '*finished*'—when it is allowed to go on to its legitimate issues—'*it bringeth forth*' that intensity of misery, transcending our present powers of conception, which John calls 'the second death,' and which the Lord Himself, 'the Faithful Witness,' describes as 'outer darkness, where shall be weeping and gnashing of teeth.' Oh, my brethren, may God in His infinite mercy grant that to all of us the depth of meaning in these awful words may for ever remain an undiscovered secret!

Observe how fully and strikingly the apostle exhibits the contrast between God's work and that of sinful desire; and how conclusively he has established his proposition, that though *trial for man's good* is from God, *temptation to sin* cannot be from Him. Trial 'worketh patience'—this is God's purpose in sending it; and when 'patience has its work perfect,' when the tried 'endure' their trials, God pronounces them 'blessed,' and gives them at last 'the crown of *life*.'[1] But wicked desire, when man's will has yielded to it, 'bringeth forth sin; and sin, when it is finished, bringeth forth *death*.' God gives life; but by man himself always comes death.[2]

[1] See verses 3, 4, 12.
[2] Compare Gen. ii. 7; Rom. vi. 23; 1 Cor. xv. 21.

V.

GOOD GIFTS FROM GOD.

'Do not err, my beloved brethren. 17 Every good gift and every perfect gift is from above, and cometh down from the Father of lights, with whom is no variableness, neither shadow of turning.'—JAMES i. 16, 17.

THE expression rendered here '*Do not err*' occurs several times in the New Testament, but in all the other places is translated 'Be not deceived.' It has always a reference to what has preceded, and at the same time introduces a new and impressive aspect of the truth on which it is said to be of importance not to err, or an argument in its support. It always intimates that the matter under consideration is one of great moment; thus: 'Be not deceived: God is not mocked; for whatsoever a man soweth, that shall he also reap:' 'Be not deceived: evil communications corrupt good manners' (Gal. vi. 7; 1 Cor. xv. 33). Here, accordingly, it sets forth the vast importance of right views regarding the origin and growth of sin. Our views on this subject cannot but most materially affect our feelings and our life. Where the blasphemy that God is the author of sin is in a defined form thoroughly entertained by the mind, the man cannot be a Christian: where the thought, when it rises, is not at once with horror repelled, religious vitality must be very low, if life can exist at all. If a right estimate be wanting of the fulness of man's moral responsibility, there can manifestly be no correct appreciation of the nature and evil of sin, of the divine character, of the nature of the Saviour's work, or of His claims on our gratitude and devotion. Thus by false conceptions here the whole structure of Christian faith and hope and holiness is undermined. In every aspect in which the thought that God tempts to sin can be presented, however modified or disguised, it is utterly impious, unspeakably dishonouring to God, and destructive to the soul. Good cause, therefore, has the apostle for his earnest appeal, 'Do not err'—'Be not deceived.'

This warning, you observe, naturally brings up before our minds the great importance everywhere ascribed in Scripture to correct views of religious truth generally. It is the teaching of the Bible that, while the spring of evil in man is a perverse will, a desire to disobey God, yet wicked emotion and action arise immediately from false views with which the mind is filled through the blinding influence of the perverse will on the judgement,—false views of God, and of ourselves, and of the relation in which we stand to God. 'Wherefore doth the wicked contemn God?' asks the Psalmist; and he proceeds to give the answer: 'He hath said in his heart, Thou wilt not require it.' Misconception regarding God as a living God, who marks men's hearts and lives, and will judge them, can alone account for so monstrous a state of soul. Error being thus the source of sin, the suitable instrumentality for His purpose, who 'gave Himself for us, that He might redeem us from all iniquity, and purify unto Himself a peculiar people, zealous of good works,' is a revelation of truth; and in exact proportion as this truth is understood and believed—its meaning clearly seen, and its importance vividly realized—is the removal of sin from our hearts and lives. 'The truth shall make you free,' was the Lord's declaration to the sin-enslaved Jews; and His prayer for His people was, 'Sanctify them through Thy truth; Thy word is truth.' It may be safely said, that there is no error in religious doctrine which is not in its nature fitted to affect injuriously religious feeling and conduct. The digression from truth may seem slight, as a footpath may start from a high road at a very small angle of divergence; but follow it up, and you might soon find yourselves far away from any point on the high road, travelling through a different region. It is grievously uncharitable to attribute to a man who professes a particular opinion all either of doctrinal inferences or of practical results which you see, or think you see, to follow legitimately from his opinion: for many counteracting agencies may be at work to neutralize the poison of error. Thus many men are much better than their creed, and if they saw all the fair deductions from their avowed opinions, would fling these from them with horror, like one who suddenly discovered that he had been cherishing a serpent in his bosom. But for *ourselves*, brethren, we cannot be too careful in the formation of our religious opinions; and this with reference not merely to cardinal matters of faith, but even to what may seem subordinate points. 'Let us not err, my beloved brethren:' let us not be led away by glittering plausibilities, but *think* earnestly and conscientiously, looking at subjects and statements not simply in the aspect in which they are first presented to us, but all round, praying much always for God's Spirit, that we may walk 'in the light of the Lord.'

Observe the affectionate manner in which the apostle makes his appeal: '*my beloved brethren.*' We have a fine example here for all controversial dealing. Passionate denunciation raises up in opposition all the fierceness or sullenness of a man's nature, and thus deafens the soul to the voice of truth. Love is by many degrees the most powerful solvent of obstinacy and prejudice. It is with the 'bands of love' that the erring are by far the most likely to be drawn back to the right way. 'The servant of the Lord,' says the Apostle Paul, 'must not strive; but be gentle unto all men, apt to teach, patient; in meekness instructing those that oppose themselves; if God peradventure will give them repentance to the acknowledging of the truth; and that they may recover themselves out of the snare of the devil, who are taken captive by him at his will.'

I said above, that wherever the expression 'Do not err' ('Be not deceived') occurs in the New Testament, it always has a reference to what has preceded, and at the same time introduces a new and impressive aspect of truth on the point under discussion, or an argument in its support. Here, accordingly, having in the previous verses stated negatively the truth on the matter he has in hand,—thus: 'God is in no sense or degree the author of sin,'—the apostle proceeds now to exhibit such positive truth regarding the divine character as puts in the strongest light the folly and wickedness of the supposition that God could tempt to sin. 'God is love; and, in accordance with this His nature, His conduct to men is characterized by boundless benevolence. In particular, the awakening and fostering of spiritual life in men is wholly His work. Must it not, then, be utterly foolish and blasphemous to ascribe the authorship of the death in sin to Him who is the Author of life in holiness, and who, from His nature, is in all things consistent and immutable?' Such seems to be the argument exhibited in the 17th and 18th verses.

In addition to this logical connection of these verses with the preceding section in the line of argument now stated, there is also a connection in the form or way of setting forth the truth. It is important to notice this, as it shows the naturalness of phraseology which at first sight might appear somewhat unnatural. The apostle's mind is occupied with the thought of birth, generation, fatherhood. He has told us that when man's will has been 'drawn away and enticed' by his lust, then lust, conceiving, 'bringeth forth sin; and sin, when it is finished, bringeth forth death.' This mode of looking at the matter is carried on; and thus God naturally comes before us as a *Father*, 'the Father of lights,' who '*begat* us with the word of truth.'

The first statement of the apostle in his positive teaching regarding God's relations to men is, that '*every good gift and every perfect gift is from above, and cometh down from the Father of lights.*' No very substantial or obvious distinction can be drawn between '*good gift*' and '*perfect gift*' (or rather, perhaps, 'perfect boon,' for the words are different in the original, though as nearly as may be synonymous). The apostle wishes to state the truth very emphatically and impressively, in opposition to the falsehood that evil influences are from God. 'Nay, my brethren, every gift that is *good*, every boon that is *perfect*, this is from heaven; but not what is evil.' Such seems to be the force of his words.[1]

The statement is true, taken with the most general reference. All the beauty, and comfort, and joy in our lives come from God; and this as bounties, as free gifts to us, the undeserving. Whatever intermediate agencies He may have chosen to employ, yet to Him the gifts are wholly due; and we should never rest in the view merely of secondary agencies, but rise in thought to the great Fountain of life and joy, and praise the

[1] The peculiar fulness and pleasantness of the form in which the subject is expressed ('every good gift and every perfect boon') suggest naturally that the words are perhaps quoted from a poem; and this is confirmed when we find that in the original we have here an hexameter line. Winer speaks of it as 'a current poetic sentence from an unknown source.'

divine love. It is God that 'healeth our diseases, redeemeth our lives from destruction, and satisfieth our mouths with good things.' 'The earth is full of the goodness of the Lord.' 'O Lord, Thou preservest man and beast. How excellent is Thy loving-kindness, O God! Therefore the children of men put their trust under the shadow of Thy wings.'

It is evident, however, from the nature of the argument on which the apostle is engaged, that he speaks of God's gifts here with special reference to their action on the soul of man; for he is setting forth the truth which stands opposed to the error that God is the author of sin. It is by no means improbable that the direct influences of the Holy Ghost were primarily in his thoughts, in speaking of '*good gifts*.' At least the expression would very naturally suggest to him—or be suggested to him by—the words of Jesus in the Sermon on the Mount, 'If ye, being evil, know how to give good gifts unto your children, how much more shall your Father which is in heaven give good things to them that ask Him?' (Matt. vii. 11); of which last expression the Lord Himself, by the form in which He repeated the declaration on another occasion, showed the chief reference in His mind to be to divine influence on the heart: 'How much more shall your heavenly Father give *the Holy Spirit* to them that ask Him?' (Luke xi. 13). I have before had occasion to remark that the Sermon on the Mount had evidently made a peculiarly deep impression on this apostle, and exercised great sway in the formation of his cast of religious thought, and over the language of the Epistle. In the verse before us, then, as it appears to me, he says: 'All the influences brought into action on men's hearts which are in their nature good and perfect, and tend to make men good and perfect, all the enlightening and quickening dealings of the Holy Ghost, are from God.' But, further, everything which God has created may, under certain circumstances, exert power over our moral nature. All these things too, then, the apostle would have us understand, are in their original tendency, as designed by God, '*good*,' and helpful to man's soul. As they come from the divine hand, they are, as regards moral influence, as well as in all other respects, '*perfect*' in their kind; and if, in the influence they actually exert on men, there be anything bad or imperfect, drawing to sin and not to holiness, this element has entered from another source than God—even, as the apostle has already told us, from man's perverse desires. 'Corruption is in the world *through lust.*' The harvest-field, waving with golden grain, is in itself a 'good gift,' a 'perfect boon,' fitted and designed to fill the soul with thankfulness and love to the great Giver, though the fertility *may* swell the possessor's heart with sinful pride and self-confidence, tempting him to say, 'Soul, thou hast much goods laid up for many years; take thine ease, eat, drink, and be merry.' 'Every gift that is good, and every boon that is perfect, is from above, and cometh down from the Father of lights.'

This peculiar name here given to God, '*the Father of lights*,' calls now for consideration. By the statement that 'every good gift is *from above*'—'from that world yonder,' as we instinctively conceive the apostle saying, pointing upward—the thoughts of any reflective and imaginative person might very easily be carried at once to that glorious effulgence of light which the sun is pouring forth on the world from day to day, quickening and gladdening all nature, as both in itself a 'good gift' of God, and a lively type or picture for the heart of that boundless outflow of kindness, that golden radiance of blessing, ever streaming forth from heaven to undeserving men. To a Hebrew, to whose warm Eastern imagination the language of figure and symbolism was almost as natural as the plainest prose is to us, the thought which I have mentioned could hardly fail to occur, remembering as he did that everywhere in his ancient Scriptures *light* is the favourite image for every kind of 'good and perfect gift'—for knowledge, for holiness, for happiness, for all excellences of mind and heart, for whatever is most noble, and beautiful, and precious. '*Light* is sown for the righteous, and gladness for the upright in heart.' 'The Lord is my *light* and my salvation; whom shall I fear?' 'There be many that say, Who will show us any good? Lord, lift Thou up the *light* of Thy countenance upon us.' To 'the twelve tribes scattered abroad,' therefore, nothing could appear more natural than the apostle's expression, 'Every good gift and every perfect boon is from above, and cometh down from the *great Creator of the lights*,'—the grand primal Fountain of all that illumines, and enlivens, and gladdens in the universe. The reference is in the first place, no doubt, to the material luminaries, particularly the two great lights which God has set in the sky—the sun 'to rule the day,' and the moon 'to rule the night;' but this simply as the starting-point of thought regarding all those joys and excellences, those myriad 'good gifts and perfect boons,' of which light is the type. The use of the term '*Father*' for 'Creator' is due, as I have already explained, to the figure of birth or generation which runs through the whole passage, and which we find showing itself again in the next verse, in 'begat.' It is not impossible that James had in his mind the words spoken by Jehovah Himself to Job out of the whirlwind, 'Hath the rain a father? or who hath begotten the drops of dew?' (Job xxxviii. 28).

In the words which follow, '*with whom is no variableness, neither shadow of turning*,' there is an implied contrast between

God, the Creator of the lights, and all the lights He has created, material or spiritual. The 'gifts,' which are 'good and perfect' as they come from Him, are marred by the weakness and folly of man; and the lights of the firmament, which symbolize these, have, by God's appointment, revolutions and variations. The sun is not always with us. He leaves us to the gloom of night—a night at some seasons longer than the day; and this gloom of night is not always dispelled by the moon, 'walking in brightness,' for she, too, has her times of darkness. Sometimes, also, in the revolutions of the earth, and of its satellite the moon, the sun is eclipsed from us by the intervention of the moon, or the moon by the shadow of the earth. But '*with the Father of lights there is no variableness, nor any shadow from turning,*'—any shadow, that is to say, caused by revolution; for this appears to be the meaning, and not what the English words 'neither shadow *of* turning' most readily import, 'not the slightest turning,' 'not a shadow of change.' The statement is obviously substantially equivalent to that of John, 'God is light, and in Him is no darkness at all' (1 Ep. i. 5).

We have here, you observe, an important link in the apostle's argument, which may be stated thus: 'God cannot be in any sense or measure the author of sin; for sin is darkness,[1] whereas God is light, light that knows no darkness, no shadow, —essentially, eternally, immutably light.' He is 'the same yesterday, and to-day, and for ever,' the Giver of 'good and perfect gifts,' of *nothing but* 'good and perfect gifts.' Storm and earthquake have great ends of kindness to work out. Afflictions, as God designs them, are among His choicest blessings. The final judgements on the obstinately impenitent

---

[1] Compare 1 John i. 6, and indeed the whole of the first part of that Epistle.

are designed and needed to maintain the honour of the divine government, and thus to secure the highest and everlasting good of the moral universe. 'Every gift that is good, and every boon that is perfect, is from above, and cometh down from the Father of lights, with whom is no variableness, neither any shadow from turning.'

In a world such as this is—a world of confusions, of sins and struggles and sorrows—even the 'lights' which the church of God enjoys will always be subject to 'change' and 'shadow,' though their Creator knows none; but it will not be so with her always. She counts Him faithful who hath promised: 'Thy sun shall no more go down, neither shall thy moon withdraw itself: for the Lord shall be thine everlasting light, and the days of thy mourning shall be ended.'

VI.

REGENERATION.

'Of His own will begat He us with the word of truth, that we should be a kind of first-fruits of His creatures.'—JAMES i. 18.

THIS is a verse of very great interest. The truth set forth in it is in itself one of unspeakable importance; and the statement of it here has a special value for students of this Epistle, from the fact that it exhibits more clearly and fully than any other passage what sceptically-inclined persons have often questioned—the perfect harmony between the teaching of James and that of the other apostles respecting the way of salvation, the essence of evangelical truth. The object James had mainly in view led him to draw the attention of his readers chiefly to the fruits of piety; here its roots are described, very briefly, but with marvellous completeness and beauty, and in a form so Pauline, that probably most persons who heard the words quoted apart from the context would look for them first in Romans or Ephesians.

The statement is, that 'God, the Father or Originator of all enlightening and quickening influences, has of His free will originated a new life in us Christians, by means of the word of His truth, and to the intent that we might be a kind of first-fruits of His creatures.' The connection with the previous argument is somewhat on this wise: 'Consider the greatest of all His good and perfect gifts; He has given us *life:* how is it conceivable that He, immutable, always consistent, without variableness or shadow from turning, could be the author of *death?*'

We have brought before us in this verse, then, the subject of regeneration or the new birth, that great change of heart elsewhere spoken of as a new creation, or a resurrection from the dead, a dying to sin and becoming alive to righteousness,—the subject which, of all that can occupy our attention, is of incomparably the greatest practical moment. Formal division will aid us in clearness of exposition.

I. The *nature* of regeneration is set forth by the apostle in the words, 'God *begat* us.'

It consists, then, in the *origination of a new life.* For a moral creature to *live,* according to the grand Bible use of the word, is for him to give up all the powers and capacities that God has bestowed upon him to those ends for which God bestowed them,—to devote all his faculties to serving God, and to seek happiness in God's favour and fellowship. If this be life, then certainly observation and candid self-scrutiny will give to all who listen to their teaching the same testimony as that implied in the apostle's words, that by nature we are all destitute of this life, all '*dead* in trespasses and sins,' being prone to what is evil, and averse to whatever is in the highest sense good. According to Bible teaching, nothing is morally good in God's sight but what springs from love to Him and regard for His will. What man calls his natural goodness, then, the 'good-heartedness, good temper, good humour,' which is found in many that care nothing for religion, is not goodness before God; for it is but a product of indolence, or self-indulgence, or, at the best, nervous constitution. 'The heart is deceitful above all things, and desperately wicked.' 'In Thy sight shall no man living be justified.' By nature, men are spiritually dead.

But Christians have spiritual life. They have been 'begotten' by the Father of lights—'born again.' Their views and feelings on every point connected with the moral relations between them and God have been radically changed. They now admire, love, trust, and delight to obey Him whom formerly they dreaded, hated, shunned to think of. They have been 'transformed by the renewing of their minds,' so as to 'prove' in personal experience how 'good and acceptable and perfect' the will of God is. The desires and tastes of the soul are different now from what they were before. In the heart, where sensuality or greed or frivolity held sway, purity and seriousness and noble aims now reign; and out of the purified heart are pure and holy issues of life. Many objects of former affection are loved still, but for new reasons substituted or added, and with new wishes respecting them. Thus, to the natural instinct of parental love now conjoins itself, as the ruling element, a tender devotedness and watchful anxiety for the spiritual interests of those regarding whom Jesus is now heard saying to father and mother, 'Feed My lambs.' Many objects which formerly engaged interest engage it no more, or in a greatly lessened degree. Many things that were before looked at with satisfaction, or pursued with eagerness, now excite loathing and horror. Companions who were merely hearty, jovial men of the world, are cherished companions no longer, and occasional association with them brings sadness rather than satisfaction. Excess now and again in some form of animal enjoyment, which was once deemed but a trifle, is now seen to be sin and abomination in the sight of God, and looked upon with disgust. The study of the Bible has now a genuine and deep interest. Prayer is enjoyed, because it is a real approach of spirit to God. Work done for the Saviour, be it preaching the gospel in the wilds of Africa, or quietly handing in a tract from door to door at home, is felt to be reasonable and sweet. Our passing into this new state of thought and feeling is regeneration.

You will observe, then, that, being the introduction of a new life, a new life for the whole man, spirit, soul, and body, regeneration is plainly a *radical* change. The heart is 'directed into the love of God.' The fountain is purified, that by all the channels of the nature a pellucid stream of holiness may be carried throughout the whole being, to refresh and beautify. A change of external conduct, therefore, however striking and pleasant, is not, *taken by itself*, the 'great change.' Reformation, in our ordinary use of the term, does not *necessarily* prove regeneration. When a drunkard or a licentious man becomes sober, chaste, industrious, a good citizen, a kind father or son or friend, this is an admirable change, a change for which the man deserves high respect, and which gives very good ground for hope that he has been 'born again.' Yet it *may be* the result of influences not at all of a religious kind, but belonging strictly to this world. Reformation proves regeneration, only where it springs from regard to the will of God, loved as a pardoning God in Christ Jesus.

Being a radical change, regeneration is altogether distinct from a respectable development of natural character. We often see a boy, reared by discreet, especially Christian parents, ripening under kind providential influences into a useful man, an honoured member of society. As he grows, he 'puts away childish things.' Manly thought awakens manly sensibility; he acquires some sense of the seriousness of life, as a scene of difficulty and conflict; emergencies rouse up slumbering energies; and a certain dignity of character is formed, which commands respect. But if this be *all*, then there is here no regeneration. There may be in an unregenerate man refined sensibilities, magnanimous impulses, and even some interest in religion. 'One thing is needful;' and it is possible to have very many things which are beautiful and pleasant, and yet not to 'choose that good part.' A certain ruler came to Jesus, and, kneeling, 'asked Him, Good Master, what shall I do that I may inherit eternal life? And Jesus said unto him, Thou knowest the commandments, Do not commit adultery, Do not kill, Do not steal, Do not bear false witness, Defraud not, Honour thy father and mother. And he answered and said unto Him, Master, all these have I observed from my youth. Then Jesus, beholding him, loved him, and said unto him, One thing thou lackest: go thy way, sell whatsoever thou hast, and give to the poor, and thou shalt have treasure in heaven: and come, take up thy cross, and follow Me. And he was sad at that saying, and went away grieved, for he had great possessions.' How much must have been beautiful in this young man's character, when Jesus 'loved him'! And yet he was not regenerate. He was 'grieved,'—'very sorrowful;' *but he 'went away:'* he could not give up all for Christ—could not take the will of God as his rule in everything. 'One thing he lacked,' but that was the 'one thing needful.' His attractiveness of character was the work of God, indeed (for from Him come all things that are beautiful and noble,—'every good gift'), but not by way of regeneration: it was only a fair flower springing from the root of nature, under peculiarly favourable circumstances in divine providence, and 'like the flower of the grass' to pass away. Now regeneration is the introduction of a new life, a life imperishable, everlasting.

And *this life is that of children of God.* This most wonderful and precious truth also is evidently involved in the apostle's declaration that 'God *begat* us.' In a true sense all mankind are children of God, as being His moral creatures, made by

Him in His own image, and continually sustained by His care and goodness. 'As certain even of the heathen poets have said, We are His offspring.' But, alas, we have not remained in our home; we have wandered away into the 'far country' of sin, and have striven to forget our Father's house and our Father's love. Yet that love yearned over the prodigals; and His grace in Christ Jesus raises believers to a new and blessed relation of sonship, in which His covenant love secures the eternal continuance of a filial spirit, and thus that we shall abide in our Father's house for ever. 'As many as received Jesus, to them gave He power to become sons of God, even to them that believe on His name.' 'Come out from among the wicked, and be ye separate, saith the Lord, and touch not the unclean thing; and I will receive you, and will be a Father unto you, and ye shall be My sons and daughters, saith the Lord Almighty.' How illustrious is this dignity, my brethren! When Cowper, in his exquisite 'Lines on receiving his Mother's Picture,' says:

> ' My boast is not that I deduce my birth
> From loins enthroned and rulers of the earth,
> But higher far my proud pretensions rise,
> The child of parents passed into the skies;'

we feel that there is here shown a true appreciation of essential worth and dignity. If the richest spring of honour, then, connected with earthly parentage be to be descended from those whose characters bore the charm of Christian goodness, how ineffable the dignity must be to be His children, of whose infinite radiance of holy beauty the highest moral loveliness of earth is but a faint reflection! 'Behold what manner of love the Father hath bestowed upon us, that we should be called the sons of God!'

II. The apostle exhibits to us the *instrumentality* of

regeneration, in the statement that 'God begat us *with the word of truth.*'

The gospel of Jesus Christ—the Bible, of which the gospel is the substance—is emphatically and by pre-eminence 'the word of truth,' 'to which whatever is contrary is imposture, and whatever is compared to it insignificant.'[1] Now the constant statement of Scripture is, that the new life is produced by this 'word of truth,' understood and believed. Thus Peter tells us that men are 'born again, not of corruptible seed, but of incorruptible, by the word of God, which liveth and abideth for ever, the word which by the gospel is preached unto you,' and that it is 'by God's exceeding great and precious promises' that we 'become partakers of the divine nature;' and the Lord Jesus Himself says, 'The words that I speak unto you, they are spirit, and they are life.'

Wilful ignorance—wilful misconception of the divine character, and of our own, and of the relations in which we stand to God—is the immediate spring of sinful feeling and action. Wilful ignorance of God is described by the Apostle Paul as one great distinguishing characteristic of those who shall finally be condemned, 'when the Lord Jesus shall be revealed from heaven, with His mighty angels, in flaming fire, taking vengeance on *them that know not God.*' The unregenerate man shrinks from the thought of God, a living, observing, judging God. In all his difficulties and sorrows he would seek refuge anywhere rather than in the counsel and help of God, because he does not know Him to be 'merciful, and gracious, and long-suffering,' but, having become 'vain in his imaginations, with his foolish heart darkened,' deems Him to be a cold and austere being, whom it is impossible to please or to love. Or perhaps, shrinking as really from the thought of the

---
[1] Robert Hall.

sin-hating Being that the instincts of his conscience assure him God in truth is, he succeeds in half-persuading himself that he has to do with a God weakly placable, like those many earthly parents whose self-indulgent, foolish fondness is so often proved by results to be in reality terribly cruel. Now, as from ignorance of God springs sin, with its constant fruits, sorrow and fear, so from the knowledge of God arise holiness and joy, life and godliness. As to 'know not God' necessarily involves to be wicked and to be unhappy, which are the essential elements of *death*, so 'this is *life* eternal, to know the only true God, and Jesus Christ, whom He hath sent.' Such knowledge can be obtained only through the faith of the gospel, a hearty acceptance of God's testimony concerning Himself as gracious in Jesus Christ. When a man believes the 'word of truth,' it convinces him of sin : for no man, looking at his character in the 'light of God,' can help crying out, 'Unclean, unclean!' 'God be merciful to me, a sinner!' His suspicion and dread of God, too, which aforetime barred his heart against even honest consideration of the divine claims on his service, are removed by the gospel, telling us that in Christ He is ready to 'receive us graciously,' to guide and watch over us with Fatherly love, and to make us happy in His presence for evermore. The icy barriers of suspicion are melted by the rays of the sun of righteousness, and the streams of filial affection ripple joyously on towards God. Thus through the 'word of truth' we enter into spiritual life.

III. We have set before us the *Author* of regeneration, the *Originator* of the new life, in the apostle's statement that '*He (the Father of lights)* begat us with the word of truth.' This indicates not merely that God gave us the Bible, the 'word of truth,' itself a 'good and perfect gift,' but also that it is He who, by an influence graciously exerted on the soul, leads men to believe it. The communication of truth in Scripture is full and clear, fitted to convince and satisfy a candid mind; but by nature our souls, instead of being candid, are so beclouded by wilful prejudice, that, left to ourselves, no one of us would with seriousness and openness of heart consider the truth. The mental eye could see, but, amid sunlight streaming all around, the sinner obstinately keeps his eyes closed. But God by His action on the will induces men to open their eyes, and thus see the truth and feel its force. Thus He regenerates. His spiritual children are 'born not of blood, nor of the will of the flesh, nor of the will of man, but of God.' 'God, who is rich in mercy, hath quickened us—made us live—together with Christ; for by grace are we saved, through faith, and that not of ourselves: it is the gift of God.'

This divine action on the soul is through the Holy Spirit. In the blessed economy of grace, the Father is set forth as originating the plan of redemption; whilst the Spirit applies the blessings purchased by the Son. Our deliverance is *of* the Father, *by* the Son, *through* the Spirit. The Holy Ghost is the grand immediate Agent in regeneration. Through Him we are 'renewed in the whole man after the image of God.' To Him are due alike the beginning and the growth of spiritual life. As with the old creation, so with the new: but that He 'breathes into man the breath of life,' our souls would continue utterly torpid and insensate, 'dead in trespasses and sins.' It is He who clears away the mists of prejudice, who impels to attention to the truth, who bends the stubborn heart, and turns it from iniquity. Blessing the means of grace, He makes the good seed of the word germinate, waters the tender plant continually with the genial rain of His heavenly influences, and makes it bring forth the fruits of godliness and peace. Or, according to another scriptural representation,

God's people are 'temples of the Holy Ghost,' in which 'He dwells,'—not fitfully, as an uncertain lodger, now here, now there, but as in a home which He delights to make beautiful and happy.

Regeneration, then, is *of* God, 'the Father of lights,' *through* His Spirit.

IV. The *ultimate cause* of regeneration is set forth in the words, '*Of His own will* begat He us.' It is from *spontaneous kindness* that God originates this new life. If we were to trace the history of kind deeds among men, we should often find that the persons who perform them receive the impulse to some extent from others. But it cannot be so with God. 'Who hath directed the Spirit of the Lord, or being His counsellor hath taught Him?' And there is in us by nature nothing to attract the affectionate interest of a holy Being: everything to avert it. *Death* we have *earned* as *wages;* 'eternal *life* is the *gift* of God,' the gift of free grace. 'Not by works of righteousness which we have done, but according to His mercy God saves us, by the washing of regeneration, and renewing of the Holy Ghost.' 'Blessed be the God and Father of our Lord Jesus Christ, who hath blessed us with all spiritual blessings in heavenly places in Christ, according as He hath chosen us in Him before the foundation of the world: having predestinated us unto the adoption of children by Jesus Christ to Himself, according to the good pleasure of His will:' 'That, according as it is written, He that glorieth, let him glory in the Lord.'

The words 'of His own will' have, as you will observe, a special emphasis from their position; and this corresponds to the original. The apostle would have us see that a portion of the force of his argument is found here. The argument is this: 'God cannot be in any sense or degree the author of sin, for from Him come *good* gifts, and nothing but good gifts. Look in particular at the most precious blessing any of us have or can have—spiritual life: this is from God, and *given in spontaneous kindness*, proving it to belong to the very nature of God to do good. How is it conceivable, then, that He should be the author of spiritual death?'

V. The apostle brings before us *God's purpose* in regeneration, in the words, 'Of His own will begat He us, *that we should be a kind of first-fruits of His creatures.*' By some expositors the reference of this '*we*' is supposed to be exclusively to the first Christians—those of the age when James wrote; and some have been disposed to limit it to but a portion of these,—namely, the primitive *Jewish* Christians, because the message of glad tidings was 'to the Jew first.' Now, beyond doubt, a certain fulness and specialty of significance are thus gained for the word 'first-fruits;' yet I cannot but think that, had such a limited reference of the clause been intended by the apostle, the limitation would have been marked in some way, especially seeing that the words occur at the close of a paragraph exhibiting principles of universal validity and importance. Besides, if the chronological position in the history of God's church of certain believers be thought of as constituting them 'first-fruits of His creatures,' it would seem that Abel and Enoch and the other faithful antediluvians have this dignity. It appears to me altogether unnatural to regard the '*we*' as having any other sense than 'believers in Christ' generally; and taking this reference we shall find the apostle's statement rich in precious teaching.

The grand ultimate purpose of all God's doings—the end in which is summed up all good— is 'the praise of His glory.' That set forth here is a subordinate purpose, and one the statement of which was eminently fitted to touch and impress the apostle's readers. In the Jewish ceremonial law — 'a shadow of good things to come'—it was enjoined that the first-fruits of the ground should be taken to the tabernacle or temple, and there presented by the priest as an offering to God. 'Thou shalt take of the first of all the fruit of the earth, which thou shalt bring of thy land that the Lord thy God giveth thee, and shalt put it in a basket, and shalt go unto the place which the Lord thy God shall choose to place His name there. And the priest shall take the basket out of thine hand, and set it down before the altar of the Lord thy God. And thou shalt speak and say before the Lord thy God, A Syrian ready to perish was my father; and he went down into Egypt, and sojourned there with a few, and became there a nation, great, mighty, and populous: and the Egyptians evil entreated us, and afflicted us, and laid upon us hard bondage: and when we cried unto the Lord God of our fathers, the Lord heard our voice, and looked on our affliction, and our labour, and our oppression: and He hath brought us into this place, and hath given us this land, even a land that floweth with milk and honey: and now, behold, I have brought the first-fruits of the land which Thou, O Lord, hast given me. And thou shalt set it before the Lord thy God, and worship before the Lord thy God' (Deut. xxvi. 2, 4–7, 9, 10). The meaning of this usage was an acknowledgement that *all* the harvest was God's; and, more widely, that 'the earth is the Lord's, and the fulness thereof.' Even so, Christians are regenerated, and thus spiritually brought nigh to God, 'presented' (speaking in Scripture phrase) by God 'to Himself,'[1] as representing *all* His creatures, which are His by every right, though His sinful moral creatures refuse to acknowledge His right.

In this description of Christians there are thus implied two things in particular. One is *special consecration;* and this, as

[1] Eph. v. 27; compare Col. i. 22, Jude 24.

you know, by cheerful, loving self-surrender. The regenerate, impelled by the mercies of God, 'present their bodies living sacrifices, holy, acceptable unto God,' feeling that this is 'their reasonable service.' The other is *special dignity and preciousness*, such as was always considered to attach to the first-fruits, from the close relation into which they came to God. The spiritual Israel are 'the Lord's portion,' 'a peculiar treasure unto Him,' 'kings and priests unto the God and Father of our Lord Jesus Christ.' Our dignity is higher even than that of angels, through our peculiar union to Christ— through the fact that One in our nature sways the sceptre of the universe. Neither the measure of self-consecration nor the manifestation of dignity is complete here below; but by and by will be attained the fulness of both, when 'the hundred and forty and four thousand shall sing the new song before the throne.' 'These,' says he who saw the visions of the Lord in Patmos, 'are they which follow the Lamb whithersoever He goeth; these were redeemed from among men, being *the first-fruits* unto God and to the Lamb' (Rev. xiv. 4).

The figure here may be looked at also in a somewhat different aspect. I have observed that God 'presents' the regenerate 'to Himself.' As the great Husbandman—if I may so speak—He brings these first-fruits to the temple of the glory of His own grace. So, as a Jewish farmer recognised in the sheaf he brought to God a cheering pledge of the rich harvest which, through the divine kindness, would fill his garners, similarly God looks with complacent joy on the regenerate as the first-fruits of a great harvest to come [1]—and this

---

[1] This particular force of the figure had of course a special fulness in the first age of the church, yet it holds amply still; and, seeing that the harvest is in some way to include the lower creation also, will hold till the consummation of all things.

not of men only, but of all the 'creatures' of God. The reference of James's word *creatures* cannot naturally be taken as less wide than that of 'creature,' or, more exactly, 'creation,' in the familiar passage of Paul: 'For the earnest expectation of the creature waiteth for the manifestation of the sons of God. For the creature was made subject to vanity, not willingly, but by reason of Him who hath subjected the same in hope; because the creature itself also shall be delivered from the bondage of corruption into the glorious liberty of the children of God. For we know that the whole creation groaneth and travaileth in pain together until now' (Rom. viii. 19–22). What the meaning of these wonderful words is, or of James's, which manifestly set forth the same truth in a condensed form, we can but very faintly conjecture. But they plainly point to the 'new heavens and new earth, wherein shall dwell righteousness,' and intimate that, at 'the manifestation of the sons of God,' all nature, according to its capabilities, will be invested with beauty and filled with sympathetic joy. Paradise will be restored. From every creature of God all trace of the curse will be removed, except from those moral creatures who, by obstinate unbelief, refused to have it taken away, and chose death rather than life.

You see now, brethren, the conclusiveness, the irresistible force, of the apostle's argument: 'Since the purpose of God is to bring His creatures into joy and beauty, and since ye Christians have, through His spontaneous kindness, received a new life, and that the life of His children, to the intent that ye might be the first-fruits of His ransomed creation,—can anything be conceived more foolish and blasphemous than to count Him the author of sin, which is the spring of wretchedness and death?'

VII.

RECEIVING THE INGRAFTED WORD.

'Wherefore, my beloved brethren, let every man be swift to hear, slow to speak, slow to wrath: 20 For the wrath of man worketh not the righteousness of God. 21 Wherefore lay apart all filthiness and superfluity of naughtiness, and receive with meekness the ingrafted word, which is able to save your souls.'—JAMES i. 19-21.

THESE verses introduce a new subject,—one, however, into which the last statement of the previous paragraph naturally leads, as the writer indicates by his 'Wherefore.'[1]

[1] The reading here is uncertain. Instead of ὥστε, the oldest MSS. have ἴστε, and after ἔστω read δέ,—giving this sense, 'Ye know it' (or, taking the form as imperative, 'Know it'), 'my beloved brethren, but let every man,' etc. Whether the verb be viewed as indicative or as imperative, this reading seems to be hard, unnatural, altogether unlike James's style. The indicative appears the less awkward of the two; but against it lies the fact that elsewhere (iv. 4) our apostle has the form οἴδατε. The connection of thought, 'Ye know it' (God's regenerating grace, mentioned in the previous verse),—'but, instead of being puffed up, let every man,' etc., is not altogether unsatisfactory; but the direct inference, 'Ye have been regenerated by the word of truth,—*wherefore* let every man,' etc., seems much more natural. This latter, it may be observed, too, is the connection (distinctly marked by οὖν, ii. 1) in a passage of First Peter, i. 23-ii. 2, so kindred to the present in the course of thought as to suggest a likelihood that Peter had James's words in his mind. Considering these things,—remembering the risk of textual error through the assonance with ἔστω following, and that, in fact (as is shown particularly when the reading of Codex A is examined), some confusion must have entered very early,—and bearing in mind also that ὥστε is very unlikely to have been a copyist's intentional *correction*, because the construction of this particle with an imperative is not common in classical Greek,—there seems fair ground for still holding by ὥστε.

'The word of truth,' as we have seen, is the instrument of regeneration; by this the new life is begun; by this also it is—so the thought of the apostle, and, as he knows, of all his intelligent readers, advances—that Christians *grow* in wisdom and holiness. It is through 'the truth,' as our Lord Himself tells us, that we are 'sanctified,' through 'the truth' that we are 'made free,' emancipated from the bondage of guilty fears and of depraved tendencies. 'If you wish, then,' the apostle proceeds, in that paragraph on the consideration of which we now enter, 'to attain to the maturity of Christian manhood, to the measure of the stature of the fulness of Christ—and it belongs to the very essence of genuine religion to be dissatisfied with present attainments, and reach forth towards higher, even towards complete spiritual likeness to the Lord—then, with such strong longings as new-born babes have for their natural sustenance, desire the sincere milk of the word, that ye may grow thereby; for in no other way can ye grow. Watch and pray, too, that everything in your state of heart which is fitted to obstruct your seeing truth or feeling its force may be removed, so that with godly simplicity you may wait on the Lord, and listen to His word.' Such appears to be the substance of the paragraph.

'*Wherefore, my beloved brethren, let every man be swift to hear.*' This injunction and the others with which it stands connected, the apostle would have us understand, are intended by him for *all* members of the Christian society—for those of considerable attainments in knowledge and strength of character, as well as for the ignorant and immature. '*Every man*' is to be '*swift to hear*'—ready and eager to avail himself of all opportunities of increasing his acquaintance with the 'word of truth.' The reference of the apostle is, of course, to every mode of obtaining such knowledge. In his days, and for many centuries after, so long as books could be multiplied only by the slow and laborious process of transcription, and were consequently very costly, the ear was, in the case of all except a very few, the sole avenue by which the knowledge and thoughts of others entered the mind. In philosophy, politics, religion, or any other sphere of thought, instruction was almost exclusively oral. Hence such an exhortation as that of the apostle here, to study truth, to seek instruction, most naturally assumed the form of an injunction to '*hear.*'[1] In our time, through the marvellous and most blessed agency of the printing press, Bibles abound, and can be procured at such a trifling cost that they are within the reach of the very poorest of the people. On every subject, too, there are books in great numbers, and but few among us cannot read. Instruction from books is therefore very largely open to us; and to it also the spirit of the apostle's injunction extends, its force plainly being, 'Let every man be eager to grow, by every means, in knowledge of the truth.'

As we have already seen, it is clear from the connection that we are to fill up the terms of the injunction with 'the word of truth,' as the thing to be 'heard' or studied. There are many things in which we act wisely in being *slow* to hear: there is much in current talk and literature which is profane, impure, and false; much, too, that is utterly trifling and unprofitable, —no more fitted to benefit either head or heart than the shouting of the Ephesian mob, when 'all with one voice about the space of two hours cried out, Great is Diana of the Ephesians.' As far as possible, my brethren (and I appeal especially to the young, who in this matter are under peculiarly strong temptations), let us avoid—unless when, from particular circumstances, duty appears clearly to call us to it—reading or listening to

[1] For illustrative modes of expression see, *e.g.*, John xii. 34; Rom. ij. 13.

what is opposed to sound religion or good morals. Even persons who, on the whole, are settled in right principles, are liable to serious injury from influences of this kind; and vast multitudes who, from the peaceful enclosure of a quiet and orderly childhood's home, have gone forth into the desert of a wild and wicked life, could trace the beginning of their deplorable wanderings to their being 'swift to hear' what they knew their parents and their God disapproved. Then with regard to talk and literature which is simply light, not wicked, let us remember that life is too short, and has too much that claims to be learned and to be done in it, to justify our giving a *very* large portion of it to what at the best, in our expressive popular phrase, can but 'kill time.' Those whom God has taught the value of time feel that it has little need to be 'killed:' it goes away from us all too quickly without that. The wise Apostle Paul would have us '*redeem* the time'—buy it back from worldliness and indolence at the cost of self-sacrifice.

The best way to keep ourselves right in these respects is to be 'swift to hear' 'the good word of God,' anxious through the diligent use of all our opportunities to grow in the knowledge of divine truth. This implies having the ear open to the voice of creation and providence, telling us of God's wisdom, and power, and goodness. The Christian alone can study nature and history to the *highest* ends, for 'the secret of the Lord,' as Creator and Ruler as well as Saviour, 'is with them that fear Him;' and every judicious believer will, so far as his opportunities permit, give heed, as 'day unto day uttereth speech, and night unto night showeth knowledge.' He who gives obedience to the apostle's precept will read the Bible diligently too; and this with the earnest purpose of one who knows that he is digging where hidden treasure lies, and with the reverence and affectionate interest of one who in the written word hears God's voice, 'a voice from the excellent glory,' addressing to him personally a message of warning and of peace. James's appeal calls upon us also to give regular attendance at the house of God. No cause should keep us at home which we should be afraid to plead before Him; and, in hearing a discourse on Bible truth, let us brace ourselves up to definite serious listening, with a real wish to grow in knowledge and in grace. The Bible lying unused on the shelf from one Lord's day to another, the wilful half-day's or occasional whole day's absence from public worship, the wandering eye or habitual sleepiness in the sanctuary in persons whose eye is always bright and their mind alert in the shop or the counting-house, —the commonness of these things among us, my brethren, gives very saddening evidence that it is possible for men and women to bear the Christian name, and yet be very far from '*swift*' to hear that truth which, if their profession means anything, it declares that they believe to be the only sustenance of the life of their souls.

'*Slow to speak*,' continues the apostle. It is an old saying, that 'many a man has had to repent of speaking, but never one of holding his peace.' There is very much truth in this; still, no doubt, like many such terse proverbial expressions of human experience, it is not to be taken in all its breadth. Whilst, beyond question, far more ground for repentance has been given by speech than by silence, yet sometimes a right-minded man finds much cause for regret that he failed at the proper moment to say a needed word of counsel, or comfort, or reproof. God's command to all of us is, 'Let him that heareth say, Come'—'Exhort one another daily, while it is called to-day, lest any of you be hardened through the deceitfulness of sin.' In the dark days of ancient Israel, the remnant 'that feared the Lord spake often one to another; and the

Lord hearkened and heard it, and a book of remembrance was written before Him for them that feared the Lord, and that thought upon His name.' This is an aspect of truth which needs to be brought prominently forward; for there is reason to fear that, in the case of many Christians, indolence and constitutional reserve lead to much sinful neglect of opportunities given by God in His providence for uttering a word in season. But the judicious Christian will be very careful when, and where, and what he speaks on any subject, and especially on religion. Knowing the power of words for good or evil, and their solemn irrevocableness, feeling strongly how fragmentary and mingled with misconceptions the knowledge of even the best informed and most thoughtful of us is, the wise believer will be much 'swifter' to hear than to speak; so that, not shrinking from speaking, where to speak is plainly his duty, he will at the same time never be rash, will not speak except where he sees duty clear, and then will carefully weigh his words. Such is evidently the meaning of the apostle's counsel to be '*slow to speak*,' taken in a general sense.

But I think there can be little doubt from what follows that there is a particular reference here to keen religious controversy, and to the unkind insinuations and personal reflections to which it often leads. When important truth is assailed, it must be defended; but then, most of all, caution, thoughtfulness, and self-control are necessary. From various allusions in the New Testament, it appears that, whilst certain of the elders of each church were set apart to 'labour in the word and doctrine,' yet in the meetings for public worship of the Christians of the first age the proceedings were to some extent of a conversational kind, the assembly being regarded as a religious *conference*. This system has some obvious advantages, but it has also some equally obvious dangers, into which, it is clear from statements and advices in various parts of the apostolic writings, many of the congregations fell. The meetings too often became scenes of wrangling, of attempts at self-display, of the manifestation of unchristian tempers in the midst of debates on Christian truth; and the evils were found so to predominate over the good, that the practice was soon altered to that followed in most Christian assemblies now. The special immediate force of our apostle's injunction here, then, seems to me to be this: 'In your assemblies for worship, or wherever, under any circumstances, religious conversation, particularly the discussion of religious doctrine, springs up, let your great desire be to have your minds instructed and your hearts warmed. Let each brother listen kindly, respectfully, and thoughtfully to what his brethren say; and if he feel called on himself to take part in the discussion, let him not be rash or inconsiderate, let him not be influenced by vanity or the mere love of controversy and excitement, but by a simple desire to help on the ascertainment of truth for the spiritual benefit of all. Thus *let every man be swift to hear, slow to speak.*'

But further—'*slow to wrath.*' This counsel may be intended to have some bearing on both the injunctions preceding, for anger may spring up both in hearing and speaking of religion. Unpalatable truth often excites in a hearer's mind ill-will to him who sets it forth. Paul asks the Galatians, 'Am I therefore become your enemy, because I tell you the truth?' Persons who are pricked in their consciences, but kick against the pricks, are always ready to admit some such hard thoughts of faithful ministers. But the danger of unholy wrath is mainly with those who are 'swift to *speak*,' and the precept now before us seems to rise immediately out of the reference to speaking. A man who delights to put himself forward in debate, whether with tongue or pen, whether on the floor of the hall of an ecclesiastical assembly or in a gathering of Christian friends by a fireside, is extremely apt to be carried away into undue heat of feeling, and thus both himself show an unholy temper, and stir it up in those around.

You will observe that the apostle does not teach that anger in itself, in all circumstances, is wrong. As we are to be '*slow* to speak,' but must sometimes speak, so we are to be '*slow* to wrath.' There is such a thing as 'being angry and sinning not.' The Lord Jesus on one occasion, we are told, looked round on a group of narrow-souled, uncharitable, wicked men '*with anger*, being grieved for the hardness of their hearts.' A Christian's soul may and should be stirred with holy indignation, when he sees or hears of illustrations of the unutterable meanness or revolting cruelty to which depravity sometimes debases the enemies of God. But it becomes us to be 'slow' —very slow—'to wrath.' There is no instinctive feeling of the soul into which oftener or more easily sinful elements enter,—none more apt to be indefensibly excited, or, even when the grounds are reasonable, carried to an unreasonable degree,—none more prone to wither the peace and beauty of our own Christian life and that of all around us. The wise and loving Christian 'is not easily provoked.' 'He that is slow to anger is better than the mighty; and he that ruleth his spirit than he that taketh a city.'

The 20th verse gives a weighty reason for compliance with this last injunction: '*For the wrath of man worketh not the righteousness of God.*' The expression, '*the righteousness of God*,' is employed in Scripture in various senses. Here it denotes that 'righteousness' or holy character in man which God loves to see, and which He forms through the 'word of truth' and the influences of His Spirit. '*Worketh*' has very much the force of 'produces;' as above, in the 3rd verse, 'The trying of your faith *worketh* patience.' You observe the antithesis: 'man's wrath—God's righteousness.' As I have said, the 'righteousness' is 'God's,' not merely because He approves it, but because it comes from Him. Being the chief element of spiritual life, it is in regeneration originated by God through the 'word of truth,' and is by Him, through means of that same 'word,' sustained. As this righteousness, then, comes wholly from God, and opposes itself at every point to man's depraved nature, it is plain that words and deeds which are prompted by the anger that wells up from the fountain of *man's depravity* cannot be helpful to *God's righteousness*, either in ourselves or in others, but must have a blighting, deadening power. As we have seen, there may be a righteous anger, an anger which belongs to the 'righteousness of God' here spoken of; but the apostle assumes that anger, as it actually shows itself among us, has always in it more or less that is wicked, carnal, of man, not of God. Such anger cannot work out God's righteousness. It rouses up the evil principles in our souls into greater activity than at other times. Amid the tempest of passion, the thoughts and feelings even of a genuine servant of Christ seem almost to break loose from that grasp by which they are commonly held in sweet 'captivity to the obedience of Christ.' To men around it presents a most unalluring misrepresentation of the gospel's influence, and evokes from their hearts those mists of pride and prejudice which are most fitted to hide God and His truth from them. Controversy, even among Christian brethren, is no doubt sometimes useful, and indeed necessary; angry feeling in such controversy, never. 'Wrath' is surely utterly out of place in the discussion of a religion which is based on the atonement of the 'Lamb of God,' and built up in the soul by the working of that Spirit who descended as a 'dove.'

The very solemn and impressive statement of the 20th verse leads naturally into another precept, in which the line of duty indicated in the 'swift to hear, slow to speak, slow to wrath,' is still further marked out. 'The wrath of man worketh not the righteousness of God: *wherefore lay apart all filthiness and superfluity of naughtiness, and receive with meekness the ingrafted word.*' '*Naughtiness*' is a word now scarcely ever employed except of children's misdeeds, but in the older English it was in common use in the general sense of 'wickedness.' The original word which it here represents, while denoting 'wickedness' generally, is often used with the special sense of 'malice, malignity;' and the dependence, shown by 'wherefore,' of this verse on the preceding statement regarding 'anger,' proves, as it seems to me, that this special meaning is intended here. '*Filthiness*' may be, and has been by some expositors, taken by itself, as indicating 'moral pollution' of every kind; but both the course of thought and the mode of expression appear to suggest that we should join it, as well as 'superfluity,' with 'naughtiness;' the two things spoken of being thus not 'filthiness' (the one) and 'superfluity of naughtiness' (the other), but 'filthiness of naughtiness' and 'superfluity of naughtiness.' The words '*superfluity of naughtiness*' have a decidedly odd sound to our ears, and the meaning is not altogether clear. They do not imply, I need scarcely say, that there can be any measure of 'malice' which is not 'superfluous' and wrong. By some, the expression 'all superfluity of naughtiness' has been supposed to denote 'every form in which malice *overflows* into the feelings and life.' Again, the whole, 'all filthiness and superfluity of naughtiness,' or 'all naughtiness's filthiness and superfluity,' may very well mean, I think, 'all the malice which is so *polluting* and so *abundant*' in our hearts by nature. But I am rather disposed to consider the horticultural figure, which shows itself plainly in 'ingrafted,' as in the apostle's mind throughout the whole verse; and that the meaning of the first clause is, 'Put away (from the garden of your moral life) all the defilement and rank growth which are found in malignity,' or, more simply, 'all malignity's defilement and rank growth.' We should strive to have 'every root of bitterness' extirpated, that the tree which yields 'the fruits of the Spirit' may grow.

Accordingly the injunction goes on, '*Receive with meekness the ingrafted word.*' Every one of us is called to be, in a subordinate sense, the keeper and tiller of his own vineyard; and as such we have just been enjoined to remove the disfiguring and destructive weeds of malice and passion. But when God is regarded as the Husbandman, or when the 'Son of man' is set prominently before us as the Sower of the good seed, then our souls are simply the field or garden in which the divine Agent works. This aspect now presents itself. The thought of labouring on the soil of his own heart, and that of being simply soil on which God works, are both so perfectly familiar to the Christian, and so clearly seen to be but two sides of the same religious life, that to a spiritual mind there is not the slightest unnaturalness or incongruity, when the apostle passes on at once from speaking to us as tillers, to address us as ground. As ground we are to '*receive the ingrafted*' (or rather '*implanted*') '*word.*' Elsewhere described as seed, the 'word of truth' is here represented as a scion or cutting of a tree. Now, as the seed is 'sown' in every proclamation or exhibition of the gospel, so the scion is 'implanted' in the soil, whenever God brings the truth within our knowledge. But the scion, like the seed, must be *welcomed* by the ground, '*received*' gladly—through faith the truth must become *rooted* in us—if the fruit of righteousness is to be brought forth. The apostle's charge is, accordingly, that we should 'receive' it in such a spirit as that it may be rooted; and this spirit, with particular reference to the 'wrath' and 'malice' which he has been forbidding, he describes as a spirit of '*meekness.*' Immediately, this no doubt denotes willingness to learn from all who can teach, without wrangling or arrogant self-assertion. But child-like docility in relation to God is plainly included also; for only a heart which has already been and longs to be more fully 'taught of God' to be humble and gentle, can thus be 'meek' towards men.

The excellence of that 'word' which has been by God's kindness 'implanted' in his readers, and thus the transcendent importance of putting away everything from heart and life which may prevent its being fully, meekly, lovingly 'received' by us, are set forth by the apostle in the last clause of the verse, '*which is able to save your souls.*' 'The gospel of Christ is the power of God unto salvation, to every one that believeth,' —being His appointed instrumentality for uniting men to Christ, and thus obtaining for them forgiveness, sonship, and the sanctifying influences of the Spirit. In specially adverting to the salvation of the '*soul*' (as in Peter, 'the end of your faith, even the salvation of your souls'), the apostle, we may suppose, intends to bring out prominently the *radical* and therefore gloriously complete nature of the deliverance. It is no mere amelioration or adornment of the outward life, but reaches that inmost and noblest part of our nature out of which are 'the issues of life,' and by the condition of which, accordingly, is determined the condition of the whole man; for the body follows the state of the soul, to destruction or to salvation. At the same time, in thus putting forward the truth that God's salvation is fundamentally a *spiritual* deliverance, the apostle suggests to all intelligent readers that no mere formal respect to the 'word,' His instrument, but the reception of it *into the soul*, will bring men into the enjoyment of its blessings; thus illustrating the meaning as well as the reasonableness of his precept, 'Receive the word with meekness.'

This 21st verse has an interesting parallel in the beginning of the 2nd chapter of 1 Peter: 'Laying aside all malice' (the same word rendered 'naughtiness' in James), 'and all guile, and hypocrisies, and envies, and all evil speakings,—as new-born babes, desire the sincere milk of the word, that ye may grow thereby.' In both, the importance of knowing divine truth—so knowing it, being 'received with meekness,' that it becomes a power, as spiritual nourishment, to make the new man in Christ 'grow'—is set forth very clearly; and at the same time the needfulness, in order to our so knowing the truth, of shunning unchristian tempers and practices. There are here continually action and reaction. Nothing can really eradicate 'malice' and other forms of sinful desire except the influence of the truth; but again, as these evil propensities are subdued, the power of the truth grows in us. By thoughtful, prayerful, earnest effort to vanquish sin, the dimming, begriming incrustations which have gathered on the windows of the soul are removed, and the beams of heavenly light shine in.

VIII.

THE SPIRITUAL MIRROR.

'But be ye doers of the word, and not hearers only, deceiving your own selves. 23 For if any be a hearer of the word, and not a doer, he is like unto a man beholding his natural face in a glass : 24 For he beholdeth himself, and goeth his way, and straightway forgetteth what manner of man he was. 25 But whoso looketh into the perfect law of liberty, and continueth therein, he being not a forgetful hearer, but a doer of the work, this man shall be blessed in his deed.'— JAMES i. 22–25.

THE apostle continues here his treatment of the subject taken up in the verse immediately preceding. The connection marked by the introductory '*But*' may be paraphrased as follows : ' But whilst I thus enjoin upon you to be swift to hear, ready to receive with meekness the implanted word, bear in mind what this "receiving" means, and that *mere* hearing is by no means all that is implied in it. The word, I have said, is able to save your souls. Now precious, inestimably precious, as are tidings of pardon and peace through believing, the experience of peace does not wholly fill up the idea of the salvation of the soul : one element, indeed the grand element, of this salvation is transformation of character,—a radical alteration in the convictions, and feelings, and tendencies of the soul itself,—a change from the love and service of sin to the love and practice of holy obedience. Wherefore, brethren,'—

'*Be ye doers of the word, and not hearers only, deceiving your own selves.*' It is obviously implied here, that the word of which the apostle speaks is in its nature *practical*, intended and fitted to act on the hearts and lives of those who become acquainted with it. There is, as you know, much truth on many subjects which, in its place, is valuable, but which has no immediate bearing on the conduct of life. There is, no doubt, a vast multitude of facts mentioned in Scripture, of which, looked at simply by themselves, the same may be said. That Sihon was king of the Amorites, and that Rabbah was a strong town of the children of Ammon, are truths which cannot well affect our feelings or life. But 'the Scriptures *principally* teach' *religious* truth, of which it is of the very essence to have an immediate bearing on the conduct of life. And the one kind of religious truth revealed in the Bible, 'what man is to believe concerning God,' is such as, when believed, to prompt us, through reverence, gratitude, and love, to hearty compliance with what is also therein made known as 'the duty which God requireth of man.' 'Be ye, then, *doers* of the word, and not hearers only.'

'To *be doers*' has a force of its own, distinct from that of the simple 'to do.' You feel that the expression exhibits *an habitual occupation*. It sets before us as being real Christians persons who make the 'doing of the word of God' the main business of their lives,—a business affecting, penetrating, pervading all other business and all pleasure; so that just as, when you speak of an ordinary trade or profession, you say that a man is a teacher, a manufacturer, or the like, so speaking of character, those who know a Christian intimately should always be able to say of him, 'He is a doer of the word of God.' In every department of his life such a man will show clearly that he makes this 'the principal thing,' in matters which men call secular as well as in those which they call sacred; for he knows that nothing is really beyond the sphere of religion, beyond the sphere illuminated by the teaching of the Holy Spirit in the Bible. In health and sickness, therefore, in his family circle and in general social intercourse, in the shop or the counting-house no less than at the prayer-meeting or in positive and direct labouring and giving for Christ's cause,—everywhere, in a life of holy energy, humility, love, and patience, according to the measure of his faith, he will be a 'doer of the word.'

The apostle enforces his injunction by setting forth the solemn consideration, that persons who are 'hearers only' '*deceive their own selves.*' Such persons evidently altogether misconceive the nature of true religion, and thus cheat themselves with reference to their position before God. Knowing that the study of divine truth, through reading the Bible, giving attendance on the public ordinances of grace, and otherwise, is a most important duty,—is, indeed, the road leading towards the gate of everlasting life,—they allow themselves, through man's natural aversion to genuine spirituality, to be persuaded by the wicked one that this is the sum of all Christian duty, and itself the gate of life, so that in mere 'hearing' they enter in, and all is well with them. To rest satisfied with the means of grace, without yielding up our hearts to their power as means, so as to receive the grace and exhibit its working in our lives, is manifestly folly of the same class as that of a workman who should content himself with possessing tools, without using them,—madness of the same class as that of a man perishing with hunger, who should exult in having bread in his hands, without eating it,— but folly and madness as immeasurably greater than these, as the 'work of God' (John vi. 29) transcends in importance the work of an earthly artisan, and 'life with Christ in God' the perishable existence of earth. Yet, alas, brethren, there is reason to fear that, with great numbers of professing Christians in all sections of the church—persons who attend the house of God, listen with a fair measure of diligence to the proclamation of truth, and, it may be, in intercourse with their friends rather love to talk of sermons and ministers and orthodoxy—this is *all;* whilst yet they are impressed with the conviction that they are certainly Christians,—nay, perhaps singularly excellent Christians,—forgetting that any degree of religious profession, where the heart is destitute of the love of God, and the life not consecrated to His service, is in His sight utter mockery. On no point are the warnings and appeals of our Saviour and His apostles more earnest and solemn than on this. Remember the words of the Lord Jesus, how He said: 'Not every one that saith unto Me, Lord, Lord, shall enter into the kingdom of heaven; but he that doeth the will of My Father which is in heaven. Therefore, whosoever heareth these sayings of Mine, and doeth them, I will liken him unto a wise man, which built his house upon a rock: and the rain descended, and the floods came, and the winds blew and beat upon that house; and it fell not,—for it was founded upon a rock. And every one that heareth these sayings of Mine, and doeth them not, shall be likened unto a foolish man, which built his house upon the sand: and the rain descended, and the floods came, and the winds blew, and beat upon that house; and it fell; and great was the fall of it.' 'When once the Master of the house is risen up, and hath shut to the door, then shall ye begin to say, We have eaten and drunk in Thy presence, and Thou hast taught in our streets. But He shall say, I tell you, I know you not whence you are: depart from Me, all ye workers of iniquity.'

In the verses which follow, the apostle brings forward with considerable fulness the great reason for the injunction here given,—the fact which is implied in his statement that those 'deceive themselves' who are 'hearers of the word only.' Such persons show that *the word has no power over them.* It remains outside them; for though it may have entered the mind, yet it plainly has not penetrated into the affections and will, which morally constitute the man. Whatever impression is made on the heart is but transient. Now, only when the word 'dwells' (Col. iii. 16) in the heart, not fitfully but permanently, and when, consequently, it regulates the life not fitfully but permanently,—only in this case does the word bring the blessings and glories of salvation. This is substantially the meaning of the paragraph; but the truth is presented, as you see, in a very interesting and graphic way, under the figure of a mirror and a man looking at himself in it.

'*For if any be a hearer of the word, and not a doer, he is like unto a man beholding his natural face in a glass.*' The expression '*his natural face*'—literally, 'the face of his birth'—seems intended to suggest, through the specialty made prominent, the line of interpretation for the figure. We are, in expounding, to think of the *spiritual* countenance, the face of the soul, as contrasted with 'the natural face,' which obviously is in meaning practically the same as 'bodily face.'

As a general rule, a person looks into a mirror for a definite end, which can be soon attained; and then goes away to the work or the pleasures of life. He glances at his features, makes those little arrangements in his personal appearance for which a mirror is helpful, and then leaves the glass, and thinks no more of it or of what he had seen in it. So little of definite and lasting impression, indeed, has been made on him, that he is better acquainted with the features of his friends than with his own. Such, no doubt, is ordinary experience, except where persons are under the influence of a silly vanity with regard to their personal appearance. Taking the facts to be as now described, the apostle says that people contemplate the features of their souls as carelessly, if they be 'hearers of the word, and not doers.' The force of the illustration, regarded as an argument, is somewhat as follows : ' To make but a brief survey of the natural face in the glass—to spend but a little time on that bodily adornment for which the mirror is intended as an aid, and thus to receive but a slight and evanescent impression of our bodily appearance—may be very fitting, since the body is in every point of view the inferior part of man, and is appointed to moulder to dust. But the case is altogether different with the soul. To know the features of our souls intimately, to look at them carefully, to bear them much in mind, and to strive by every means that their beauty may be increased,—this is the part of a wise man, and is a sacred duty : for the soul is immortal, and according to the care we bestow on it here, will be its condition in eternity. The soul which, by divine grace, is through faith and prayer and earnest Christian effort cleansed, beautified, and adorned, shall in heaven stand before God clothed in the beautiful garments of salvation ; whilst the soul that is heedless of holy beauty, and by the love and practice of sin disfigures itself, marring its lineaments more and more from day to day, shall appear in His presence in nakedness, uncomeliness, and fear. One day certainly a voice of power shall say, He that is holy, let him be holy still ; and he that is filthy, let him be filthy still. Let the mirror which God has given for our souls, then, be used with conscientious and loving diligence. Study yourselves therein, and let the remembrance of its revelations of your spiritual features be ever present with you, that, knowing your natural sinfulness, you may grow into the likeness of God's holiness.'

According to the figure, every one who 'hears the word' beholds his spiritual image, the features of his soul, in a glass; which glass evidently is the 'word' spoken of, the testimony of God in Scripture. Conscience might to some extent serve as such a mirror; but, alas, through the influence of our depravity, this mirror has been greatly flawed, and become very dull in its reflection. Now in the graphic delineations of the divine word we see ourselves as we really are. He who 'compasseth our path and our lying down, and is acquainted with all our ways,' who 'searcheth all hearts, and understandeth all the imaginations of the thoughts,' has in the Bible given His declaration of our spiritual condition. Thus every man who with any attention reads the Bible, or waits on a gospel ministry, must see with some degree of clearness both the defilement and uncomeliness of the countenance of his soul, and at the same time—for, through God's grace, more is shown in this glass than man's depravity—how alone purity and beauty can be obtained.

The seeing of these things in God's mirror is common, though with very varied degrees of clearness, to all persons who in any measure attend to the word. From this point, however, we have two distinct classes. The *mere* hearer—the hearer that 'doeth not'—follows in every respect, in his use of the mirror which God has given for the soul, the same course as men generally follow in using the mirror which shows the 'natural face;' '*for he beholdeth himself, and goeth his way, and straightway forgetteth what manner of man he was.*'

He '*beholdeth himself,*' but not with much interest, not as if it were a matter of vital importance to see himself as God sees him. He could look at a machine, or a picture, or an Act of

Parliament, so intently as to have the whole accurately and vividly before his mind. He can look at himself, too, with much enjoyment, in the picture painted by his own vain fancy. But the countenance which the faithful mirror shows, with all its hard lines and all its traces of pollution—this he does not care to contemplate minutely. Pride and unbelief enter in; and so he '*goeth his way*' to his farm or his merchandise, his library or his ball-room. He gives but little time to God's mirror. If each of us were to construct a time-table for any average week of his life, setting down honestly in separate lines the number of hours spent in secular work, in recreation of one kind or another, and in studying God's will, 'looking not at the things which are seen, but at the things which are not seen,' many a gospel hearer would be most painfully startled by the results brought out. Nay, even confining the inquiry to the day which God claims as peculiarly His, what proportion of its hours is given to religious reading or thinking, carried on with anything like definite and earnest purpose, with the 'loins of our mind' girded up,—the statement of facts would often not be pleasant for us to look at. We are all too ready to 'go our way' from God's mirror.

'*And straightway forgetteth what manner of man he was.*' His mind never having been very earnestly occupied with the truth, his thoughts regarding it, such as they were, are soon driven out by thoughts on more congenial matters. 'He that received seed among the thorns is he that heareth the word,— and the cares of this world, and the deceitfulness of riches, and the lusts of other things entering in, choke the word, and he becometh unfruitful.' The forgetfulness occurs '*straightway.*' The man has been listening, it may be, to a faithful, searching sermon, and under it has been somewhat impressed with a sense of his sinfulness and helplessness; yet before he reaches home, perhaps, the seriousness has gone from him. Oh, how many of us, brethren, know from experience the frequent and deplorable evanescence of religious impressions! In our Sabbath exercises every voice seems to say to the Lord of the vineyard, 'I go, sir;' but the morrow tells another tale. 'O Ephraim,' cries the Lord through His prophet, 'what shall I do unto thee? O Judah, what shall I do unto thee? for your goodness is as a morning cloud, and as the early dew it goeth away.'

'But whoso looketh into the perfect law of liberty, and continueth therein, he being not a forgetful hearer, but a doer of the work, this man shall be blessed in his deed.'

In contrast with the careless, unbenefited hearer of God's word, whom the apostle has sketched for us in the two previous verses, we have here exhibited the wise hearer, and this mainly in unfigurative language; though the 'looking' is an evidence that the image of the mirror is still in James's mind, at least at the outset. In place of the 'glass,' however, we have the thing signified by the glass described to us by the very striking expression, *'the law of liberty.'* The reference of this name has been understood in more than one way; yet if we regard the connection of the verse with what precedes and what follows, and also attend to the apostle's use of the same expression in the 12th verse of the next chapter, as illustrated by the immediately preceding context, we cannot have much doubt, as it appears to me, what was in his mind. The 'law of liberty' is evidently, from the course of the argument, another name for the 'word of truth,' by which God regenerates, and the hearty acceptance of which constituted 'the faith of our Lord Jesus Christ' and was the root of the 'religion' professed by James's readers (i. 18, 27, ii. 1). But, no less evidently, while it is the gospel that is in his thoughts, it is the gospel regarded specially in its sanctifying aspect, as 'the power of God unto salvation' from spiritual debasement and pollution. More exactly, 'the law of liberty' is the divine law considered as taken up into the grand redemptive system, which has for its purpose to make men spiritually like God, 'holy and without blame before Him in love,'—the divine law, as those who are in Christ see it, exhibited under the gospel with new motives and in connection with new spiritual influences,—the 'old commandment, which we had from the beginning,' and yet 'new' in Christ.

The code of morals exhibited by God in 'the word of truth' is for the Christian a binding '*law.*' Recognising God as his rightful and absolute King, the believer feels that every expression of His will with regard to the conduct of His human subjects has for him obligatory force. In accepting Jesus as his Saviour, he has renounced all trust in obedience to the law *as a means of earning eternal life*, acknowledging that for a depraved creature this is hopeless work, but rejoicing that Christ, as his representative, has yielded perfect obedience, which God's tender mercy will reckon as his. In this respect, then, he is 'not under the law, but under grace' (Rom. vi. 14). Yet his knowledge that he is 'under grace' only leads him to feel the more deeply his subjection to the divine law *as the rule of life:* he is 'not without law to God, but under the law to Christ' (1 Cor. ix. 21). And through this '*to Christ*'—through the fact that all the relations of the believer to God are *in Christ*—the law is for him 'the law *of liberty.*' We are sensible of a vagueness in this language which contributes to its grandeur. Every relation binding closely together these two, which to the unwise seem foes, law and liberty, is implied here. The divine law, as seen by the Christian, exhibits liberty, gives liberty, is liberty.

The 'light of the Lord' shows sin to be a slavery—a cruel bondage. Nought but slavery could keep that noble creature of God, the soul of man, alienated from the absolutely Good and Beautiful, indisposed to think of Him, occupied continually with things which cannot by possibility afford any rational or lasting happiness. Sin is an oppressive power, malignantly holding our spirits back from their true good, degrading them and weighing them down, so that they cannot soar towards those lofty objects of contemplation and effort for which they were made. The clearest proof of the crushing nature of this bondage is the fact that, till the light of Christ illuminates the soul, the chains are almost wholly unseen. In lands where the accursed system of man holding his fellow as a chattel exists, the thoughtful mind sees the clearest evidence of the utter abominableness and monstrousness of the iniquity, not so much in looking at those slaves who feel and lament their condition, as in the case of those whose whole natures from their infancy have been so degraded by the sight and experience of cruelty and pollution, that their hearts scarcely rise to the vague idea that all this is unnatural, or that God made such as they are to be other than beasts of burden. Like this is the slavery of sin; nay, so completely are things spiritual inverted before the sinner's mind, that he counts himself free, and deems obedience to God a thraldom. 'Let us break asunder the bands of the Lord and His Anointed,' he says, 'and cast away Their cords from us.' 'Promising' to themselves and all who act like them 'liberty,' unbelievers 'are the slaves of corruption; for of whom a man is overcome, of the same is he brought in bondage.'

But the Christian sees things as they really are, and his will is brought into unison with God's will, so that he loves to do what he ought to do. He finds that in obedience to God, and there only, all the powers of his nature find full, free play, and all his capacities of happiness full gratification. This is spiritual freedom. Such freedom has been enjoyed under all the stages of the revelation of God's grace, in the measure in which the love and beauty of His character were apprehended. 'I will walk at liberty, for I seek Thy precepts,' says the Psalmist. Yet, no doubt, from the comparative darkness which prevailed during the Old Economy, the buoyant feeling of freedom was attained to in any high degree by but few. Lighted up by the meridian beams of the Sun of Righteousness as, since Pentecost, have been the richness and tenderness of the divine love in Christ, all believers in Jesus should, in a measure far exceeding that which was possible for ancient saints, exult in the sense of liberty; 'for we have not received the spirit of bondage again to fear, but have received the Spirit of adoption, whereby we cry, Abba, Father.' 'My yoke is easy,' said the Master, 'and My burden is light.' 'This is the love of God, that we keep His commandments; and His commandments are not grievous.' To the servant of God under the Christian dispensation, then, the King's law is, with peculiar fulness, 'the law of liberty'—of freedom to live up to the capabilities of his being. He enjoys

> ' A liberty unsung
> By poets, and by senators unpraised,
> Which monarchs cannot grant, nor all the powers
> Of earth and hell confederate take away;
> A liberty which persecution, fraud,
> Oppressions, prisons, have no power to bind;
> Which whoso tastes can be enslaved no more.
> He is the freeman whom *the truth* makes free,
> And all are slaves beside.'

By the epithet '*perfect*,' which the apostle applies to the 'law of liberty,' some interpreters suppose him to point out the superiority in fulness and clearness of the exposition of moral duty given by the Lord Jesus and His apostles to that contained in the Old Testament. Now, no doubt, the whole of the expression here employed, especially the reference to 'liberty,' was fitted and intended to bring up before the minds of the readers the glorious completeness of the revelation of duty as well as of grace which had been granted to them, as contrasted with that which their fathers had enjoyed. Still nothing in our apostle's course of thought, either here or in any other part of the Epistle, leads us to think that he means this to be more than suggested in a secondary and incidental way. He plainly thinks primarily of the moral law of God, as made known under all the Economies,—under all of them a 'law of liberty' for those who apprehended its spirit and 'walked with God,'—under all of them '*perfect*,' as being a transcript of the divine character. His object in drawing attention so prominently to the grandeur and sweetness of the law is, evidently enough, to impress his readers with the transcendent importance for their own good of 'not hearing only, but doing' God's will. Indeed, for all the thoughtful, his words anticipate the express declaration which comes afterwards, that 'the doer' of the law 'shall be blessed in his deed.'

In the apostle's description of the wise gospel hearer, we find made prominent three points of contrast with the conduct of the foolish man delineated in the previous verse. In the first place, this man '*looketh*' into the spiritual mirror. The word rendered 'behold' in the 23rd and 24th verses does not necessarily, taken by itself, imply carelessness; but that used here does seem, according to New Testament usage (and this naturally, from its etymology), to imply intentness of gaze,[1]—

[1] In classical Greek παρακύπτειν is often 'to take a slight side glance;' but in New Testament use the meaning seems unquestionably to be 'to look earnestly,'—the exact idea being 'to bend so as to see distinctly.' Compare Luke xxiv. 12; John xx. 5, 11; 1 Pet. i. 12.

and as the apostle passes with marked purpose from the use of the one word to that of the other, this idea is obviously meant to stand out distinctly. The case here is not that of an object casually meeting the eye, and thus being 'beheld.' This man 'stoops down beside' the word of God (such is the precise force of the term); he alters his position with definite intention to contemplate the object carefully. The grand obstacle to the progress of Christ's cause is man's natural aversion to serious religious thought—an aversion springing from pride, or fear, or pure frivolity of spirit. If men would only gravely and honestly look at their own character and prospects, and at the gracious offers made by God in Christ, all would be well. Seriousness is the true 'mother of devotion.' Seriousness, then, we have here in the way in which this man '*looketh* into the perfect law of liberty.'

But again, whilst the foolish hearer, having 'beheld himself,' 'goeth his way,' the wise man '*continueth* (looking).' The '*therein*' which our translators have supplied is somewhat misleading; for it means (most naturally at least) 'in the law, in obedience to the law,'—a sense which dislocates the antithesis, and makes the next clause tautological. The man 'continues looking,' looks not earnestly only, but perseveringly. There are those who, having listened to the word attentively, 'anon with joy receive it, and dure for a while; but, having no root in themselves, in time of temptation fall away.' These persons have seen some sides of gospel truth, and been attracted by them; but not having prosecuted the study of the word, they find by and by that difficulties occur for which the view they had taken of truth had not prepared them, and thus they are 'offended.' The true disciple of Christ is always learning of Him.

We have yet one point more in the contrast. The foolish

hearer 'straightway forgetteth what manner of man he was,' as shown in the glass of divine truth; whilst the crowning excellence of him whom we are now contemplating is that he is '*not a forgetful hearer, but a doer of the work,*' or rather, simply, '*a doer of work.*' This is the third feature in the conduct of the wise hearer; but it holds such a relation to the first two, that, as you will observe, it is not connected with them, in the apostle's sentence, quite as they are connected with each other. A man may 'look' who does not 'continue looking;' and therefore the apostle is careful to describe the person who is before his mind as one who 'looks, *and* continues looking.' But, these two things being given, the third follows of necessity, from the power on man's mind and heart of divine truth, earnestly and perseveringly looked at. Accordingly he brings in the last feature in such a way as to express this: 'being ("thus" or "consequently" we might supply) not a forgetful hearer, but a doer of work.' The man who avails himself sedulously of all opportunities of growing in the knowledge of God's will, carries the remembrance of what has occupied his attention into all the scenes of life. In the bustle and strain of daily work we naturally and reasonably lose all thought of the mirror for the 'natural face;' but the revelations of the spiritual mirror, often and with deep interest contemplated, remain with him who saw them, and, more or less consciously, are powers over him at all times, in all circumstances. He is the very opposite of the 'forgetful hearer;' and his remembrance— necessarily operative, from the nature of the truth seen and believed—leads him to shun sin, and in every way, as God gives him opportunity, to labour in His cause. From the very nature of the case, he is 'a doer of work.' To speak of a candid and persevering student of God's will who does not in practice try to do God's will, is to utter that which is absurd, self-contradictory.

Having described wise dealing with the word of God, the apostle pronounces him who so deals with it 'blessed.' 'Whoso looks—and that perseveringly—into the perfect law of liberty, and thus comes to have the remembrance of it ever with him, and to be a doer of the work it enjoins,'—'*this man*,' says James emphatically, as if to concentrate on him, for admiration and imitation, the eyes of all readers, '*shall be blessed in his deed*,' or, more exactly, as the margin has it, '*in his doing*' of the work. The 'blessedness' of the righteous will have its glorious completeness only in heaven, when the King says, 'Well done, good and faithful servants, enter ye into the joy of your Lord.' Yet even here, '*in the doing*' of God's will the saint experiences 'a joy that is unspeakable and full of glory.' 'The judgements of the Lord are more to be desired than gold, yea, than much fine gold, sweeter also than honey and the honeycomb; and *in keeping of them there is great reward*.' 'Our rejoicing is this, the testimony of our conscience that in simplicity and godly sincerity, not with fleshly wisdom, but by the grace of God, we have our conversation in the world.' The supreme 'blessedness' of every Christian, brethren, is to know himself growing liker his Lord. Now, as he 'continues looking' into the 'glass' of Scripture, he sees ever more and more clearly, not the likeness of himself merely, but that of the Master, who has come to stand very near His servant; and thus, 'beholding in the glass the glory of the Lord,' he is, by the energy of the Spirit, through the transforming power of love, 'changed into the same image, from glory to glory.' By and by contemplation of the reflection of the Altogether Lovely will give place to the 'open vision.' We shall see Him no longer 'as in a glass, darkly,' but 'face to face.' Then the 'blessedness' will be perfect, because 'when He shall appear, we shall be like Him, for we shall see Him as He is.'

IX.

TRUE RELIGIOUS SERVICE.

'If any man among you seem to be religious, and bridleth not his tongue, but deceiveth his own heart, this man's religion is vain. 27 Pure religion and undefiled before God and the Father is this,—to visit the fatherless and widows in their affliction, and to keep himself unspotted from the world.'—JAMES i. 26, 27.

THESE verses are closely connected with what precedes. The apostle wishes to impress on his readers the vast importance of being 'doers, and not hearers only;' and he knows the great advantage of exhibiting a particular example illustrative of any general principle, not merely from its making the meaning clear, but because, in morals especially, general principles are apt to slip from thought, whilst examples lay hold of heart and conscience like grappling irons. A general principle of duty is to our feelings very often like an exquisitely chiselled and most beautiful statue in a gallery of art, looked at with admiration, but cold, dead, destitute of all connection with our daily life,—an example, like a living, loving, wise friend and adviser, whom we meet at every turn in our life. The apostle proceeds, accordingly, to show what 'doing God's word' is by special cases: and this first negatively, mentioning one easily recognised feature which characterizes the *non-doer;* then positively, describing modes of conduct which, with more or less fulness, are found in *doers*.

First, negatively: '*If any man among you seem to be religious, and bridleth not his tongue, but deceiveth his own heart, this man's religion is vain.*' Our Authorized Version, admirable on the whole alike for accuracy and for perspicuity and beauty of expression, appears to lack somewhat of its customary excellence in the rendering of this verse; for in one or two points it is obscure, if not misleading. The sentence would have been clearer, if in the middle clauses the participial form, which they have in the original, had been retained, thus: 'whilst bridling not his tongue, but deceiving his own heart.' Again, the question very naturally arises, How can a man *seem* at all to be religious—how could any person take him for religious— when his religious pretensions are completely and obviously refuted by his unbridled tongue, 'his speech bewraying him'? But the word translated '*seem*' has reference merely to the existence of an opinion, not to the existence of any apparent ground for this opinion; and in the present case the opinion is the man's *own*. The meaning therefore is, 'seem to himself' or 'think himself;' just as, for example, in Paul's words to the Corinthians: 'If any man among you *seemeth* to be wise in this world, let him become a fool, that he may be wise' (1 Cor. iii. 18). But after these little things have been rectified, there still remains the chief misleading element in the translation,—which, however, is not due to any ignorance or carelessness on the part of the translators, but to a change since their days in the meaning of the words '*religion*' and '*religious.*'

Change of meaning is a source of error which has affected a considerable number of words in the English Bible; and there is plainly more danger of misunderstanding passages where these occur, than passages where words occur which are now entirely out of use. When you meet such a word as 'ouches,' 'taches,' 'days-man,' you see at once that it is a stranger in modern English; and if you wish to understand what you read, and do not merely go over a chapter mechanically, under the idea that you are serving God and benefiting yourselves by passing the eye over the words, you ask a well-informed friend, or consult a book, what the obsolete word means. But when you read, 'If any widow have children or *nephews*,' and do not know that everywhere in our version this word means 'grandson;' when you are told that Paul and his company 'took up their *carriages*, and went up to Jerusalem,' or that 'David left his *carriage* in the hand of the keeper of the *carriage*,' and forget that with our translators 'carriage' meant 'baggage;' when you hear Paul saying to the Athenians, 'As I passed by, and beheld your *devotions*, I found an altar,' and do not know that by these the translators intend the outward objects connected with what we now call devotion—temples, images, and the like;[1]—in these and other similar cases you might easily go unconsciously altogether astray as to the sense of the passage. Words wholly unused in the English of our own time 'are like rocks which stand out from the sea: we are warned of their presence, and there is little danger of our making shipwreck upon them. But words like those which have been just cited, as familiar now as when our version was made, but employed in quite different meanings from those which they then possessed, are like hidden rocks, which give no notice of their presence, and on which we may be shipwrecked, if I may so say, without so much as being aware of it.'[2]

[1] 1 Tim. v. 4; Acts xxi. 15; 1 Sam. xvii. 22; Acts xvii. 23. Some interesting and valuable remarks on this source of error are to be found in the second chapter of Archbishop Trench's work entitled, *On the Authorized Version of the New Testament.*
[2] Trench.

By far the most serious of the misconceptions arising from this source of error are those connected with the words '*religion*' and '*religious*,' especially in the passage before us. At the time our translation was made, these words seem to have been generally, if not always, employed with reference to the *outward forms* in which what we now usually call 'religion'—reverence and love to God—showed itself. The words do not occur often in our Bible,—nowhere in the Old Testament, and but a few times in the New; but in every case they refer to what we may call the *body*, not the *soul*, of religion—to forms of worship, under which there might or might not be true piety. 'Godly' and 'godliness' are the terms our translators employ for the *spirit* of religion. In the verses before us, the words in the original which 'religion' and 'religious' are used to represent, unquestionably refer to *worship*, or, generally, to the *form* or *embodiment* of religion. I have gone into this matter with some fulness, because I am persuaded that the last verse of this chapter, misunderstood, has often been applied as an opiate to their consciences by persons who, feeling that they loved the world and the things of the world more than they loved Jesus Christ, would fain believe that a life of outward decency and some kindness to the poor constitutes the whole of religion — the whole of piety. What the apostle states is that, where piety exists in the soul, stainless morality and earnest philanthropy form its proper and legitimate outward expression.

Gathering up what has been said with regard to various points in the rendering, we may give the translation of the verse thus: 'If any man among you think himself to be observant of religious service, whilst at the same time bridling not his tongue, but deceiving his own heart, that man's religious service is vain.'¹ The case supposed is that of a 'hearer of the word,'—a person, say, who attends the house of God with considerable, perhaps great, regularity, to whom the Bible is not by any means an unfamiliar book, and who regards his character with complacency, but all the while has a tongue which is '*unbridled*,' unrestrained by Christian judgement and feeling.

The tongue, you observe, *needs to be 'bridled.'* Like all the other members, it is by nature yielded up as an 'instrument of unrighteousness,' under the impulse of unholy passions. By nature its course is wild and destructive, like that of a spirited horse, infuriated, and free from bit and bridle. The apostle assumes, too, that *Christian principle will bridle it.* 'For this purpose the Son of God was manifested, that He might destroy the works of the devil,' and among them falsehood, profanity, unkind, unclean, unprofitable talk. The gospel of Christ is 'the power of God' to effect this, to save the soul from the corrupting power of the devil, to bring men to yield up the tongue, with all the other members, 'as instruments of righteousness unto God.' 'Whoso,' then, 'looketh into the perfect law of liberty, and continueth looking, he being not a forgetful hearer, but a doer of work, this man bridleth his tongue.'

The apostle's statement here implies still further, that *bridling the tongue is a peculiarly excellent test of genuine religion.* From drunkenness, uncleanness, and other gross and obvious vices, many are led to abstain through influences unconnected, or but indirectly connected, with religion; but whilst every true Christian—every person really spiritually-minded—will

---

¹ The Revised Version—unhappily, as it seems to me—retains 'religious' and 'religion:' 'If any man thinketh himself to be religious, while he bridleth not his tongue but deceiveth his heart, this man's religion is vain. Pure religion and undefiled,' etc.

with more or less thoroughness and success bridle his tongue, there must be very few cases, if any, in which this is habitually done by an unconverted person. The government of the tongue is a task so difficult, that he who has grace to accomplish it, has grace to accomplish anything. Think of *the facility and rapidity with which sins of the tongue are committed.* Almost before we are conscious that a thought has entered the mind, before we have taken a moment to ponder its nature or the consequences of uttering it, it has leaped into outward life as a spoken sentence. Again, think of *the great scope there is for going wrong.* To most of the other sins which take an outward form temptations present themselves but occasionally; and, if we desire it, we may to a considerable extent keep ourselves clear of those circumstances in which the temptations occur. But business and the general intercourse of life cannot be carried on without speaking, and therefore there is always abundant scope and temptation for offences of the tongue. The words which any one of us speaks during one day of average talkativeness would, I suppose, if printed, go far to fill a fairly-sized volume. Speech is continually passing from us on the most varied subjects; and thus, as it is far more difficult for a military commander to keep a post to which there are many approaches, than one where he is safe if his force is concentrated on two or three, so the habitual and thorough government of the tongue is a singularly difficult duty. Still further, consider *how little help one has to the right discharge of this duty from popular feeling on the subject.* 'You know how very little importance men generally attach to sins of the tongue. Is not the tendency of our minds to reason thus: A hasty word, vented in a moment of excitement, a slight misrepresentation, a profane joke, an impure innuendo—why, it is all empty breath, nothing serious is intended by it, and a man may be a very good man who indulges in such words occasionally?'[1]

When you think of these things, my brethren, is it not plain that nothing but deep, decided piety will habitually, thoroughly, on all subjects, in all circumstances, bridle the tongue? This *can* do it, this *will* do it. Every believer, according to the measure of the intelligence and liveliness of his faith, bridles his tongue; for he knows that God's judgement on words is not as man's. 'I say unto you,' was the solemn declaration of the Lord Jesus, 'that every idle word that men shall speak, they shall give account thereof in the day of judgement. For by thy words thou shalt be justified, and by thy words thou shalt be condemned. A good man, out of the good treasure of the heart, bringeth forth good things; and an evil man, out of the evil treasure, bringeth forth evil things.' It is evident that, however lightly men may regard the conduct of one who speaks words which ought not to be spoken, 'the Lord will not hold him guiltless.'

Thus, looking into the matter closely, you see that nothing could well be either a truer or a more easily consulted index of the character of the heart than the character of the tongue —lawless, or 'bridled,' regulated constantly by reverence and love for God and His law.

Hence it follows that a professor of Christianity, a man who believes himself to be an acceptable worshipper of God, and who yet 'bridleth *not* his tongue,' necessarily '*deceiveth his own heart;*' for through such conduct he plainly takes rank, not among the 'doers of the word,' but among the 'hearers

---

[1] Dean Goulburn, in a sermon preached in the school chapel at Rugby, and printed as an appendix to his excellent little book, *The Idle Word*. To this sermon I have been indebted, in writing the present lecture, for several valuable hints.

only,' of whom the apostle has already said, in the 22nd verse, that they 'deceive their own selves.' Such a man cheats himself, in that he fancies that a decorous observance of ordinances and a freedom from some of the coarser vices prove piety, though all the while his corrupt, unhallowed speech betrays a corrupt, unhallowed heart.

Or, if the apostle's reference in 'bridling not the tongue' be, in the first instance, and especially—as, from the connection of the verse with what precedes, I am inclined to think—to unchristian bitterness in religious discussions,[1] then these persons may even, and no doubt often do, '*deceive their own hearts*' to the extent of fancying that their unbridled speech itself, their fierce and uncharitable declamation on behalf of what they deem orthodoxy, is a service rendered to God—that their 'wrath' is fitted to 'work His righteousness.' This special reference of the 'deceiving'—'cheating themselves with the idea that their angry and arrogant speech is honouring to God'—appears to me almost certainly the true one, because thus a distinct and impressive thought is brought out; whilst, if we give the word only the general sense—'cheating themselves with the thought that they are Christians, when they are not'—then it is difficult to discriminate this from the force of the closing statement in the verse, to which we now come.

'*This man's religion*'—that is, as we have seen, 'religious service'—'*is vain*,' 'empty and profitless.' The apostle, experienced in human weakness, would be very far from saying that all who sometimes, or even often, are guilty of violent or otherwise unguarded utterances, are thereby absolutely proved to be irreligious. Yet, certainly, those with whom this is

[1] One can hardly help feeling the figure of 'bridling' to have a *peculiar* appropriateness, if passion, bursts of angry invective, be the sin of the tongue particularly in the writer's mind.

frequent have much cause to doubt of their piety. Persons who look largely to their theological bitterness, or their keen denunciation of the moral halting of their neighbours, as evidence of their standing before God, are trusting to a broken reed. And wherever a man's tongue is *habitually* unbridled, then, many though his prayers may be, great his knowledge of truth, high his hopes, decorous his general life, still 'his religious service is vain,'—it lacks life and power,—it is a body without a soul,—and it meets no acceptance with God: for 'out of the abundance of the heart the mouth speaketh,' and therefore a mouth full of wrath and bitterness cannot but reveal a heart full of envy, malice, uncharitableness,—a heart which has not yet felt how marvellous is the love of Christ, and thus by the divine 'gentleness' been made truly 'great.'

Having thus pointed out the *non-*'doer of the word' by describing a feature easily recognised, and which evidently was to be seen lamentably often among the professing Christians of that age,—and in most ages of the church since too, for men slow to hear, but swift to speak, and to speak arrogantly and unlovingly, have never been wanting in her ranks,— the apostle goes on now to depict the 'doer,' and thus show how Christ would have men serve Him. 'The religious service' of the man who has been set before us in the 26th verse—very fair in his own esteem—was in truth, before the eye of God, sullied with a broad black stain,—a stain which came from within, from a polluted heart, and thus made the whole 'vain.' In what follows we have in contrast a description of '*religious service pure and undefiled.*' These two epithets are as nearly as possible equivalent in meaning,—the one exhibiting the idea positively, the other negatively; and they seem to be joined here simply to give emphasis to the thought. But further, the 'religious service' now to be depicted is 'pure and undefiled *before God'*—that is, 'in His sight or estimation.' The views of men on the nature of acceptable worship are very varied; but it is God 'with whom we have to do.' It is His view on the subject which alone will be regarded at the great judgement: how transcendently important, then, that we should accept that view now! By the words rendered '*God and the Father*' is meant, undoubtedly, '*our God and Father*'—He who 'begat us with the word of truth.' Now, wherever in Scripture an addition is made to the simple name of God, there is implied in the addition something by way of argument or illustration specially bearing on the point before the writer. This special force here is obvious and striking. 'To us Christians God has given life, and the life is that of His *children*. This is our supreme dignity, the chief spring of our joy. Now, what can be a true or acceptable embodiment or exhibition of this new spiritual life, except such an outward life as bears the image of our Father, mirroring His love and holiness who is *Father of the fatherless, and Judge of the widows*, and *of purer eyes than to behold evil?*'

In accordance with what is thus, as we see, naturally suggested by the name 'our God and Father,' the 'pure and undefiled religious service' of His children is set forth by the apostle as falling into two great divisions—active philanthropy and personal holiness. This is not altogether exhaustive, but sufficient for his purpose. He wishes to bring impressively before his readers those elements of true 'service' in which many of them were grievously lacking. The third great division, attention to 'religious ordinances'—in our ordinary limited application of the expression—attention to prayer, to the study of the Bible, to public worship, and to the sacraments, he leaves unmentioned; because, as the whole course of his previous remarks has shown, those for whom he primarily wrote were not seriously neglectful of these duties, regarded simply as outward services, but in too many cases deemed them the sum-total of the proper embodiment of religion.

'*The fatherless and widows*' are clearly enough representative classes. Their case is meant to suggest the general category of 'all who need temporal or spiritual help—all who, from any cause, require the active display of Christian love.' Thus, as I have already said, this branch of 'religious service' is active philanthropy. 'The widow and the fatherless' are often referred to in the Bible as claiming peculiar sympathy, and the feelings of all of us attest the justice of this representation. An Oriental widow (particularly when through any cause cut off from the aid of her natural connections—father, brother, and the like — as, no doubt, among the Jewish Christians was often the case through the woman's conversion) 'presents a case of even more absolute destitution than with us : for, in the East, any resources of remunerative occupation to a woman can scarcely be said to exist; and the comparatively secluded habits of life which custom exacts, prevent her from pressing her claims and wants upon the attention of others with vigour and effect.'[1]

True piety, the apostle says, will impel us '*to visit*' the destitute, in order to give comfort and aid. The word is one employed of God's manifestations of grace. 'Blessed be the Lord God of Israel,' exclaims good Zacharias, 'for He hath *visited* and redeemed His people, and hath raised up an horn of salvation for us.' So, when Jesus raised from the dead the widow's son at Nain, 'there came a fear on all, and they glorified God, saying, A great prophet is risen up among us, and God hath *visited* His people.' The employment of the term in the passage before us, regarding God's children, has manifestly

[1] Kitto's *Daily Bible Illustrations*, viii. 58.

reference to visits made in their heavenly Father's spirit of tender love and pity. The need and the purpose of the 'visit' which constitutes an element in true 'religious service,' are further defined by '*in their affliction.*' Many visits—many visits to 'the fatherless and widows' even—may have nothing of religion connected with them; but when the existence of need draws men, through the working of Christian love, to strive to satisfy the need, there is a religious deed.

Christians act in the spirit of the principle here laid down, when they give money to build and maintain asylums for the sick and destitute, and to send Bibles and missionaries to the heathen at home and abroad. But this is not all that is required. The apostle's statement evidently intimates that vital religion in the soul will reveal itself by *personal exertion* in the way of Christian help to others, as its legitimate embodiment. In our age, at least as fully as in any previous age of the world, men believe in the power of money,—and money certainly can do many things; but it cannot buy the position before God of Christians; nor, in the case of true Christians, can it buy advancement in the divine life. Too many are disposed to compound for personal effort, by giving to charitable institutions. The sound principle on the subject, I apprehend, is that 'this we ought to do, and not to leave the other undone.' Town missionaries and Bible-women are most necessary and most useful; yet I cannot help believing that the Christian who, because there are such agencies, and he helps to maintain them, abstains from personally '*visiting* the fatherless and widows in their affliction,' sinfully darkens and enfeebles his own spiritual life. And persons who can take time for much recreation of various kinds, and who, in the midst of a day which they would declare to be quite full of business, could yet certainly *make* time to consider some new remunerative piece of business which unexpectedly presented itself, and accomplish all the rest besides,—such persons cannot at the bar of conscience plead want of time for the discharge of Christian duty. Few things, dear brethren, are more quickening and strengthening to the life of the soul than a visit made in a Christian spirit to a house of mourning. We meet Jesus there: '*I* was sick, and ye visited Me: inasmuch as ye have done it unto one of the least of these, My brethren, ye have done it unto Me.'

The other great division of 'pure and undefiled religious service' to which James draws our attention, is personal purity of life: '*and to keep himself unspotted from the world.*' This covers the whole range. '*The world*' here, as often in Scripture, particularly in the writings of the Apostle John, designates the men and things here below, regarded as pervaded and controlled by the great evil spirit whom Jesus Himself called the 'prince of this world.' By nature we are all 'of the world;' but 'as many as receive Jesus Christ, to them gives He power to become sons of God, even to them that believe on His name,'—and these 'are not of the world, even as He is not of the world;' for to this end 'He gave Himself for our sins, that He might deliver us from the present evil world, according to the will of our God and Father.' Yet, being not taken 'out of the world,' but left in it for a time, to be its 'lights,' its 'salt,' and for these ends expressly called on to have much intercourse with the men of the world, we are liable to be contaminated by its evil, and thus be but dim 'lights'—'salt' which has almost 'lost its savour.' Hence the urgency of Bible pleading with Christians, 'Be not conformed to this world;' 'Love not the world, neither the things that are in the world,' and the like. The duty of the child of God is '*to keep himself unspotted* from the world,'—his character ever a garment of stainless white. God alone can so 'keep' us, and His gracious help will be bestowed abundantly; for the prayer of the great High Priest for His people—Him whom the Father 'heareth always'—is, that God will 'keep them from the evil.' But while *power* is only from Him, there must be *care* with us. 'Keep thyself pure,' says Paul to Timothy. We must 'work out our own salvation with fear and trembling,' for the very reason that we know 'it is God'—the God of all grace—'which worketh in us both to will and to do of His good pleasure.'

It is important to observe that the two characteristics which James describes—active love to the needy, and personal purity—belong both to every truly Christian life. There are, I doubt not, non-Christian people, who, from a certain constitutional delicacy of spirit, favoured by education and surroundings, live a life of beautiful personal purity, but have little love or care for others. On the other hand, there are not a few kindly worldlings and sensualists—men personally given to drunkenness perhaps, or uncleanness, or profanity, or utter frivolity—who yet, simply from natural temperament, from impulse and not from principle, pity and help those who are in trouble. But in 'religious service pure and undefiled,' in the life which is the legitimate 'issue' from a renewed heart, are found both benevolence and purity of character. Active love is an essential element in it no less than self-restraint, and self-restraint no less than active love.

Looking over the whole of the apostle's statement in this verse, then, brethren, we find him here, as so often, echoing declarations made by his Master in the Sermon on the Mount; for Jesus too has told us that piety exhibits its presence in us—that we take rank among the 'blessed' of God—when we are 'merciful,' and when we are 'pure in heart.' How perfect such teaching! How divine! And how gloriously complete is the model that the Lord's own earthly life has set before us! His coming from heaven was 'to visit the fatherless in their affliction,' the fatherless who had criminally made themselves such by wilful alienation from their true home,—and to bring them gladness by recalling them to their Father's presence and grace. 'He went about doing good;' and when imagination calls Him up before our view in His ministry, the ear seems at once to hear a 'Son, Daughter, be of good cheer: go in peace; thy faith hath saved thee.' If we seek a representative scene from the records of that wondrous life, none more naturally occurs than this: 'When He came nigh to the gate of the city, behold, there was a dead man carried out, the only son of his mother, and she was a widow: and much people of the city was with her. And when the Lord saw her, He had compassion on her, and said unto her, Weep not. And He came and touched the bier: and they that bare him stood still. And He said, Young man, I say unto thee, Arise. And he that was dead sat up, and began to speak. And He delivered him to his mother.' Certainly no embodiment in 'religious service' of love and consecration to such a Saviour can be more fitting than '*to visit the fatherless and widows in their affliction.*' And amidst the freest converse with the men of the world—often the most depraved—for the working out of His purposes of love, yet the exquisite beauty, the unsullied purity, of His character, stood out clear and glorious. By His bitterest foes the challenge remained and remains unanswered, 'Which of you convinceth Me of sin?' He '*kept Himself unspotted from the world;*' so that, 'when the prince of this world came, he had nothing in Him.'

X.

RESPECT OF PERSONS.

'My brethren, have not the faith of our Lord Jesus Christ, the Lord of glory, with respect of persons. 2 For if there come unto your assembly a man with a gold ring, in goodly apparel, and there come in also a poor man, in vile raiment; 3 And ye have respect to him that weareth the gay clothing, and say unto him, Sit thou here in a good place; and say to the poor, Stand thou there, or sit here under my footstool; 4 Are ye not then partial in yourselves, and are become judges of evil thoughts? 5 Hearken, my beloved brethren,—Hath not God chosen the poor of this world, rich in faith, and heirs of the kingdom which He hath promised to them that love Him? 6 But ye have despised the poor. Do not rich men oppress you, and draw you before the judgement-seats? 7 Do not they blaspheme that worthy name by the which ye are called?'—JAMES ii. 1–7.

A NEW section of the Epistle begins here,—connected, however, naturally and obviously with the preceding. 'Genuine religion in the heart,' the apostle has said, 'will express itself in holiness of life—in a lofty morality, comprising personal purity and earnest devotion to the glory of God through the good of men: if a man love God, he will strive to keep God's law of liberty.' But certain serious violations of this law had become lamentably common among the Christian communities, and were doing much to neutralize their influence for good. One of these James proceeds now to point out and reprove.

'*My brethren, have not the faith of our Lord Jesus Christ, the Lord of glory, with respect of persons.*' The words which are

VER. I.] *Respect of Persons.* 141

last in our version stand in the original immediately after 'My brethren,' and on them rests the emphasis: thus, 'Do not with respect of persons have your faith.' A peculiar pungency, which can hardly be represented in an English translation, is given to the reproof in the original by the particle rendered '*with*,' strictly '*in*.' Its force is similar to that which it has in Chap. i. 6, where '*in* faith' means 'enveloped in faith as in an atmosphere.' So here, 'in the midst of, or environed by, respect of persons,'—respect of persons, too, shown in many ways, for the noun in the original is plural. The meaning is pretty fully brought out by such a free rendering as, 'Let not respect of persons be a characteristic of the manner in which you maintain faith in our Lord Jesus Christ.'

You observe how clearly the apostle teaches here that the primary or fundamental element in religion—the root of the divine life in man—is faith in our Lord Jesus Christ. His particular purpose in writing the Epistle leads him to dwell mainly on the practical side of Christianity, the 'pure and undefiled religious service before our God and Father,' of which he has just spoken—the fruits rather than the root. But in this verse, especially taken in connection with the singularly rich and precious statement of truth which he has given in Chap. i. 18, we are very plainly taught that hearty acceptance of God's testimony concerning His Son is the spring from which reviving, fertilizing, purifying streams flow forth throughout the whole man. Christians, like all their fellow-men, were by nature dead in sins; but of His own will God originated life in them, and this through the word of truth regarding Jesus, received by faith. This is manifestly the doctrine set forth in these two verses. To be a Christian, therefore, is fundamentally to have faith in Christ. To the anxious sinner inquiring the way of salvation, James, no less decidedly than

Paul, says, 'Believe on the Lord Jesus Christ, and thou shalt be saved.' James, no less decidedly than Paul, 'counted all things but loss for the excellency of the knowledge of Christ Jesus his Lord,—yea, counted all things but dung, that he might win Christ, and be found in Him, not having his own righteousness, which was of the law, but that which is through the faith of Christ, the righteousness which is of God by faith.' It is of importance to notice this, because the last verses of the first chapter have been taken by many as containing a description of the *whole* of religion, and therefore as teaching a doctrine which the apostle would have rejected with abhorrence; and because in the latter part of the present chapter there are modes of expression which many have deemed to be directly opposed to the doctrine of justification by faith alone, as fully set forth by Paul.

To all candid thinkers on the subject, it must be evident that a character, however outwardly beautiful, of which love to God is not the grand animating principle, cannot be pleasing in His sight; for moral beauty which springs only from earthly motives is but a subtler form of that disloyalty to the King of the universe which elsewhere reveals itself in gross outward sin. The first and great commandment in the moral law—inevitably such, our consciences tell us, if there is a God at all—is, 'Thou shalt love the Lord thy God;' and a scheme of morality which puts this out of view is as defective as a scheme of the planetary system which should leave out of account the relation of the planets to the central sun. Now sin has prejudiced men against God, and nothing but that sight of His true character which faith in Christ gives will teach us to love and revere Him. To believe in Christ, to have affiance of the heart in Him, is therefore the very first step towards a true morality — a morality pleasing to God.

'Then said they unto Him, What shall we do, that we might work the works of God? Jesus answered and said unto them, This is the work of God, that ye believe on Him whom He hath sent.' 'Abide in Me, and I in you. As the branch cannot bear fruit of itself, except it abide in the vine, no more can ye, except ye abide in Me: for without Me ye can do nothing.'

> ' Talk they of morals? O Thou bleeding Love,
> The grand morality is love of Thee.'

On the believer in Jesus, God looks with complacency and tender Fatherly affection; and his good works, being prompted by his faith, are really a religious service, a worship, a sacrifice, with which 'God is well pleased.'

In speaking of 'the faith of our Lord Jesus Christ,' our apostle goes on to add to that ordinary name the designation, '*The Lord of glory.*' The words '*The Lord*' here are, as you see from their being printed in italics in our Bibles, a supplement inserted by the translators from the preceding designation. Now the connection of the expression '*of glory*' may be, and has been, supposed to be different. For example, it may be brought into immediate dependence on 'faith,' and we may construe thus,—'the faith of the glory of our Lord Jesus Christ,' that is, faith in His exaltation, regarded as an expression of the Father's perfect satisfaction with His Son's atoning work; or thus,—'faith (resting on our Lord Jesus Christ) in the glory,' that is, in the future glory of His people. The latter of these very well brings out the argument which we shall see to be involved in the words 'of glory;' but this is done with at least equal clearness and force by the construction of our translators (retained by the Revisers),—which seems to be, on the whole, the most natural. Jesus is 'the Lord of glory,' in all the grand generality of this expression:

the Possessor, as God, of an essential, infinite glory: the King of glory, who as Mediator has 'sat down at the right hand of the Majesty in the heavens, all power given Him in heaven and in earth, and a name which is above every name; that at the name of Jesus every knee should bow, of things in heaven, and things in earth, and things under the earth; and that every tongue should confess that Jesus Christ is Lord, to the glory of God the Father:' the Fountain of glory, from whom, in whom, alone we can have true glory.

'Of your faith in the Lord Jesus Christ, the Lord of glory,' then, says our apostle, '*let not respect of persons be a characteristic.*' To a thoughtful Christian mind this simple statement of the injunction contains overwhelming argument in its support. Faith in Christ and respect of persons are diametrically opposed to each other; so that in proportion as the one is cherished, the other necessarily is weakened. To speak of respect of persons, therefore, as a 'characteristic' of faith in Christ, or, more exactly, of having our faith 'enveloped in respectings of persons,' is almost a contradiction in terms. Thus the form into which the apostle throws his precept exhibits with singular pungency and force the inconsistency and absurdity of professing Christians whose conduct seemed to show that they were attempting to combine the two. Faith in Christ is a cordial acceptance of the gospel of God's mercy, which is not a message to this or that class of men, but to men universally, to men regarded from that moral point of view in which we all by nature constitute one class,—sinners, who have earned death as our wages. A man who believes the gospel has come to feel himself the fellow-sinner of all around, has become convinced that his relations to God are of immeasurably greater moment than any he can hold to his fellow-creatures, and has passed into a sphere in which he recognises all his fellow-Christians as in a high and peculiar sense his *brethren*, members with him, through the grace of their common Saviour, of the family of God. In this family, rich and poor, wise and feeble-witted, those who aforetime were respectable worldlings and those who aforetime were bold sinners, meet together on terms of perfect equality. Their salvation is a 'common salvation.' The faith of poor Joseph is 'like precious faith' with that of the Apostle Paul.

Groaning under the inequalities and oppressions of the world, political enthusiasts have thought that by simple changes in forms of government complete deliverance could be attained. A foolish fancy! Wisely devised political arrangements can do something to benefit men's condition; but so long as sin reigns, true brotherhood can be only a vision, for the tendencies of moral evil are always to disunion and hatred. Satan 'was a murderer from the beginning.' That the revolutionary convulsions of France in the end of last century, which were expected by so many honest spirits to bring in an age of liberty and equality and fraternity, should in fact bring in a 'reign of terror' and a crushing despotism, was nothing more than natural, when sin and unbelief were rampant, religious influences contemptuously thrust aside, and nought leant on but the arm of flesh. But the church of Christ *is* a brotherhood, a 'fraternity,' distinguished by true 'equality,' and regulated by the law of 'liberty.' For 'respect of persons' to enter here, for regard to worldly distinctions to intrude itself as a governing influence in the sphere of religious feeling and action, is utterly alien from the spirit of the gospel. The incongruity of this with 'the faith of our Lord Jesus Christ' is especially obvious when we remember that He is the 'Lord of glory.' In the light of His glory, all worldly distinctions are seen to be very trifling. In His house, among His brethren, to give importance to the fleeting glories of earth should be deemed an insult to the riches of His grace, from which comes true lasting glory to *all* His people. For even now *all* true believers, though they may be clothed in rags, and glad to receive the crumbs which fall from rich men's tables, are children of God, sons and daughters of the Lord Almighty; and there awaits them all 'an exceeding and eternal weight of glory,' seeing that 'when He shall appear we shall be like Him,' and He will take us home 'to sit with Him upon His throne,' and enjoy all the blessedness and honour of the heavenly kingdom. 'My brethren, have not the faith of our Lord Jesus Christ, the Lord of glory, with respect of persons.'

I need hardly say that nothing in the apostle's precept is intended to forbid the fullest recognition in ordinary life of the distinctions of society. It can never be wrong—indeed, the whole spirit of Scripture, and many express injunctions, call upon us—to give to those whom God in His providence has placed in positions of authority, or of greater prominence and influence than ourselves, the customary marks of respect, not in any spirit of mean subservience, but in the spirit of freemen—'the Lord's freedmen.' We are to 'render to all their due, honour to whom honour.' The principle stated by our apostle here is, that in matters where Christians have to act *simply and distinctively as professors of Christianity, members of Christ's church*, not as citizens or members of general society, they are not to allow worldly considerations of any kind to sway them.

In the verses which follow, he illustrates his meaning by an instance. The case is given in the form of a supposition; but it is plain that James knew well that such an incident as he describes often occurred in the meetings of the Christians.

VER. 2.]　　　*Respect of Persons.*　　　147

'*For if there come unto your assembly a man with a gold ring, in goodly apparel, and there come in also a poor man in vile raiment; and ye have respect to him that weareth the gay clothing, and say unto him, Sit thou here in a good place; and say to the poor, Stand thou there, or sit here under my footstool:*[1] *are ye not then partial in yourselves, and are become judges of evil thoughts?*'

By some expositors the scene of the incident here depicted by the apostle is supposed to be a sitting of the congregation, or of the body of elders, as a kind of *court*, to investigate disputes among the members of the church; and that the fault pointed out is as if in an ordinary court of justice, in the trial of a case between a rich and a poor man, the judges were at the very outset to show marked favour to the rich. This view is founded mainly on the word '*judges*' in the 4th verse, and is thought to be supported by '*synagogue*,' which is the strict rendering of the word in the 2nd verse given by our translators as '*assembly*.' We know that in the Jewish synagogues trials were held, and sometimes punishment inflicted; and there are in the New Testament several allusions to this practice.[2] This view of the reference here, however, is not by any means required by the fact that these words are employed, and, on the whole, appears unnatural. '*Judges*' may, without any difficulty, be taken quite generally and loosely; and the use of '*synagogue*' in an Epistle addressed to 'the twelve

[1] The meaning of the last part of the 3rd verse may be, 'and say to the poor man, Stand thou there, or (say to him), Sit under my footstool.' But it seems preferable to take the whole from 'Stand' to the end, including the 'or,' as words of address to the poor man,—the utter carelessness of the officers of the church as to where he put himself, provided only that it was not 'in a good place,' being thus forcibly set forth.

[2] See, for example, Acts xxii. 19.

tribes which are scattered abroad,' seems merely to prove what of itself might have been thought very likely,—that in many cases the Jewish members of Christian churches retained for their place of religious assembly the old name, familiar and dear to them in Judaism.[1] Very similarly, we ourselves, if explaining to children what 'synagogue' means, should naturally enough describe it as 'a Jewish *church;*' just as, not unmisleadingly for some readers perhaps, the assertion of the town-clerk of Ephesus, that Paul and his company were innocent of pillaging *heathen temples*, takes with our translators the form of a statement that they were not ' robbers of *churches*' (Acts xix. 37).

There can be little doubt, I think, that James refers to one of the ordinary meetings of the Christians for worship, which, like our own, were open to any person who chose to come;[2] and you observe how with two or three firm strokes the picture is made to stand out before us. The arrangements of the house for the public worship of the Christians are, we must suppose, similar to those of the synagogue. There are some seats more prominent than the rest, probably a little elevated; and on these, the 'chief seats,' which in the synagogue the scribes and Pharisees loved to occupy, sit, no doubt, the elders and deacons of the church. On these brethren, among other more serious responsibilities, rests the duty of assigning seats to strangers who may come into the meeting,—and who may be either unbelievers, heathen or Jewish, or Christians from other places. The ordinary congregation has assembled, then, and the seats are pretty fully

---

[1] On more than one extant inscription the name 'synagogue' is found, with distinct reference to a Christian church: see Schürer's *Jewish People in the Time of Christ* (E. T.), div. ii., vol. ii., p. 69, footnote.
[2] See 1 Cor. xiv. 23.

occupied, when the door opens, and two strangers enter, one evidently from his dress and demeanour a person of considerable wealth, the other as plainly a poor man. One of the office-bearers immediately rises, and beckoning to the well-dressed man to come forward, courteously invites him to sit beside himself, 'in a good place;' while to the poorly attired he says carelessly, 'Stand yonder, or sit on the floor beside my footstool.'

Now, says the apostle, when a scene like this occurs, '*are ye not partial in yourselves?*'—rather, 'do ye not (or, yet more exactly, the case being conceived as a fact, and the question here put as if a narrative had been related, 'did ye not') *waver* in yourselves?' The word is the same as that used in Chap. i. 6, and there rendered 'waver.' The force of the question is, clearly, 'Did you not show that your faith in our Lord Jesus Christ, the Lord of glory, was very weak, or very dim? Did you not evince forgetfulness of the grand principles which you profess to believe? Did you not, by your special desire to secure, through your deference and attention, the rich man as a member of the church, show a want of trust in Jesus, and a reliance on an arm of flesh, as if His kingdom *were* of this world?'

'*And are (ye not) become judges of evil thoughts?*' The natural meaning of the Authorized Version is: 'Have you not constituted yourselves judges that evil thoughts exist in the mind of the poor man, so as to call for your exhibition of coldness or harshness, but that such are absent from the soul of the rich man?' But the more natural and probable construction is to regard the 'evil thoughts' as belonging to the 'judges' themselves,—as we speak of 'judges of integrity,' 'of wisdom,' or the like, in the sense, 'who are men of integrity,' or 'of wisdom.' In Luke xviii. 6, 'the unjust judge' is, strictly rendered, 'the judge of injustice;' and similarly, in Chap. i. 25 of our Epistle, 'a forgetful hearer' is, strictly, 'a hearer of forgetfulness.' So, in the verse before us, the meaning is 'evil-minded judges.' The apostle here charges those who acted in the way which he has described with two faults. The one was their constituting themselves judges of character at all. Here, I apprehend, as so often in the Epistle, we have a reminiscence of words in the Sermon on the Mount, 'Judge not.' 'When one calmly considers such conduct as I have described,' James says, 'it means that you gratuitously and rashly made yourselves judges of character, and expressed your judgement by your doings.' But secondly, they had judged on altogether false and immoral principles, such as that the soul of a man who has good clothes and a gold ring is therefore a better soul, more worth saving, than the soul of a poor man,—that this world's wealth of itself, apart from all other considerations, entitles a man to prominence among the brethren of the Lord Jesus.

Partiality of this kind was nowise confined to the time of James. Springing as it does from the carnality which is found by nature in every human heart, and which leaves some of its roots of bitterness even in regenerate souls, its fruits show themselves in the church in all ages. Literal parallels to the case here described by the apostle would not be hard to find among us. You find exactly the same tendency often showing itself, too, when congregations are called on to elect their spiritual office-bearers. Certainly, the mere fact that they elect a man of wealth or general influence by no means proves, of itself, that this spirit has been at work; for where the essential spiritual qualifications are present — true and ardent piety, and Christian intelligence and judgement—then wealth and influence are to a certain extent additional recommendations, seeing that they are in themselves means of usefulness, which can be turned to special account by one occupying a prominent position in the church. Yet there is always great danger of a congregation being led away by external glitter to elect persons spiritually unsuitable. Again, spiritual overseers are in hazard of paying but slight attention to delinquencies of the rich, whilst under similar circumstances the poor would have been sharply dealt with. Ministers are under some temptation, too,—occasionally, I could suppose, very strong temptation—to keep back, or exhibit with modified colouring, aspects of truth which they have reason to believe unpalatable to some of the wealthy among their hearers. Everything of this kind obviously comes under the sweep of James's rebuke in the passage before us.

Observe the stress which God lays on what we are apt to deem little things. For our 'idle words,' He tells us, we shall be called to account. Looking over the incident which James has described, we can suppose it very likely that neither the rich man, nor the poor man, nor the person who assigned them their respective places, would think much on the subject; but God marked it with condemnation. In a ship becalmed near the shore, one can imagine the captain intently watching pieces of loose sea-weed as they drift past: they are small and worthless, but they show the experienced eye the direction and the rate of dangerous currents. Even so, little things in conduct often show the direction and the force of strong currents of character.

In the three verses which follow, the apostle exhibits the wickedness and the folly of such conduct as he has described, bringing out forcibly the justice of his statement that persons guilty of it were 'evil-minded judges,'—acting on utterly unchristian principles. Affectionately and earnestly he solicits their diligent attention to his observations: '*Hearken, my beloved brethren.*' The particular incident he had sketched might seem an absolute trifle; but the state of feeling which revealed itself by that incident was seriously dishonouring to God, and antagonistic to the progress of His cause in the world. The principles involved, therefore, claimed very careful consideration. The argument following—which, according to a favourite style of James, is set forth in a series of pointed questions—is to this effect: 'In your church procedure you pay much attention to the wealthy, but disregard the poor. Now, while such conduct under any circumstances reveals a mean soul, yet for a man who seeks his portion simply in this world it is no doubt natural, and often from his point of view prudent. But you, according to your profession, have loftier aims; and, regarding heaven as your home, you desire to breathe even on earth a heavenly spirit, taking God's estimate of everything as yours, and trying to be in character like Him. Think, then, how very far you are, in this respect of persons which you practise, from reflecting the divine image; nay, how directly opposed your conduct is to His whom you call your Father. Has not the whole history of the church proved that mainly from the class of those whom the world, according to its standard of reckoning, counts poor, God in His sovereignty has chosen men and women to be, through faith, truly and enduringly rich, and, as His children in Christ, heirs of the blessedness and glory of the heavenly kingdom? But the poor man of my story, who came into your assembly—a representative of the class so honoured by God—you treated with dishonour. On the other hand, rich men, simply because they are rich, you honour. As Christians, you profess to believe that the only thing truly worthy of honour in God's creatures is holiness, devotion to His service, helpfulness to His cause,—

the reflection of His character, which you honour supremely. Now, is wealth moral excellence, or is it necessarily connected with moral excellence? Have the rich, as a class, been in any age conspicuously God-fearing? Nay, in your own experience, is it not the rich who oppress you Christians? Is it not they[1] who drag you into courts of justice, harassing you by accusations, simply because you believe in Christ? Is it not they who blaspheme the infinitely honourable name of the Lord Jesus, which was named over you when in baptism you severed yourselves from the world, and became His? If you give special honour to that class who, as a class, thus dishonour Him and oppose His cause, do you not make yourselves sharers in their misdeeds, and seem to be ashamed of being associated with that worthy name?'

The fulness of this paraphrase, and the general simplicity of the passage, render it unnecessary to say much more in the way of explanation. You observe that the apostle speaks of 'the rich' and 'the poor' *as classes*, in order to show clearly the wickedness of the conduct of those whom he is reproving; for they too looked at the *classes*, despising this man simply because he was one of the poor, and paying special respect to that, simply because he was one of the rich. His statements, then, being made generally of the two classes, naturally admit exceptions, it may be many. A vast number of the poor, it is to be feared, are not spiritually rich; and some of the rich are truly honourable, because they love and revere the worthy name of Jesus. Yet, beyond all question, wealth has been in all ages a serious obstacle to men's becoming religious. The

---

[1] The αὐτοί in this verse might bear the translation 'themselves,' but that in the next would have no meaning, so rendered. It is clear, therefore, that the force of both is such as is given in the paraphrase above.

abundance of present and tangible good, instead of awakening thankfulness and devotion to the Giver, far oftener deadens all longing after nobler and abiding sources of pleasure. In the Psalmist's days the church was 'the congregation of God's poor;' the apostles of the Lord Jesus, and plainly all but a very few of those who 'heard Him gladly,' were poor men; and in every age since, it has been found that 'not many mighty, not many noble' enrolled themselves under the banner of the Captain of salvation, or at least so 'fought the good fight of faith' as to prove that they were sincerely on the Lord's side.

The spiritual exaltation of the outwardly poor James ascribes, in language as explicit as Paul ever employs, to God's sovereign election. Poverty is not an excellence or ground of desert, any more than wealth is in itself a demerit; and the impenitent poor will receive righteous condemnation and punishment as well as the impenitent rich. 'God hath *chosen* the poor.' Our Lord pointed to the fact that by Him 'to the poor the gospel was preached,' as one evidence that He was 'He that should come,' God's commissioned and anointed Servant; and that any of them welcome the glad tidings proclaimed to them, is due to God's spontaneous grace, for 'of His own will begat He us with the word of truth.' 'Even so, Father, for so it seemed good in Thy sight.' Accordingly the being '*rich in faith*' is the *result* of the 'choosing' by God. 'Blessed be the God and Father of our Lord Jesus Christ, who hath blessed us with all spiritual blessings in heavenly places in Christ; according as He hath *chosen* us in Him before the foundation of the world, *that we should be holy and without blame before Him in love.*' The full exhibition of James's meaning is, 'Hath not God chosen the poor in this world *to be* in faith rich;' as when we say, 'The men of Israel chose David king,' that is, '*to be king*.'[1]

'The poor as regards the world'[2] (for this seems the most natural meaning of the reading found in the oldest manuscripts) become, through God's grace, '*rich in faith.*' 'Faith' here may be conceived as the wealth in which they are rich, as elsewhere (Eph. ii. 4) God is described as 'rich in mercy:' and this is undoubtedly the sense which first suggests itself for the words. The apostle's purpose, however, is evidently to set over against worldly poverty spiritual riches generally, not merely wealth in one particular grace; and thus it seems better to take the meaning 'rich through faith,' or 'rich in the sphere of faith,' as contrasted with that of sight,—which the original words will bear quite as well as that first mentioned. The treasures, then, are all the gifts of the Spirit—the peace, and wisdom, and holiness, which Christians enjoy through their faith. They have this spiritual wealth even now, and their prospects are ineffably lofty. Being through faith children of God, they are, 'if children, then heirs, heirs of God, and joint-heirs with Christ,' '*heirs of the kingdom,*' to whom Jesus 'will grant to sit with Him in His throne, even as He is set down with His Father in His throne.' To every true believer this glorious future is absolutely secured by the assurances of Him who cannot lie. '*He hath promised the kingdom to them that love Him.*' Has not Jesus said in express words, 'Fear

---

[1] In ἐξελέξατο πλουσίους the construction is exactly analogous to that in Rom. viii. 29, προώρισε συμμόρφους, 'did predestinate *to be* conformed:' comp. also 2 Cor. iii. 6.

[2] Τῷ κόσμῳ, which is the best supported reading, may mean 'in the judgement of the world;' but the antithesis suggests rather that more common use of the dative, according to which it expresses the sphere or range to which a general predicate is to be confined, 'in (that is, as regards) the world.'

not, little flock; for it is your Father's good pleasure to give you the kingdom'? And, indeed, as He tells us elsewhere, in a solemn and sublime passage of which our apostle's words are plainly a reminiscence, 'the kingdom' which 'the blessed of His Father' are to 'inherit' (receive as 'heirs') has been '*prepared for them* from the foundation of the world.'

XI.

UNITY OF GOD'S LAW.

'If ye fulfil the royal law according to the scripture, Thou shalt love thy neighbour as thyself, ye do well : 9 But if ye have respect to persons, ye commit sin, and are convinced of the law as transgressors. 10 For whosoever shall keep the whole law, and yet offend in one point, he is guilty of all. 11 For He that said, Do not commit adultery, said also, Do not kill. Now, if thou commit no adultery, yet if thou kill, thou art become a transgressor of the law.'—JAMES ii. 8-11.

THE first two of these verses obviously sum up the teaching of the paragraph, enunciating the grand general principle regarding our duty to others, and declaring that respect of persons is opposed to this. In the 8th verse there is in the original an introductory particle which our translators have passed over, probably because they took it as equivalent to another (one of the components of this), which simply indicates the first part of an antithesis, and is often left unrendered. But in every other place in the New Testament where that here employed is found, it introduces something which modifies what has preceded, or is in some way divergent from the line of observation previously pursued, having the force of 'but,' 'nevertheless,' 'however.' It seems reasonable to take it in the same sense here. The connection of thought I apprehend to be somewhat as follows: 'I have spoken severely, knowing that deference to mere earthly distinction has sadly intruded itself among you. *Still* many of you may in this matter be acquitted by your consciences, and these I praise.' 'I have expressed myself sharply. If, *however*, ye (any of the Christian churches to which the letter was written) fulfil the royal law, then ye act as Christians should. But (ver. 9) let me repeat my solemn testimony and warning,—If ye have respect to persons, ye commit sin.'[1]

The particular law of God which the apostle quotes he calls '*royal*' or 'kingly,' because it is that which has been given to govern with supreme authority our conduct to our fellow-men, and to control absolutely all principles and precepts on this subject. To this law all schemes and rules of duty to our fellows are subordinate. However beautiful and justly influential they may be in their own sphere, this has a 'glory that excelleth,' this wears the crown and sways the sceptre. To it, on every matter of doubt and difficulty in this department of morals, lies an appeal; to it the appeal ought always to be carried; and its decision is final. By '*fulfilling*' this kingly law the apostle means, as is plain from the whole tone of his address here, honest and earnest endeavour, in reliance on divine strength, to keep it. This passage gives no sanction to

---

[1] The connection intended by the adversative μέντοι is somewhat obscure. Tyndale, followed by the Authorized Version, has left it untranslated, apparently considering it as simply equivalent to μέν: Wycliffe, rightly, has 'netheles,' and the Rheims 'notwithstanding.' By Calvin, Beza, Huther, Wiesinger, and others, the sense is supposed to be semi-ironical, thus: 'If, however, (in caring for these rich as ye do) ye are (according to your own conceptions) fulfilling the royal law, so far well.' Alford takes the meaning to be, 'If, however, (notwithstanding these cruelties and blasphemies of the rich) ye (in your dealings with them as with others) fulfil the royal law, that is well.' The view of the thought which is illustrated in the paraphrase given in the text above seems to be simpler and more natural than either of these,—namely, that the apostle merely pauses for a moment in his strain of exposure and rebuke of sin, to throw in the kindly remark that, though addressing his readers generally in this strain, still he knew there were many among them who did not merit condemnation in reference to the matter in hand.

the unscriptural and dangerous opinion, that it is possible in this life perfectly to obey God's law. He speaks, too, of 'fulfilling the law *according to the Scripture*,' in distinction from those glosses and perverted readings of it which the carnal wisdom of the world has devised. The truly wise man goes to God's own authorized statute-book; and those who 'fulfil' the law, as found there, '*do well*,' act worthily of the Christian profession, 'adorn the doctrine of God their Saviour.'

The great precept here called 'the royal law'—'*Thou shalt love thy neighbour as thyself*'—occurs first in the book of Leviticus, in the midst of a number of injunctions on points of detail (Lev. xix. 18). It was taken by the Lord Jesus and placed in conjunction with the command, 'Thou shalt love the Lord thy God with all thy heart, and with all thy soul, and with all thy mind;' and these two together were set forth by Him as comprehending all moral duty,—a summary of that law which God had at first written on man's heart, but which now, through the fall, is so sadly defaced and perverted. 'On these two commandments,' said Jesus, 'hang all the law and the prophets' (Matt. xxii. 37-40). The '*neighbour*' spoken of in the law is shown by the parable of the good Samaritan, put forth by the Lord in reply to a question on the subject, to be every fellow-member of the human race, or more particularly, with reference to the active display of love, every human being whom God places us in circumstances to benefit. Our sentiment of humanity is to be co-extensive with the race of humanity.

The '*as*' of the precept is naturally taken as expressive both of measure and of mode. We are to love our fellow-men in the same *degree* as we love ourselves; and we are to love them in the same *way;* our love for them is to have the same characteristics—sincerity, activity, and constancy—which belong to the love we entertain for ourselves. By many interpreters the element of *degree* is excluded altogether from the meaning, on the ground that, 'from the constitution of human nature, obedience to such a precept is impossible.' But I may appeal to your own feelings, when the law is quoted to you, whether *degree* be not one idea—indeed the foremost idea—you attach to the 'as;' so decidedly, I am sure, in the case of every one of you, that very strong reasons would be needed to prove that this thought was not intended to belong to it. If by 'human nature,' in the argument just cited, be meant fallen human nature, even when brought under the control of Christian principles, then this line of reasoning would go much further, and would exclude at least the reference to thought and feeling of any of God's commandments; seeing that it is impossible for us in this life to keep our souls absolutely pure—to refuse unvaryingly the sanction of the will, even for a moment, to desires of a kind offensive to God. Yet, as you know, our Lord's teaching everywhere, and very fully in the Sermon on the Mount, is express in regard to this spiritual reference, this exceeding breadth, of all God's moral laws. If by 'human nature,' however, be meant our first nature, our nature apart from depravity and simply as it came from the hand of God, and if, from the constitution of this, it is impossible to love our neighbour in the same degree as ourselves,—then the argument is conclusive, for between God's creatures as He made them and the laws intended for them by Him, there cannot be any incongruity. But is the assumption true? Do you not think, my brethren, that in heaven, where God's ideal of human character is realized, we shall love our neighbours as much as ourselves? Shall we not rejoice in their joys as warmly as in our own? Now God's moral laws always have the ideal perfection of character in view. They exhibit holiness without defect as man's duty, though divine grace bears long with much defect in the actual obedience to them of Christ's people, and is preparing us, through the *growth* of earth, for the perfect ripeness of heaven.

The practical application of this law, looked at as implying equality of degree (as of that other rule, which sets before us a yet loftier and more wonderful measure of love : 'This is My commandment, that ye love one another, as I have loved you'), will be somewhat on this wise. When the icy fingers of selfishness chill the soul, and the whisper rises, 'Have I not loved my neighbour, my brother, enough?' the still small voice of conscience answers, 'Be not weary in well-doing: hast thou loved him with the intensity of thy love to thyself? Hast thou cared for his interests with the same ardour as for thine own? Hast thou shown to him the same devotedness as to thyself, or affection like the love with which Jesus devoted Himself for thee?'

Extremely difficult questions of many kinds might very easily be suggested regarding the carrying out of this 'royal law,' especially looked at with relation to degree,—difficulties arising out of the complexity of human relations and interests, and the distinctions in love itself, as an affection of instinct, of benevolence, and of complacency or satisfaction,—difficulties such as in multitudes of cases it might be impossible wholly to solve. The solution of many of them, I am persuaded, is to be looked for in the force of the word 'neighbour,' by which God Himself intimates that those who are brought *near* to us in various ways have the first claim on our love, considered as a practical energy. To the priest and Levite and Samaritan the poor wounded man was given by God in His providence as 'neighbour,' more than, at the time, to any other people in the world. The one recognised and accepted the gift and the duty; the others failed to do so. So by kinsmanship, and many other connections of life, which the Christian judgement must discern for itself, God in His providence brings some of our fellows peculiarly close to us, and constitutes them 'neighbours' in a special sense, and with a special claim. Christian love embraces the world in its interest and sympathies; but its practical action is outward, in widening circles. 'Andrew first findeth his own brother Simon, and saith unto him, We have found the Messias.' 'If any provide not for his own, especially for those of his own house, he hath denied the faith, and is worse than an infidel.' 'As we have therefore opportunity, let us do good unto all men, especially unto them who are of the household of faith.'

Besides equality of degree, the '*as*' of the 'royal law' enjoins also similarity in mode. Love to our neighbour is to have the same characteristics—the same sincerity, activity, and constancy—as self-love, and to display itself in similar ways. In this aspect, the precept before us is obviously equivalent in force to that of our Lord in the Sermon on the Mount, 'All things whatsoever ye would that men should do to you, do ye even so to them: for this is the law and the prophets;'—that is, whatsoever things you might reasonably expect from them, were they in your place, and you in theirs. Observe the singular wisdom and beauty of such rules as these, by which that self-love which is ever present with all of us, and the irregularities and excess of which are the main sources of sin, is laid hold of and itself employed as a guide to holiness. By your zeal for the maintenance or advancement of your own health, property, and reputation, by your shrinking from anything which approaches to self-injury, by your eager desire (if you be a true Christian) for your own spiritual welfare, your growth in holiness and peace,—by these things be directed as to your duty to your neighbour: love him after the same fashion.[1]

Oh, brethren, if this 'royal law' were carefully and constantly followed by all in the world who are servants of Christ,—for them and those immediately around them the blessedness and beauty of the 'new earth' would seem almost already come. Speedily, too, the waste places everywhere would 'rejoice and blossom as the rose,' for consistent obedience to this precept throughout the church would be of itself an evangelistic power immeasurably surpassing anything else she could bring into action. 'If ye fulfil the royal law according to the Scripture, *ye do well.*'

In the 9th verse, the apostle returns to the supposition which he had dwelt upon in the earlier verses. He knew that, in reference to many of the congregations to which the letter was written, it was only too well founded; and he is desirous to impress upon them that conduct of the kind he has described is in the judgement of God no trifle, but a serious moral offence. 'If ye have respect to persons, *ye commit sin.*' The expression in the original seems to convey even greater severity of condemnation. Strictly, the meaning is, 'ye *work* sin;' as elsewhere we have, 'Depart from Me, ye that *work* iniquity,' and, on the other side of character, 'He that feareth God and *worketh* righteousness is accepted with Him' (Matt. vii. 23; Acts x. 35). The force appears to be, 'habitually practise:' 'this respect of persons having become your customary procedure, and thus exhibiting a constant state of feeling, you are continually working sin.' To establish this strong statement, James goes on, '*and are convinced of the law as transgressors.*' '*Convince*' is used here, as elsewhere in our

---

[1] This thought is expanded, with characteristic thoroughness and force, by Barrow, in a sermon on Matt. xxii. 39.

version (for example, in John viii. 46), in the sense in which we now commonly employ another verb from the same root—'convict.' This clause, as I have said, is intended to account for the use of the stern word 'sin;' and this connection would perhaps be better brought out by adhering to the participial form of the original, 'being convicted by the law as transgressors,' or by 'seeing that you are convicted.' 'The law of God' (either that particular 'royal law' already mentioned, or rather the divine law in general, of a part of which that is a summary) 'judges you, and in God's sight convicts you, whether you yourselves at present recognise its decision or not. For to have respect of persons is plainly inconsistent with the principle of the commandment, Thou shalt love thy neighbour as thyself.' Respect of persons is obviously, in its very nature, to some extent a limiting of what God has expressed universally. He says 'thy neighbour,' and we say 'my rich neighbour,' 'my neighbour of exactly the same way of thinking in religious matters,' or the like. The good Samaritan did not turn away from the poor wounded traveller because his features showed that he was not a Samaritan but a Jew.

You see, brethren, how gravely our inspired apostle viewed this intrusion of worldly considerations into the sphere of purely religious thought and feeling. He evidently saw here not merely what was likely to cause some annoyance to an individual treated with neglect or contempt, but the working of that very evil and most destructive tendency under which the church has suffered deplorably all down its generations,—the tendency to distrust the support of the unseen divine King, to doubt the almighty energy of faith, to lean on man, and trust to earthly buttresses, as if Christ had never said, 'My kingdom is *not* of this world.'

The 10th and 11th verses are intended to impress yet more

deeply on the readers of the Epistle a conviction of the serious light in which the apostle—and indeed his Master, speaking by him through His Spirit—regarded such respect of persons as has been described. James has called their conduct 'sin,' and the fact that they were 'convicted by the law as transgressors' showed it to be such; for, as we are expressly told elsewhere, 'sin' and 'the transgression of the law' are convertible terms, co-extensive (1 John iii. 4). But to James's readers this would appear 'an hard saying.' All men are prone to think that the law of God, strictly so called—the law as a stern condemning judge—takes cognizance only of *large* matters. There is a vast number of acts into which our consciences tell us that an element of moral wrongness enters, which yet, counting them little, we consider to be scarcely *sins*, or transgressions of God's law. Society often calls sins of this kind by half-jesting names, attenuating and palliating, that, by the subtle power of words, the feeling may be deepened which the heart desires, that these are trifling matters, not within the sweep of *law*. When, for example, the fulfilment of a disagreeable engagement is evaded through the pretence of illness, or when a lady instructs her servant to tell certain persons, if they call, that she is not at home, whether she be really at home or not,—this class of falsehoods is named 'white lies.' Among the Jews, the teaching of the scribes and Pharisees, which dwelt mainly on isolated precepts instead of broad principles of duty, had a tendency to produce the impression that, whenever men could persuade themselves that any act or course of conduct did not fall within the *exact letter* of any particular prohibition, then it was not within the range of the law at all. Accordingly, having called the respect of persons 'sin,' 'transgression,' James anticipates an objection arising from such views and feelings to this effect: 'This may be a violation of a single point of propriety or duty; but surely it is not *sin*, not a breach of *law*.' The apostle's answer is: '*Whosoever shall keep the whole law, and yet offend in one point, he is guilty of all. For He that said, Do not commit adultery, said also, Do not kill.*[1] *Now, if thou commit no adultery, yet if thou kill, thou art become a transgressor of the law.*'

Here he shows the supposed objectors, you observe, that God's law constitutes a grand unity; that everything which in any measure is morally wrong, is a violation of this one glorious body of law; and consequently, that even if a man could keep, and did keep, all the commandments of God except one, the breach of that one makes him, in the fullest sense of the words, a *violator of God's law*, and liable to punishment. The only difficulty in the verses lies in the words '*guilty of all.*' They must be explained by the course of thought, and particularly by the words 'transgressor of the law,' in the end of the 11th verse, to which plainly, from the argument, they are used as very nearly equivalent. The apostle does not mean to say that all sins are equally heinous, or that a man who has told one lie is necessarily as great a sinner as one who has broken all the commandments of the Decalogue. His teaching is that a man who has broken one commandment cannot shelter himself under the idea of having merely violated a precept isolated from the general law of God, but is *guilty of a breach of the law which includes all the commandments*, and thus has as really, though it may be not so glaringly, placed

---

[1] It will be observed that James's mode of reference seems to imply that what (following the order in Exod. xx.) we commonly reckon the sixth and seventh commandments occurred to his mind transposed. This transposition is found also in Luke xviii. 20, Rom. xiii. 9, and perhaps Mark x. 19. Philo too has it, and rests something on the order. There was, no doubt, some traditional authority for it.

himself in opposition to God, as if he had broken all the commandments.

The apostle lays down as his fundamental proposition, that *the authority on which the law rests is one:* 'He that said, Do not commit adultery, said also, Do not kill.' We might conceive the Scripture to have been partly the word of God, partly the utterance of men unguided by God. In this case some precepts might have been from God, whilst others were only the suggestion of human wisdom. But '*all* Scripture is given by inspiration of God.' This is the general truth, of which the apostle's argument leads him to make the part prominent, that all which the Bible declares to be divine law is really such. From this fundamental proposition, it follows that *the essential principle pervading every point of the law, even the minutest, is one.* The law is a transcript of the divine character. It contains many details for our guidance; but of this *body* of law *love* is the *soul*, all-pervading: for God, whose character the law expresses, 'is love.' A breach of the law in its minutest detail, therefore, is a breach of love: as, when a man strikes another severely on one of his limbs, he hurts not that limb only, but the whole man, because life and sensation are everywhere. But further, *the spirit of true obedience to the law is one*—loving respect and submission to God as the Author of the whole law. Such obedience is necessarily implicit and impartial. If a man selects certain commandments to obey, if he 'picks and chooses' among God's precepts, it is plain that he follows his own will, not God's; and the same spirit which leads him to break one, would, under other temptations, lead him to break all. There is here no true obedience to God. His sincere servants 'esteem *all* His precepts concerning *all* things to be right.'

XII.

JUDGEMENT BY THE LAW OF LIBERTY.

So speak ye, and so do, as they that shall be judged by the law of liberty. 13 For he shall have judgement without mercy that hath showed no mercy; and mercy rejoiceth against judgement.'—JAMES ii. 12, 13.

THE 12th verse contains an earnest practical appeal founded on the whole preceding discussion; and this is enforced in the 13th by a very solemn and pointed statement of the respective results of the two courses of life which men may pursue.

The injunction in the 12th is so framed as to remind the readers of some momentous doctrinal truths. One of these is, that '*we shall be judged.*' To any one who looks at the course of history, either of individuals or nations, with an eye which sees no deeper than the outer covering of things, it may seem as if God, having created His world, and established certain general physical laws, had then left it to develop for itself its good and evil, joy and sorrow,—unheeded, uncared for. 'One generation goeth,' after a life of thoughtlessness and sin, 'and another cometh,' to idle through the same frivolous round; and still no voice of solemn rebuke comes forth from the 'excellent glory.' A Howard and a John Williams live lives full of self-sacrificing devotion to God and to their fellow-men; yet no visible diadem of heavenly beauty is set by a divine hand upon their brows, and for them too, as for the thoughtless

VER. 12.] *Judgement by the Law of Liberty.* 169

and the base, 'it is appointed to die.' In the nineteenth century of gospel light men repeat the crime of Cain,—slaveholding nations repeat the oppressions of Egypt,—the iniquities of our great cities cry to the Lord, as did the sins of Sodom and Gomorrah; and still the sky is not cleft by the destroying bolt of God's wrath. Nay, so strangely assigned seem the portions of men at times—the wicked revelling in prosperity, and God's servants draining the 'waters of a full cup' of trouble—that even believers are tempted to say, 'How doth God know, and is there knowledge in the Most High?' And scoffers, 'walking after their own lusts,' and exulting in their fancied impunity, say, 'Where is the promise of His coming? for, since the fathers fell asleep, all things continue as they were from the beginning of the creation.'

But all such thoughts are foolish and false; 'for the eyes of the Lord *are* upon the ways of man, and He seeth all his goings.' 'He knoweth the way of the righteous;' and 'there is no darkness nor shadow of death, where the workers of iniquity may hide themselves.' And though in the riches of His goodness He bears long with sinners, that His forbearance may 'lead them to repentance,' yet He has not left us without manifold witness that even *now* He is sitting in judgement. The awful visitation of the flood, when desolation swept over the world of the ungodly, who were buying and selling, planting and building, marrying and giving in marriage, and scoffingly asking, 'Where is the promise of His coming?' until the day that the fountains of the great deep were broken up and the windows of heaven opened,—how loud a voice of solemn warning has this for our modern world! National judgements, varied and most distinct, from the overthrow of the cities of the plain, to the sea of blood into which their national sin of slaveholding brought our brethren in America, have continually been attesting that God is the Governor among the nations. Every sickness, every bereavement, every stroke of adversity, should be felt by each individual as a 'coming of the Son of man' to him for gentle judgement, to remind him that, though day passes after day now in comparative quiet and monotony, yet certainly one day the Lord shall come in His glory,—'the judgement shall be set, and the books opened.' For all the judgements of time are but prelusive of one great solemn, sublime event, when time shall be no longer. The last stage in the ripening of the bitter fruits of sin, the final crisis in the history of its working among men, will then have come. All disguises shall be removed, the secrets of all hearts and lives made known, and the solemn sentence which shall have eternal issues shall be pronounced from the throne, and responded to by each heart as divinely righteous. 'Behold, the Lord cometh with ten thousands of His saints, to execute judgement upon all, and to convince all that are ungodly among them of all their ungodly deeds which they have ungodly committed, and of all their hard speeches which ungodly sinners have spoken against Him.'

But, as you see, to Christians the law which is to be the standard of judgement is a '*law of liberty*.' This magnificent expression has been already explained, in the observations made on Chap. i. 25. The way in which it is applied here, however, calls for a few further remarks. It means, as we saw, the moral law, looked at as incorporated with the gospel of salvation, in integral connection with its historical facts and its 'exceeding great and precious promises.' The only true liberty for man is that which is given by Christ, the freedom which flows from our being made partakers of the blessings of His redemption, and which indeed, when we take the word in its broadest sense, is but another name for salvation. By nature we are enslaved to base tendencies; and as we are thus morally in bondage, so legally we are criminals, 'condemned already,' prisoners in the hand of divine justice, and liable at any moment to be consigned to the 'outer darkness' for ever. The constant effort of the unregenerate to forget God, and shun all serious religious thought, is but an attempt to deafen the ear of conscience to the clank of their chains. But the Lord God has sent His Son 'to proclaim liberty to the captives, and the opening of the prison to them that are bound;' and with this 'glorious liberty' Christ 'makes His people free' through 'the truth.' Believing the truth, we are 'justified by faith;' and to be justified means to be emancipated from subjection to the curse of the law, for 'there is no condemnation to them which are in Christ Jesus.' The same faith of the truth, which thus delivers from liability to punishment, breaks also the fetters of depravity, because it arouses in the soul a supreme love of God and holiness. You observe, then, that the freedom given by Christ is not lawlessness. It was God's regard for His law, conjoined with His love to the sinner, that provided the wondrous plan of redemption; and the death of Christ, accordingly, has in every aspect 'magnified the law, and made it honourable.' 'He gave Himself for us, that He might redeem us from all iniquity,' that is to say, might deliver us from the power of our natural disposition to disobedience; and the same faith through which we pass into the condition of freedom from the curse of the law, introduces convictions and awakens desires which make that law for the first time truly the rule of our lives. We see its beauty now and love it. 'It is no longer an external thing, commanding with stern voice and terrible threats, but an internal, written on the tables of the mind, and sweetly constraining, by impulses springing up spontaneously in the heaven-born soul, to follow after holiness, to abound in all the fruits of righteousness.'[1]

Now it is by this 'law of liberty,' the apostle tells us—by the moral law looked at in vital connection with the facts and promises of the gospel—that believers are to be judged. For unbelievers the standard of the trial is the moral law simply considered, with its stern obligations, its 'Do this, and thou shalt live,' but 'Cursed is every one that continueth not in all things which are written in the book of the law, to do them.' But for all those who have truly accepted Christ as their Saviour, the law has the curse erased by their Saviour's hand. The Judge of all the earth will show in the face of the moral universe that He does all things righteously and well: the works of the ungodly shall be produced as the ground of condemnation, the works of the godly as evidences of their having cordially accepted forgiveness through free grace. Thus the decisions of the judgement-day will be a great public attestation, under circumstances of inconceivable solemnity and sublimity, that 'the wages of sin is death, but the gift of God is eternal life through Jesus Christ our Lord.'

On the facts which we have been considering the apostle founds an earnest appeal to his readers to cultivate holiness: '*So speak ye, and so do, as* they that shall be judged by the law of liberty.' Christians should remember continually their subjection to the great law which expresses for us the character of God—their being 'under the law to Christ.' We should have much before our minds and hearts the fact that to glorify God —the end for which we were made at the first, and for which we were created anew in Christ Jesus—is to keep His law; that 'without holiness no man shall see the Lord;' that sincere and growing conformity to the divine law is the only satisfactory

[1] Dr. Adam's *Exposition of James*, p. 177.

evidence of our having given ourselves up to be saved through Christ, seeing that to it will be the appeal on the great day of final account. The fact, also, that the law under which Christians are placed is the 'law of liberty,' should be much before us, as fitted, to stimulate and sustain us in the narrow way of godliness. When our hearts sink under the sense of our spiritual weakness, how cheering to remember that for all true believers the law is indissolubly incorporated with the gospel; that a Saviour who was once 'tempted like as we are' is looking down upon us with pity, and ready to give us new strength; and that, at the last, the obedience of a Christian to the law will not be rigidly and sternly scrutinized, as if claiming to be a meritorious ground of everlasting life, but lovingly surveyed as an evidence of true spiritual union by faith to the Living One. The comforts of the gospel, therefore, and the motives which it presents to holy obedience, ought to be often pondered by the child of God, that he may be spurred to ardour in the divine life, and thus experience increasingly the *sense* of 'liberty'—the joyous buoyancy of spirit which we may and should have in keeping God's law—that sweet constraint of the love of Christ which is perfect freedom.

'Think of these things, brethren,' says our apostle, 'and let the fruit of your ponderings be seen in your whole outward life.' '*So speak ye*, as they that know and consider the truth on this matter.' We commonly think little of words, because we little know their power and importance. There is perhaps no class of sins against which our Lord and His apostles give more frequent and earnest warnings than sins of the tongue. James has already urged the importance of being 'slow to speak,' and 'bridling the tongue;' and in the 3rd chapter he discusses the subject with considerable fulness. The distinct and decisive place which this particular part of morals is to have in the reckoning at the judgement is emphatically exhibited by our Lord: 'I say unto you, that every idle word that men shall speak, they shall give account thereof in the day of judgement; for by thy words thou shalt be justified, and by thy words thou shalt be condemned.' In immediate connection He gives the reason: 'O generation of vipers, how can ye, being evil, speak good things? for out of the abundance of the heart the mouth speaketh. A good man out of the good treasure of the heart bringeth forth good things; and an evil man out of the evil treasure bringeth forth evil things.' 'So speak ye,' then, watchfully, purely, truthfully, lovingly, 'as they that shall be judged by the law of liberty.'

'*And so do.*' Our actions of every kind should be such as may reasonably be expected of a man who thinks of judgement and the 'law of liberty.' An unconverted man, being spiritually in an atmosphere of darkness and falsehood,—for Satan, the 'prince of this world,' is ever a liar, and untruth the element in which he delights to envelop his subjects,—is naturally inconsistent: his deeds may often not accord with his words, and neither words nor deeds may truthfully represent his thoughts and feelings. But a Christian, a child of light and truth, having through faith in Jesus Christ received into his mind certain grand principles, which are in their nature fitted to control more or less obviously his whole life, will plainly, in so far as he yields himself up to the power of these principles —in other words, in so far as he approaches the character of a perfect Christian,—be consistent: his words and his deeds will agree, and both will truly exhibit his state of mind and heart. We must be *doers* of the word, not hearers or talkers only. He who is to sit on the great white throne, judging the world, has already given solemn warning on this point: 'Not every one that saith unto Me, Lord, Lord, shall enter into the kingdom of heaven; but he that doeth the will of My Father which is in heaven. Many will say to Me in that day, Lord, Lord, have we not prophesied' (spoken well,—taught others impressively and wisely) 'in Thy name? and then will I profess unto them, I never knew you: depart from Me, ye that work iniquity.' 'So speak ye, *and* so do, as they that shall be judged by the law of liberty.'

In the 13th verse we have a singularly striking and impressive enforcement of the injunction given in the 12th. Substantially the argument is: 'For those who now prove their faith in the Lord Jesus to be vital, by habitually speaking and acting according to the law of liberty, shall in the great day be judged by that law of liberty—the law as read in the gospel of saving grace; but those who disregard it shall be tried by the law apart from the gospel.' James, however, throws this into another form, which brings out these truths also,—truths holding everywhere the highest prominence in the teaching of the Saviour and His apostles,—that 'love is the fulfilling of the law,' and that the love to God which is 'the fulfilling' of the first table is not really found except where there prevails the love to man which is 'the fulfilling' of the second; 'for he that loveth not his brother whom he hath seen, how can he love God whom he hath not seen?' You observe, too, that instead of employing the general term 'love' our apostle specifies '*mercy*.' This does not in the Bible mean exclusively, as usually in modern English, '*forgiving* kindness,' but 'active pity,' of which forgiveness of injuries is a most important branch. The sense of the word is well illustrated by the passage which follows the parable of the good Samaritan: 'Which now of these three, thinkest thou, was neighbour unto him that fell among the thieves? And he said, He that showed *mercy* on him.' In choosing this word in place of the general term 'love,' James no doubt has in mind the contemptuous 'unmerciful' treatment of the poor in some of the Christian assemblies, with the reproof of which his present line of remark started. But he desires to remind us also that the heaven-born grace of *Christian* love, whilst elevating and purifying the natural affections, will always go further, revealing itself in active fruit-bearing compassion to the spiritually or temporally needy, *because they are needy.* This evinces the spirit of brotherhood to Him who came to 'destroy the works of the devil'—ignorance, and sin, and wretchedness.

'*He shall have judgement without mercy*,' says the apostle, '*that hath showed no mercy.*' This is a principle which we find set forth everywhere in Scripture. The chief aim of the gospel is to produce in men a spirit resembling God's, who 'is love;' and those that persistently retain the image of the 'prince of this world,' who hates love, exclude themselves thereby from salvation. 'Forgive us our debts, as we forgive our debtors.' 'But if ye forgive not men their trespasses, neither will your Father forgive you.' 'Then his lord, after he had called him, said unto him, O thou wicked servant, I forgave thee all that debt, because thou desiredst me; shouldst not thou also have had compassion on thy fellow-servant, even as I had pity on thee? And his lord was wroth, and delivered him to the tormentors, till he should pay all that was due unto him. So likewise shall My heavenly Father do also unto you, if ye from your hearts forgive not every one his brother their trespasses.' 'Then shall He say also unto them on the left hand, Depart from Me, ye cursed, into everlasting fire, prepared for the devil and his angels: for I was an hungered, and ye gave Me no meat; I was thirsty, and ye gave Me no drink. Verily I say unto you, Inasmuch as ye did it not to one of the least of these, ye did it not to Me.'

On the other hand, '*mercy rejoiceth* (or glorieth) *against judgement.*' The meaning is: 'Where a man's life is characterized by active Christian compassion towards the sinful and the suffering around him, he may, and he does, look forward to the judgement with calm confidence.' But our apostle, according to his wont, expresses the thought with much liveliness and boldness. 'Mercy' and '(condemning) Judgement' are conceived of as rulers in two distinct spheres: and with regard to all who are in Mercy's domain, cleaving to her in love, she tells Judgement confidently that he, the stern king, cannot take them away from her. She points to the cross of Christ, and Judgement confesses that all his claims on those within her bounds were indeed fully satisfied there, through the death in their room of the Son of God.

> 'The raging storm is heard no more:
> Mercy receives them on her peaceful shore;
> And Justice, guardian of the dread command,
> Drops the red vengeance from his willing hand.'

I cannot resist the impression that, whilst the mercy which reigns in a Christian's heart is undoubtedly, from the antithesis of the clause to the preceding, the apostle's primary reference, yet one end of his choosing the abstract 'mercy,' instead of the concrete 'merciful man,' was to leave room for the believing heart to expatiate on the general thought of 'fruit-bearing pity,' and in particular to trace up the human mercy to its fountain in the mercy of God. A heart full of mercy through faith in the mercy of God in Christ, and relying always and simply on that divine mercy,—this heart '*rejoiceth against judgement.*'

The force of this statement is twofold. It intimates, first, that the man who by a merciful character proves his having a vital faith in God's mercy, is through Christ *safe;* and secondly, that he has *a blissful sense of safety.* The peace which the gospel imparts grows, as a rule, with the growth of holiness—that is, of the spirit and life of love; for thus, in our becoming like Christ, evidence is ever increasing that we are Christ's. For despondent believers the best medicine is energy in Christian work, the cultivation of 'mercy.' The selfish and unmerciful man 'trembles,' as, through His providence or His word, God 'reasons of judgement to come,'— conscience recognising 'a certain fearful looking for of judgement, and fiery indignation, which shall devour the adversaries;' whilst, as the Apostle John has it in a passage strikingly parallel to that of James now before us, 'He that dwelleth in love dwelleth in God, and God in him; herein is our love made perfect, that we may have boldness in the day of judgement; because as He is, so are we in this world' (1 John iv. 16, 17).

XIII.

FAITH WITHOUT WORKS.

'What doth it profit, my brethren, though a man say he hath faith, and have not works? can faith save him? 15 If a brother or sister be naked, and destitute of daily food, 16 And one of you say unto them, Depart in peace, be ye warmed and filled; notwithstanding ye give them not those things which are needful to the body; what doth it profit? 17 Even so faith, if it hath not works, is dead, being alone. 18 Yea, a man may say, Thou hast faith, and I have works; show me thy faith without thy works, and I will show thee my faith by my works. 19 Thou believest that there is one God; thou doest well: the devils also believe, and tremble.'—JAMES ii. 14-19.

WE begin here another section of the Epistle. In the preceding section James, starting with the truth plainly exhibited in the 1st verse of the chapter, that the root of spiritual life in man is 'the faith of our Lord Jesus Christ,' has shown that a certain line of conduct which he describes is entirely inconsistent with this 'faith,'—wholly alien from the spirit of Christ's religion. He has wound up the paragraph by the awfully solemn declaration, that if a man is destitute of the spirit of kindness to his fellows, showing nothing in his character of the image of God, who 'is love,' then, however loud his profession of religion, however orthodox his creed, however high his hopes, he shall at the last be condemned, being subjected to 'judgement without mercy.' The apostle is thus led now to make some remarks on the nature of saving faith, bringing out, as one grand essential characteristic of such faith, that it is *operative, productive of the fruit holiness.*

It is evident that there were some in the Christian church of the first age, as indeed there have been in the church of every age, who with more or less fulness and consciousness rested in the thought that privilege is saving grace. Their position was that knowledge of the truth, accompanied by some measure of belief, brings salvation, however barren the belief be, though it be but that cold, uninterested assent which can hardly be otherwise described than as the absence of positive disbelief. There were then in all likelihood, as now, very few who stated such as their opinion, or even clearly defined it to their own minds; yet many, then as now, rested quietly in the soul-destroying impression that the knowledge of truth, with assent, necessarily constitutes saving faith. The Jews were very largely under its influence. Paul sets their state of feeling before us with much liveliness: 'Behold, thou art called a Jew, and restest in the law, and makest thy boast of God, and knowest His will, and approvest the things that are more excellent, being instructed out of the law; and art confident that thou thyself art a guide of the blind, a light of them which are in darkness, an instructor of the foolish, a teacher of babes; which hast the form of knowledge and of the truth in the law. Thou therefore which teachest another, teachest thou not thyself? Thou that preachest a man should not steal, dost thou steal? Thou that sayest a man should not commit adultery, dost thou commit adultery? Thou that abhorrest idols, dost thou commit sacrilege? Thou that makest thy boast of the law, through breaking the law dishonourest thou God? For the name of God is blasphemed among the Gentiles through you, as it is written' (Rom. ii. 17–24). Now, remembering that those whom James primarily addressed in this Epistle were Jews who had embraced Christianity, we can easily see how their previous training had prepared the way for satisfaction on the part of many of them with a mere inoperative assent to the truths of the gospel.

Throughout the apostle's discussion the name '*faith*' is taken in a broad and general sense, covering any degree of acceptance of Christian truth; his object being to show that the grand test of a man's impression or belief being that deep, radical, abiding conviction which alone unites vitally to Jesus Christ, is its producing the fruit of earnest devotion to God's glory.

He begins his remarks by the question, evidently arising naturally out of the reference in the preceding verse to the unmerciful professor of religion, '*What doth it profit, my brethren, though a man say he hath faith, and have not works?*' In this supposed case, you observe, James gives prominence to the man's '*saying* that he has faith,' evidently implying that persons of the class whom he has in his thoughts have usually much more of *profession* than of religious belief or feeling. Still the man is not a conscious hypocrite, a wolf in sheep's clothing, an infidel who for purposes of his own calls himself a believer. He has received some religious impressions, he assents in a loose and general way to the doctrines of the Bible, and he considers himself a Christian. The apostle's arguments throughout the paragraph all proceed on the supposition that the man whose religious position he is considering has something which, in a vague and liberal application of the word, may be spoken of as '*faith.*' But he '*has not works.*' In these words the apostle already assumes that radical vital faith will show itself in operation on the character. The person supposed may be a man of great activity, full of 'works' of a kind,—a man to whom those around point as conspicuous for energy, making his personal influence felt through every pulsation of a large business, rapidly building up for himself a great fortune. All this, we know, may be true; and yet, says the apostle, while he 'says he has faith,' and has it of a kind, he 'has not works,'—such 'works' then, manifestly, as a faith worthy of the name, a cordial, radical belief of the gospel, must from its nature produce. Impelled by the mercies of God, seen and felt through faith, the true believer 'presents his body a living sacrifice, holy, acceptable unto God,' feeling this to be 'reasonable service.' He is no longer 'conformed to this world;' but through 'the renewing of his mind' by the faith of the truth is 'transformed,' so as to obtain experimental acquaintance with the 'good, and acceptable, and perfect will of God.' 'The grace of God, bringing salvation, teaches him that, denying ungodliness and worldly lusts, he should live soberly, righteously, and godly in this present world.'

'If a man say he hath faith, but have not works, *what doth it profit? Can faith save him?*' Now, that faith can save a man, and that nothing else can, is written throughout the Scriptures as with a pencil of light. The essence of the gospel is, 'For God so loved the world, that He gave His only begotten Son, that whosoever *believeth* in Him should not perish, but have everlasting life' (John iii. 16). And the power of faith to save has already been expressly set before us by the apostle in Chap. i. 21, where we are told that 'the implanted word,' when 'received with meekness'—that is, believed with childlike simplicity,—'is able to save our souls.' You see, then, that in the clause before us the apostle is not speaking of faith universally, but of *this man's faith*, and all faith like it. Indeed, a more exact rendering of the apostle's words would be '*the* faith'—such faith as has been described, a faith that is unaccompanied by works,—'can this save him?'

The apostle propounds the question, and leaves it to the conscience and common sense of his readers to give the answer. 'When you think,' he seems to say, 'that sin is infinitely hateful to God, and in its nature utterly inconsistent with true happiness,—that sin alone brought that death into the world from which God in the gospel offers deliverance,—that the very name of "Jesus" was given expressly because He was to "save His people *from their sins*,"—can you consider it possible that such a faith as I have described, a faith which does not impel the man to good works, but allows him to continue indulging his natural sinful tendencies, can save him? Does not the simple statement of the case show the supposition to be wholly absurd?'

Observe, brethren, the suggestiveness of the conjunction of these two questions : 'What doth it profit? Can his faith save him?' His profession of Christianity and barren assent to its doctrines might 'profit' him in some things. It might as an opiate lull the soul to a treacherous and fatal repose, mistaken by him for the 'peace of God which passeth all understanding.' It might also under certain circumstances, such as those which exist in our country at present, be helpful to his worldly advancement. But this is not the 'profiting' to be thought of in connection with religion. In self-examination, the one point to be ascertained is whether our faith, our religion, is such as will bring 'profit' at the judgement; whether it is 'a house founded on a rock,' which will stand when 'the rains descend, and the floods come, and the winds blow and beat thereon,'— a house which, being built of stone, and not of 'wood, hay, or stubble,' will endure the trial by fire in the 'great and terrible day of the Lord.' 'As a snare,' said Jesus, 'shall that day come on all them that dwell on the face of the whole earth. Watch ye therefore, and pray always, that ye may be accounted worthy to escape all these things that shall come to pass, and to stand before the Son of man.' 'And now, little children,' urges the beloved apostle, 'abide in Him, that, when He shall appear, we may have confidence, and not be ashamed before Him at His coming.' No religion should satisfy us, my brethren, which will not '*save*' us,—no religion, therefore, which is not distinguished by the graces of Christian character, for these are 'things that *accompany salvation.*'

In the 15th and 16th verses the apostle illustrates the emptiness and uselessness of a barren faith, such as has been described, by a comparison drawn from ordinary life, and with reference to another spiritual principle—that of charity. It is plainly a most efficient mode in many cases of bringing clearly before the mind the true character of conduct towards God, to look at something similar in the relations of man to man. What with reference to God we fail to see clearly, through the mists of prejudice, is visible and tangible with reference to man. 'If ye offer the blind for sacrifice, is it not evil? and if ye offer the lame and sick, is it not evil? *Offer it now unto thy governor:* will *he* be pleased with thee, or accept thy person? saith the Lord of Hosts.'

James supposes the case of a '*brother or sister*' (that is, in all likelihood, according to ordinary Scripture usage, not 'a fellow-member of the human race' merely, but 'a fellow-Christian, a fellow-member of the household of faith') who is '*naked*' (by which is meant, no doubt, 'thinly clad,' according to a frequent use of the original word) '*and destitute of daily food.*' To such a one, having not only the general claims of a destitute fellow-creature, but the special claims of a fellow-Christian, he supposes one of his readers (observe how pointedly the case is put: 'one *of you*,' possibly implying a rebuke for some notorious neglect on this very head), to whom the sufferer makes application, or who at least in some way comes into contact with him, to say, '*Depart in peace, be ye warmed and filled.*' 'Peace be to you' has been in Western Asia, all down the ages, the ordinary salutation and parting wish. The words of address here, you see, are courteous and kind: 'Farewell; I hope that Providence will open up a way for your obtaining food and clothing, and that soon you will enjoy every comfort.' As *words*, they are excellent. Now, brethren, kind words from a kind heart are in themselves very good things, often falling on the bruised spirit with such refreshing and strengthening power as the wine and oil of the good Samaritan exerted on the traveller's poor bruised body. We deny ourselves and others much happiness, when we are niggards in the use of an instrument of good which is ever so ready at hand and so fitted to benefit. Even in the case mentioned by our apostle, if we suppose nothing given but simply these words spoken to the poor brother by another obviously nearly as poor as himself, unable to give material help, but sincerely sympathetic, how full of sweetness and refreshing the words would be—'as cold water to a thirsty soul'! But the person meant in the apostle's illustration is clearly one able to help as well as to speak kindly. Now for such a man, with a well-filled storeroom and an ample wardrobe, to use great swelling sentences of benevolence, and yet send away the poor brother or sister starving with hunger and shivering with cold—to be liberal of good words, which cost nothing, but altogether averse from giving to the poor of the worldly goods which God has given to us,—how utterly hollow and heartless this is!

We all know, brethren, that this illustrative case is not drawn from anything peculiar to the age or country of the apostle, but from a form of the working of human depravity sadly common in every age and country. The type of charity, cheap and contemptible, which he here holds up to view, is by no means extinct. Modern society—the modern church—also has its men who are fluent in the language of generosity, its women who would weep over a scene of wretchedness touchingly described in a novel,—and yet of their abundance give to the poor only most scantily and grudgingly, or, it may be, in their pecuniary dealings with the persons they employ, and in other ways, even 'grind the faces of the poor.' What a destitution of all right principle and noble feeling is here! '*What doth it profit?*' asks the apostle. What good is there for anybody? Will the hunger of the poor brother or sister be appeased by generous words? Will good wishes serve the place of clothing to them? Will expressions of sympathy, coming from the lips of one who has so evidently a hard, unsympathizing heart, bring them comfort? And to the man himself, who puts good words in the place of kind deeds, can his utterances of benevolence yield permanently the satisfaction of a good conscience? Will not every indulgence of such idle sentiment under the name of charity make the heart harder, and draw the chains of selfishness closer round the soul? And if kind words unsupported by kind deeds continue till the end, will not the Judge's declaration on the great day be, 'Inasmuch as ye *did it not* to one of the least of these, ye did it not to Me; depart from Me, ye cursed?' What, then, doth it profit? 'Whoso hath this world's good, and seeth his brother have need, and shutteth up his bowels of compassion from him, how dwelleth the love of God in him? My little children, let us not love in word, neither in tongue, but in deed and in truth.'

In the 17th verse the apostle applies the illustration to the matter in hand: '*Even so faith, if it hath not works, is dead.*'

He assumes, you observe, by his '*even so*,' that in the judgement of all his readers the charity in the case supposed, which went no further than words, was '*dead*.' Life worthy of the name involves action, fruit-bearing: here there was plainly a mere image of love, as destitute of energy as a corpse, or a tree withered from the roots. A sentiment there might be, but it was an utterly valueless and contemptible thing, because unproductive. Now a faith which does not rule the life, is exactly like such charity. '*Faith, if it hath not works, is dead*.' To this statement James adds the words, as our translators tell us in their margin, '*by itself*,' which in their text they render '*being alone*.' 'Alone' is a meaning which the expression may bear, as in the statement that 'Paul was suffered to dwell *by himself*' (Acts xxviii. 16). But the supplement '*being*,' which is needed to make the words yield the sense our translators intend, is hardly justifiable, constituting them, as it does, a separate clause. The sense itself, too, even supposing it legitimately obtained, is not very satisfactory, for it is simply a repetition in another form of 'if it hath not works,' and this without adding strength or clearness to the argument. It seems preferable, therefore, in every way, to take the sentence thus: 'Faith, if it hath not works, is *in itself* dead.' This rendering is quite as accordant with usage as the other, and suits better the position of the words. It gives advance to the argument also, for thus we move onward from observation of phenomena to a judgement as to the cause. Life has evidences. If in that which has the appearance of a man we can find no activity, no pulse, no breath, no vital heat, we know certainly, however great the resemblance to a living man in many things, that there is no life there. It may be a statue, where life has never been, or a corpse where life was but yesterday,—but beyond doubt there is no life now. And not less certainly than a living man breathes, and a living tree puts forth leaves, does a living faith prompt to holiness of life. Wherever, then, a faith 'hath not works,' a candid thinker will not merely recognise the fact that the outward beauty of leaf and fruit is wanting, but that the tree, the faith, '*is in itself dead.*'

This statement carries with it the solemn significance that such faith cannot save. For salvation is life, given through our being 'quickened together with Christ;' and it cannot but be that the faith through which this life is originated and sustained is itself an energy, a living power. From no 'dead faith' can eternal life spring.

The first words of the 18th verse, which, strictly rendered, are, '*But some man will say*,' lead one to expect an objection to the apostle's argument, such as Paul supposes made to his teaching regarding the resurrection, in 'But some man will say, How are the dead raised up? and with what body do they come?' (1 Cor. xv. 35). It is plain, however, on examining the statement made, that the person introduced as speaking holds precisely the apostle's views, and argues, as the apostle has been doing, with the man who trusts in an inoperative faith. It thus appears that we have here simply an illustration of that liveliness of style which pervades the whole Epistle, the discussion being thrown for a little into a dramatic form.[1] The force of the introductory particle seems

---

[1] Dean Scott inclines to regard the words 'But some man will say' as meant to be in antithesis with 'though a man say' in ver. 14, the intermediate verses being parenthetic. Thus the expression will have its usual force, introducing an objection to the first speaker's statement. But the parenthesis, and the bringing in of a formal antithesis after a long interval, in the midst of pleading so intensely earnest, are so unnatural that a much greater difficulty is thus constituted than that which the supposition is intended to clear away.

to be 'But further,' or, as our version has it excellently, '*Yea;*' the connection of thought being, I think, somewhat like this : 'What I have now stated, that inoperative faith is dead, may appear to you an hard saying; *but* something even stronger may be put forward on the subject. A Christian whose life shows the fruits of faith may reasonably, in this controversy, question the very existence of a faith which bears no fruit, and challenge the man who trusts in such a faith to prove its existence. Not merely is it dead, but one may doubt whether there is even a corpse or a statue— whether there is anything of faith — whether, instead of intellectual assent, there be not a kind of torpid unbelief.'

The Christian whom the apostle introduces to maintain the cause of truth opens his case thus, addressing the man of unproductive faith: '*Thou hast faith, and I have works.*' The point of distinction in the controversy is thus put forth into prominence : 'I strive by God's help to live a holy life; and thou assertest thyself to have, and at the outset I assume that thou hast, faith, but no holy life.' Now comes the challenge, '*Show me thy faith without thy works, and I will show thee my faith by my works;*' or rather, according to the best authenticated reading, '*Show me thy faith without the works* (which are its proper fruits), *and I will by my works show thee the faith* (from which the works naturally spring).' This challenge proceeds on the assumption that in true religion, of which faith is the root, there will inevitably be something visible; and that this is, or should be, admitted by all professing Christians. Whilst the supreme relations of religion are between the soul and God, it is also plainly intended by God, that by every one in whom religion is found a power should be exerted on society. Jesus says to His people, 'Ye are the light of the world.' 'Fulfil this necessary condition of religion, then,' says the challenger before us; 'make thy faith visible, let it be a light of the world,—without the works which it legitimately produces, seeing that thou disregardest these: I, on my side, will show thee by my works the faith which gives them birth.' As the fruit on the tree demonstrates to all beholders the existence of a root, though it is hidden; as our seeing light proves to us that there is a luminous body somewhere; as from the streamlet on the mountain-side we know that far up there is a spring; so, by a consistent life of holy earnestness and patience, we have shown to us the faith of the heart which prompts it. But if a so-called fire sends out no light or heat, if a so-called spring gives forth no water, we not merely lack evidence of their being what they are said to be, but we have positive proof against it, and therefore disbelieve it. There can be no doubt, then, of the issue of the challenge, 'Show me thy faith without the works.' The thing cannot be done. Now, according to the clear teaching of Scripture, faith has visible results: therefore what calls itself faith, but is unable to *show* its existence, cannot in any proper sense be considered faith—indeed, is not a reality.

Throughout several verses following this, the form of direct address to an individual, who represents all that trust in a mere unproductive faith or assent, is continued. At first sight, it seems most natural to suppose that the whole passage is to be regarded as the discourse of the intelligent fruit-bearing Christian whom the apostle has introduced in the 18th verse. Closer examination, however, leads to doubt on this head. In the 24th verse, plainly enough, we have James himself addressing his readers generally—'Ye see;' and that verse closes the argument from Abraham's history, the first part of which has the form of address to a single person.

It seems clear, therefore, that at some point he sets aside the 'man' of the 18th verse, whilst retaining the pointed 'thou' which the 'man' had begun. By some interpreters this point is fixed at the beginning of the 19th verse. To me it appears more natural to place it at the beginning of the 20th, where another section of the argument commences. Of course, as regards the sense, this is a matter of entire indifference, the 'man' being in everything intended as an exhibitor of James's own views.

He has shown the nullity of his opponent's 'faith;' yet in Christian love he will not leave him without another appeal, in which, going back, he takes him up on his own ground: 'Suppose, however, that the faith thou claimest has an existence, what then? Such a faith, which does not purify and elevate the moral nature, will not bring happiness; and this the experience of the most wretched class of God's creatures abundantly illustrates.' *Thou believest that there is one God.* This cardinal article of the belief both of Jews and Christians he selects as representing an orthodox creed generally, — as certainly held by the Jewish professing Christian whom he addresses, even if in some respects his creed might be unsound, — and as one which fully and pointedly, without weakening modifications and explanations, he could ascribe also to the evil spirits. '*Thou doest well.*' 'Thus far, good. It is a truth, and one of transcendent importance. But observe, *the devils also believe (it)* —*and tremble.*' The devil 'abode not in the truth, because there is no truth in him;' and therefore 'when he speaketh a lie, he speaketh of his own, for he is a liar, and the father of it.' Yet, whatever falsehoods he has persuaded himself and his angels to receive, he and they have no doubt 'that there is one God.' But their belief exerts no beautifying effect on their character,—awakens no love or reverence for the one true God. Indeed, in their hatred to Him, they have striven with deplorable success to induce men to worship many gods; for behind the deadness of the stocks and stones is everywhere the energy of the spirits of the abyss, so that, in fact, 'the things which the Gentiles sacrifice, they sacrifice to devils, and not to God' (1 Cor. x. 20). And as their *character* remains unimproved by their 'faith,' so is it also, according to the infinite rectitude of the divine administration, with their *position and prospects*. Their belief in the unity of God only deepens their anguish, since they know that no help to them can come from any quarter, and that, however they may oppose themselves to Jehovah, yet they struggle in vain against the One Almighty,—who, as they themselves confess (Matt. viii. 29), will at last deprive them even of the measure of wretched liberty they now have, and 'cast them into the lake of fire and brimstone, to be tormented day and night for ever and ever.' 'The devils believe—*and tremble.*' One may safely say that there is nothing in all literature more perfect, rhetorically, than this tremendous and utterly withering close of the first part of the discussion.

XIV.

JUSTIFYING FAITH A WORKING FAITH.

'But wilt thou know, O vain man, that faith without works is dead? 21 Was not Abraham our father justified by works, when he had offered Isaac his son upon the altar? 22 Seest thou how faith wrought with his works, and by works was faith made perfect? 23 And the scripture was fulfilled which saith, Abraham believed God, and it was imputed unto him for righteousness: and he was called the Friend of God. 24 Ye see then how that by works a man is justified, and not by faith only. 25 Likewise also, was not Rahab the harlot justified by works, when she had received the messengers, and had sent them out another way? 26 For as the body without the spirit is dead, so faith without works is dead also.'—JAMES ii. 20-26.

ON the surface of this passage there lies obviously a seeming contradiction of that element in the teaching of Scripture elsewhere which we often call distinctively 'evangelical,' and, in particular, of many express statements of the Apostle Paul, especially in Romans and Galatians. Thus in Romans we read, 'Therefore we conclude that a man is justified by faith without the deeds of the law' (Rom. iii. 28); and in Galatians, 'Knowing that a man is not justified by the works of the law, but by the faith of Jesus Christ, even we have believed in Jesus Christ, that we might be justified by the faith of Christ, and not by the works of the law: for by the works of the law shall no flesh be justified' (Gal. ii. 16). Here, on the other hand, James says, 'Ye see how that by works a man is justified, and not by faith only.' Now, believing, as we do, that the Bible is the Word of God,—that though the subordinate human authorship was various, yet the whole is the utterance of the one Divine Spirit,—it necessarily follows that we cannot suppose any statements in it to be *really* contradictory of each other. The existence of such would plainly unsettle the whole basis of our faith. But in His revelation of Himself to us in the Bible, just as in His revelation of Himself in providence, God has not entirely withheld difficulties. In both He offers a knowledge of Himself, His character and will, to candid souls—to minds and hearts which are willing to be fair and reasonable—which are truly desirous to know Him, and therefore ready to read text in connection with context. Such souls find the difficulties helps to faith, not hindrances. 'It is one of the great beauties of the Scriptures, that the sacred writers, in the calm consciousness of truth, in the use of popular as distinguished from philosophical language, affirm and deny the same verbal proposition, assured that the consistency and intent of their statements will make their way to the heart and conscience.'[1]

Seeing that there is a verbal opposition between the statements of Paul and James, we must look for the reconciliation either in the employment by the writers of the same words in somewhat different senses, or in their contemplating the matter under discussion from different points of view, or perhaps partly in the one and partly in the other. Some interpreters find the solution of the difficulty in a twofold use of the word 'justify;' holding that, whilst Paul undoubtedly speaks of the act of God's free grace in which a sinner is accepted as righteous in His sight, James uses the word to designate what takes place when a man is to himself or those around him *proved* or *shown* to have been thus accepted by God, which is done by the consistent holiness of his life. The one

[1] Hodge, on 1 Cor. viii. 1.

is *actual*—a justification of the *man;* the other is *declarative* —a justification of the man's *faith*. Other expositors believe the solution of the difficulty to be found in the supposition, not of a different use of words, but of a different point of view. This opinion appears to me the true one. I cannot but think that the 'justification' of which our apostle speaks is acceptance before God; while there is perhaps also, but quite in a subsidiary way, a lively reference in his mind to the attestation of this justification to the individual himself—the witness of the Spirit that he is a child of God. The verses before us are, beyond a doubt, as it seems to me, intended as an illustration of the point raised in the 14th verse, the first of this paragraph, 'Can his faith save him?'—which again stands in closest connection with the truth set forth in the 12th and 13th verses, that 'we should live as those who are to be judged.' The course of the argument therefore requires that the 'justification' be taken as substantially equivalent to 'being *saved*,' —as that justification which will be of supreme moment when we come to be '*judged*.'

It is important to remember that the apostolic epistles are not, in the technical use of the phrase, 'confessions of faith,'— not systematic bodies of divinity built up with passionless exactness,—but effusions warm from the hearts of men glowing with zeal for souls, and who warn, teach, plead with their fellow-men in their letters, just as they did in their sermons, in forms varying according to the particular requirements of those whom they addressed. Paul, and Peter, and James are not geographers seated on a hill-top, quietly mapping out the features of the country round, but soldiers in intense earnest fighting on the plain for the honour of their Lord, captains marshalling their troops of arguments and appeals against various manifestations of error and sin. The form of their line is of necessity constantly regulated in great measure by the form of that of the enemy. Thus sometimes, in the progress of the fight, two of the Lord's captains, with their bands, might seem to a spectator at a distance as if they were facing each other in opposition; whereas, looking more closely, we find that in truth there is an enemy between, whom they are assailing,—the one in front, and the other in rear. The case before us is somewhat of this kind. In the passages quoted above from Romans and Galatians, and indeed in a great part of his writings, Paul opposes *legalism*, or self-righteousness,—the error of those who, under various disguises of their real position, cling to the covenant of works, and are disposed to trust wholly or partially to their *earning* heaven by holiness. To these foolish dreamers Paul exhibits the glorious truth that justification is of grace through faith. James, on the other hand, in the paragraph before us, and more or less obviously and directly throughout the whole Epistle, opposes *antinomianism*,—the error of those who theoretically, or in far greater numbers practically, without defined views on the subject, put holiness of life aside, as if assent to the truths of the gospel, or a conviction that they are certainly Christians, released them from the obligation to live 'soberly, righteously, and godly.'[1]

[1] Bp. Lightfoot, in a long note on 'The faith of Abraham,' in his *Commentary on Galatians* (pp. 156-162), gives some interesting and valuable information regarding the rabbinical discussions on that subject. He shows that Gen. xv. 6 'was a common thesis in the schools of the day' (the age of Paul and James), and that 'the meaning of *faith* was variously explained, and diverse lessons drawn from it.' A Christian apostle and a rabbi 'might both maintain the supremacy of faith as the means of salvation; but faith with St. Paul was a very different thing from faith with Maimonides, for instance. With the one its prominent idea is a *spiritual life*; with the other an *orthodox creed*: with the one, faith is allied to liberty; with the other, to bondage'—the bondage of subjection to an external rule of ordinances. It is to be remembered that James's readers had been brought up under rabbinical teaching.

The full doctrine of Scripture on the subject under discussion is, that a sinner is justified not on the ground of anything in his personal character, but by divine grace, solely through faith in Jesus Christ,—such faith, however, as 'worketh by love,' and is thus a 'victory overcoming the world,'—a potent principle, revealing its energy in producing devotion of life to the service of God. In the writings both of Paul and James there is evidence that each of them held and taught the whole of this doctrine in its integrity; but, from the nature of the error most prevalent and clamant among those whom respectively they had immediately in view, Paul specially maintains the first part of the truth, James specially the second. Or, putting it in another form: To those who, being 'ignorant and out of the way,' ask, 'What must we do to be saved?' Paul answers, 'Believe—have faith—on the Lord Jesus Christ, and ye shall be saved.' To those who, knowing this, and professing to rest their hopes on it, ask, 'Is *all* faith saving; and if not, how shall we ascertain whether our faith is?' James replies, 'Faith without works is dead.' To unbelievers in Christ, Paul says, 'Ye can be justified only through faith; your best works, apart from faith, are *dead works.*' To professed believers in Christ, James says, 'If ye have not the works of faith, then ye are not justified: a faith which is alone—which has no works—is a *dead faith.*' Both apostles teach that true spiritual life is found *always* and *only* where faith reigns in the soul, and reveals its power in the life. Rightly understood, understood according to the drift of the context and the general spirit of his Epistle, this passage of James no more makes justification dependent on works as its meritorious ground, than the teaching of Paul connects it with an inoperative faith—a barren, uninterested assent to truth. 'Oh, it is a living, quick, mighty thing this faith,' says

Luther in his preface to the Epistle to the Romans;[1] 'so that it is impossible but that it should do all good things without intermission. It does not ask whether good works are to be done; but before the question could be asked it does them, and is always doing them. He who does not these good works is a man without faith; he is looking about him for faith and good works, but knows neither the one nor the other: all his words without them are idle babbling. Faith is a living confidence in the grace of God,—so confident that it would die a thousand deaths in reliance on it. And this confidence and knowledge of the grace of God make the heart merry and alert towards God and all His creatures. Hence man is free without force to do what is right, to serve every one, to bear all sufferings, out of love to God and in His praise, who hath shown him such grace. Yea, it is *impossible to separate works from faith*—as impossible as to separate burning and shining from fire.'

James has already illustrated in various ways the truth which he wishes to impress on his readers—that of the operative, fruit-bearing nature of saving faith. In the present paragraph he illustrates it by instances. These are introduced by a stern and searching question addressed to the professing Christian who believes in the sufficiency of a barren faith. With deep solemnity and loving severity, the apostle, in the very form of address he employs, exhibits to the man his true condition before God: he was a '*vain man*'—'utterly empty, destitute alike of vital religion and of good sense.' Then he asks him, '*Wilt thou know that faith without works is dead?*' The '*Wilt thou*' has its full significance—'Art thou willing?' It was here that the real difficulty lay, not in any obscurity of the subject. 'If any man *be willing to do* God's will, he shall *know* of the doctrine, whether it be of God;' but those who are unwilling

---
[1] Quoted by Stier.

to *do* are unwilling to *know*, for they 'love darkness rather than light, because their deeds are evil.' The force of this 20th verse, in connection with what follows, is obviously this: 'If you have a willingness to know, then listen, and you will hear irresistible evidence.' You observe, then, that what follows is plainly meant to prove the proposition stated in this verse, that 'faith without works is'—as the best supported text reads—'barren' or 'unproductive' (unproductive, that is, of the blessings of salvation).[1] This, in substance, and yet more pointedly, we find repeated at the close of the argument, as the sum of the whole matter : ' For as the body without the spirit is dead, so faith without works is dead also.'

The nature of the argument now brought forward I apprehend to be this: 'Let us look at any of the cases of piety mentioned in Scripture, and which we are in the habit of referring to as illustrations of justification by faith, and you will find that in all of them the faith was operative.' Both of the cases which are here cited are mentioned also in the catalogue of the eminent for faith contained in the 11th chapter of Hebrews, which is no doubt simply a reduction

---

[1] Both the readings νεκρά and ἀργή are well supported, but probability is decidedly in favour of ἀργή, because while there was considerable chance of a transcriber changing it into νεκρά, which occurs in verses 17 and 26, there was very little of his altering νεκρά into a word which does not occur elsewhere in the Epistle, and indeed but rarely in the New Testament. Ἀργή plainly does not mean here merely 'idle' with regard to the works of holiness which faith ought to produce, for thus we should have only the statement that 'faith without works is without works.' It is obviously employed with a reference to the great question which is the subject of the whole discussion, ' Can a faith which has no works save a man ' (ver. 14)? Ἀργή, then, means (compare its use in 2 Pet. i. 8) 'unfruitful,' unproductive, of the blessings of salvation ; and thus the connection with what follows is most natural and close, for the apostle proceeds to show that in all cases where faith is known to have been justifying, 'productive' of salvation, such as those of Abraham and Rahab, it evidently had works.

to writing of instances often brought up in preaching, especially to congregations of Jews. The first example adduced by James is naturally that of Abraham, 'the father of all them that believe,' the representative man of faith. ' Now,' asks the apostle triumphantly, ' was not he whom we Jews proudly and affectionately call our father, the great founder of our race, *justified by works, when he offered Isaac his son upon the altar?*' He puts the matter first in a general form, '*by works,*' and then specifies that one ' work ' in the patriarch's history which all readers of his life would at once single out as the preeminent evidence of his devotion to the will of God,—his offering Isaac on the altar,—a sacrifice completed, so far as the father's entire subjugation of self-will was concerned, and arrested only by the divine command.

This statement in the 21st verse (for statement it obviously is, though expressed interrogatively) does not contain the whole argument ; and in order to understand this part correctly, we must look at what follows, and then come back to it. The proposition, you remember, which the example has been adduced to support, is that 'faith without works is dead ;' or, which is the same thing, and the aspect looked at in the examples, that 'all living faith has works.' In the 21st verse Abraham's '*works*' have been mentioned, and one of them specified. In the two verses which follow, James goes on to show the connection of '*faith*' with these 'works.' '*Seest thou*' (rather, perhaps, as in the margin, ' thou seest') '*that faith wrought with his works,*'[1]—prompting, operating on and by them. 'Whenever you seek for Abraham's *faith*, you find it at *work ;* and, on the other hand, whenever you contemplate his

[1] Or, which is substantially the same thing, 'wrought with him in his works,'—that is, 'so influenced him that his works were such as without his faith they would not have been.'

works, and ask for the principle producing them, you find that to be *faith.*' '*And by the works the faith was made perfect,*' —that is, either simply 'was exhibited in glorious fulness' (as when Jesus says to Paul, 'My strength is *made perfect* in weakness'—2 Cor. xii. 9), or 'attained its legitimate development or completion.' The meaning is not that works supply anything defective in the grace of faith itself, but that they reveal it in its fulness of wealth and beauty, as by the leaves and fruit a tree is made perfect.

The passage which, in the 23rd verse, James quotes from the Old Testament (Gen. xv. 6), is expressly cited by Paul both in Romans (iv. 3) and in Galatians (iii. 6), *as a most distinct and explicit statement of the doctrine of justification by faith alone.* The precise form of the thought presented in the words is somewhat doubtful. They may mean : 'Abraham believed God, and it (his faith) was reckoned to him, unto (that is, so as—not meritoriously but instrumentally—to bring into) the position of being righteous in God's sight.'[1] Abraham had 'believed God,' and through his faith been justified, long before the wonderful transaction in the land of Moriah ; and, indeed, the words quoted here from Genesis have reference, in their original application, to an incident which occurred many years before that. When our apostle, then, says that at the offering up of Isaac (for obviously of it he is still speaking) this '*scripture was fulfilled,*' the meaning must be, that the faith which had been 'imputed to Abraham for righteousness' long before, and also God's approval of that faith, were *exhibited with special fulness and clearness.* God's justifying *act* introduces the believer into a justified *state*, in which he is 'kept by the power of God through faith'—that same faith by which he was

---

[1] Compare the use of εἰς δικαιοσύνην in Rom. x. 10 ; and see Hodge's exhaustive note on Rom. iv. 3.

brought into the state—'unto salvation, ready to be revealed in the last time.' The patriarch's perseverance, then, in justifying faith was signally illustrated in his willingness to offer up his son at God's command. The divine approval of it—the fact of its being 'imputed to him for righteousness'—was also most distinctly attested on the same occasion: for 'the angel of the Lord called unto him out of heaven, and said, Now I know that thou fearest God, seeing thou hast not withheld thy son, thine only son, from Me; and because thou hast done this thing, in blessing I will bless thee, and in multiplying I will multiply thy seed as the stars of the heaven; and in thy seed shall all the nations of the earth be blessed; because thou hast obeyed My voice.'

As a further evidence of God's approval of the faith which 'wrought with Abraham's works,' and which exhibited itself in such glorious strength under the terrible test, James proceeds to recall to the minds of his readers the closeness and dignity of the patriarch's relation to God, shown by the fact— one which 'the twelve tribes scattered abroad' knew well and delighted in—that their great father '*was called*' (that is, according to the constant Scripture use of the expression, 'was, and was acknowledged to be') '*the Friend of God.*' This name—which Isaiah uses in a well-known passage, where God says, 'Thou, Israel, art My servant, Jacob whom I have chosen, the seed of Abraham My friend' (Isa. xli. 8)—was a favourite designation for Abraham with the Jewish Rabbis, and became, indeed, so current in the east, that now in the Mohammedan countries 'El-Khulil-Allah' (the friend of God), or more usually simply 'El-Khulil' (the friend), has superseded altogether his proper name.[1]

[1] This is now the name in ordinary use for Hebron, the town with which, in life and death, Abraham was so closely connected.

Now, gathering up the apostle's statements regarding Abraham, what we find, as you observe, is simply this, that his faith was *operative*, and specially showed its power in that amazing work of self-sacrifice in the land of Moriah. No other principle, indeed, could have triumphed over the appeals of natural affection, carnal reason, and seeming self-interest, as faith on that occasion so completely did. Works were the flower or fruit of his faith; and at the altar in Moriah that scripture obtained a most striking fulfilment or verification, which says that Abraham *was justified through faith*. When in the light of these statements, then, we look back to that made in the 21st verse, that '*Abraham was justified by works,*' what *can* it mean, but that by the faith which showed itself in his works he was justified,—the works being regarded not as in any degree meritorious, but simply as *the evidence of a real and vital faith?* If this be not the sense, then what follows, and particularly the citation in the 23rd verse, is wholly irrelevant and meaningless.

In the 24th verse James states the inference to be drawn concerning the subject in hand from these reasonings on the case of Abraham: '*Ye see how that by works a man is justified, and not by faith only.*' By this he means, that, in considering our relations to God and prospects for eternity, we should not be contented if we see in our minds some such assent to divine truth as in a liberal use of the word may be called faith, but should carefully examine whether it be an operative, fruit-bearing belief; for only this is saving faith. Startling and unevangelical as the words of the apostle here seem to be, taken by themselves, no one who has candidly and intelligently followed the train of his argument can be misled as to his meaning, or as to the perfect harmony between his teaching and that of the Apostle Paul. The great cardinal doctrine that justification is by faith alone, was, beyond reasonable question, well known and, professedly at least, fully received by the readers of this Epistle, as by all others of the primitive Christians; and it could never enter their minds for one moment that James or any of the apostles entertained the slightest doubt of its being the very truth of God. Differences of opinion and practice on some points there might be among the first teachers of Christianity; but no inspired servant of Him who summed up His gospel in the words, 'God so loved the world, that He gave His only begotten Son, that *whosoever believeth in Him should not perish, but have everlasting life*,' could for an instant be held to doubt that *salvation is through faith alone.* That the full theological expression 'justification by faith' was current in its well-defined sense at a very early period in the history of the church, too, is shown by the language which, in Galatians, Paul mentions his having addressed to Peter at Antioch: 'We who are Jews by nature, and not sinners of the Gentiles, knowing that a man is not justified by the works of the law, but by the faith of Jesus Christ, even we have believed in Jesus Christ, that we might be justified by the faith of Christ, and not by the works of the law; for by the works of the law shall no flesh be justified' (Gal. ii. 15, 16). Under these circumstances, our apostle could, without danger of misleading his readers, throw his statement of most important truth into the form which he has here given it. He could with safety expose a deplorable abuse of the doctrine of justification by faith alone, and exhibit the nature of saving faith, in a way which, by its seeming at first sight to contradict the doctrine, would lay hold of men's memories and excite them to thought.

The apparent opposition and real harmony between the declarations of James and Paul may be illustrated by an analogy. Suppose a thunderstorm, by which lives and property have been destroyed,—and that an intelligent child in the desolated district, whose ears had been stunned by the peals of thunder, and his eyes dazzled with the glare of the lightning, should ask a friend, 'Was it the thunder or the lightning that caused the destruction?' The answer would be, that 'terrible as the noise of the thunder is, yet the *destruction is caused by lightning alone, without the thunder.*' But if the further question be proposed, 'Is *all* lightning of a destructive kind?' then the answer will be, 'No; *destruction is not caused by lightning alone, without thunder,*'—the noiseless 'summer lightning,' as it is sometimes called, which we often see playing near us in sheets of flame, at the close of a sultry day, being harmless. The two answers, when we look at them simply as isolated statements, flatly contradict each other, you observe; but when we regard them in connection with the respective questions which elicited them, they are both true, and both fitted to help the inquirer to a full view of the subject in which he is interested. Similarly, to him who asks, 'Is it faith that justifies, or works?' Paul replies, 'Faith alone justifies, without works.' To him who, knowing and believing this, asks further, 'But does *all* faith justify?' James answers, 'Faith alone, without works, does *not* justify,'—for an inoperative faith is dead, powerless, unprofitable. Both statements, looked at in connection with the questions they are respectively meant to answer, are true, and both of vast importance. *Faith alone justifies, but not the faith which is alone.*[1]

Our apostle proceeds to bring forward another instance of justifying faith, and to show that in that case also the faith produced works. As has been already mentioned, Rahab is

---

[1] The illustration given in this paragraph is simply an amplification of a hint contained in a letter of Frederick Robertson of Brighton, printed in his Life (vol. ii. p. 64).

one of the heroines of faith commemorated in Hebrews. It is probable, therefore, that her case was one not unfrequently cited in the discussions of the Jews regarding the nature and power of this grace. James's object in here referring to it in particular is not far to seek, and is suggested indeed in the original by an introductory particle marking slight contrast, which our translators have not rendered. The position which the apostle is maintaining is, that all justifying faith is operative; and it is plain that the wider the range of classes represented by his illustrative instances, the more effective is his argument. Now no persons could well be further apart in everything except their faith than Abraham, the illustrious father of God's chosen race, and poor ignorant Rahab, brought up in the midst of heathenism, and actually at one time living a life of immorality. If genuine justifying faith bore in her as well as in Abraham the fruit of good works suitable to her circumstances, then it may fairly be concluded—these persons representing the extremes—that the faith of *all* the justified is fruit-bearing. Rahab, in Jericho, pondering the reports which had reached her of the character and doings of the God of Israel, had come through the teaching of His Spirit to have faith in Him,—justifying faith, our inspired writer tells us,—faith, the approval of which by God was evinced by His raising her to a position of dignity in Israel, and giving her the lofty honour of being an ancestress of the Messiah. Now her faith, like Abraham's, had very manifest visible effects. She '*received*' Joshua's messengers kindly, because they were servants of the God of Israel. She exerted herself, too, at much personal risk, to deliver them from the danger to which they were exposed in a hostile city, '*sending them out*' with urgency, in deep anxiety for their safety,[1]—and this by '*another*

---

[1] Urgency is implied in the original word translated 'sent out.'

way,' showing her heartiness and her inventiveness in the cause of Israel by not leaving the men to the hazard of an attempt to pass out through the well-guarded city-gate, by which they had come in, but letting them down from her window, which overhung the wall. *All* justifying faith, then, we see, in whatever class of persons it is found, produces works, varying in kind according to circumstances, but all expressive of love to God, and trust in Him.

From the nature of the case—from the nature of God, and man, and salvation—it must be so : '*for as the body without the spirit is dead, so faith without works is dead also.*' James here closes his discussion of the great subject by repeating, as now conclusively demonstrated, the proposition with which in the 20th verse this section began. The form of his comparison somewhat startles us, habituated as we are to think of faith as the spirit or animating principle of religion, and godly works as the body. But, as you will remember, throughout the whole disquisition from the 14th verse the term 'faith' has been taken in a very wide sense, as including any measure of assent to divine truth, from the barest and coldest to the most intense and influential; and the persons for whose benefit mainly the apostle's observations have been intended were such as the man spoken of in the 14th verse, who '*said* he had faith, but had not works.' Naturally enough, then, in the image before us, faith, thought of as the holding and professing of a creed, is represented as a '*body*,' which '*without the spirit*' of love, and trust, and obedience, '*is dead.*' Strictly speaking, you observe, the 'spirit' is not 'works' themselves, but rather the principle in the soul, the energetic convictions and affections, by which 'works' are produced; but the apostle, to bring his argument home, adheres to the term which he has employed throughout the discussion, the sense being sufficiently clear. The solemn and impressive statement made in this verse very fittingly winds up the great argument. No one who has honestly and thoughtfully followed the apostle's discussion can entertain any doubt that the only faith which can be pleasing to God is such a profound and influential belief of His truth as reveals its presence in the soul by moral beauty and earnest devotedness in the outward life. A supposed and professed faith which has no such results is a dead thing; and only where there is spiritual life in God's moral creatures, can He regard them with complacency. An inoperative faith is a corpse passing to corruption—utterly loathsome in His sight.

XV.

RESPONSIBILITY OF TEACHERS.

'My brethren, be not many masters, knowing that we shall receive the greater condemnation. 2 For in many things we offend all. If any man offend not in word, the same is a perfect man, and able also to bridle the whole body.'—JAMES iii. 1, 2.

IN this chapter the apostle discusses the sins of the tongue, —a new subject, but one naturally arising out of the preceding. Whenever mere adherence to a creed becomes the matter mainly regarded among a body of professing Christians, and the influence of the creed on heart and life sinks almost out of view,—whenever questions of orthodoxy, however important in themselves, exclude vital religion from the foreground of thought,—talk on points of doctrine and church procedure will superabound, and, through the absence or feebleness of Christian love, will lead to bitter wrangling and many forms of sin. The history of the church affords a multitude of illustrations of this tendency. Many of the Jewish Christians to whom James wrote, no doubt brought with them into their Christianity much Pharisaic leaven received from their training in Judaism. Among them, consequently, one can easily suppose the tendency which I have mentioned to have been peculiarly strong; and from the apostle's tone it is obvious that, in fact, it had shown itself to a considerable extent. James's strong feeling on the subject of religious wranglings has already spoken out again and again: 'My beloved brethren, let every man be swift to hear, slow to speak, slow to wrath;' 'If any man among you seem to be religious, and bridleth not his tongue, but deceiveth his own heart, this man's religion is vain' (i. 19, 26). In this chapter, however, he takes up the subject more fully, and by touching on the dangers connected with over-fondness for talk on religious matters, is led to enlarge on the sins of the tongue generally.

He begins his remarks with the advice, '*My brethren, be not many masters.*' It is not improbable that, from the ambiguity of the English word '*master*,' some of you have failed to attach a definite sense to these words, or perhaps have attached a wrong one. The radical idea of the word is that of superiority and government; but in the particular relations of an instructor, the 'master' of a school, to his pupils, the idea of *teaching* becomes the most prominent. Very often in the New Testament the word has this special meaning, as when Jesus is addressed as 'Master,' when Nicodemus is spoken of as 'a master of Israel,' and the like. In these cases the word in the original means simply 'teacher,' not a master as contrasted with a servant or slave. So also in the passage before us the reference is not (immediately at least) to lordship over others— to conduct and character like that of Diotrephes, who 'loved to have the pre-eminence' (3 John 9)—but simply to teaching. James's injunction is, '*Be not many of you teachers,*' or, according to the force of the rendering in our Authorized Version, '*Be not* (each congregation of you) *a multitude of teachers* (instead of learners).' It is not easy to decide which of the two renderings brings out the exact shade of meaning intended.

We gather from various statements in the apostolic writings, that in the first age the public religious services of the church were to some extent of a conversational character. From the beginning the apostles gave the churches a regular organization, ordaining elders, on whom—particularly on one or more of them whose gifts seemed specially to qualify them for 'labouring in the word and doctrine' as well as ruling—rested mainly the duty of conducting public worship and instructing the congregation; but, at the same time, an opportunity was freely given for exposition or exhortation by other members. 'Despise not prophesyings,' is an instruction given by Paul to his spiritual children at Thessalonica; and we cannot doubt that, so long as extraordinary gifts of the Holy Ghost for prophesying and other modes of benefiting the brethren were bestowed on believers, the system of free converse in the public assemblies was on the whole advantageous. It is evident, however, that even then it offered to many a strong temptation to display and disputatiousness; and gradually everywhere, the miraculous gifts ceasing, it was found needful to introduce that system which has ever since prevailed in the church. James's advice in the words before us, then,—an advice plainly implying that serious abuses of the privilege of free speech in the meetings of the church already existed,—is that his readers should not in great numbers press forward as exhorters and instructors in the public assemblies of the brethren. There were grave spiritual hazards connected with this, even where men had considerable religious knowledge; and for very many the proper place was manifestly that of learners, not teachers.

From the mode in which the public services of religion are generally conducted in the church now, our apostle's advice to the congregations of his time is not usually, with exactly its original reference, applicable to a modern congregation. With regard to these public services, however, in the form in which we have them, the spirit of the injunction might not unfaithfully, I think, be given thus: 'Cultivate a teachable and impressible disposition, — a disposition to seek spiritual good rather than to criticise.' But observe what I mean by 'criticise.' Every minister whose heart is in his work, and who has sound ideas regarding the objects of the work and the way in which these are to be gained, delights in an intelligent congregation, attentive and thoughtful, disposed to weigh what he says to them for themselves, bringing it all to the touchstone of 'the law and the testimony.' It is truly mournful that so many members and adherents of Christian churches seem to throw away upon the world all the understanding God has given them; so that, while thoughtful and inquiring among their goods and merchandise, shrewd and penetrating, taking nothing on trust, but sifting carefully everything which concerns their secular prosperity, they put their minds to sleep when they open their Bibles or enter the sanctuary. In saying that the spirit of the apostle's advice here may partly be represented by 'My brethren, be not a multitude of critics,' I am as far as possible from referring to that criticism which is involved in considerate, discriminative hearing of the word by candid and right-hearted persons. Would that the Divine Head of the church would make such criticism abound!—for this is the life of a congregation. Ay, and the knowledge, too, that there are among one's flock members here and there who, from their abilities and education, are qualified to analyse their minister's arguments, or review for themselves his expositions,—this is a most healthful stimulus to exertion, not unneeded at times even by the most conscientious servant of God.

But there is another kind of criticism, very different in spirit from that of which I have spoken, and wholly opposed to it in tendency. The spiritual evil, or at least one prominent among the evils, against which James's exhortation was directed, was, no doubt, the indulgence of the pride of knowledge—of an arrogant conviction, very often in persons who were really extremely ignorant and foolish, that they had no need to learn anything from their brethren, but were fully equipped as teachers. Now I am afraid that a carping and supercilious spirit, which, if those who indulge in it thought out the matter, they would find to rest very much on the same basis, is far from uncommon in our congregations. These people come to God's house not to receive food for the mind and heart, but to judge composition, and orthodoxy, and manner of delivery. They act rather as if they were members of a court of examiners, trying a student's qualifications for the ministry, than either as enlightened Christians or anxious inquirers after salvation, hearing for the good of their souls the word of eternal life from their pastor and God's servant. To a minister visiting a member of his congregation, on whom the shadow of death had fallen, the dying man said, 'I think, sir, the word of the Lord makes comparatively such little way among church-goers mainly because so many hear sermons to criticise rather than to learn; and so on the way home, or during the Sabbath evening afterwards, if they speak on the subject at all, it is far oftener about little matters connected with the preaching, than about the truth declared as truth for their hearts.' These words are weighty, I think,—weighty with such solemn truth as the shadow of death is calculated to bring out into special vividness before the soul.

But looking to the *form* as well as the spirit of the apostle's words, we find in them thus also very important instruction for ourselves, no less than for the churches of 'the twelve tribes scattered abroad,' to which they were primarily addressed. We must not press his principle further than he himself, and the Holy Ghost, speaking through him, intended it to go.

His meaning clearly is, that whenever in any Christian community a large proportion of the members give themselves to teaching rather than learning, there is much reason to fear that something is weak and wrong somewhere; just as, in a civil community, if a very great number of persons put themselves forward to act as magistrates, giving their time and thoughts more to the regulation of the affairs of others than to the regulation of their own, there would, beyond question, be a good deal of unsatisfactory regulation, and much detriment to the commonwealth in various ways.

Were the Apostle James living in our day, he would no doubt remember and echo his Lord's words, who, 'when He saw the multitudes, was moved with compassion on them, because they fainted, and were scattered abroad, as sheep having no shepherd. Then saith He unto His disciples, The harvest truly is plenteous, but the labourers are few: pray ye therefore the Lord of the harvest, that He will send forth labourers into His harvest.' He would lament that, with unparalleled openings among the nations for the extension of the gospel—with the cry sounding out from every side in the ear of the church, 'Come over and help us'—still comparatively such a small number of young men are found in our schools of theology preparing for the work of the ministry. He would seek earnestly to impress on our Christian youth, that slight—in very many cases most miserably and inexcusably small—as are the worldly inducements connected with the ministerial office, and awfully solemn and weighty as are its responsibilities, yet the work is in its nature incomparably the noblest of all work, and the joys springing from the conscientious discharge of its duties will certainly in the eternal world be peculiarly lofty and sweet; whilst even on earth, amid many things to sadden and discourage a faithful minister, he has often comforts specially refreshing and cheering. Remembering, too, and echoing Paul's injunction to '*all* the saints in Christ Jesus at Philippi'—the private members as well as the 'bishops and deacons'—to 'shine as lights in the world, holding forth the word of life,' and the command given by the Saviour in the Apocalypse, 'Let him that heareth say, Come,'—James, were he living now, would rejoice to see multitudes of believers, gifted with discretion, and self-knowledge, and intimate acquaintance with Scripture, teaching the ignorant, pleading with the wayward, or trying to instruct Christian brethren less enlightened than themselves, at their homes, or in classes or meetings of various kinds. With regard to labour of this sort by Christians of this sort, James would say, as Moses did when Eldad and Medad prophesied in the camp, 'Would God that all the Lord's people were prophets, and that the Lord would put His Spirit upon them!'

Yet, while all this is true, and truth of the highest practical importance, still, on the other hand, the Divine Spirit says to us through our apostle, 'My brethren, be not many masters.' There are most serious spiritual dangers connected with the rash assumption of the position of a religious teacher,—dangers both for the persons themselves who take the position, and for those whom they undertake to instruct. This is a fact which needs to be borne in mind particularly in seasons of religious excitement. At such times numbers of young and inexperienced converts, in the ardour of their first love to their Saviour (a flame, as Dr. Wardlaw well observes, 'usually blended with more or less of smoke'), are impelled by their feelings to come forward into considerable prominence as 'masters of Israel.' In cases of this kind,—the ballast to the moral nature which Christian experience supplies being wanting, in many instances also that which is afforded by a good general education,—little religious knowledge showing itself, and perhaps less prudence, there is obviously very great peril that the teacher may be puffed up into a most arrogant and foolish self-confidence, that his pupils may be miserably ill-taught, or indeed, simply through their master's ignorance, seriously misled, and that in various ways no little occasion may be given to the enemies of the Lord to blaspheme.

Both sides of the truth on this subject need to be carefully pondered by us, brethren: on the one hand, the clear injunction, 'Let him that heareth say, Come;' and on the other, the no less clear injunction, 'Be not many masters.' The decision with regard to each Christian's immediate duty must be left to his own judgement, through which, if he candidly weigh the matter, and pray for God's guidance, the Spirit will give him light. But this one general principle, at all events, will, I apprehend, be in all cases a safe one,—that no person is called upon to become in any formal way a 'master' until, for a considerable time and with considerable success, he has been a learner.

James supports his injunction by a very solemn and impressive argument: '*Knowing that we shall receive the greater condemnation.*' Teachers have a specially heavy responsibility. The universal principle in God's dealings with His moral creatures is, that according to the measure of opportunity is the measure of responsibility. Now the office of a religious teacher is necessarily one of considerable influence, and consequently of proportionate responsibility for the exercise of the influence. Truth is God's instrument for quickening, comforting, and sanctifying men; and hence, when one who is looked to as an instructor fails 'rightly to divide the word of truth,' others, many perhaps, are led astray by him, and thus withheld to some extent from experiencing the blessed power of the gospel. In many cases this may be done through culpable ignorance merely; but there are strong temptations also at times, through motives of worldly interest, to conceal or slur over some portions of the divine testimony. How incalculable is the evil which may thus be wrought! The deviation from the King's highway of truth may seem very slight, yet some hearers of this teaching may, by temperament or circumstances, be induced to follow the divergent path right on, every step carrying them further from the way of peace, until 'their feet stumble upon the dark mountains.' In olden days in Canaan, had a man, fleeing to a city of refuge, been misdirected with regard to the road by one who professed to know it, and been therefore overtaken by the avenger of blood, and slain, what a heavy burden of responsibility would have rested on the head of the misleading guide! How, then, shall we estimate the awfulness of the guilt contracted in giving misleading directions to a soul anxious to flee from the wrath to come! Twice in the prophecies of Ezekiel have we the solemn warning: 'Son of man, I have made thee a watchman unto the house of Israel: therefore hear the word at My mouth, and give them warning from Me. When I say unto the wicked, Thou shalt surely die, and thou givest him not warning, nor speakest to warn the wicked from his wicked way, to save his life, the same wicked man shall die in his iniquity: but his blood will I require at thine hand. Yet if thou warn the wicked, and he turn not from his wickedness, nor from his wicked way, he shall die in his iniquity; but thou hast delivered thy soul.' And you remember Paul's declaration before the elders of Ephesus regarding his ministry among them: 'I take you to record this day that I am pure from the blood of all men; for I have not shunned to declare unto you all the counsel of God;' implying that in the New Testament church he felt the same blood-guiltiness, the guilt of the death of souls, to rest on an unfaithful minister.

You will observe, however, that the apostle's words are not 'greater responsibility,' but 'greater *condemnation.*' It is true, indeed, that the strict meaning of the term employed in the original is 'judgement,' which our translators give in the margin as an alternative rendering; but New Testament usage leaves no room for doubt that where the word is connected, as here, with 'receive,' a condemnatory judgement is intended. Some interpreters take '*condemnation*' here in a very wide sense, including not merely the doom of the lost, appointment to positive suffering, but also deprivation of the highest rewards of grace, as in the case of the man in the parable, who, having with his pound earned five pounds, was made ruler of only five cities, while his neighbour, who with his pound had earned ten pounds, obtained from his gracious master the dominion of ten cities; or of those teachers of whom Paul speaks, who, having built on the one foundation, Jesus Christ, are saved, but having through culpable ignorance and folly built into the wall of the temple 'wood, and hay, and stubble,' see their work burned, and thus 'suffer loss,' and are themselves saved only like persons dragged 'through fire.' On this view, the logical connection between the clause before us and the next is immediate and perfect; thus: 'We who are teachers—all of us, apostles as well as others—shall receive greater condemnation than those who in positions of less influence err like us,—*condemnation*, I say, for in many things we all offend.' Even the most faithful teacher, the man who, 'having turned many to righteousness, shall shine as the stars for ever and ever,' stands in regard to wisdom and devotedness far below the position to which, had he used his opportunities to the full, he might have attained, and 'in many things offends.' This wide sense of 'condemnation,' however, does not seem to accord with Scripture usage, and indeed appears to oppose itself to express Scripture teaching; for 'there is no condemnation to them which are in Christ Jesus'—even to those of them who are 'saved so as by fire.' The real meaning and connection, I apprehend, may be thus exhibited: 'Knowing, as ye do or ought to do,[1] that if we who are teachers act unfaithfully, we shall receive greater condemnation than others,—and condemnation, alas, is no impossible or even unlikely issue, for in many things we all offend.' The sternest sentence will certainly be for him who not merely is himself without the wedding garment, but has by his teaching or his example kept others out of the feast-chamber, or induced them to enter without the wedding garment. The apostle's humility leads him to class himself with the other teachers, in speaking of their spiritual hazards ('*we* shall receive'), just as similarly, through tenderness of conscience, he says in the 9th verse of this chapter, 'With the tongue bless *we* God, and with the tongue curse *we* men.'

The proper meaning of the word '*offend*,' which exactly represents the term employed in the original, is to strike the foot against some obstacle—'to trip' or 'stumble.' In the metaphorical application the idea obviously is, that for the exercise of all the powers which God has given us He has appointed a way in which we should walk; that is to say, He has bestowed these powers upon us for certain ends; and to 'offend' or stumble is simply to employ them for other ends, or at least to fail to employ them for those appointed by God. Now, '*in many things we all offend.*' The ground here pointed to by James for his assertion of the risk of 'condemnation,' is

---

[1] The '*knowing*,' being closely associated with the command, 'Be not many masters,' may be held to have itself somewhat of an imperative force.

one which will be recognised as valid by all who either believe the Bible or know themselves. A man who counts himself sinless simply illustrates the deceitfulness of the heart; for 'if we say that we have no sin, we deceive ourselves, and the truth is not in us.'

To the argument derived from the universal weakness and sinfulness of man our apostle appends another, founded on the peculiarly great facility with which men fall into offences of the *tongue*. '*If any man offend not in word, the same is a perfect man, and able also to bridle the whole body.*' The exact connection of these words with the preceding, and their argumentative force, may be brought out thus: 'In many things we all offend; and to avoid offending with the tongue is peculiarly difficult—so difficult, indeed, that it may safely be said, that a man who has sufficient strength of principle and spiritual vigilance to offend not in word, is able also to bridle the whole body. Now, as regards speech, a person who occupies the position of a teacher obviously has particularly great spiritual dangers, seeing that so much of his work has to be done by speaking; that in prosecuting it he is liable to be drawn into heated controversy; and that, from the prominence given him by his office, the influence for evil upon others of his offences of the tongue is likely to be great. Considering these things, brethren, do not rashly assume this heavy responsibility.' But whilst such appears to be the relation of the latter part of the 2nd verse to what goes before, the statement contained in it is expressed in the widest form, and leads from the remarks regarding teachers and their responsibilities into that most interesting and impressive paragraph on the power and untameableness of the tongue generally, which constitutes the larger part of this chapter.

The essence of the passage, looked at in its logical relation to the injunction in the 1st verse, is simply the truth that 'it is extremely difficult to avoid sinning with the tongue;' but instead of putting it in this bald form, James supposes the case of a man who is free from offences of this class, and remarks that one who has reached this point of excellence is '*perfect*' —the master of all his constitutional tendencies to evil. To the moral power of a man who can govern his tongue there are no limits. By '*perfect*' appears to be intended here, as in Chap. i. 4, a maturity of religious life, a ripeness and richness of knowledge and character, such as may be supposed to mark the full-grown man, as contrasted with the babe in Christ. In the other passage just referred to, 'perfect' is explained by the added words, 'entire, wanting nothing;' which teach us that whilst intensity, depth in the action of religious principle and feeling, is implied, yet breadth of range, the action of godliness over every department of our inner being and our outward life, is also an essential element, and in that passage the most prominent. Similarly, in the present place, the explanation is appended, '*able also to bridle the whole body.*' The '*and*' which introduces this last clause in our version is merely a supplement by the translators, and the meaning would really be clearer without it. A 'perfect' man is one who, through the energies of his Christian principle, can '*bridle*,' or hold in firm restraint, his '*whole body*,' all its organs of voluntary action, and the propensities which work in them,— one in whom not certain classes of passions merely are duly governed, but the whole man, the whole life, is regulated by religion.

To 'offend,' we have seen, is to employ our powers for other ends than God has appointed, or at least to neglect employing them for the appointed ends. Now the purposes for which speech has been bestowed upon us are these: to carry on the business of life, to minister to the needful mental refreshment of ourselves and others, to help our fellow-men by instruction, encouragement, and comfort, and (the highest use of all) to praise God and hold direct communion with Him. When speech is devoted to these ends in suitable proportions, and to no other ends, there is freedom from 'offending in word.' Addressing Christians as he is, one can hardly suppose that the apostle, in here speaking of the extreme difficulty of avoiding offences of the tongue, has mainly before his mind such gross offences as profanity or deliberate calumny; for sins like these one can scarcely imagine committed by any one who has given himself to the Saviour, at least except under circumstances of the very strongest temptation. But however true this is in regard to the grossest forms of sin of the tongue, yet even for experienced Christians there is great hazard of falling into many offences in word, through the sudden temptations which are continually emerging in the ordinary intercourse of life. How often the fretting cares of business strike out the sparks of angry words! In our social gatherings for the solace of life, how strong the temptation is frequently found to be to argue for victory rather than for truth, to give interest and pungency to conversation by running down the character of absent acquaintances, to point a joke at the expense of perfect truthfulness, and in some society at the expense of perfect purity or perfect reverence for the word of God! If we were candidly, before we retire to rest, after any day of lively intercourse with our fellows, to look back, trying to recall what we had said, and how we had said it, and surveying these in the light shed by conscience and divine revelation on the proper purposes of speech, would many of us have great satisfaction in our review?

One prominent cause of 'offences in word' is undoubtedly

the tendency, which is very strong in the vast majority of people, to speak much more than is needful or desirable. 'In the multitude of words,' says the wise man, 'there wanteth not sin; but he that refraineth his lips is wise.' The exhortation given by our apostle, in the first chapter, with particular reference to religious discussions, is of great importance and value for the intercourse of life generally: 'Let every man be swift to hear, slow to speak.' If we review the talk in which we have taken part in any one day, what an amount do we find to have been spoken that was not at all worthy to be said, not at all fitted either to instruct or to give rational amusement! what a mass of mere 'idle words,'—words not perhaps having anything wrong in them, as we say, yet wholly inoperative with reference to any of the great ends of speech! ay, what a multitude too, in many cases, of positively hurtful wrong words! For example, are not nine-tenths of what we say or hear said on personal character usually hurtful and wrong? Conversation turns on such subjects largely because really valuable thoughts are wanting, whilst yet there is a desire to say something,—something which may interest at least the lower if not the higher elements of our nature. Is conversation on personal character often *perfectly* truthful and charitable, *perfectly* free from the imputation of imaginary motives, or from some form of detraction which ministers by comparison to the vanity of the speaker? The more we think of this matter, the more we shall be humbled, by feeling how little we have used God's noble gift of speech for the noble purposes for which it was bestowed—how much we have abused it to the dishonour of God, and the injury of ourselves and our fellows. To be free from 'offending in word,' to employ the tongue for those great ends for which God intended it, and for no other ends,—this will task the highest energies of the most experienced Christian.

The case which the apostle supposes, of a man who 'offends not in word,' is one which will not with absolute exactness be realized: for, beyond question, speech is among the 'many things' mentioned in the previous clause in which we 'all offend.' Indeed, as we have already seen, the truth underlying and forming the basis of the argument here is, that we are more apt to 'offend in word' than in anything else. But James would have us take home this thought, that in proportion as a Christian advances towards complete government of the tongue, does he grow in spiritual maturity. We all know that nothing is generally esteemed to be a better evidence of the state of a man's heart, than the habitual tone of his conversation. Just as we see the measure of his intellect by the subjects on which he can speak, and loves to speak, so from the usual character of his talk we form decided conclusions, legitimately enough, at least within certain limits, regarding his amiability, his manliness, his piety. As naturally as a fountain sends out into the channel of the stream such water as gushes up from the depths, and thus by tasting the water in the stream we know the sweetness or the bitterness of the water in the fountain, however hidden it be; so 'out of the abundance of the heart the mouth speaketh.' 'How can ye, being evil, speak good things?' 'A good man, out of the good treasure of his heart, bringeth forth good things; and an evil man, out of the evil treasure, bringeth forth evil things.' It is impossible *permanently* to prevent this. 'My heart was hot within me,' says the Psalmist; 'while I was musing, the fire burned: then spake I with my tongue.' Hence the best test of the moral condition of the affections is the ordinary tone of conversation. To a youth of a fair countenance Socrates said, 'Speak, friend, that I may see thee.' An habitual purity, lovingness, and discreetness of language, then, proves that the heart is filled with love to God and man. In regard to Jesus, the only absolutely perfect man, it is written not only that He '*did* no sin,' but also that 'no guile was found in His mouth;' that 'when He was reviled, He reviled not again; when He suffered, He threatened not;' and that 'grace was poured into His lips.' In the degree in which our holiness of language approaches His, we have reason to believe that our inner nature has been 'changed by the Lord the Spirit into His image.'

But whilst thus, like pure water from a pure fountain, a wise, chastened, godly use of the tongue is a direct and natural issue from holiness of heart, the apostle's words present prominently the aspect of *restraint*—'*bridling*,'— which must be one aspect of all holiness in man so long as he is here below. Now that power to control the tongue is an evidence of ripe godliness, appears when we consider such points as these: the facility and rapidity with which sins of the tongue are committed; the great scope for 'offending' afforded by the manifold needs and applications of speech; and the strong influence exerted against earnest effort in this department of morals, by the light opinion generally entertained even in Christian society of this class of offences. You know how little is thought of a 'hasty word,' 'a slight exaggeration or misrepresentation,' or the like. Men are apt to say, or at least to speak as if they thought, 'Our lips are our own, who is Lord over us?' and hence multitudes who would recoil with horror from the thought of being unpunctual or dishonest in matters of money, and who count themselves harmless and kindly, are most unjust and cruel in language,—cheating their neighbour, without scruple, of his reputation—murdering the good name which may be to him more precious than his life. Considering all these things, then, it is plain that if a man takes a grave view of this subject, and is watchful against sins of the tongue, he will certainly be in all other departments also vigilant, upright, pure, godly, — that he who has grace to 'offend not in word,' has grace to accomplish anything.

Besides being a most satisfactory *evidence* of general moral discipline, Christian government of the tongue is also an efficient *instrument* of such discipline— a *means* of 'bridling the whole body.' That this thought is involved in the apostle's words in the latter part of the 2nd verse, is clearly shown by the illustrations which he goes on to adduce,—the bit, and the helm, which direct the 'whole body' of the horse—the whole mass of the ship. To suggest this, indeed, and thus lead the way to those other important and impressive statements regarding the tongue which it was his purpose to lay before his readers, may have been the chief reason for his giving the passage before us the peculiar form it has,—a form certainly not the most natural if merely the argumentative connection of the words with the injunction in the 1st verse be regarded.[1] The point in morals to which he here calls our attention is one of much interest, and one with which every person who has with any considerable measure of seriousness and success endeavoured to rule himself has some acquaintance. Energetic effort directed towards the regulation of the tongue has a most healthful influence on the whole nature. A man of violent temper, who, when the gust of passion comes, has Christian wisdom and power of will enough to 'keep the door of his lips,' will find not merely that he is saved from speaking words which might cause him and others sorrow, but that through prayerful, persistent efforts of this kind, the power of the evil spirit within him is broken,—as certainly as, in cases

---

[1] This argumentative connection, indeed, he intimates to be not solely, perhaps not even mainly, in his mind, by omitting an introductory particle of dependence or conjunction.

where passion finds free utterance, the power of the demon steadily grows. Or again, where vanity is a besetting sin, in no direction is the action of a manly Christian will more likely to be helpful, than in the endeavour to suppress all words of self-exaltation, — or of self-depreciation, which is very often, and in persons of the class supposed would almost certainly be, only a very thinly disguised egotism. Whatever be our special spiritual weakness and peril, it is the part of true wisdom to say, with David, 'I will take heed to my ways, that I sin not with my tongue; I will keep my mouth with a bridle;' praying with him always, at the same time, 'Set a watch, O Lord, before my mouth.'

XVI.

POWER OF THE TONGUE.

'Behold, we put bits in the horses' mouths, that they may obey us; and we turn about their whole body. 4 Behold also the ships, which, though they be so great, and are driven of fierce winds, yet are they turned about with a very small helm, whithersoever the governor listeth. 5 Even so the tongue is a little member, and boasteth great things. Behold how great a matter a little fire kindleth! 6 And the tongue is a fire, a world of iniquity: so is the tongue among our members, that it defileth the whole body, and setteth on fire the course of nature; and it is set on fire of hell.'—JAMES iii. 3-6.

THESE verses abundantly illustrate a fact which must strike every attentive reader of this Epistle, rigidly practical though its substance is—that the writer had in a high degree a poet's eye and sympathies. He had a keen and delicate perception of the analogies between the spiritual and the outer world, and felt that for one who could understand them these are often not merely interesting and pretty, but fitted to instruct and impress,—to *illustrate*, in the true sense of the word—casting *light* for mind and heart on what by itself may seem obscure. He went through the world with his eyes open. He was at once reflective and imaginative; and to a soul of this natural temperament—and which by the gracious work of the Divine Spirit had been made sensitive to religious impressions—everything around had something to show of God, truth, duty,—something to warm the heart, or guide the laggard, erring feet in the ways of holiness and peace. In some respects we see in the world very much what we look for. A man who has not thought seriously and savingly of death, and sin, and Christ, could tell you, on returning from a visit to some great city, of the vast traffic, the magnificent buildings, the gay attire of the people; if an educated and observant man, he might be able to speak also of recent inventions and improvements in the arts which he had seen: but ask him how the work of the Lord prospered there, and you would find that he had seen very little casting light on that matter. But Barnabas, when he was at Antioch, '*saw the grace of God*, and was glad: for he was a good man, and full of the Holy Ghost and of faith.' The last clause explains the first. And so it is everywhere, alike in the observation of inanimate nature and of life. With many there is nothing but the mere physical act of vision; no learning, no growth of the soul in wisdom, or energy, or happiness. As with the peasant of whom Wordsworth sings,—

> 'A primrose by a river's brim
> A yellow primrose was to him,
> And it was nothing more;'

so with a vast number of men and women. The beauty of creation tells them nothing of the beauty of the character of the Creator; the grandeur of creation nothing of His glory. Even in Christians, partly from mental indolence, partly from spiritual carelessness, the ear is but too often deaf to the rich harmonies of nature; the eye blind to the writing with the finger of God on His creation and His providence—those myriad and most valuable illustrations of truth and duty which the eye unsealed by the Holy Ghost should see all around. Power to discern the analogies between the outward world and the inner life is given to men in very varied degrees; yet something of this poetic power, I believe, is possessed by all, and true religion is most of all things fitted to quicken and purify it. Were our minds and hearts more exercised in this direction, a new interest would, beyond doubt, be given to every department of our lives, and spiritual strength and wisdom and joy would grow.

You remember how constantly the Lord Jesus illustrated His teaching by analogies from the material world; and you know how instructive and precious these illustrations are felt to be, both by the babe in Christ and by the wise and experienced believer. The sheepfold, the corn-field, and the vineyard, the candlestick in the house and the children playing in the market-place, the sublimest objects in creation and the commonest acts and scenes of human life, were made tributary to the elucidation and enforcement of spiritual truth. The manner in which the Lord and His inspired servants speak of these analogies, and reason from them, suggests that that is but an imperfect view which regards the images as, whilst happily chosen and highly useful, yet only incidentally, and for the time, accommodated to this purpose of illustration. Are we not rather to consider that to serve for this very use of casting light on spiritual truth was a definite purpose, perhaps the grand purpose, of the existence and the form of external nature, of the material laws which man applies in his inventions, of the necessities which govern human life, individual and social? As the earthly tabernacle was made according to the pattern shown on the mount, so the persons and things and relations of our outer world are *images*, in the full sense of the word—reflections—of profound spiritual truths, —a sacred writing, intelligible only to the eye which is enlightened by faith.[1] The Christian eye and mind and

---

[1] Archbishop Leighton thus begins his fifteenth Theological Lecture (on 'Regeneration'):—'The Platonists divide the world into two, the

heart, therefore, should be far more occupied than they usually are in studying this commentary, if I may so phrase it, given us by God Himself on His own Bible teaching. Our apostle evidently had much enjoyment in this study. He loved to read the writing of his heavenly Father on the 'wave of the sea driven by the wind and tossed'—on the 'flower of the grass that passeth away'—on the mirror which reflects the 'natural face'—on the horse and its bridle, the ship and its helm, the fire and its fuel.

The illustrations of the horse and the ship stand in immediate connection with the statement made in the close of the 2nd verse. This, as we have seen, exhibits not merely an *evidence*, but a *means*, a *most efficient instrumentality*. To those who have not thought on the subject, it may be a startling statement, that by the regulation of the tongue, such a little member,—by self-restraint with regard to words, so quickly spoken, so soon forgotten,— the whole body, its organs and propensities, may be kept under sway; 'yet,' says the apostle, 'if you will only look around, you will see at once a striking analogy, in the way of physical restraint by means

sensible and intellectual world. They imagine the one to be the type of the other, and that sensible and spiritual things are stamped, as it were, with the same stamp or seal. These sentiments are not unlike the notions which the masters of the cabalistical doctrine among the Jews held concerning God's *sephiroth* and seal. Therewith, according to them, all the worlds, and everything in them, are stamped and sealed. And these are probably near akin to what Lord Bacon of Verulam calls his *parallela signacula* and *symbolizantes schematismi*. According to this hypothesis, those parables and metaphors which are often taken from natural things to illustrate such as are divine, will not be similitudes taken entirely at pleasure, but are often in a great measure founded in nature and the things themselves.'

Leighton does not commit himself to acceptance of the view; but it seems clear, from the way in which this passage is connected with the rest of the lecture, that it had at least much interested and pleased him.

of the tongue, to that spiritual restraint by its means of which I have spoken,—an analogy singularly exact in all its details. I have said that the man who offends not in word is able to *bridle* the whole body. This word "bridle," if you think of it, brings before your minds a strong and fleet horse, an animal naturally wild and ungovernable, self-willed and capricious, like human nature under the impulses of depraved lusts and passions. But man, guided by his reason, obtains complete control over the animal, so that he can make it follow his will instead of its own,—compelling the lower nature to be submissive to the higher. Now how does he do this? He puts a bit in its mouth, he bridles its tongue, and so controls the whole body. By having command of the mouth, he has command of all.'

Looking at this illustration as an argument, it plainly does not prove all that the apostle has stated in the previous verse. He does not intend it to do this. But it does clearly enough show these things, at least,—that a little instrument applied at the right point will often effect great results; and that man signally evinces the power and grandeur of the reason which God has given him, when he makes such applications. The bearing which these facts have on the apostle's counsel to be careful in regard to words, if we wish to have universal holiness, is not far to seek. In the analogy itself, too, there is for all whose eye and ear are opened to every form of God's teaching something very suggestive; the truth which the apostle brings up, you observe, being this, when stated in its most general form,—that *it is by restraining the mouth, the tongue, that man obtains and keeps control over the animal nature.*

Another illustration, most graphic and complete, that man often controls a vast and most complicated machine by a very small instrument applied at the right point, is drawn from the steering of a ship. Even in the apostle's days many of the vessels trading in the Mediterranean were of what we still call considerable size, probably from five hundred to a thousand tons burden. The vessel in which Paul suffered shipwreck at Malta, carried, in crew and passengers, nearly three hundred persons; and Josephus tells us that six hundred were on board a ship in which he sailed. In our day, when ships are built of a size sufficient for the conveyance, if need be, of small armies, whatever argument the apostle founded on the largeness of the vessels of his time is plainly intensified many-fold. In looking, then, at one of these great floating houses (or, as one might describe some ships of modern times, floating towns), and remembering not merely their unwieldiness in themselves, but their exposure to the furious tempests of ocean, the thought connected with them most astounding and most suggestive is that one man—the '*governor*' of the ship, as our older English called the steersman—should, by the movements of a small instrument at the stern, sway the whole, direct the vessel over thousands of miles to her intended port, and often make even seemingly opposed winds and billows serviceable to her progress in the desired course. Man's strength, even at its fullest stretch, applied directly in any way, would be utterly vain; yet the man who has control of the helm which reason has constructed governs, by the exertion of comparatively but little strength, the whole of the vast mass. The bearing of the illustration on the apostle's purpose is plainly this: 'Let no one deem the statement extravagant, that he who governs his tongue will thereby regulate his whole body; for a power applied at the right point is often incomparably more efficient than a far greater power brought into action directly on the whole mass.'

Besides this general teaching, however, it seems to me,

taking both of the apostle's illustrations together, that he probably had in his mind the two great causes of difficulty in the way of man's bridling the whole body: the power of natural perversity, or what I have already spoken of as the animal nature; and the power of temptation, the evil influences of the world and the world's prince, driving us hither and thither. To the man who governs the little instrument, the tongue, he has ascribed the power of governing the whole body; and with reference to both classes of difficulties in the way of doing this, he exhibits striking and instructive analogies. With the little bit man controls the horse's self-will; with the little helm he governs and directs the ship, even amid the external and often most violent impulses 'of fierce winds.'

In the 5th verse we have the formal application of the illustrations to the point in hand: '*Even so the tongue is a little member,*'—very small in proportion to the whole body, or even when compared with many other parts of the body; just as the bit in a horse's mouth is but a little thing when compared with the horse, and the helm when compared with the ship,—'*and (yet) boasteth great things.*' This is not precisely what we expect. The statements and illustrations hitherto have had reference to the actual possession of power, not to mere claims or boasts regarding its possession; and therefore we look rather for the assertion that the tongue, though so small a member, '*doeth* great things,' as the bridle and the helm do; and in particular, that the wise regulation of the tongue does much to secure wise control over the whole man. This is the logical drift of the apostle's statements and illustrations, and is a *part* of what he says here. Seeing, however, that the tongue is the organ of speech, he, in accordance with his usual liveliness of style, introduces it as *asserting* its own power. Little as it is, yet it claims, truthfully enough, to be the accomplisher of '*great things.*' It can sway 'the fierce democracy.' It can still wild passions, excite high hopes, rouse flagging energies to bright activity. It can proclaim the gospel of Christ, crying, ' Ho, every one that thirsteth, come ye to the waters;' and thus bring rest, joy, and godliness to sinful, sorrowing hearts. All this is true, and yet the apostle's spirit is sad; for he remembers that in the vast majority of cases the tongue is ungoverned, and exercises much of its power not for good, but for evil. This is the thought which is amplified in the passage that follows, and it finds some expression even here in the use of the word '*boast*,' a term naturally suggestive of extravagance and vainglory. The apostle's idea in his words here, therefore, fully developed, appears to be something of this kind : ' Like the bridle and the helm, the tongue, though so small, wields great power, which might be, and under the firm government of a Christian spirit is, productive of great good; but, alas, as a rule this little member is braggart and wicked, and thus its power is exerted for evil.'

In immediate connection with this last thought, implied in 'boasteth,' James proceeds now to illustrate the measure of *evil* which a little thing uncontrolled may effect. Nothing is smaller than a *spark;* yet, '*behold, how great a matter a little fire kindleth !*'[1] You will observe that the marginal reading

---

[1] As the adjective to πῦρ, both ὀλίγον and ἡλίκον have good MS. authority, the latter, however, considerably the stronger. If ἡλίκον be read, the natural rendering is, ' How great a fire lights up how great a forest !'— the conflagration being looked at in its ultimate extent, and the smallness of the spark which originated it merely suggested by the context. So De Wette translates. With this, however, as Wiesinger points out, the verb ἀνάπτει does not suit ; for ' consumes' would be required, whilst it means ' kindles.' Most of those expositors who read ἡλίκον take it in the sense of 'how small,' translating ' How small a fire kindles how great a forest !' and in the connection it certainly seems that this must be the meaning. But

for '*matter*' is '*wood;*' and this, which is the proper and usual meaning of the original word, is greatly more in accordance with the picturesque style of the Epistle, and of this passage in particular, than the vague general term 'matter,' or 'mass of materials.'[1] The picture is one which had no doubt been seen again and again, both by James and his readers. Joel, speaking of a time of sore drought, says, 'O Lord, to Thee will I cry: for the fire hath devoured the pastures of the wilderness, and the flame hath burned all the trees of the field. The beasts of the field cry also unto Thee: for the rivers of waters are dried up, and the fire hath devoured the pastures of the wilderness.' Indeed, the picture was a familiar one in the poetry of the ancients generally, as an image of rapidity and destructiveness. Homer, for example, speaks of enemies falling below the blows of one of his heroes:

> 'As when the winds with raging flames conspire,
> And o'er the forests roll the flood of fire,
> In blazing heaps the grove's old honours fall,
> And one refulgent ruin levels all.'

---

to employ the same word in one sentence in the senses of 'how small' and 'how great' is manifestly harsh, and altogether alien from James's ordinary style. The form of expression in English most nearly corresponding, 'What a fire kindles what a forest!' is, if taken in this sense, not nearly so strained as the Greek, because 'what a' is much more a term of undecided signification than $\dot{\eta}\lambda\iota\kappa\sigma$, which always, in the first instance, clearly and distinctly suggests to the reader, 'how *great!*' Considering these things, and remembering how easily a mistake of eye or ear might lead a transcriber to substitute $\dot{\eta}\lambda\iota\kappa\sigma\nu$ for $\dot{o}\lambda\iota\gamma\sigma\nu$, seeing that, as Bengel says, *plana est alliteratio ad* $\dot{\eta}\lambda\iota\kappa\eta\nu$ *subsequens*, it appears to be a very fair question whether—even in the face of preponderant MS. authority, and of the canon of difficulty—we should not (with Bengel, Wiesinger, and others) hold likelihood to be on the side of the *textus receptus*.

[1] The primitive meaning of the word 'matter' also, as of its Greek representative, is 'wood.' The beautiful island of Madeira received its name (the Portuguese form of our 'matter') from the fact that, when first discovered, its hills were clothed to their summits with noble timber.

In the prairie region of America, sudden fires of this kind are among the most serious dangers to which travellers are exposed. A spark from the camp-fire of some careless hunter falls among the long parched grass near, which in a moment bursts into a blaze; and the flame spreads with appalling rapidity, carrying desolation and terror perhaps for fifty or a hundred miles, till it comes to places where it finds no fuel, and dies of exhaustion. Occasionally, in our own country, in summers of extreme and long-continued heat, we read in the newspapers of fires raging for days in woods—fires kindled by a mere spark from some passing locomotive on a railway, or in some other way equally casual.

'Behold, then,' says the apostle, 'how great a forest a little fire kindleth: *and the tongue is a fire.*' His reference is evidently not to the tongue as it might be, but as it is— in all men by nature, and to a lamentable extent even in many who are Christians—ungoverned, abused. 'An ungodly man,' says the Book of Proverbs, 'diggeth up evil; and in his lips there is a burning fire.' The chief points of analogy are obviously *destructiveness* and *rapidity of diffusiveness*. Fire is often spoken of by our newspaper writers as the 'devouring element;' and though the expression is so hackneyed as to have in great measure lost its force, yet it is in itself most truthful and expressive. Water, when it bursts its bounds, carries ruin, and fear, and sorrow along its course; but terrible as are its outbreaks, still the far more frequent and extensive devastation wrought by fire makes fire always rise up first in our minds when we think of destructive agencies. For it, as we know, is reserved the final destruction of our world: in the 'day of God' 'the heavens, being on fire, shall be dissolved, and the elements shall melt with fervent heat.' And to the creatures which God has made capable of feeling pain, perhaps no pain is more excruciating than that caused by fire. No more terrible torture has been devised for poor humanity by the keenest ingenuity of malevolence than that of the stake and faggots. In this element, then, brethren, so destructive and so potent to cause agony, see an image of the power of the tongue to produce ruin and wretchedness. Character, peace, health, property, — what cannot a false, calumnious, impure tongue destroy?—what does it not destroy every day, as our own observation tells us, if we only look and think? All this is done by a little word, as from a spark may come the conflagration which levels the noble forest. Again, the rapidity with which fire often spreads over a vast area plainly constitutes one of the points of similarity to which the apostle wishes to call attention. In the drought of an Eastern summer, a flame seems scarcely to have begun its destructive work on one side of a field, before it appears careering exultingly near the other. So with words. How fast and how far does calumny travel! Wise old Homer's standing epithet for 'words' is 'winged.' Like the birds of the air, they are fleet and wide of range. Or like the multitudes of little seeds which we see every autumn floating past on the breeze, each balanced on its own tiny wing, our words go far and wide, each the germ for some soul of a plant of utility and beauty, or of a useless and poisonous weed. And, impelled by the influences of a wicked world, our wicked words generally go fastest and farthest.

The principal *causes* of destructive fires, too, are the principal causes of the tongue's evil work. Sometimes the cause is definite, conscious *malignity*. A man hates his neighbour, and sets fire to his house or his stack-yard,—or he scorches his reputation by scattering lies. Now and again *desire of sport* is at the root of the matter. The Romans believed that Nero set the city on fire, that he might enjoy the sight of the blaze. So, according to the inspired proverb, 'it is sport to a fool to do mischief;' and, in particular, 'as a madman who casteth firebrands, arrows, and death, so is the man that deceiveth his neighbour, and saith, Am not I in sport?' But by far the commonest cause of destructive fires, as you know, is simple *want of care and thought*. So, too, with the tongue. A vast amount of the injury which it does is caused by words spoken in sheer heedlessness, without anything like definite, conscious ill-intent,—words spoken, it may be, merely to fill up a gap in conversation, or to give to conversation a little more sprightliness and piquancy. 'The tongue is a fire;' and, brethren, just as the man who, from malignity, or desire of sport, or simple want of thought, has kindled a conflagration, possesses often little or no power to stop its ravages, however anxious he then may be to do so,—nay, as its fury may soon become resistless by any human agency,—so with the fires which words light up. This is the most solemn thought connected with the exercise of God's great gift of speech,—that words once spoken are irrevocable. We can thereafter, in most cases, do but little to alter their tendency or check their power. They have sprung into the world as influences for good or evil, and we may hear their echo from many sides at the great Judgement.

Leaving this figure for a little, the apostle proceeds to describe the tongue as '*a world of iniquity*,' or, more exactly, '*the* world (that is, as I think the article may here be correctly paraphrased, 'that notorious world') of iniquity.' This is a very strong and startling expression, well fitted to arrest the attention of the inconsiderate, and lead them to think somewhat of the power of sins of the tongue, which by many are looked upon so lightly. The notion of *vastness* is obviously intended to be suggested by 'world.' In the ordinary use of the tongue there is an enormous mass of moral evil. Besides this general notion of vastness, however, the name 'world,' under which we comprehend in thought earth, and sea, and sky, and all things which exist in these, brings in also this idea, that *all kinds* of iniquity are to be found gathered up in the work of an ungoverned tongue. Of some sins it is the peculiar instrument; and of all sins it may be, and in a very large number of instances is, the minister, fosterer, fanner, propagator. The apostle's language here, then, has a somewhat similar force to that of Paul, when he calls the love of money 'the root of all evil;' not thereby intimating that all sin has as a matter of fact sprung from covetousness, but that that vice is of such a nature as readily to lead to the breach of any of God's commandments, and that an inconceivable number of sins of all classes do actually spring from it. So with the tongue. By it the blasphemer defies God, the liar utters his falsehoods, the seducer pours forth his destroying flatteries, the slanderer blasts his neighbour's good name, the traitor spreads sedition and disturbs the peace of nations. The tongue 'diffuses error, kindles strife, inflames the passions, stimulates to vice, originates crime. It breaks hearts, embitters families, distracts communities, divides and destroys churches.'[1]

But the apostle continues: '*So is the tongue among our members*'—such is the position of evil influence which it takes up—'*that it defileth the whole body.*' The mind of the apostle here obviously reverts to what he had said a little before, and had illustrated by the analogies of the horse's bit and the ship's helm,—that the man who rules his tongue can 'bridle also *the whole body.*' The actual state of things among all men by nature, and to a sad degree even among Christians, shows

[1] Dr. Adam's *Exposition of James*, . 234.

a deplorable contrast with this ideal. The tongue *has* power over 'the whole body;' but it is power for evil—power not for purifying and ennobling, but for defilement. The introduction in the previous clause of 'world' shows that the apostle is not confining himself strictly to the image of fire; yet from the last clauses of the verse it is manifest that this is mainly in his mind, and it seems therefore most natural to suppose the idea in '*defileth*' to be that of sullying, blackening like smoke. Not merely does the flame of the tongue's fire scorch and consume, as has been already suggested, and as is fully exhibited in the next clause, but its smoke *pollutes* the whole body. This is an instructive and impressive aspect of sin, which the young in particular would do well to ponder. We care much for these perishable bodies of ours—for their comfort and their adornment; and within certain limits this is needful and right: yet let us ever bear in mind that to the eye of God, and of all in the universe who see things in the light of God, there is no true beauty, no adornment which will bear minute examination, except that of holiness. When the bodily powers are instruments of sin, when the eyes range to and fro after vanity, when the mouth utters or the ear greedily drinks in false, impure, uncharitable words, when the feet 'walk in the counsel of the ungodly,' and the hands carry out that counsel,—then, however great the physical loveliness, however elaborate and tasteful the outward adorning, in God's sight the 'whole body' is 'defiled,' repulsive, loathsome. 'Now,' says our apostle, 'the tongue has such an influential position among our members, that by its utterances of malignity, greed, uncleanness, it excites the lusts which act through all the various bodily organs, and thus brings universal pollution.' This is a statement confirmed by the experience and observation of us all.

The tongue, moreover, '*setteth on fire the course of nature.*' It is not easy to define the precise significance of this expression. As it stands, it appears to mean,—'sets the world, or the whole creation, in flames.' To this these objections present themselves,—that such a strong hyperbolical statement is hardly consistent with our apostle's style, either in the context or elsewhere; and especially, that as this clause, like that immediately preceding, appears to stand in close connection with '*so is the tongue* (such is its influential position) *among our members*,' we expect a reference to its power for evil, not on the world generally, but on the character or immediate relations of the individual to whom the ungoverned tongue belongs. It seems to me that '*setteth on fire the revolving circle of our life*,' which is perhaps as literal a translation of the original words as could well be given, conveys a satisfactory sense.[1] Having in the previous clause spoken of the tongue's defiling power on the whole man, looked at strictly by himself, James proceeds here, I apprehend, to its injurious power on him as a member of society; exactly according to the order followed in the 17th verse, in describing the characteristics of heavenly wisdom. The life of each of us in the world may be conceived as a 'circle' of influences of various kinds, acting on the persons

[1] The expression τὸν τροχὸν τῆς γενέσεως has received a vast number of interpretations. The idea of a 'course' may be set aside at once, for 'to set a course on fire' seems language which has no definite meaning. In the accented manuscripts, too,—which may fairly be supposed to exhibit the traditional pronunciation,—τροχόν is found, not τρόχον: now the grammarians confine the sense of 'course' to the latter (Winer, p. 62, ed. Moulton). The closeness of the relation of the participial clauses to each other, which is shown by the fact that the three have but one article, seems to require a reference in the expression before us, as in σπιλοῦσα, κτλ., to the individual life and character; and support to a certain extent is given to this conclusion by the fact, that in the only other place where James uses the word γένεσις (i. 23) it means 'the birth' of the individual spoken of. If a reference to the individual must be looked for, this at once disposes of

and institutions around us,—a circle which is in ceaseless revolution, seeing that every moment of our social life brings in some new element. All these influences, then, the apostle says, are fired, inflamed, by the action of the tongue; and, by immediate inference, those persons also with whom, as the circle revolves, the influences come into contact, are fired or inflamed by it, with anger, licentiousness, covetousness, malice, or any other passion, according to circumstances. Something like this, I think, is the meaning of this rather obscure statement; and thus understood, the truthfulness and the force of the picture are alike manifest.

There remains yet one solemn fact on the subject to be brought forward. 'The tongue lights a devastating fire all around,' the apostle has said,—'*and it is set on fire of hell.*' The figure is bold and striking, and the truth which it exhibits is a very awful one. When the prophet cried, 'Woe is me, for I am a man of unclean lips,' one of the seraphim touched those lips with a live coal from God's altar. Jesus came into the world, as He tells us, 'to send fire on the earth,' the blessed fire of the Holy Ghost, to enlighten the understanding, warm the heart, and consume sin; and at Pentecost the outpouring of the Spirit was manifested visibly in the resting

---

the view held by many, that by the image is indicated the succession of generations; and also of the rendering of De Wette, Alford, and others, 'the orb of the creation' (the words being taken as equivalent to τὸν κύκλον τῆς κτίσεως), which appears, besides, too strong a hyperbole to be really effective for James's hortatory purpose. Wiesinger takes the expression to be almost a synonym for ὅλον τὸ σῶμα; but this is a sense which the figure cannot well be brought to yield. On the whole, it seems to me that the apostle's thought is exhibited by some such rendering as is given in the text above—'the wheel, or revolving circle, of our life' (a sense in which γένεσις is found in Plato; see De Wette),—or, with the same general meaning, but keeping to the sense of γένεσις in i. 23, and regarding the genitive here, as there, as one of origin, 'the birth-given' (that is 'natural') 'revolving circle.'

on the apostles of tongues of fire. I cannot help thinking that probably both Isaiah's vision, and especially that wondrous scene at Pentecost, which must have printed itself so deeply on the memories of all who were privileged to witness it, were present to the apostle's mind when he wrote the words now under consideration. *There* was fire from *heaven* for lips and tongue: the fire which the tongue has by nature is kindled from *hell*. The evil of the tongue, like all sin, came from Satan's temptation of the founders of our race; and from him it is ever receiving fresh strength, as James's words intimate,— for his statement is not merely that the tongue 'was,' but that it '*is habitually* set on fire of hell.' You cannot but feel, brethren, that this representation is singularly impressive. How appalling the thought should be to the careless talker, the man of unchastened lips, that his words are really Satan's, for which yet he himself is responsible; that his utterances are doing on himself and those around him the devil's work; that, when he pours forth from his lips profane, or impure, or unkind language, he is, in truth, breathing out flames lighted from the bottomless pit!

XVII.

THE TONGUE UNTAMEABLE AND INCONSISTENT.

'For every kind of beasts, and of birds, and of serpents, and of things in the sea, is tamed, and hath been tamed of mankind : 8 But the tongue can no man tame ; it is an unruly evil, full of deadly poison. 9 Therewith bless we God, even the Father ; and therewith curse we men, which are made after the similitude of God. 10 Out of the same mouth proceedeth blessing and cursing. My brethren, these things ought not so to be. 11 Doth a fountain send forth at the same place sweet water and bitter ? 12 Can the fig-tree, my brethren, bear olive-berries ? either a vine, figs ? so can no fountain both yield salt water and fresh.'—JAMES iii. 7–12.

THIS passage exhibits the *untameableness* of the tongue, and its grievous *inconsistencies*. By the introductory '*for*,' the paragraph is set before us as presenting the ground of the previous statements. The apostle has been dwelling, as we have seen, on the intensity and wide diffusion of the evil wrought by the tongue, piling up figure on figure to illustrate the terrible power of this little organ ; employing language, indeed, which to a person who has not thought carefully on the working of words would seem almost extravagant. Here he proceeds to point out evidence. He has been speaking with particular fulness of the devouring and often resistless energy of the tongue, under the figure of fire ; and now he supports this, saying in substance, that if we only look abroad we shall see that this organ is indeed utterly wild and untameable.

The statement of the 7th verse simply leads on to that of the 8th, and sustains it. The greater the power and skill of man to tame are seen to be, the more, obviously, the energy and wildness of the tongue are exhibited, seeing that it defies all that power and skill. By his amplification of the preliminary statement, as you see, the apostle so floods the background of his picture with light, that no one can fail to see the untameableness of the tongue standing out against it with startling impressiveness. The general idea is, 'Man can tame all the inferior races of creatures;' but you observe how each part of the statement is expanded : '*Every kind of beasts, and of birds, and of serpents, and of things in the sea, is tamed, and hath been tamed of mankind.*' Where we have '*birds*' and '*serpents*' here, the original has the more comprehensive terms 'flying creatures' and 'creeping things,'—the one including winged insects as well as birds, and the other all classes of reptiles. The classification, which is evidently for practical purposes complete, is the same as that given in the 9th chapter of Genesis, where the grant of power over the creatures is renewed to Noah, the second father of our race. The margin of our version shows 'nature' as the strict meaning of the word rendered '*kind*' in the beginning and end of the verse; and we have here presented, in truth, a somewhat different and deeper thought than merely that of 'race.' 'Every nature,' says the apostle, 'every special temperament and instinct throughout the animal creation, can be subdued by the peculiar nature of man—his constitutional superiority through reason.' This happens now, and is a fact of daily observation: 'every animal nature *is tamed,*'—'*and hath been tamed;*' all down the ages, from the grant of dominion to Adam and the renewal to Noah, this power of man has been proved. The thought underlying this last expression, and meant to come out into the reader's full consciousness when he considers the assertion made in the next verse, is plainly this: 'During all these generations, as now, the power of man over all the lower creatures has been clearly shown; yet at what point in all these ages could you find any man able to tame the tongue?' Of course the apostle does not intend to say that actually representatives of each of the almost innumerable species of living creatures have been tamed by man, neither does the force of his illustration at all require any such extreme supposition. All he means to say is, that ample evidence of this power over all classes of creatures is afforded by observation and history. The lion and the elephant have been taught to draw man's chariot, the hawk to hunt for him in the air, the fishes to come near him with trustfulness for their food, the serpent to submit to the charmer, and even the savage crocodile (the 'leviathan' of Job, 'who is made without fear, and is a king over all the children of pride') has been made by obedience to acknowledge the supremacy of man. Such cases as these supply the fullest proof that nothing of this kind is to be counted beyond the power of human skill and patience, firmness and gentleness.

'*But the tongue can no man tame.*' The tongue became a wild creature at the same time as the lion and the tiger. In paradise it and they were lovingly obedient to man; but when sin came, it and they revolted. The grant of superiority to the creatures was renewed, under an altered form—the dominion of fear, not of love. '*The fear of you and the dread of you,*' said God to Noah and his sons, 'shall be upon every beast of the earth, and upon every fowl of the air, upon all that moveth upon the earth, and upon all the fishes of the sea: into your hand are they delivered.' This did not extend to the tongue. Vast as the taming powers of man are, and have ever been proved to be, all experience shows that this wild creature '*no man can tame.*' The statement, you observe, is put in the most general way: 'No man has skill or strength to tame either his neighbour's tongue or his own.' I need scarcely remark that, so far as regards each man's own use of the glorious gift of speech, this inability is purely moral, due simply to a weakness of will. Were there as real, clear, decided a desire to tame the tongue as there is on the part of any man who undertakes the taming of one of the animals to succeed in the enterprise, and consequently similar perseverance and patience, there would be success here as well as there; but the will is weakened and perverted through depravity. 'Joseph's brethren,' the sacred historian tells us, 'hated him, and *could not* speak peaceably to him.' That 'could not' may fairly stand as a representative of all cases of the tongue's untameableness; and thus the apostle's teaching here, like all teaching everywhere in the Bible on man's moral condition, leads us up directly to our dependence on God. 'No *man* can tame the tongue:' 'With *man* this is impossible; but with God all things are possible.' Let the unconverted man, then, who has found resolution after resolution to bridle his tongue fail utterly, see in this failure 'a schoolmaster to bring him to Christ,' that in Him he may receive strength from above. And let the Christian remember that in nothing is the natural wildness of the flesh more apt to show itself than in the use of speech, and be especially earnest in laying hold, by the prayer of faith, on the strength of God for dominion over the tongue. In the statement made in this verse, you will see, is presented fully the basis of that which is made in the 2nd verse of the chapter, and with which, from the similarity or indeed identity of the figure employed, it seems to have been immediately connected in the apostle's mind: 'If any man offend not in word, the same is a perfect man, and able also to bridle the whole body.'

The apostle, continuing his sketch of the tongue's characteristics, says that '*it is an unruly evil*'—an unrestrainable, ungovernable instrument of wickedness. This is simply a forcible summing up of the previous statement. Modern editors of the Greek Testament, however, following the authority of the oldest and best manuscripts, have substituted in the text, for the word rendered 'unruly,' another, differing from it only by two letters, and which thus might easily be mistaken by transcribers. The approved reading means 'restless,' 'continually changing,'—the same epithet which in the 1st chapter is applied to the 'double-minded man,' and there rendered 'unstable.' This gives a new, interesting, important thought; a thought which presents one reason for the untameableness of the tongue just spoken of, and at the same time leads the way into the statements which follow regarding its inconsistencies. The tongue, says the apostle, is '*a restless evil :*' it flits constantly from one subject to another, from one sphere of wrong-doing to another. From slander it glides into impurity, from impurity into arrogance, from arrogance into frivolity, from frivolity into anger: so that, when a man is trying to tame it in one sphere, it suddenly escapes him, and exults in its wild freedom in another. Yet further, the tongue is '*full of deadly poison.*' It is like a serpent highly charged with venom, and from which no one can extract the fangs. As David has it, 'Evil men have sharpened their tongues like a serpent; adders' poison is under their lips.' And this poison of error, profanity, calumny, unclean language, is '*deadly* poison.' Slowly it may be, but surely, it kills reputation, or peace, or hope for eternity. It was the poison of the old serpent's words to Eve, 'Ye shall not surely die,' which made her and all of us die in trespasses and sins; and like Satan's tongue are in a degree the tongues of all his children. Standing as these words of the apostle do between the description of the tongue as a 'restless evil,' and his detailed illustration of its inconsistencies, it seems to me probable that its restlessness particularly in the form of inconsistency on the part of professing Christians, was prominent in his mind when he wrote them,—and that thus the special idea which we are to attach to them is that the careless, wicked language often heard from the lips of those who have named the name of Christ, is perhaps above all other language 'full of deadly poison.'

This remark brings us to the consideration of the *inconsistencies* of the tongue, of which James speaks in the next four verses.

Inconsistency is not by any means necessarily a bad thing. We not unfrequently hear public men condemned simply on this ground; whereas the truth is, that inconsistency is often most beautiful and honourable. Not to speak of the fundamental opposition between earlier and later utterances on religious subjects,—which may prove that the great vital change of thought and feeling has come between,—the man who on any question of importance and difficulty does not hold, and if need be express, at forty years of age opinions somewhat, it may be considerably, different from those he entertained at twenty, can scarcely have thought much regarding them, or allowed the light of experience to illuminate his mind. Or, to take a case more nearly analogous to that before us,—often when a man's soul is deeply stirred, and conflicting emotions are struggling within him, most obvious inconsistency, even in the same conversation, is felt by candid hearers to be at the least pardonable, because it is so natural. But the inconsistency of which our apostle speaks in this paragraph,—to 'bless God, and with the same tongue to curse men, which are made after the similitude of God,'—*this* is in the very highest degree sinful and injurious.

To '*bless God*'—to praise Him with thankfulness and love—to pronounce Him ineffably blessed in the possession and exercise of His own perfections—is the noblest use of speech, as it is the loftiest act of the soul. To 'bless the Lord, who forgiveth all our iniquities, who healeth all our diseases, who redeemeth our lives from destruction, who crowneth us with loving-kindness and tender mercies, who satisfieth our mouths with good things,'—to sing, 'O Lord, I will praise Thee; behold, God is my salvation: I will trust and not be afraid; for the Lord Jehovah is my strength and my song,'—for this use, above all others, the tongue was given us. 'Therewith,' says the apostle, 'bless we *God even the Father;*' or rather, adopting the best supported reading, 'our Lord and Father.' This is the peculiarly close and endearing relation in which the believer delights to think of God, and to address Him—as our reconciled Father in Jesus Christ; and only those who thus know Him as their Father can truly, lovingly, and gratefully 'bless' Him. Its mention here is peculiarly appropriate. The designations of God in Scripture are never selected at random, as, I am afraid, they often are in our prayers and other religious utterances. The study of the connection in which they stand will always discover a delicate beauty in them, or a special argumentative force. That before us has occurred already in this Epistle, in the last verse of the 1st chapter, where the apostle speaks of 'true and undefiled religious service before our God and Father' being 'to visit the fatherless and widows in their affliction.' There the name most manifestly involves an enforcement of the duty enjoined, irresistibly cogent to the Christian's heart, seeing that he is called on to care for those destitute ones who, *as children of the common Father*, are his own brothers and sisters. In the present place the same thought of God's common Fatherhood is that which we are to carry with us into the consideration of the latter part of the verse, where it casts a broad and strong light on the wickedness of the inconsistency described.

'With the tongue,' says the apostle, we 'bless our Lord and Father, and with the tongue *we curse men.*' To '*curse*' is strictly to imprecate evil on a person—to pray for injury or destruction to come upon him. Language of this kind has always been sadly common in the East; and very probably even professing Christians, of whom plainly James is here speaking, might at times, under the influence of depravity and their surroundings, fall into the practice. Peter, in the high priest's palace, 'began to curse and to swear,' the evangelists tell us. On our own streets, alas, my brethren, the swearer's awful prayer is lamentably familiar to our ears,—the words in which, if they have any meaning, he prays for everlasting destruction on himself or his neighbour. As James employs the word here, however, it obviously includes much more than this,—utterances of any sort which show unkind feeling to our neighbour—our neighbour '*made after the similitude of God.*' 'God said, Let us make man in Our image, after Our likeness. So God created man in His own image,'—with the sublime dignity of a moral nature, a mind and heart which could apprehend and love truth and holiness. This image has not been wholly lost. Though sadly blurred by the fall, yet in reason and conscience all men still show God's likeness. This fact was made prominent, you remember, in one of the laws given to Noah, as summing up man's dignity and value: 'Whoso sheddeth man's blood, by man shall his blood be shed; *for in the image of God made He man.*' The same argument is employed here. How utterly monstrous it is to 'bless our God and Father,' and with the very tongue which does this to 'curse' those who, by bearing His image, prove that they are His children! For, 'as certain even of the heathen poets have said, We are also His offspring.' The argument becomes stronger yet, when we bear in mind that Jesus was a man, and by His incarnation lifted up all the members of our race into the position of His 'kinsmen after the flesh.' Oh, how this fact should ennoble to our feelings universal humanity! All this, you observe, applies to men without distinction. But the awfully wicked inconsistency of the conduct described is most glaring of all when the curses are imprecated on the heads of those who by faith are God's children in the covenant, 'predestinated to be conformed to the image of His Son.' No more gross inconsistency can be conceived, no evidence more complete that the tongue is 'full of deadly poison,' than for a man to bless God, to praise the Father with glowing words of gratitude and affection, and to curse, to slander, or insult His children in Christ Jesus.

In the first words of the 10th verse the statement of inconsistency is summed up in a terse and pointed way : '*Out of the same mouth proceedeth blessing and cursing.*' There are people professing godliness, people who every Sabbath-day in the song of praise lift up their voice and bless God for His boundless Fatherly love, who yet during the week often give way to most unhallowed anger against their fellow-men and God's children, or in whose company you cannot be for a few minutes without hearing some ill report against a neighbour, communicated as venomously as the measure of apparent sympathy among the auditors with the speaker permits. All of us have met persons of the kind, and in every one of us there is somewhat of this inconsistency—too much, far too much, for in any degree it is altogether opposed to the will of God. 'My brethren,' says the apostle, '*these things ought not so to be.*' It is true that 'the tongue can no man tame,' yet its untamedness is not the less sin. Wherever there is humble, sincere desire and effort to obey the will of God, strength is given by the Almighty. 'Stretch forth thine hand,' said Jesus to a man who had his hand withered; '*and he stretched it forth.*' For a professed child of God, then, to mingle with his more becoming utterances the language of the children of the wicked one—this is conduct which calls for the severest condemnation. Bitter words are fruit from a 'root of bitterness' in the soul. The tongue of such a professing Christian praises God for the Sun of righteousness, with its glorious light and heat; but his angry denunciations of brethren show that his heart meanwhile is shutting itself up in darkness and biting cold. 'My brethren, these things ought not so to be.'

In the two verses which follow, the apostle, as is his wont, directs our attention to analogies, for some hints on the matter in hand. Nature, he would have us bear in mind, is to some extent a revelation of spiritual truth, but a revelation written in strange characters, the key to which is given only in the Bible. That same 'opening of the eyes' which enables a believer to 'behold wondrous things out of God's law,' gives him power also to behold wondrous things out of God's works all around. 'Now,' says James, 'if you who, being members of Christ's church, thus assert that you can read the hieroglyphics of nature, will but look at them carefully, you will see that everywhere they declare the utter monstrousness of such inconsistencies of the tongue as have been mentioned,—seeing that God, whose children you call yourselves, is not the author of confusion, but of order.' '*Doth a fountain send forth at the same place sweet water and bitter?'* 'You know that it is not so. Near each other may be bitter springs and sweet springs; nay, in the salt sea one may find a jet of fresh water thrown up to the surface by a strong spring;[1] but no fountain sends forth at one mouth sweet water and bitter.'

Not merely as a matter of fact is such inconsistency not found in the physical sphere, but it is contrary to the laws which God has given to nature, and therefore *cannot* occur. From the 'doth' of the 11th verse we now advance to the '*can*,' regarding which, in the first instance, reference is made to an analogy from the vegetable kingdom: '*Can the fig-tree, my brethren, bear olive-berries? either a vine, figs?*' In this illustration the apostle's intention is to set forth simple incongruity or confusion of products, without any contrast of bad and good species, such as appears in our Lord's similar question: 'Do men gather grapes of thorns, or figs of thistles?' '*So can no fountain both yield salt water and fresh.*' With these words James closes his remarks on the inconsistencies of the tongue. Seeing, then, that the fact and physical law regarding springs have been referred to merely by way of illustration, whilst the statement before us has all the appearance of a weighty observation on the main subject, it seems clear that the apostle has passed from an illustrative allusion to natural phenomena into a metaphor. More exactly, perhaps, the two are conjoined, but the metaphor is the more prominent before his mind. Under the '*fountain*' he thinks of the heart of man, 'out of which are the issues of life'—issues of the '*salt water*' of angry speech, bitter

---

[1] In the Gulf of Spezzia, a branch of the Gulf of Genoa, there is a powerful jet of fresh water rising from the bed of the sea. On the south coast of Cuba also, at a considerable distance from the shore, there are fresh-water jets of such force that boats cannot approach them without some danger.

to the taste, and destructive to the flowers of joy and holiness, or of the '*fresh water*' of loving, truthful, earnest utterances, sweet and life-giving. With reference to this fountain, his declaration is, that what holds in outward nature holds in the moral sphere also: it '*cannot* both yield salt water and fresh.' It may *seem* to do so; but where the habitual outflow is bitter, the apparently 'fresh water' of gracious speech, which comes at times, is not really in its nature quickening and fertilizing; for though the praises of God are spoken, they 'come out of feigned lips.' Thus the charge of *inconsistency*, in anything beyond a superficial sense, is removed from those slanderous, abusive professors of Christianity to whom the apostle has been addressing himself,—but only by the substitution of something yet more awful. He does not *say* all this, you observe, but he *suggests* it all; and, for those who are willing to think, the suggestion is perhaps even more impressive than the explicit statement would have been.

According to another reading, supported by the oldest manuscripts, the statement takes this form: '*Nor can salt water yield fresh.*' The force of this is, in substance, the same as that of the other, and expressed even more pointedly. The fountain of the heart obeys laws as fixed as those by which the fig-tree bears figs, not olives, and the vine grapes, not figs. A heart renewed by the Spirit of God is a spring of living water, 'a well of water springing up into everlasting life.' Its outflow in speech, as in conduct, will be pleasant and healthful. There may be indeed, since depravity is not wholly subdued here, *jets* of bitter water, but the *habitual* issues are sweet. An unrenewed heart is a deep well of bitterness; and '*salt water cannot yield fresh.*'

XVIII.

EARTHLY WISDOM.

'Who is a wise man and endued with knowledge among you? Let him show out of a good conversation his works with meekness of wisdom. 14 But if ye have bitter envying and strife in your hearts, glory not and lie not against the truth. 15 This wisdom descendeth not from above, but is earthly, sensual, devilish; 16 For where envying and strife is, there is confusion and every evil work.'—JAMES iii. 13-16.

THE connection of these words with the preceding is natural and close. The apostle, you remember, was led into that exposition and condemnation of sins of the tongue which has thus far occupied the chapter, by his knowledge of the fact alluded to in the 1st verse, that in those churches to which he wrote a strong disposition to put themselves forward as teachers was manifested by many persons who were not qualified for the work by knowledge and Christian experience. Various most serious evils resulted from this. In particular, the meetings of congregations were occasionally scenes of most unseemly wrangling, instead of means of edifying and comforting the brethren. Many argued for victory instead of for truth; angry stinging words were spoken; ill-feeling was produced, which not merely poisoned happiness and prevented any spiritual advantage at the time, but led to alienations and outbreaks of bitterness in ordinary social intercourse. It is plain from several passages in Paul's writings, that he had been much distressed by faults of this kind in some of the churches to which his Epistles were sent. They obviously weighed much on the heart of James also. Very early in his Epistle we find his convictions and feelings on this subject uttering themselves thus: 'My beloved brethren, let every man be swift to hear, slow to speak, slow to wrath: for the wrath of man worketh not the righteousness of God. Wherefore lay apart all filthiness and superfluity of naughtiness, and receive with meekness the ingrafted word, which is able to save your souls' (i. 19–21). In the remarks on the sins of the tongue which started from the injunction given in the 1st verse of this chapter, 'My brethren, be not many masters,' the presumptuous and turbulent discussion of *religious* questions has naturally been mainly in the apostle's mind; and, in the last few verses, particularly the monstrous and grievously sinful incongruity of the warm words of devotion toward God, and the wrathful language toward men, which were often mingled in the Christian assemblies. Now these painful and discreditable scenes arose from an impression on the part of men who neither in head nor heart were fitted for the position of Christian teachers, that they were so qualified, having spirituality and large acquaintance with truth. From the point which we have now reached, therefore, to the end of the chapter, James directs the attention of his readers to the nature and evidences of true heavenly wisdom, and the inconsistency with it of everything like bitterness and hatred.

The subject is thus introduced: '*Who is a wise man, and endued with knowledge among you? Let him show out of a good conversation his works with meekness of wisdom.*' In substance the meaning is evidently this: 'If there be truly wise and instructed men among you, they will prove their wisdom by a holy life—a life distinguished by Christian meekness.' But the first part of the sentence is thrown into the form of a question, the construction of the whole being similar to what we find, for example, in the 34th Psalm: 'What man is he that desireth life, and loveth many days, that he may see good? Keep thy tongue from evil, and thy lips from speaking guile. Depart from evil, and do good: seek peace, and pursue it' (Ps. xxxiv. 12-14). You feel that the interrogative mode of stating a supposition has a peculiar force in the discussion of morals, from its directness of appeal. Many of the apostle's readers were conscious that they had taken up a position of prominence which only persons who were 'wise and endued with knowledge' could rightly fill. Many of his readers in our time, too, may be conscious of a similar persuasion in regard to themselves, of fitness for a prominent position, though perhaps modern ecclesiastical usages may have prevented its being exhibited exactly in the same way. To each conscience goes straight home the question, 'Who is a wise man and endued with knowledge among you?'

'*Let him show*,'—that is, 'The proper course for such a one is to show; and (for this thought is plainly implied in the injunction) every one who is truly wise and well instructed *will* show.' 'Let him show,' then, what? We expect 'his wisdom,' but the apostle expresses himself differently. He says, '*his works*,'—that is, 'his works *as a wise man*,' or, substantially, 'the works or fruits of his wisdom.' We have here again what may be described as the central thought of this Epistle, that where religion has real saving hold of a mind and heart, it cannot from its nature but powerfully influence the outward life; and that the more a Christian has of true wisdom and spiritual knowledge, the more manifestly will his life at all points be governed by his religion. Talk of orthodoxy and Christian experience, however fluent and animated and clever, does not of itself prove wisdom; the really wise man will 'show his *works.*' '*Out of a good conversation,*' James continues. The word '*conversation,*' as employed in modern English, designates one element of our social life—the interchange of thought by speech: but at the time our version of the Bible was made, it meant generally 'a course of life or conduct,' and wherever it occurs in the Bible, which it does often, this is its meaning. The line of thought will in most cases lead readers of any intelligence instinctively to give the word something like its correct force, except perhaps in 2 Pet. ii. 7, where, in the statement that 'just Lot was vexed with the filthy conversation of the wicked,' there may be a risk of its being taken improperly in the modern sense, which covers only a portion of the meaning. '*Out of*' here represents the same original particle which is rendered '*by*,' in 'I will show thee my faith by my works' (ii. 18). The meaning seems to be similar, and the same translation would be clearer here: 'Let him show by a good course of life his works.' The 'works' here spoken of and the 'good (beautiful, noble) course of life,' are the same, but looked at in different lights. The 'works' are the separate acts of holiness, of godly earnestness and godly patience, which constitute the 'noble life;' and each such act, when we know it to be not isolated, but consistent with the whole life, is to be regarded as a new fruit and evidence of wisdom.

We have here, you observe, the truth brought before us, that genuine Christian wisdom, whether it lead a man to become a teacher in the church or not, will, at all events, in all cases find expression through giving spiritual loveliness to the whole daily life. He is the *wisest* Christian, whether he occupy the pulpit or the pew,—he exhibits the most knowledge of God, and of himself, and of Christianity,—he shows the broadest and profoundest views of the philosophy of religion, of the chief end of man, and the way to obtain happiness,—who walks most closely with God, and is most perfectly changed into His likeness.

The apostle, having before his mind the angry, turbulent, arrogant spirit often exhibited by professing Christians who fancied themselves wise, and because they fancied themselves wise, gives prominence to that characteristic of true wisdom which is most directly opposed to this: 'Let him show out of a good conversation his works *with meekness of wisdom*,' or more exactly, '*in* wisdom's meekness.' Meekness is thus set before us as that disposition of heart in which alone men can show works of real Christian wisdom,—that element or atmosphere in which alone a truly good, noble, beautiful course of life can be maintained. This grace of '*meekness*'—freedom from the spirit of wrathfulness, revenge, sullenness, under any kind of trouble, and this with relation both to God and man—is closely allied to humility, and patience, and love. I do not know that at any point the opposition between the spirit of the world and the spirit of Christ is more marked, more obviously diametrical, than with regard to this feature of character. That 'the *meek*' should 'inherit the earth'—they who bear wrongs, and exemplify that love which 'seeketh not her own,'—to a world which believes in high-handedness and self-assertion, and pushing the weakest to the wall, a statement like this of the Lord from heaven cannot but appear an utter paradox. The man of the world desires to be counted anything but 'meek' or 'poor in spirit,' and would deem such a description of him equivalent to a charge of unmanliness. Ah, brethren, this is because we have taken in Satan's conception of manliness instead of God's. One Man has been shown us by God, in whom His ideal of man was embodied; and He, 'when He was reviled, reviled not again; when He suffered, threatened not, but committed Himself to Him that judgeth righteously:'

He for those who nailed him to the tree prayed, 'Father, forgive them; for they know not what they do.' The world's spirit of wrath, then, must be folly; whilst than a spirit of meekness like His, in the midst of controversy, oppositions, trials of whatever kind, there can be no surer evidence that 'Jesus is made of God to His people *wisdom*.'

In the 14th verse, the other side—the case as it actually stood with a great number of the readers—is presented with much pointedness and force : '*But if ye have bitter envying and strife* (more exactly, *factiousness*) *in your hearts, glory not and lie not against the truth*.' James probes here to the quick for the patient's good. He tears off the tissue of plausibilities (zeal for God's glory, ardour on behalf of truth, and the like), in which an envenomed, arrogant, bigoted spirit often enwraps itself, and lays bare the moral deformity and defilement— '*bitter envying and strife*.' We have not here the pleasant 'water of life' (the image of the 12th verse is perhaps still in the apostle's mind), but 'bitter waters' of hatred. 'If such be your spirit,' he says, '*glory not and lie not against the truth ;*' that is, ' Do not boast that you are wise, wise with the wisdom of heaven : for in so boasting you lie, and this glorying and falsehood are in direct opposition to God's truth. The gospel of Christ' (for this is what is here, as so often in the New Testament, meant by '*the truth*') 'has for its spirit love, meekness, long-suffering; and thus the wisdom which Christ gives through that truth reveals itself in these graces. If ye, then, have in your hearts envy, and self-seeking, and contentiousness, to boast of these as being His wisdom is to lie against Him and His truth.' I need hardly observe that we are not to take these words of the apostle as a declaration that controversy on religious points is always a bad thing. The life of our Lord, and the lives and writings of His inspired followers, all prove the reverse to be true. It is often the duty of Christians, in 'holding fast the form of sound words,' to 'contend earnestly for the faith once delivered to the saints.' Yet our apostle's teaching in this passage will not have its full and proper effect on our minds, unless it leave a distinct impression that a so-called zeal for religion may be a very irreligious zeal, that controversy always involves serious spiritual hazards, and that wherever love fails and a spirit of bitterness enters in, there is sin.

The statement that to give the name of Christian wisdom to a condition of mind and heart such as has been described in the first clause of the 14th verse, is 'to boast and lie against God's truth,' is supported and illustrated in the two verses which follow. '*This wisdom,*' says James, '*descendeth not from above, but is earthly, sensual, devilish.*' The wisdom which displays itself in bitterness—and alas, brethren, in the history of the Church of Christ, how often has fancied wisdom displayed itself in bitterness! how much of real knowledge and mental power has been wasted in such bitterness!—this wisdom is not from heaven; but as it displays itself on earth, so it is also of '*earthly*' origin. Moreover, being 'earthly,' it is '*sensual.*' The word so translated occurs in the New Testament several times, and is rendered 'sensual' only here and in a verse in Jude, where 'mockers, walking after their own lusts,' are described as 'sensual, having not the Spirit' (Jude 19). Elsewhere the rendering is 'natural,' as in the contrast between the 'natural body' and the 'spiritual body' in the 15th chapter of First Corinthians, and in the statement in the 2nd chapter of the same epistle, that 'the natural man receiveth not the things of the Spirit of God' (1 Cor. xv. 44, ii. 14). According to its derivation, the original word strictly means '*belonging to the soul.*' The contrast with *spirit* and the *spiritual,* which is expressed in the passages that I have quoted from First Corinthians and from Jude, and implied in that now before us, is the key to the exact meaning. Sometimes in Scripture, as commonly among ourselves, man is spoken of as consisting of a body and a soul, in which case 'soul' is used in the widest sense. Sometimes, however, we have three constituent elements mentioned or alluded to—the spirit, soul, and body.[1] According to this division, the '*soul*' comprehends only those energies and capacities of mind and heart which have to do with the world known by our bodily senses,—man's mental and emotional nature in so far merely as he is the highest of the animals—an animal able to buy and sell, as the beaver can build a hut and a dam; the '*spirit*' is that highest power of a rational being by which it can apprehend the idea of God, and hold communion with Him,—by which through faith it can live under the influences of an unseen world. The 'spirit' *should* be the governing principle, holding the whole nature under a firm and healthful sway. But, as you know, brethren, in man, as he now is by nature, the spirit is darkened, perverted, and weakened; it is dethroned through sin; and only the enlightening and strengthening energy of God's Spirit can enable our spirits to take their rightful dignity and rule. Where the spirit does not rule, the *soul*—that is, as we have seen, the mental and emotional nature in so far as it is occupied with the world open to the senses—tends to become ever more and more subject to the lowest element of our constitution, the appetites of the body. Hence Paul, in Romans, distinguishes all men into two classes—those who are 'in the flesh,' and those who are 'in the spirit;' the standard on which the division is based being that which I have now indicated: 'Ye are not in the flesh, but in the spirit, *if so be that the Spirit of God dwell in you*' (viii. 9).

[1] See 1 Thess. v. 23, Heb. iv. 12.

You see, then, that when James here calls the wisdom which bore bitter wranglings as its fruit a wisdom '*of the soul*,' with an implied and well understood contrast to that wisdom of the *spirit* which ought to regulate all the thoughts and feelings, words and actions, of Christians, he means that it belongs entirely to the lower elements of our nature. Its characteristics are simply those of the wisdom belonging to the men of the world, whose aim is personal honour and aggrandisement. The words which this wisdom utters may be of God's glory, but their real aim is man's glory. Its plans and procedure have all reference to self and to this world of the senses, though the subjects it discusses may belong to the invisible world, the world known to faith. Rightly understood, then, brethren, you cannot but feel how searching and scathing this word of the apostle is; and it is interesting to notice, that the very same tempers which are here denounced as *unspiritual*, merely ' of the *soul*,' are those which the Apostle Paul specifies as peculiarly grieving to that Divine Spirit through whose indwelling alone man's spirit has rule over his lower nature. 'Grieve not the Holy Spirit of God, whereby ye are sealed unto the day of redemption. Let all bitterness, and wrath, and anger, and clamour, and evil-speaking, be put away from you, with all malice; and be ye kind one to another, tender-hearted, forgiving one another, even as God for Christ's sake hath forgiven you' (Eph. iv. 30–32). From the completeness with which the distinction between *soul* and *spirit* has been lost to our modern thought, it seems impossible to give the idea of the word before us exactly in any translation. 'Sensual' and 'animal' suggest too exclusively the action of the very lowest propensities of our nature,—though, as we have seen, the tendency of the 'soul,' when ungoverned by the 'spirit,' is steadily towards subjection to these. Perhaps, on the whole, 'natural,' in its well understood opposition to 'spiritual,' is the best word.

But something more awful still has to be said of this wicked wisdom. Like all wisdom among men on moral questions which is only 'earthly,' only 'natural,' it is *'devilish'*—demon-like. Our first parents yielded to the temptation to sin, because they considered that the tree was 'to be desired to make one wise;' and *this* was the wisdom—a wisdom kindred to that of Satan, whose lie seduced them—full of envy and falsehood, moving ever in the atmosphere of selfishness and malignity. Where zeal even regarding religion shows itself in unholy tempers like these, the fire of this zeal is fire from the bottomless pit. The 'spirit' of man is in action here as well as the 'soul;' but, alas, the grandeur of the capabilities of this constituent of our being only deepens the debasement. The spirit 'made but a little lower than the angels' of light, links itself with the lost angels of darkness.

The 16th verse justifies the strong statements of the 15th: '*For where envying and strife is,*' such as in the beginning of the 14th verse has been supposed, '*there*'—always, both in the envious persons themselves and in others whom their spirit influences—'*is confusion,*' turbulence and distraction of every kind—mental, moral, and social. Ah, brethren, from the day when envy and self-seeking—springing up, too, in immediate connection with religious worship at God's altar—desolated Adam's family, what ruin has this spirit wrought in families, churches, communities of every kind! Now 'God is not the author of confusion, but of peace'—peace in the individual heart, and in the societies, where the gospel rules. He is the 'God of peace,' and His revelation is the 'gospel of peace.' What produces 'confusion,' then, cannot be from Him. Moreover, not 'confusion' only, but '*every evil work,*' may naturally spring from this bitter root of envy and contentiousness. If love be 'the fulfilling of God's law,' as He Himself declares it to be, then lovelessness in any of its forms cannot but, if persistently indulged, sap, poison, destroy the whole moral nature. This wisdom is certainly not 'from the Father of lights, from whom cometh down every good and every perfect gift,' and *nothing but* good and perfect gifts. It is 'earthly, sensual, devilish.'

XIX.

HEAVENLY WISDOM.

'But the wisdom that is from above is first pure, then peaceable, gentle, and easy to be entreated, full of mercy and good fruits, without partiality, and without hypocrisy. 18 And the fruit of righteousness is sown in peace of them that make peace.'—JAMES iii. 17, 18.

THE apostle passes on now to depict for us the features of real wisdom,—that only satisfying wisdom for immortal creatures of which 'the fear of the Lord is the beginning.' This wisdom is '*from above.*' That with which James has contrasted it was described as 'earthly,' having its origin in the blinded minds and corrupt hearts of men themselves; but this is a 'good and perfect gift,' such as only the 'Father of lights' bestows. It comes through faith in Jesus Christ, which is 'not of ourselves, but the gift of God.'

James proceeds to exhibit some of its main results and evidences in heart and life. You observe that he does not dwell on its basis, or the way in which it is attained. In speaking of '*the* wisdom that is from above,' he assumes that his readers know of such a wisdom, and believe in its heavenly origin. He assumes, indeed, we may say, as generally throughout the Epistle, that they were familiar with the central truths of the religion of Jesus which they professed, his aim everywhere being to show how the vital reception of these truths will reveal itself in man's moral nature. The question which he answers in the verse before us is this: 'If a man, feeling that he lacks wisdom, has asked of God, who giveth to all liberally; if a man has been begotten again with the word of truth, and thus has the faith of our Lord Jesus Christ, the Lord of glory, so that the secret of the Lord is with him,— how will this celestial wisdom show its presence?' The characteristics are set forth under two heads, which, with logical precision, James marks with the notation '*first*' and '*then*,' that is to say, 'in the first place,' and 'in the second place;' the first division having reference to the influence of heavenly wisdom on a man looked at simply by himself, the other to its influence on him considered as a member of society.[1] The division is the same, only in the inverse order, as that before given by the apostle of the features of 'true and undefiled religious service:' 'to visit the fatherless and widows in their affliction, and to keep himself unspotted from the world.'

Under the first head, the influence of heavenly wisdom on a man's moral nature, looked at simply by himself, James mentions only one characteristic, but that a most comprehensive one. 'This wisdom,' he says—that is, as of course the meaning must be in speaking of the moral results of wisdom, the man who possesses it—is '*pure*.' The Christianly wise man shrinks from moral defilement of every kind. Nothing less wide of range than this is involved in the word 'pure' here. One great fundamental characteristic of the morality taught in the Bible is, that it occupies the whole nature.

[1] A discreditable misapplication of the apostle's logical terms 'first' and 'then,' is sometimes made in the interests of bigotry and uncharitableness. He does *not* say that one whom we cannot doubt to be a Christian must 'first' have his doctrine in every minute point what we think 'pure,' before our relations to him can be 'peaceable.' His teaching throughout the whole passage is, in substance, the saying of the very reverse.

'Blessed are the pure *in heart*, for they shall see God:' 'Blessed are the undefiled *in the way*, who *walk* in the law of the Lord.' The truly wise man is he who has conformity of spirit to the 'only wise God,' who believes what God teaches, loves what God loves, lives as Jesus lived—He who was the express image of the invisible God. 'Purity,' as required by God, and exemplified in the measure of their faith by all Christ's people, implies a superiority of soul, which will show itself continually in word and deed, to everything low and sensual, selfish and mean,—a freedom from petty views and sinister ends, and, on the contrary, a relish and love of everything really great and good. By such moral convictions, and feelings, and conduct, a man is proved to be wise with that heavenly wisdom which consists in a true, vital, energetic apprehension of his relations to God, of the chief end of man, of duty and happiness. How sadly unwise, then, my brethren, a very large proportion of those who call and deem themselves Christians must be; and how much of folly must mingle with the wisdom even of the wisest here below! The divine ideal of the church for which Jesus gave Himself up to death, is 'a bride adorned for her husband' with all the graces of holy beauty,—'a glorious church, sanctified and cleansed with the washing of water through the word,' and thus freed from 'spot and wrinkle, and every such thing.' How lamentably different from this divine ideal the reality seems to be, if we take it to be set before us in the visible church now!

Under his second class of the characteristics of heavenly wisdom, those in which are exhibited its moral influence on man as a member of society, the apostle mentions six. In the first place, it is '*peaceable.*' 'Envying and strife,' James has already said, prove a so-called wisdom to be not heavenly, but, in the worst acceptation of the term, 'earthly.' So also

Paul says to the Corinthians, 'Whereas there is among you envying, and strife, and divisions, are ye not carnal, and walk as men?' (1 Cor. iii. 3). The wisdom which is really from above leads a man to delight in peace. The spirit of love will reign in his heart, and, so far as his influence extends, turbulence and contention will be discouraged, whether in business, in ordinary social intercourse, in religious or political procedure. Perpetual and uncompromising war with sin in ourselves and in the world, but love to our neighbours as to ourselves, tender pity for their weaknesses such as we need for our own, forgiveness for their trespasses against us such as we ask of God for ours against Him,—this is wisdom.

The spirit of peace, a disposition and longing for peace, the wise man always has, in so far as he is wise; but the existence of the external condition of peace necessarily depends to some extent on the will of others. Our part is, as Paul puts it in Romans, wherever it 'is possible,' and always 'as much as lieth in *us*, to live peaceably with all men.' But there are worse things, incomparably worse things, than the non-existence of external peace; and it would evince anything but the possession of heavenly wisdom not to recognise this fact. Had external peace been the best of all things, Jesus would not have come among us with His work and gospel of grace; for so certain is the resistance which sin makes to the gospel to interrupt in innumerable cases and ways external peace, that He Himself, the Prince of peace, testified, 'Think not that I am come to send peace on earth; I came not to send peace, but a sword.' 'There are many sacrifices which must not be made by Christians, even to secure peace. We must not flatter nor imitate what we think wrong in men's opinions and conduct, in order to have peace with them; we must not buy peace at the cost of truth and justice; we must not omit duty for it, nor commit sin. If men will not be at peace with us but on principles which infer our disloyalty to the Supreme King, and are thus inconsistent with our primary and paramount obligations, then peace, however desirable, must be parted with, for the plain reason, that to have God for a Friend is a greater good, an immeasurably greater good, than to have all the world as our enemies is an evil.'[1]

This wisdom is '*gentle*' also. The exact idea intended by the original word is ' considerate and forbearing.' The Christianly wise man loves to make allowances for the ignorance and weakness of others, knowing how great need he stands in constantly of having allowances made for himself both by God and man. In his business dealings with others, for example,—knowing that human laws, however carefully made, yet, if always rigidly enforced, will often act cruelly and unjustly, he guides himself by the broad principles of equity in the sight of God. In his judgement of the conduct of men, he takes a kindly view wherever it is possible, never believing evil of them until he cannot help it. In his judgement of men's opinions, he remembers how inadequately the loose language of many represents their real views, how many men are much better than their professed creed, and how unfair the practice so common in controversy is, of ascribing to a man as held by him views which *we* may think legitimately deduced from his avowed principles, but which he himself may hold in abhorrence. In every department of his thought and life, the possessor of the wisdom which is from above is 'considerate and forbearing.' Many professing Christians may tremble to think of this characteristic.

Again, it is '*easy to be entreated.*' The wise man is free from everything like repulsive austerity, neither has he aught

---

[1] Prof. John Brown, *Commentary on Romans*, p. 475.

of headstrong self-sufficiency and obstinacy. He is accessible and open to remonstrance from persons reasonably entitled to give it, regarding any opinion which he has formed or anything which he has done or proposed, especially affecting others. We see a fine example of this feature of heavenly wisdom in David, when, though extremely irritated by the insolence and ingratitude of Nabal, he yielded to the pleadings of Abigail, and said: 'Blessed be the Lord God of Israel, which sent thee this day to meet me; and blessed be thy advice; and blessed be thou, which hast kept me this day from coming to shed blood, and from avenging myself with mine own hand.' The wise man never nurses anger; but, even when he has just ground of complaint, longs for kindly relations with his brother. The offender therefore finds the offended not disposed to insist on humbling him in the dust of penitential acknowledgements, but ready to meet him half-way, rejoicing in the prospect of concord.

Another feature of this wisdom is, that it is '*full of mercy and good fruits.*' The wise man pities all who are called on to suffer, and this is the feature of character here indicated: for, as I have had occasion to show in a previous lecture, where mercy is spoken of in Scripture as a Christian duty, it does not refer merely to the forgiveness of those who have wronged us, but more widely to *active compassion* for those who are in trouble and sorrow. He whom God has made wise 'weeps with them that weep,' and 'remembers them that are in bonds, as if bound with them;' and these tears and remembrances are no mere self-indulgent exercise of sentiment, but conjoined with earnest and persevering effort and self-sacrifice for the relief of the suffering. This wisdom is 'full of *good fruits*,' you observe. While this expression naturally suggests a richness of holy and beautiful fruitage of every kind contrasting with the 'every evil work' which in the previous verse is ascribed to 'envying and strife' as their legitimate result, yet the close connection of the 'good fruits' with 'mercy' plainly indicates a special reference to *its* fruits. Christian wisdom exerts herself actively for the relief of sorrow in private, in the sphere which God has given to each individual; and helps onward by every means within her reach enterprises of combined effort for breaking any of the shackles with which sin has bound humanity. In all genuine believers, according to their faith and their opportunities, John Howard and Elizabeth Fry have true fellow-labourers, true brethren and sisters,—nay, He has, who 'went about doing good.'

Heavenly wisdom is '*full* of good fruits:' it abounds with them. Hence, whenever it is present, you cannot fail to find them; or, if you do fail, the wisdom must be miserably stunted and blighted by the influence of worldliness. On the healthy tree every branch is laden with the fruits of mercy. By them will the reckoning be at the judgement. 'Whosoever shall give to drink unto one of these little ones a cup of cold water only in the name of a disciple, verily I say unto you, he shall in no wise lose his reward.' And let not any poor, or unlettered, or uninfluential Christian think that from the narrowness of his sphere he cannot be '*full* of mercy and good fruits.' The Lord's mode of reckoning is not like man's. In casting into the temple treasury the two mites which came out of deep poverty and deep love, the widow was far more 'full of good fruits' than the rich men who cast in many times the sum with no self-sacrifice and little true love. Ever and anon, on a Highland hill-side, one passes a little rocky cup filled with cool crystal water from a deep unfailing spring. The little cup barely affords a draught to the traveller, and yet, because it fails not, what a multitude of weary wayfarers does it refresh

VER. 17.] *Heavenly Wisdom.* 275

and invigorate, generation after generation ; and how green and beautiful the little rill that trickles from it keeps a long stretch of the mountain-side ! So, however little the cup of cold water be which you are able to give in Christ's name, it will refresh many hearts in a lifetime if it be kept ever full, ever ready.

The last two characteristics of heavenly wisdom which James mentions are shown by the form of the words employed in the original, as well as by their meaning, to be very closely allied to each other. The sense of the first of the two words appears to be something more comprehensive than the '*without partiality*' of our version. Freedom from partiality is included, but more. The exact idea seems to be that of freedom from the 'doubting' or 'wavering' of spirit of which the apostle has already again and again, and with much earnestness, pointed out the evil.[1] '*Without wavering and without hypocrisy*,' then, —'steady and sincere,'—these are the two closing features in the description. The man who is really wise has fixed principles. He is no dogmatist, but always open to light ; yet the grand principles which God has distinctly revealed in His word are so firmly believed by him, that with regard to all moral questions and relations these principles are settled,

[1] There is some uncertainty respecting the precise meaning of ἀδιάκριτος. The Authorized Version, having 'without partiality' in the text, has 'without wrangling' in the margin. The Revised has 'without variance' in its text, and in the margin two alternative readings, 'without doubtfulness,' and 'without partiality.' The word occurs here only in N.T., and not at all in LXX. ; and with regard to the present case classical usage is not of much help. The fact that ἀνυπόκριτος is unquestionably equivalent to οὐχ ὑποκρίνεται (middle voice) naturally leads us to regard ἀδιάκριτος, which is so closely associated with it here, as meant similarly to have the middle force : and it is reasonable to suppose that that sense of διακρίνεσθαι which is found elsewhere in the Epistle is to be taken here also. On the meaning of the verb see footnote on p. 42: compare also the exegesis of ii. 4, p. 149. The translation 'without wrangling,' or 'without variance,' seems to be here somewhat tautological, after 'peaceable, gentle.'

unalterable, unassailable *data* for his reasonings. They are pillars on which all the details of his character are built up and rest. The moral life of such a man is therefore simple and stable. A person who does not take the absolutely wise and absolutely harmonious will of God as his rule of judgement and action, must have an utterly discordant character. Selfishness, in some one of its myriad forms, is its basis; yet there are yearnings in the soul now and again after what is noble and beautiful, and good influences of many kinds act upon it. Thus the man's views and aims are a congeries of inconsistencies and contradictions; and accordingly in his conduct there is no steadiness or congruity,—his procedure in cases essentially similar being by what is merely casual swayed in altogether opposite directions, and possibly neither of them the right one. Too many Christians, through want of decision, share largely in this instability, their moral judgements and conduct being to a great extent determined, at least modified or coloured, by circumstances having no real connection with the merits of the case in hand, instead of resting on the everlasting verities. With the truly wise Christian the case is altogether different. One who knows him can never be in doubt what his opinion will be, or his course, in any matter where a moral principle is clearly involved; for the *principle* is what he mainly regards always, and he will not allow himself to be diverted from what he sees to be right by any considerations arising out of non-essential circumstances. His views, feelings, and conduct are consistent. In every department of his life he displays this consistency and stability; and in his dealings with other men, in particular, there is nothing which more decidedly than this constitutes him an epistle of Jesus Christ,—telling the truth to all beholders regarding the ends and energies of the gospel. His standard of value for men is moral excellence, because he knows this to be God's standard; and he applies it according to his light, faithfully, cautiously, with tenderness and charity. Wickedness he hates and condemns, whether it show itself under purple and fine linen, or under rags. He 'honours all men,' but he 'loves the brotherhood' with a peculiarly strong affection, because they are Christ's; and as they are Christ's, and honoured by Him, whether they live in a garret or in a palace, the wise man's love for them also is not dependent on their outward position. Thus, through his being '*stable*' in principle, he is 'without partiality.'

The Christianly wise man is '*without hypocrisy*' too. Bearing ever about with him the thought, 'Thou God seest me' —a joyful thought for one who in God recognises his gracious Father,—he strives in everything to be sincere, to shun all mere stage-play, to speak and act according to his real views and feelings, to have seeming and being in true accordance. As a rule, the world deems some measure of hypocrisy a prudent thing, and indeed essential to success; but 'the wisdom of this world is foolishness with God.'

All moral beauty in God's creatures is a reflection of the ineffable radiance of His holiness. In every feature of that heavenly wisdom which we have been contemplating, we discern the image of Him who is 'of purer eyes than to behold evil,' who loves to be known as the 'God of peace,' whose 'gentleness' makes His servants great, who is 'good, and ready to forgive, and plenteous in mercy unto all them that call upon Him,' and 'who cannot lie.' 'Beholding His glory,' may we be 'changed into His image, from glory to glory, by the Lord the Spirit!'[1]

---

[1] 'The seven qualities which James attributes to the wisdom from above are nothing but the seven colours of the one ray of light of heavenly truth,

The 18th verse corresponds in the description of the true wisdom to the 16th verse in the description of the false. As the false, exhibiting itself in 'envying and strife,' brings in 'confusion and every form of evil,' and in this way proves itself to be from beneath; so the true wisdom, showing itself in 'peace' and peacemaking, brings in 'righteousness,' and thus proves itself to be from above. *'The fruit of righteousness,'* then, you observe, does not mean the fruit which springs from righteousness; but 'the fruit (true wisdom's fruit) which is—consists in—righteousness;' just as we read in Hebrews that 'affliction in those who are rightly exercised thereby bears the peaceable fruit (of) righteousness.' When James says that 'the fruit righteousness is *sown*,' the expression is one implying a lively anticipation of results; as if a man planting acorns were to tell you that he was sowing an oak forest, or a farmer should this spring be said to sow next winter's bread.

The field in which the seed is sown is the human mind and heart, immeasurably the noblest and richest soil to be found on earth. The grandest created thing certainly must be a soul which can grasp the idea of a Creator, and can love that Creator as a Father. But this glorious field has manifestly in great measure gone to waste. It is not merely barren of good, but overspread with all noxious weeds. Made to be an Eden of beauty and fertility, now certainly it is by nature a dreary desolation, full of briers and thorns. We gather in the field the bitter fruit of unrighteousness.

Now the fruit desired by the sowers spoken of in the verse before us is *'righteousness.'* This word is evidently to be taken here in the sense which it very often bears in Scripture, as

which has been revealed and has appeared in Christ Himself. He is therefore supremely entitled to the name, "the Wisdom of God" (Luke xi. 49).'
—OOSTERZEE.

simply another term for 'holiness,' conformity of character to the will of God, and this both as regards our immediate relations to God Himself and our relations to our fellow-men. The fruit desired is that which God made man to bring forth, affections loose from the vanities of earth, and set supremely on God Himself, and on those true, lasting, satisfying riches and glories which are at His right hand,—lives full of holy love and energy and patience. If this fruit is to be obtained, it is evident that special heavenly influences must be brought into action; for the tendency of our fallen nature, left to itself, is to depart ever further from the production of good fruit. All the mere earthly influences of every kind, material, intellectual, and moral, which a creature like man in a state of depravity could conceive of as likely to give him advancement, have in turn or unitedly been brought into play in the history of the world; and the result, so far as regards moral and spiritual elevation, has always been a total failure. Wherever Christ is unknown, the world lies in wickedness, 'gross darkness covering the people;' and in Christian countries, unbelievers who live a blameless outward life, and have elevated views on moral subjects, would be obliged to acknowledge, if they fairly thought the question out, that these are due to the indirect influence on their minds of Christianity.

The seed from heaven from which 'the fruit of righteousness' will spring, is divine truth. The weeds which by nature cover the field of the human heart spring from falsehood, from the belief of what is not true regarding those matters on which it is of the highest importance that we should know and believe what is true. The ultimate source in man, no doubt, of evil affections and unholy living is a perverted will, a desire to please himself rather than to obey God. But, according to our strong natural tendency to believe readily what we want to believe, from the desire to disobey God there arise false views regarding His character and our relations to Him. These false views are the immediate cause of sinful feeling and conduct; for we cannot conceive of a human being in his senses, if possessed of clear and correct ideas respecting God and himself, defying the supreme Lord of the universe. 'Wherefore doth the wicked contemn God?' asks the Psalmist; and the answer is, 'Because he hath said in his heart, Thou wilt not require it,'—he does not know, or does not believe, that God is a God of judgement. 'Wherefore lieth he in wait to catch the poor?' 'Because he hath said in his heart, God hath forgotten, He hideth His face, He will never see it.' Moral evil being thus the fruit of falsehood, what God gives to be the seed of righteousness is truth. Now if the field of our hearts were clear from bad growths—if man were merely in intellectual ignorance, without a depravation of his moral nature—then the communication of truth respecting God's relation to us as Creator and Governor would be sufficient to call forth love, and trust, and devotion. But for fallen creatures more is needed. Nothing but a message of *mercy* will suffice for us—glad tidings of pardoning grace— awakening love through hope and thankfulness. 'The gospel of Christ is the power of God unto salvation to every one that believeth;' 'and righteousness,' likeness of character to God, is the grand element of salvation. No man can truly believe the gospel without experiencing to some extent the 'constraining' power of Christ's love, so as, impelled by the mercies of God, to be no longer 'conformed to this world,' but, in the measure of his faith, 'transformed by the renewing of his mind.'

As thus the seed is from above, 'the glorious gospel of the blessed God,' so He Himself is the Sower. The incarnate

God tells us that this is His work: 'He that soweth the good seed is the Son of man.' He 'began both to do and to teach' when 'He dwelt among us,' and He carries on the work still. But men are His agents; and this, like all His arrangements, is 'very good.' The diffusion of the gospel might have been effected by God's bringing it Himself in some way immediately to the knowledge of each of His chosen ones, without any human intervention; but we are sensible of a peculiarly winning power, a peculiarly exquisite sweetness, in the way which He has chosen. Paul and James and Peter call on us to come and share in experiences which they themselves have already had. 'Come and cast yourselves on Christ,' they cry, 'that ye may find rest to your souls. We, who were labouring and heavy-laden, as ye now are, have cast our burdens on the Lord, and entered thereby into blessed rest—joy unspeakable and full of glory. Come over with us to the happiness of the life eternal.' The word of Christ, as preached to us through the epistles of these holy men, comes thus with the wondrous power of sympathy; and the appeals of ministers or other pleaders with souls have a similar enforcement to the heart.

The labour of the spiritual sower is rich in blessing, and this for himself no less than for the field into which he casts his seed. Divine judgement gave labour as a curse ('In the sweat of thy face shalt thou eat bread'), but into all labour divine mercy has introduced many elements of blessing. In the sphere of nature, it is good for us that we have to sow before we reap. It might have been the divine arrangement that man's food came to him without labour. In the sunny islands of the Pacific the case is almost so; and the savages exult in the spontaneous abundance,—and remain savages, except new wants be brought in which call for labour. We have cause to be grateful, then, that God 'gives bread to the eater,' not immediately, but through 'giving seed to the sower.' In the spiritual sphere also, the man who becomes 'a fellow-labourer with God' feels how great a privilege this is, and blesses Him who has called him to it. He finds that the work refreshes and invigorates the life of his own soul, and that as he sows the seed of truth, which he trusts may bear 'the fruit righteousness' in others, the harvest in his own heart is becoming ever richer.

For the fruit of *civilization and social improvement* many philanthropists are sowing in the world, who care little for Christ; for '*righteousness*,' according to its grand idea, as James has set it forth elsewhere, 'the righteousness *of God*' (i. 20), Christians alone sow, for they alone value it. And *all* Christians are sowers, in so far as they understand the nature and grandeur of their calling. Our appointed work is to be the 'salt of the earth;' to 'shine as lights in the world, holding forth the word of life;' to sow seed in the hearts of men who, learning to love the Saviour, may again in their turn sow.

Our apostle shows us the spirit in which the wise sower of the heavenly seed labours. He does his work '*in peace.*' 'The wrath of man worketh not the righteousness of God,' for it misrepresents entirely the gospel of love and good-will; and thus, instead of furthering the progress of Christ's kingdom, puts obstacles in its way. Would the messenger who bears a king's pardon to vanquished rebels, or an assurance of forgiveness from a father to a prodigal son, be likely to win confidence for his tidings in the suspicious, alienated hearts of his hearers, by introducing himself with frowns and angry reproaches? Love is the true spirit of a herald of the God of love. 'He is kind unto the unthankful and to the evil; be ye therefore merciful, as your Father also is merciful.' Of the great Messenger of God it was foretold by Isaiah, 'He shall not strive nor cry, neither shall any man hear His voice in the streets; a bruised reed shall He not break, and smoking flax shall He not quench; and in His name'—the name of such a Saviour as this—'shall the Gentiles trust.' It may at times be needful, in love, to proclaim 'the terror of the Lord:' Christ did it, and His apostles; but this must always manifestly be *in love*, and by way of exception. The *rule* for those who would be successful sowers must certainly be, 'gracious words' from a gracious soul.

The work of the spiritual sowing James describes as '*making peace*,'—striving by consistent example, kindly counsel, help of every kind, to promote true peace and love in all upon whom in any way we can bring influence to bear. Now, the only trustworthy basis of peace is the gospel of Jesus Christ, accepted by faith. All therefore who aim wisely at the increase of peace, strive to gain their end by leading men to the knowledge of Christ, and to ever deeper impressions of the sweetness and beauty of His truth. From the seed of the 'gospel of peace,' sown 'in peace,' the 'fruit of righteousness' will spring.

XX.

ORIGIN OF STRIFES.

'From whence come wars and fightings among you? come they not hence, even of your lusts that war in your members? 2 Ye lust, and have not: ye kill, and desire to have, and cannot obtain: ye fight and war, yet ye have not, because ye ask not. 3 Ye ask, and receive not, because ye ask amiss, that ye may consume it upon your lusts.'—JAMES iv. 1–3.

EVERY reader must feel the power of the apostle's sudden transition from the beautiful picture of the Christian life as it should be, 'sowing in peace the fruit of righteousness,' to the sketch of the church as it actually was in many places, a community full of turbulence, disgraced by 'wars and fightings.' The scene exhibited to us by the apostle's words is so dark, that at first doubt naturally rises whether his reference is to Christians, and not rather to unbelieving Jews. But the context proves that, according to all natural interpretation, we must hold professing Christians to be spoken of. What is described here is but a fuller development of that wicked spirit described in the 10th verse of the preceding chapter, which out of the same mouth sent forth cursing as well as blessing; and there the persons guilty of this sin are expressly named 'brethren.' In the paragraph which is introduced by the verses now before us, too, those addressed are designated in the 4th verse as spiritually 'adulterous,' and in the 8th as 'double-minded,'—terms implying that these persons professed to love God, and to be wedded to Him. In the 11th verse, again, we have the name 'brethren' employed, without the slightest indication that those so addressed are different from the persons reproved and pleaded with in the earlier paragraph.

We are apt to misconceive considerably the character of the primitive church, through a vague impression that the exquisite outflow of Christian love at Jerusalem, of which the early chapters of Acts tell us, lasted all through the first ages, and had its counterpart in every congregation. A study of the Epistles is fitted to give us a different idea. Much holy beauty there was, doubtless; but also not a little defect and defilement. 'I fear,' says Paul to the Corinthians, 'lest, when I come, I shall not find you such as I would, and that I shall be found unto you such as ye would not; lest there be debates, envyings, wraths, strifes, backbitings, whisperings, swellings, tumults; and lest, when I come again, my God will humble me among you, and that I shall bewail many which have sinned already, and have not repented of the uncleanness, and fornication, and lasciviousness, which they have committed.' Christians, in truth, are always in much hazard of falling back to some extent into those sins which more especially beset them before conversion; and this particularly when they are surrounded by persons who indulge in these sins. To missionaries, labouring either among the heathen or among those in Christian lands who are 'ignorant and out of the way,' this tendency in their converts causes great and constant anxiety, and necessitates unceasing watchfulness over them. For an Asiatic, for example, living among people who scarcely feel at all that truth is morally preferable to falsehood, it is extremely difficult, even when he is brought under the power of the gospel, to become thoroughly truthful and straightforward, — the tendency to revert to the old type frequently asserting its power. Now the Jews as a race were very prone to violent language, as indeed has been the case with all the races of south-western Asia in all ages; and during the half-century preceding the destruction of Jerusalem, particularly the latter part of it, there was great political excitement and turbulence among them. The atmosphere in which James's readers lived, therefore, was highly charged with the spirit of strife. Thus one can easily believe that in many of the Christian congregations of the 'Dispersion' there were painful dissensions between individuals, or between factions, occasionally leading to outbreaks of passion of the grossest kind. The history of the church in all times and countries can show too many illustrations of the working of the same evil tendencies, not unfrequently bringing about actual wars. For a century and a half after the beginning of the Reformation, almost every war in Europe, whether civil or international, was partly due, and many were due almost solely, to differences of view regarding religion.

Our apostle's words assume the existence of '*wars and fightings*' among his readers, and that in some instances they were fierce enough to be very notorious. It is possible, indeed probable, considering how quick the Western Asiatics have been in every age to follow up violence of language with violence of hand, that James had knowledge of cases in which there had been actual physical struggles; but, whilst including these, his words are obviously meant as a startling and impressive description of all kinds of dissension. Similarly, Paul enjoins upon Timothy (2 Tim. ii. 23) to 'avoid foolish and unlearned questions, knowing that they do gender *strifes*' (the same word which is rendered in the verse before us by 'fightings'). By '*wars*' the apostle means plainly the general condition of hostility, and by '*fightings*' the particular outbreaks of hostile feeling. The immediate causes of the quarrels were in all likelihood various. Some, perhaps, sprang from the virulence of rival teachers, assailing each other with bitterness like that exhibited to Paul by his Judaizing opponents; others from the keen partisanship of the followers of different teachers, who might themselves be friends, as at Corinth one said, 'I am of Paul,' and another, 'I am of Apollos.' But what is said in the 2nd and 3rd verses appears to show that James had mainly in his mind disputes connected with efforts for worldly advancement. It seems not unlikely, when we remember the low and carnal conceptions of the nature of the Messianic kingdom which had taken possession of the Jews universally, that something of this evil leaven wrought still even among the converts to Christianity. Thus, here and there, probably, among the poorer members of the churches, there was discontent with their position, as being unsuitable for the friends of Messiah the Prince, and consequent murmuring both against God and against their wealthier brethren. In many ways, indeed, in all the Christian communities, whether Jewish or Gentile, jealousies might easily arise between the rich and the poor,—as they do still.

'Wars and fightings,' jealousies and animosities, were not confined to the primitive church. They are painfully familiar to us also. Men and women who on the Sabbath have sat side by side at the Lord's table, and drunk of the common cup of love, will scowl at and calumniate and thwart each other all the week. And the feeling between congregations or denominations, which are but different companies or brigades in the army of the Captain of salvation, is not unfrequently such as to remind one of the Midianites in the night of Gideon's victory, when 'every man's sword was turned against his fellow, throughout all the host.'

'*Whence,*' then, are these unseemly strifes? the apostle asks. He would have his readers consider the radical principles of their procedure. Men often slide or drift imperceptibly into positions which are productive of much harm to themselves and others. It is wise, therefore, to stop and turn aside for a little from the excitements and distractions of our social life, and ask ourselves *whence* and *whither* are our moral movements.

James answers the question himself. Had he asked the quarrelling Christians, he would have been told, no doubt, that their being involved in strife was due to 'circumstances,' to 'provocations,' to 'the need of asserting their rights.' The apostle tears off the veil of plausibilities, and shows them, as the real originators of the dissensions, the '*lusts*' of their depraved hearts, especially greed of wealth, and greed of prominence and influence. The apostles have had many successors in the church, so far as regards their discreditable striving with each other, in the early stages of their Christian life, which of them should be the greatest. The race of Diotrephes, who troubled the churches of Asia because he 'loved to have the pre-eminence,' is by no means extinct. Ambition, avarice, and sister lusts, are the true root of all wars—of all disputes which become envenomed. The world without presents the temptation; but the power of the temptation is from within, from the deceitfulness and wickedness of the heart. 'Let no man say, when he is tempted, I am tempted of God; for God cannot be tempted with evil, neither tempteth He any man. But every man is tempted when he is drawn away of his own lust and enticed. Then, when lust hath conceived, it bringeth forth sin.'

These lusts are '*in the members*'—standing in various ways in close connection with the animal nature. Hence Paul says, 'Let not sin reign in your mortal body, that ye should obey it in the lusts thereof; neither yield ye your members as instruments of unrighteousness unto sin; but yield yourselves unto God, as those that are alive from the dead, and your members as instruments of righteousness unto God.' 'In the members,' too, 'the lusts *war*,' or 'campaign.' In all men by nature there is struggle,—the perverse will striving with the conscience, the 'fleshly lusts' quelling spiritual aspirations and yearnings, and thus in the fullest sense '*warring* against the soul.' The lusts 'war' among themselves also. Everywhere, and in every respect, Satan proves himself the author, not of peace, but of confusion; and thus we often see contradictory lusts, such as covetousness and prodigality, co-existing in a man, and leading to strange confusions of life. In a Christian soul the lusts 'war' with the impulses of the new life. 'The old man, which is corrupt according to the deceitful lusts,' contends with 'the new man, which after God is created in righteousness and true holiness.' 'I delight in the law of God after the inward man, but I see another law in my members, *warring* against the law of my mind.' The thought exhibited by the apostle here, however, seems to have reference, not to the war which is waged in the individual soul, but to a conflict of the desires or lusts of different persons—those lusts which 'campaign' in the animal nature of each. The lusts of these different persons, or companies of persons, are directed towards the same object, one particular position of dignity and influence, perhaps, or the acquisition of wealth in one particular way. Hence comes collision. The 'campaigning' of the lusts with a view to a common object naturally leads to outward opposition,—just as, if two kings both covet a hitherto independent territory which lies between their dominions, and simultaneously lead their armies into it to take possession, the matter will have to be decided by a battle.

In the 2nd verse the answer to the question, 'Whence come the wars and fightings?' is given more fully, in a way very similar to that in which the apostle has, in the 14th and 15th verses of the 1st chapter, described the genesis of sin and of death. The general answer already given is, 'From your lusts;' now, in detail, '*Ye lust, and have not: ye kill, and desire to have, and cannot obtain: ye fight and war.*'

The first step is longing, without satisfaction: '*Ye lust, and have not.*' Desire for some particular worldly enjoyment enters men's hearts,—and they find that possession does not immediately come with the desire. What, then, naturally follows, unless through faith the spirit of love and true wisdom reign in the soul? '*Ye kill, and desire to have, and cannot obtain.*' The word rendered '*desire to have,*' whilst it has sometimes the meaning of 'to wish eagerly for,' and thus is rightly translated, for example, by 'covet earnestly' in 'covet earnestly the best gifts' (1 Cor. xii. 31), yet in other places signifies the base passion of envy, as when we are told that 'charity envieth not' (1 Cor. xiii. 4). The course of thought in the verse before us shows clearly that the word is employed here in its bad sense, for otherwise there would be no advance at all from the feeling spoken of in the first stage, 'Ye lust.' The sense, then, is, 'Ye kill, and *envy*, and cannot obtain.'

The '*kill*' startles every reader,—as no doubt it was intended to do. When we bear in mind the Jewish temperament, and the exciting circumstances in which, as already mentioned, the nation was placed at this time,—and when we remember how often in the history of the church the hands of professed followers of Christ have been stained with bloodshed, and this indeed not seldom in the name of Christ's sacred cause,—it will be felt by us as not at all improbable that, in some of those quarrels to which the apostle refers, actual slaughter of opponents had been committed in the heat of passion. On such a supposition, his word '*kill*' would come home to his readers with more naturalness and force than otherwise. But, considering the nature of Christianity, and the little inducement in those early days for other than true believers to connect themselves with the church, it is utterly inconceivable that 'killing' in the literal sense was anything but altogether exceptional, or that the apostle means to charge his readers generally with such a crime. A glance at his words, indeed, shows that actual murder was certainly not mainly, if at all, in his mind; for if it had been, he could never have followed up such a charge with 'ye envy,' which would in this case be a thought immeasurably less impressive, and thus constitute a feeble anti-climax. By '*kill*' he means, no doubt, cherishing that deep hatred of which, under the temptation of opportunity, literal murder is the natural manifestation, and which is therefore murder in heart. 'Whosoever hateth his brother is a *murderer*,' says the Apostle John; and the same is the teaching of the Lord Himself in the Sermon on the Mount: 'Ye have heard that it was said by them of old time, Thou shalt not kill, and whosoever shall kill shall be in danger of the judgement; but I say unto you, that whosoever is angry with his brother without a cause, shall be in danger of the judgement.' Every attentive reader of this Epistle observes the frequency with which it echoes the thoughts and the language of that great Sermon,—a discourse that had evidently made the deepest impression on James's mind. The case before us is one among the many illustrations of this. The use of the word 'kill,' as I have said, certainly startles, and was meant to startle. The apostle desired to lead men who were at ease in the indulgence of sins of the heart, and who perhaps threw up their hands in horror when they heard of any literal murder, to bethink themselves in what position they really stood before the eye of God. We see throughout the whole Epistle his love of terse, telling language; and in the immediate context, with its 'wars and fightings,' and its 'ye adulteresses,' this is very specially exemplified. Thus the 'kill (in heart)' is introduced here by no means unnaturally, and has its meaning lighted up to an attentive reader by its surroundings.

From unsatisfied lust, then, sprang *murderous hatred and envy*. The two do not form a climax, but are co-ordinate. Each illustrates the other, and the general state of heart—a state of intense longing and intense bitterness.

But no intensity of feeling can ensure satisfaction; and so we find it here: '*and cannot obtain.*' In His providence, God in righteous anger withholds the coveted object; or even if it be received, the anticipated enjoyment is wanting. For, in truth, intense feeling of the kinds here described not merely cannot ensure satisfaction, but from its nature ensures on any issue dissatisfaction. The lusts, like 'the daughters of the horse-leech,' still cry, 'Give, give;' for envy 'enlargeth her desire as hell, and is as death, and cannot be satisfied.'

We come now to the last stage in the genesis of the 'wars and fightings.' The first was 'lust,' conjoined with want; the second, hate and envy, still conjoined with want. From this immediately, and by most manifest sequence, come 'wars and fightings.' Thus the question 'whence?' is fully answered: '*Ye lust—ye hate murderously and envy—ye fight and war,*'—this is in brief the natural history of all envenomed dissension.

In the text of this passage, as found in all the oldest manuscripts, there is no particle connecting the words that follow with those which we have just been considering. The '*yet*' of our translators must therefore be omitted, and a new sentence begun with 'Ye have not.' The beauty of the structure of the passage now shows itself. Having closed the series of statements exhibiting the real origin and growth of strife, James goes back to that sense of *want* which he had spoken of as an active element in all the stages, and sets forth clearly the cause of the want, and the means of obtaining all needed supplies. This exposition consists of two members, which do not, however, as in the case of the previous series, form a gradation, but stand side by side as alternative explanations, applicable to different persons, or to the same person under different circumstances : ' *Ye have not, because ye ask not : ye ask, and receive not, because ye ask amiss, that ye may consume it upon your lusts.*'

When James says, ' *Ye have not, because ye ask not,*' we can hardly fail to recognise an allusion to the teaching of Christ in the Sermon on the Mount. He seems to appeal to his readers to 'remember the words of the Lord Jesus, how He said, Ask, and it shall be given you ; for every one that asketh receiveth.' We cannot suppose that the apostle, by his '*ye ask not*' here, means to charge them with being utterly prayerless, for this would be to declare all of whom he speaks to be mere empty pretenders to Christianity,—not misguided Christians simply, but utter hypocrites or self-deceivers. The force of his words seems to be limited by the connection in which they occur to an assertion that, *in regard to their worldly circumstances and wants*, many of his readers did not ask God ; otherwise that discontent and restlessness which generated the dissensions he has been speaking of would have been removed : 'for there is no want to them that fear Him.' Many Christians—all Christians probably to some extent—shrink from prayer respecting outward necessities. Our spiritual wants we carry to the throne of grace; but in the cares of this world, in the disappointment of cherished hopes, the thwarting of carefully devised plans, the anxieties of narrow income, we too frequently nurse our depression, instead of laying the matter before God. Now, can we trust Him with our eternal welfare, and not with the interests of earth? Can we depend upon Him for the everlasting life, and not for the care of the life here? 'Consider the lilies of the field, how they grow; they toil not, neither do they spin: and yet I say unto you, that even Solomon, in all his glory, was not arrayed like one of these. Wherefore, if God so clothe the grass of the field, which to-day is, and to-morrow is cast into the oven, shall He not much more clothe you, O ye of little faith?' 'Our Father which art in heaven, give us this day our daily bread.' Look not for supernatural manifestations in answer to prayer—for manna or quails, for visible angelic visitors or obvious and direct inspirations; but certainly we have every ground to believe that, in regard to the outward as well as the inner life, 'the fervent prayer of a righteous man availeth much,' and will bring down showers of blessing, in views cleared, external obstacles removed, and wishes accomplished, so far as it shall serve for God's glory and the true good of the petitioner. Whatever interests God's people, interests Him. Defective apprehension of this truth was the cause of the want felt by James's readers. Had they prayed, they would have received what they desired, if it was good for them; and certainly the feeling of want and discontent would have been removed, for the heart would have had rest in God's Fatherly love.

But some might say, 'We *have* asked God, and still we are in want.' To these the apostle replies that the solution of this difficulty is not far to seek. Their supplications had lacked one essential element of true prayer—desire to consecrate all

God's gifts to His glory : '*Ye ask, and receive not, because ye ask amiss*' (or 'wickedly'), '*that ye may consume it upon your lusts.*' It is a distinctive characteristic of the true Christian, that in his thoughts and feelings he subordinates the temporal to the spiritual. The ideal of the Christian life is to be able to say with full truthfulness, 'For me to live is Christ,'—to have always such a constant and influential sense of the truth that in the manifestation of God's glory is summed up all good for His creatures, as leads us in the discharge of even the commonest duties of life, in 'eating and drinking, and whatsoever we do,' to 'do all to the glory of God.' A Christian prayer, then, in regard to worldly things, is one which comes from a heart prepared to dedicate to God what is asked from God,— a prayer in which entreaty that our heavenly Father will give us grace to do this with His gift, is associated with the supplication for the gift. Such prayer is answered. When we 'seek *first* the kingdom of God and His righteousness, all these things shall be added unto us.' But where a petition is sent up with no thought of the kingdom of God, no longing for the advancement of His glory through the increase of the holiness and happiness of our fellow-men, but simply with a view to self-gratification, to the 'consuming' of what we ask 'upon our lusts ;' such a petition will obtain no boon. 'If I regard iniquity in my heart, the Lord will not hear me.' Or the gift craved may be bestowed, but no blessing with it,—given in judgement, not in mercy ; as, when Israel 'lusted exceedingly in the wilderness, and tempted God, He *gave them their request, but sent leanness into their soul.*'

XXI.

WORLDLINESS ENMITY TO GOD.

'Ye adulterers and adulteresses, know ye not that the friendship of the world is enmity with God? Whosoever therefore will be a friend of the world, is the enemy of God. 5 Do ye think that the Scripture saith in vain, The spirit that dwelleth in us lusteth to envy? 6 But He giveth more grace: wherefore He saith, God resisteth the proud, but giveth grace unto the humble.'—JAMES iv. 4–6.

THE statements and appeals contained in these verses follow up the remarks in the verses immediately preceding. By '*the world*' here James means obviously, according to a very frequent use of the word in the language of Jesus and the apostles, man and his institutions and surroundings considered as penetrated and controlled by malignant moral influences. God made the world 'very good,' with beauty and harmony everywhere. All things around contributed to man's rational happiness, ever sending up his thoughts and his affections in admiration and love to the great Creator; so that he, in the sublimity of reason and free-will the lord of the creatures, led the chorus of the world's praise. But sin, alluring his heart from his heavenly Father, brought in jarring and discord. The devil became 'the prince of this world,' and what God had made order he made chaos. The world was now enveloped in a distorting and misleading atmosphere of falsehood. All things presented themselves to man's mind and heart in untrue dimensions and relations; and instead of drawing him towards God, and leading him into 'the land of uprightness,' guided him further away into the 'far country' of wickedness and death. Thus now God, and the world which He created, are morally in opposition to each other.

Our apostle, then, makes a statement concerning '*the friendship of* (or 'with') *the world*,' as thus understood. Experience shows that there is considerable possibility of mistake as to what is meant by this 'friendship.' One form of error, for example, is what may be called the monkish. Seeing that we reckon those to be friendly whom we often see by choice in each other's company, the monk concludes that, if not the only, at least the highest, form of a life which aims to escape 'friendship with the world,' is one of retirement, as far as possible, from intercourse with it—one which shuns all association with the accursed thing. This has 'a show of wisdom;' and beyond doubt, here and there, perhaps in many places, the flower of true piety has bloomed very beautifully in the garden of a monastery. Yet this type of religious life is essentially morbid. It might almost be described as baptized selfishness, for it proceeds on the view that a man's religion is to be a self-contained thing, having no ends or influences beyond his own personal growth in spirituality: whilst the constant teaching of Scripture is, that we are to 'let our light shine before men, that they, seeing our good works, may glorify our Father which is in heaven,' and that we are to 'hold forth the word of life,' as well as hold it fast. This can be done, in all ordinary circumstances, only by a life in the world, but under the government of a faith which plainly soars above the world. The great High Priest's supplication for His people was, 'I pray not that Thou shouldest take them out of the world, but that Thou shouldest keep them from the evil.' The tendency of monkery is to utter uselessness; and naturally the energies of the monks themselves grow dull, and all the good which may be in them rusts from want of exercise. There have been monks in the famous monastery at the foot of Mount Sinai for some fourteen hundred years, and not the slightest approach to missionary effort among the darkened tribes around seems ever to have been put forth. Nay, the descendants of some hundreds of professed Christians, who in the early ages were given to be servants of the monks, have been so neglected religiously as to lapse into Mohammedanism; whilst the monks themselves are described by travellers as having countenances deeply marked with melancholy, and singularly destitute of intellectual expression. This is the legitimate working of the system, for the want of a free natural life amidst their fellow-creatures has a most debasing and narrowing influence. Now, brethren, although we from our training and circumstances have no temptation to become monks, yet we must remember that this is but the extreme form of a tendency which under a diseased state of feeling may obtain some dominion over us,—the tendency to shrink from a free and energetic outward life, and to brood in indolent solitude on our spiritual condition. Our Master ever and anon retired to the wilderness and to lonely mountainsides, to commune with His Father, and receive strength for labour; but His life was pre-eminently one spent in the world, in constant and close contact with men. 'Friendship with the world,' then, does not mean simple presence in the midst of the activities of the world, and taking part in its work.

Another error on this subject, by way of *defect*, to which in our time professing Christians are much more liable than that we have now been speaking of, is the belief that 'friendship with the world,' or conformity to the world, is shown *only* in attending balls, card-parties, theatres, and the like; so that among those who shun these scenes there is necessarily nothing of what the apostle here condemns. Now, no thoughtful Christian, as it seems to me, can doubt for a moment that there is some hazard to spiritual life, and to influence for good, in even occasional visits to scenes of mere frivolous excitement and amusement, and that the habitual or frequent resort to them shows concentrated and deplorable worldliness,—involving, as such conduct does, much waste of precious time, an outlay of money wholly inconsistent with adherence to the Scripture principle of stewardship for God, and much social intercourse of a spiritually debasing kind. But 'friendship for the world' may exist, and even rule, apart from any indulgences like these, and in connection with a most quiet and decorous life; for worldliness is the *spirit* of a life, not its outward form, and may be in full activity as the spirit, where the body of the life has been moulded by the pressure of education and circumstances into a form which one might expect to find inhabited by a spirit of heavenly-mindedness.

The question then, you observe, is strictly one with regard to the state of the *affections*. Friendship implies substantial accordance of opinion and of aims. 'Two cannot walk together'—that is, be intimate friends—'except they be agreed' in their views on all matters which they deem of primary importance. Now the unregenerate world plainly considers that the great object of each man's life should be to aggrandize, and glorify, and enjoy himself, and that, thinking as little of God and of a future life as he can, he should seek his portion on the earth. The riches which it believes in and seeks are those which 'perish with the using;' the honour, that 'which comes from men, and not from God only.' With innumerable varieties in detail, these are the great and unvarying general articles of the world's creed,—a creed held, alas, there is every reason to fear, by multitudes who would be greatly astonished, and think themselves greatly wronged, if they were told that they held it, and which many will never see to be theirs until they read their hearts by the light shining around the Judge as He seats Himself on the throne. Now, where there is sympathy with this creed of the world, and with the world's desires, there, in the measure of the sympathy, is an approach to that 'friendship with the world' of which our apostle speaks, and under the power of which he intimates that many of his readers—if one might judge from their 'wars and fightings' for earthly advantages—had fallen, or were in imminent danger of falling. Where this sympathy is so strong that there is more love for the world and its pursuits than for God and His cause, there is the 'friendship' in fulness.

This 'friendship,' James says, 'is *enmity with God.*' Observe the strength of the expression. Occasionally in the world we see a man having a friendship of a kind with both of two parties who are opposed to each other; and often the friend of one who is hostile to another may remain in a relation at least of indifference to that other. But in the case before us nothing of this sort is possible. '*Enmity*' is merely a short form of 'enemy-ty,' the state of an enemy. Thus we have the matter clearly set before us: 'The friendship of the world is the condition of an enemy to God.' There is a direct opposition between the views, desires, aims, of the world and those of God; and from the relation in which we stand to Him there can be no neutrality of position or feeling. If we are the friends of the world, then we are God's enemies; for, through the simple fact that we are His moral creatures, we are under obligation to be His loving servants, and we 'cannot serve God and mammon.' 'The carnal mind'—the spirit of the world—'is enmity against God; for' (here we have the sum of the whole matter) 'it is not subject to the law of God, neither indeed can be.'

For professing Christians to have 'friendship with the world' involves, James intimates, a peculiar criminality. They are '*adulterers and adulteresses*,' or, according to the best authenticated reading, simply '*adulteresses.*' A little consideration of the scope of the passage shows that this name is not intended to be taken literally, as charging the apostle's readers with violation of the marriage-bond. To such a charge there is not the slightest allusion anywhere in the verses, and what follows equally with what precedes has plainly reference to worldliness of spirit and life. But James speaks according to that very common Old Testament figure, familiar to all his Jewish readers, in which God, with infinite condescension and grace, represents Himself as the Husband of Israel,—who was, alas, an unfaithful spouse. Similarly, the Lord Jesus spoke of the Jewish church of His time as 'a wicked and *adulterous* generation.' In James's individualizing word, '*adulteresses*,' there is something very startling and rousing. When, according to the ordinary form of the image, a *church* is accused of being 'adulterous,' each member is apt to hide himself in the crowd, and shake off the thought of personal guilt. But our apostle presses the matter home to every conscience, reminding his readers that each professing Christian soul which, yielding to the lust of the eyes, or the lust of the flesh, or the pride of life, turns aside to love the world more than God, is unfaithful to its sacred vows, and has the sin, the debasement, of adultery. The use of the simple '*adulteresses*' for 'adulterous souls'—of course of men as well as of women, the feminine form being employed merely to suit the proprieties of the image—is strange, but for that very reason pointed, stinging, and memorable. Every reader feels the force and liveliness with which the figure employed here depicts the enormity of the sin of worldly professors of Christianity, in that they cast such flagrant dishonour on Him whom they have called their 'Beloved,' and to whom they have publicly united themselves by the closest and tenderest bonds. The repentance of such should be like the horror and loathing with which a wife, who has been disloyal to a true and loving husband, regards herself, if God's grace bring her back to a sound mind.

The second part of this verse contains a practical application of the general principle enunciated in the first: ' *Whosoever therefore will be a friend of the world, is the enemy of God.*' This is, of course, involved in the previous general statement ; yet we feel it to be a weighty addition, sending the truth home to the conscience, calling on us to look it fairly in the face, and study its bearing on ourselves. 'If such be the general principle,' the apostle says, 'then stop, each of you, and think what your religious position is.' The word '*will*' in this sentence has the force of 'is minded,' and by it James suggests to us the duty of honestly and unflinchingly considering what is the disposition of heart which underlies and reveals itself through our conduct. No professing Christian, perhaps, would say definitely to his own soul, 'I am minded to be a friend of the wicked world ;' but many allow themselves to drift into a mode of life which shows that such a spirit has been gaining strength. The 'will' which thus makes itself known, James would have men candidly contemplate, and bethink themselves what is its import, and what will come of it. One who 'will be a friend of the world' thereby '*constitutes himself* (for this is the exact force of the word rendered in our version '*is*') *an enemy of God.*' If we balance profit and loss, then, what do we find? Without doubt, the 'friendship of this world' has attractions, strong attractions; but of necessity, because they are of 'this world,' death breaks them off utterly; and even here the heart of immortal man is not fully satisfied with them. Eating the world's bread, the soul still hungers; drinking from the world's fountain, the soul still thirsts; warming herself by the world's fire, the soul still shudders with cold. And to 'constitute oneself an enemy of God' is to remain in spiritual death, and grow more meet daily for eternal death,—to have the Almighty King of the universe as our Foe through life, our Foe at the judgement-seat, our Foe for ever,—and to choose this relation to Him, whilst in Christ He is pleading with us in tones of the tenderest love and pity to come to Him and be His 'friends,' to sit down at His table as His 'sons and daughters,' to 'cast our burdens upon Him,' and 'find rest to our souls.'

The 5th verse and the first clause of the 6th are hard of interpretation, and indeed are classed by some with the most difficult passages of the New Testament. The causes of the difficulty are these,—that no such passage as James seems to quote is found in Scripture,—that the words of the apparent quotation may, with more or less naturalness, be very variously understood,—and that, on perhaps any view of their meaning, the force of the word '*more*' in the 6th verse is not clear.

Various passages have been suggested as possibly referred to in a general way by the apostle, such as, 'The imagination of man's heart is evil from his youth,' or, 'The soul of the wicked desireth evil;' but there is none so similar in sentiment and expression to the statement here made as to be regarded as the original from which James quoted. Some commentators rid themselves of the difficulty connected with the quotation, by making 'God resisteth the proud, but giveth grace unto the humble,' the only passage cited,—putting all the words between 'the Scripture saith' and these into a parenthesis. The quotation is suitable enough, but the parenthesis is utterly unnatural; and this view will not bear examination.

On the supposition that the apostle merely intends a general reference to a truth taught in Scripture, there are various views of the meaning. Before we look at these, however, it is proper to notice that the '*dwelleth*' of our translation is a free rendering of the original word,—the exact meaning being 'settled,' 'came to dwell.' Our translators evidently supposed the '*spirit*' spoken of to be the *natural human spirit*, the depraved state of feeling which settled in man at the fall. In this case the sense is, 'Do you think' (or rather, rendering a particle which our translators, taking it as merely indicating a question, have passed over, '*or* do you think') 'that the Scripture has no meaning when it tells us—as it does everywhere, for this is involved in all its teaching regarding our duties to our fellowmen—that desires which take the direction of envy are from our own depraved nature, not from God, and hence belong to His enemies, not His friends?' Against this view lie the strangeness of the expression, 'the spirit that settled in us,' for our carnal nature, and the fact that no reason is apparent why such a peculiar paraphrase was chosen, instead of the simple designation 'our depravity.' The idea that *Satan* is the 'spirit' here spoken of answers some of the requirements of the context well. The line of thought would thus be: 'If ye be worldly-minded, ye are enemies of God; for envy, which belongs essentially to worldly-mindedness, is always said in the divine word to come from the great enemy of God, the devil; but God gives grace greater (more powerful) than Satan's impulses to envy.' And thus we are very naturally led on to 'Resist the devil, and he will flee from you.' But the same objection lies against this view as against the preceding—that the mode of expression is not natural; and besides—an argument which has some force against the preceding view, but much more against this—the antithesis would, according to the laws of the original language, require an *expressed* subject to 'giveth grace;' whilst, as a matter of fact, the subject is not expressed. Moreover, whilst Scripture distinctly teaches the universal depravity of man, yet that Satan 'dwells' in all men by nature is not a scriptural representation. Paul, in Romans, says that '*sin* dwelleth in us' (vii. 20); and the Lord, in the epistle to the angel of the church in Pergamos, speaks of that city as a place 'where Satan's seat is,' and 'where Satan dwelleth' (Rev. ii. 13). But such language as that which is employed by the Evangelist John regarding Judas — 'After the sop, Satan entered into him'—appears to imply that the *indwelling* of the devil belongs to those who have *completely* given themselves up to iniquity.

We seem shut up to the conclusion that in the passage before us the apostle refers to the *Divine Spirit.* The glorious doctrine that the Holy Ghost 'dwells' in Christ's people is one of the commonplaces of our faith. 'Dwell' is the word usually employed in the writings of the apostles to express this most wondrous privilege,[1] and was no doubt also the ordinary term used in their oral teaching. In all ages of the church, then, the thought most readily conveyed to the minds of well-instructed Christians by the words, 'the spirit that came to dwell in us,' taken by themselves, would unquestionably be 'the Spirit of God.' This view of the meaning is supported by a various reading of the original text, found in several of the oldest manuscripts, and accepted by most of the modern critical editors,—a reading differing from the

[1] See Rom. viii. 9, 11; 1 Cor. iii. 16; 2 Tim. i. 14. Compare also 2 Cor. vi. 16; Eph. iii. 17; John xiv. 17; 1 John iv. 12.

received text only by a single letter, but giving for 'dwell' a transitive sense—'made to dwell:' thus, 'the spirit that (God) made to dwell in us,' or 'settled in us.' You will see, too, that this view exactly suits the 'he' of the first clause of the 6th verse, because the Holy Spirit is Himself the God who 'giveth grace;' and therefore, there being no antithesis, but a reference to the same Divine Agent, an *expressed* subject is not needed. This at least, then, I think, must be held as certain regarding the meaning of the verse, that by the words, 'the spirit that came to dwell' (or 'that He caused to dwell') 'in us,' the apostle, addressing professing Christians, and assuming that they were what they professed to be, designates the Holy Ghost, who at their conversion had been given by God to dwell in them.

We must now look at the question what, according to the apostle, the 'Scripture saith' regarding the Holy Ghost in Christ's people. By some this has been thought to be that He 'desireth or longeth *against envy*.' The original words might in certain circumstances have this meaning; but as they stand here it is so unnatural, that nothing but a positive impossibility of obtaining a satisfactory sense from the passage in any other way would justify our taking it. An idea favoured by some prominent modern expositors is that the apostle, having in his mind the thoughts of the previous verse—and particularly that Old Testament figure to which he had there alluded by the word 'adulteresses,' according to which the tie between God and His covenant people is exhibited as a marriage relation,—refers in the words before us to the frequent Old Testament declaration that God is a '*jealous*' God. The words rendered '*to envy*' may, as our translators intimate on the margin, mean 'enviously;' and adopting this, the force of the verse is given thus: 'God, whose closeness of relation to us Christians is shown by His dwelling in us through His Spirit, *enviously*—that is, *jealously—desireth us for His own.*' This is ingenious and fascinating, and accords well with at least the preceding context. But I am convinced that the statement is forced out of the words of the verse, rather than legitimately drawn. You will notice that the last words in the rendering just given are an arbitrary supplement; and you cannot but feel how unnatural, how unlike James's simple, perspicuous style, it is to say, 'the Spirit jealously desireth,' if he meant 'the Spirit jealously desireth us for His own.' But a yet greater objection lies against the application of the phrase 'enviously.' One cannot but think, that if the intention of the apostle had been to refer his readers to the Old Testament teaching that God is a 'jealous' God, he would have used the word employed in the Greek version of the Old Testament, which was familiar to all the Jews of 'the Dispersion' from their earliest years. Now the word used by James is *never*, either in Scripture, or, so far as I am aware, anywhere else, employed in a good sense. It refers to *envy*, and no other feeling; and, applied to any sentiment of the mind of God, would certainly have sounded as repulsively and untruthfully to James's readers as 'envy' would to our ears.[1] According to a somewhat interesting variation of that view of the meaning which supposes James to allude to the marriage between God and His covenant people, the sense is given thus: 'God jealously desireth for Himself the (human) spirit which He gave to dwell in us.' This occupies ground already traversed by us; and thus it will be plain that, in addition to the argument against it derived from its taking 'enviously' as equivalent to 'jealously' (an argument in itself, to my mind,

[1] This holds, it seems to me, even if we give the words πρὸς φθόνον the force not of *invidiose* but of *usque ad invidiam*.

altogether insuperable), it lies also under the serious objection, that the familiar, well-understood phrase, 'the spirit that He gave to dwell in us,' receives another meaning than the Holy Spirit.

On the whole, it seems to me that, with Calvin and many other expositors, we must divide the verse into two distinct questions: 'Do you think that the Scripture saith it in vain? Doth the Spirit who came to dwell in us' (or 'whom He gave to dwell in us') 'lust to envy,' or 'long towards envy?' The apostle appeals first to Scripture, and then to their own consciences as educated by Scripture, *with regard to that essential antagonism between worldliness and true piety of which he has been speaking in the previous verses.* The unemphatic 'it,' which we have to supply in the first question, as often in sentences of the kind, means 'the truth which I have just been enforcing.' He does not refer to any special passage, nor does he need to do so; for, as has been already said, the diametrical opposition between worldliness and the will of God lies at the basis of the whole moral teaching of revelation, —especially worldliness showing itself in the forms which he has described—covetousness, envy, and malignity. 'Is all this teaching in the book of God,' James says, '*vain*, meaningless?' Then, in another forcible interrogation, he presses the matter home to their consciences. The force of the order of the words in the original may be brought out by stating the question thus: 'Does desire which takes the direction of envy spring from the Spirit whom God gave to dwell in us?' 'Enlightened as you are by God's word respecting His will, can you for one moment dream, when envy rises in your hearts, that this is a prompting of the Divine Spirit within you?' Thus the appeal is substantially a repetition of that made in the 14th verse of the previous chapter, 'If ye have bitter envying and strife in your hearts, glory not and lie not against the truth'—by asserting, that is to say, that such is the fruit of the heavenly wisdom taught by the Holy Ghost.[1]

To all who know anything of the spirit of the religion of

[1] The construction ἐπιποθεῖν πρός does not occur elsewhere in the New Testament, and is found in LXX. only once, viz. at the beginning of the 42nd Psalm : "Ὃν τρόπον ἐπιποθεῖ ἡ ἔλαφος ἐπὶ τὰς πηγὰς τῶν ὑδάτων, οὕτως ἐπιποθεῖ ἡ ψυχή μου πρός σε, ὁ Θεός. This passage favours the ordinary rendering of πρὸς φθόνον; and whilst perhaps it cannot be held to have much weight against the construction of the words as equivalent to an adverb, this use of πρός being common in classical writers, it certainly may be adduced with great force in opposition to the rendering of Luther, Bengel, Stier, and others, '*against* envy.' It is in the highest degree improbable that to any Hellenistic reader, accustomed to the words ἐπιποθεῖ πρός σε, ὁ Θεός, James's πρὸς φθόνον ἐπιποθεῖ would ever suggest '*against*.' To express 'lusteth against,' Paul (Gal. v. 17) uses the regular and unambiguous construction of κατά with the genitive. The use of πρός in the sense of 'against' rarely occurs except in connection with verbs or phrases containing the notion of hostility (compare Luke xxiii. 12, Acts vi. 1 ; and see Winer's remarks on this preposition), and never, one may safely say, with such a verb as ἐπιποθεῖν.

Supposing the beginning of the 42nd Psalm, which has been quoted, to have been familiar to James's first readers—a supposition in every way probable, when we consider how familiar it is now to devout Christians,—may not an explanation of the apostle's use of the peculiar expression πρὸς φθόνον ἐπιποθεῖ, and a key to the meaning of the passage, be found in the idea that he intended to carry their minds back to the psalm? The use of the words 'panteth after,' in any religious connection, would, I apprehend, at once suggest that verse to the minds of most Christians who know the English Bible at all well; and in all likelihood ἐπιποθεῖ πρός would do the same to the minds of the Jewish Christians, the more especially as ἐπιποθεῖ occurs twice in the verse, as 'panteth after' does in the Authorized Version. Putting the Psalmist's ἡ ψυχή μου in a glorious New Testament setting, by substituting for it τὸ Πνεῦμα ὃ κατῴκισεν ἐν ἡμῖν, 'the (Divine) Spirit whom He gave to dwell in us,' the apostle says that He ἐπιποθεῖ πρός—what? As the remembrance of the grand old words of the Psalmist, πρός σε, ὁ Θεός, came over the readers' minds, we can imagine the absolute self-loathing produced in their souls by the thought that in the place of σὲ, ὁ Θεός, they were in danger of putting φθόνον, the base worldly 'envying' which is directly antagonistic to God; for, as the apostle had told them in the immediately preceding sentence, 'Whosoever is minded to be a friend of the world, maketh himself *an enemy of God.*'

Jesus, these questions obviously carry their own answer; and in all the apostle's readers who were in any considerable measure impressed by what he had said to them, a feeling of deep sadness could not but enter the heart, through a consciousness how much they had neglected compliance with the great moral principles of Scripture,—how lamentably they had yielded to influences very different from those of the Spirit of God, who had been 'given to dwell in them.' Ah, brethren, in what age of the church has such sorrow not been called for? The apostle, then, as it seems to me, bends the line of his remark to respond to this feeling. He bears in mind that the heralds of the cross are pre-eminently the bearers of 'glad tidings,'—bound to remember, even amid their sternest and justest reproofs of sin and defect on the part of Christians, that in the church their great commission is, 'Comfort ye, comfort ye my people.' '*Nay but*, brethren, be not despondent'—this, I think, is the thought connecting the two verses,—'*He giveth greater grace;*' or rather, perhaps, to bring out the force of the peculiar arrangement of the words in the original, '*Nay, but greater is the grace which He giveth*,' —greater than the strength of depravity, greater than the power of the spirit of darkness, from whom temptations to envy and all forms of worldliness come. 'The impulses you feel to covetousness, and envy, and anger, are efforts of the strong one who in time past wrought in you, when ye were children of disobedience, to regain his own dominion; but the Spirit who now dwelleth in you is stronger than he, and by His grace will enable you to repel the foe.'[1]

[1] The explanation given of the comparative μείζονα is necessarily dependent mainly on the view taken of the meaning of the 5th verse. By Gataker, Winer, Kern, and many others, it is held to mean 'greater than the world can give;' by Bengel, *eo majorem, quo longius recesseris ab invidia;* by Stier, 'increasingly and ever greater, in proportion as we

VER. 6.]   *Worldliness Enmity to God.*   311

And being ready to give this sustaining grace, He *tells* us of His willingness, that we may go to Him and cast ourselves upon His love in the appointed way : ' *Wherefore He saith.*'[1] Now the apostle might have cited innumerable passages giving the assurance of God's readiness to bless ; but He chooses one which most clearly and forcibly brings forward the *terms* of the divine offer, and thus, in conjunction with the declaration of glad tidings, continues the previous strain of solemn warning : ' *God resisteth the proud, but giveth grace unto the humble.*' This passage is a verse in the book of Proverbs, translated in our version, ' Surely He scorneth the scorners, but He giveth grace unto the lowly ' (Prov. iii. 34). The apostle gives it according to the ordinary Greek version in use among the Jews. The truth set forth in the statement is one which meets us everywhere in the Bible,—that while God 'waiteth to be gracious,' yearning to ' crown us with loving-kindness and tender mercies,' yet He will have all the glory of man's deliverance ; and that only those who cordially consent that it should be so can be blessed and saved. So long as we lean on ourselves, counting ourselves the possessors of any moral excellence, we remain outside of the sweep of God's salvation. When, sensible of utter unworthiness and feebleness, we cast ourselves wholly on Him—and this very willingness to lean on Him is 'not of

believe the word and follow the Spirit ; ' by De Wette, Wiesinger, Huther, and Alford, ' greater than if He had not for us this jealous love.' In every one of these views of the meaning there appears to be a measure of unnaturalness. It seems to me that the δί, and the comparative, and its emphatic position, are all best explained by supposing—as in expounding the compositions of any lively writer in any language we so often have to do—that the reference, instead of being directly to the preceding words, is to an intermediate unexpressed but obvious thought : ' Your consciences, I know, when I remind you of these things, make you almost despond ; *but*,' etc., as illustrated in the text above.

[1] Or perhaps ' it (Scripture) saith,'—as in verse 5.

ourselves,' but 'the gift of God,'—then He rescues us by 'the saving strength of His right hand.' '*God resisteth the proud.*' He says: 'Woe unto you that are rich, for ye have received your consolation! Woe unto you that are full, for ye shall hunger!' Man was made for simple, child-like dependence on God: anything else is dishonouring to God, and certainly opposed, therefore, to our own true happiness. Now pride, whatever form it takes, is essentially a glorifying of self, and necessarily therefore, so far as it goes, is an attempt to be or to feel independent of God. This spirit, and those who cherish it, God, consistently with His own honour and the good of His universe, cannot but 'resist.' But He '*giveth grace unto the humble.*' It is the man who says, 'Father, I have sinned in Thy sight, and am no more worthy to be called Thy son,' that receives the Father's kiss of forgiveness and welcome, and restoration to all the privileges of sonship; it is he who knows and believes himself to be by nature, as regards the matters of highest moment, a fool, that is 'made wise;' he who acknowledges himself utterly weak, that is 'strengthened with might by God's Spirit;' he who sees and feels himself to be full of sin, that is 'made the righteousness of God in Christ,' and 'sanctified wholly.' As the seraphic Leighton says: 'God pours out His grace plentifully on humble hearts. His sweet dews and showers slide off the mountains to fall on the low valleys of humble hearts, and make them pleasant and fertile.'[1]

[1] *Commentary on First Peter*, on v. 5, where the same passage from Proverbs is quoted as by James here.

XXII.

SUBMISSION TO GOD.

'Submit yourselves therefore to God. Resist the devil, and he will flee from you. 8 Draw nigh to God, and He will draw nigh to you. Cleanse your hands, ye sinners; and purify your hearts, ye double-minded. 9 Be afflicted, and mourn, and weep: let your laughter be turned to mourning, and your joy to heaviness. 10 Humble yourselves in the sight of the Lord, and He shall lift you up.'—JAMES iv. 7-10.

IN the first part of this paragraph the apostle's thoughts are presented under figures drawn from the military life. This is naturally suggested by the description of worldly men which has preceded, as 'enemies' of God, and the declaration that God 'resisteth' the proud. Indeed here, as in many parts of the Epistle, we see the connection of thoughts marked by the use of kindred words; for the original terms translated 'resisteth' and 'submit' are from the same root. Thus we have the junction of thoughts: God 'takes a position of resistance' to the proud; 'take you, therefore, a position of submission' to God. The first clause of the 7th verse, '*Submit yourselves to God*,' is the theme or text of the whole paragraph. In the following verses it is expanded. Then, after the details, the theme is in the 10th verse in substance repeated, by way of summing up the whole, but with a gracious promise conjoined. This structure reminds us of that of many of the Psalms, and indeed, throughout, the passage is not unlike a psalm in its parallelism and rhythmical flow of expression.

The apostle passes here, as you observe, from argument to injunction. His readers were professing servants of God, for otherwise their conduct would not have been called spiritual 'adultery' or 'double-mindedness.' They were therefore persons who might be assumed to have thought seriously regarding the relations between God and themselves. James has shown them that not a little in their conduct was such as characterized God's enemies, since they had been living in great measure as proud worldlings do—those whom God 'resists,' against whom He places Himself in the direct opposition of battle. Such an exhibition of the true state of the case was surely sufficient for them. They knew how mad a dream it was, that any of God's creatures could oppose their Maker with success. They knew that whoever persistently defied the Lord, and rushed on 'the thick bosses of Jehovah's buckler,' could not but meet with destruction; so that the certain end of the war would be the complete subjection of all the foes of the Almighty, either by their voluntary submission or by their absolute and irretrievable overthrow. There was no third possibility. No other advice, then, could be given to them by a wise friend than this: '*Submit yourselves to God;*' 'cast away the weapons of your rebellion, and throw yourselves at His feet, praying Him to pardon you, and give you grace to live henceforth as loyal subjects.'

Of the readers of the Epistle some were true Christians, many of whom, unhappily, had been drawn away by the seductions of the world; others were self-deceivers. To both of these classes this injunction is addressed; for the Christian life consists simply in the continuance and increase of a man's 'submission' to those principles and influences, the surrender of his heart to which made him a Christian. Alike then to those who have hitherto remained utterly stiff-necked and rebellious, and to God's own people, whose consciences tell them how many uprisings there are in their hearts of arrogance and self-will, James says : 'True wisdom has but one course for you — to submit yourselves willingly and unreservedly to God. Renounce self-will, and in everything take God's will as yours.' The precept means all this; and anything less on the part of God's moral creatures is inconsistent with the highest, truest life — opposed at once to duty and to happiness.

The submission spoken of is, in the first place, to God's *grace*. For sinful creatures the primary step in submission — the root from which all the rest is to spring — must be the 'submitting ourselves,' as Paul has it, 'to the righteousness of God,' — accepting with meekness of heart His way of justification through the work of Christ. To acknowledge, and by Bible-study and self-study to grow into an ever more profound and lively conviction, that our own personal desert, even at our best estate, is God's anger, and that in no spiritual robe except the wedding garment of the great King's own bestowal can man stand with acceptance before Him, — to 'glory in the cross of Christ,' and for its excellency to 'count all things but loss,' — this is the *basis* of 'submission to God.' And on it rises submission to God's *law*. Where the first step has been taken, this certainly follows; and the more complete and intelligent our submission to divine grace, the more thorough always will be our submission to the divine law. Gratitude and love to Him who by His atoning death has delivered us from its curse, will bring us, through the influences of the Spirit, ever more fully under the sway of its principles. Until God quickens us, we deem His law a law of bondage; but when we are quickened, we see it to be 'the perfect law of liberty,' in obedience to which, and only in obedience to which, all our energies find full, free, satisfying exercise. The believer, in the measure in which he is a believer, 'esteems all God's precepts concerning all things to be right.' He desires and strives, through divine help, so to have God's will as his, as to be, and do, and bear aright all that God appoints. Ah, that *bearing* aright, how hard a part of the work it is! Yet no element of 'submitting ourselves to God' is more needful, none more precious in its results, than submission to His will in providence,—not with sullenness because we *must*, as to the deed of an irresistible foe, but true submission of the heart, as of a child to the act of a Father whose wisdom and love he trusts perfectly. It is evident that with failure here that class of sins which James has been specially rebuking stood in close connection. Many of his readers were discontented with God's providential actings in regard to their situation in life, their wealth and rank; and hence came envying and grudging at the good of their neighbours, malignity, strife, and wretchedness. Wondrously sweet is it, my brethren, to rest in the divine love. 'Cast thy burden on the Lord, and He shall sustain thee.' 'Blessed is the man that trusteth in Him.' 'Submit yourselves unto the Lord,' then, brethren,—to His grace and to His law, whether in regard to being, or doing, or bearing. This is the apostle's injunction here—the theme which he expands in the precepts that follow.

These fall to some extent into pairs. In the first pair we have a very lively antithesis: '*Resist the devil, and he will flee from you; draw nigh to God, and He will draw nigh to you.*' It would have been well, for the exhibition of the structure and connection, had the division into verses been different;

the theme or text, 'Submit yourselves, therefore, to God,' standing by itself, and then the pair in a verse together. Submission to God, the apostle here points out, involves two lines of effort for the soul,—opposition to the evil spirit, the usurper, and self-surrender to the great good Spirit, the rightful King. Then, appended to the injunction of each of these duties, you observe, there stands a promise,—according to that exquisite tenderness which belongs to all true gospel pleading, even in circumstances where of necessity stern severity is most prominent. The apostle gives us the comforting assurance that the needful spiritual efforts may be made with all hopefulness; for Satan when resisted will flee, God when approached will meet the approach.

In the mention of Satan here, James incidentally fills up the teaching which he gave in the 14th and 15th verses of the 1st chapter regarding the natural history of sin. 'Every man is tempted,' he told us, 'when he is drawn away of his own lust and enticed. Then, when lust hath conceived, it bringeth forth sin; and sin, when it is finished, bringeth forth death.' But, besides, a spirit of great power and cunning, and boundless hatred to God and goodness, is continually busy in endeavours to bring us into sin, and to baffle our efforts to serve God. Many think very little about Satan's diligence in temptation, but his zeal and power are none the less real. Perhaps one of the strangest of all the strange revelations of the Judgement-day will be that made to wicked men, how completely they were the tools of a spirit wickeder and subtler than themselves, of whom they seldom thought,—whose very existence, it may be, they derided the belief in as a mere childish bugbear.

In the 'friendship with this world,' which James has already laid to the charge of his readers, they had been under the influences of this world's prince; and this, as our Lord tells us, is Satan. Now, those who desire to 'submit themselves to God' must energetically '*resist the devil;*' for he makes the fiercest struggles to keep his subjects, and, even after they have escaped, to drag them back into the kingdom of darkness. This cruel, cunning, powerful foe must be 'resisted' in the divine strength, obtained by the power of faith. 'The weapons of our warfare are mighty *through God*,' not otherwise. He has provided for us all needed weapons for offence, and armour for defence. Let us then 'put on the whole armour of God, that we may be able to stand against the wiles of the devil; for we wrestle not against flesh and blood, but against principalities, against powers, against the rulers of the darkness of this world, against spiritual wickedness in high places. Let us stand, therefore, having our loins girt about with truth, and having on the breastplate of righteousness, and our feet shod with the preparation of the gospel of peace; above all, taking the shield of faith, wherewith we shall be able to quench all the fiery darts of the wicked one; and let us take the helmet of salvation, and the sword of the Spirit, which is the word of God.' Thus arrayed, let us be watchful, knowing that at any moment, from any quarter, with the most varied weapons, and in the most varied guises, our fell adversary may be upon us. Let us watch the avenues where we know our position to be weak. Let us watch the sides, too, where we think ourselves to be strong. Not without profound significance and tender grace was it 'written aforetime for our learning,' that Abraham, pre-eminently a man of faith, told a lie through faithless cowardice; that Moses, habitually the meekest of men, sinned through angry impatience with his brethren; that Peter, the bold and loving, denied his

Master. One can imagine a sentry on a post of danger to be faithful, and yet to betray the position by unduly narrowing the area to which he directs his attention. 'Look at him. Every look, every motion, betokens concentration of his thoughts and feelings on the danger which impends. Perhaps he is motionless, but it is only that his eye may be more stedfastly fixed upon the point from which the enemy's approach is apprehended. You can see at a glance that he is ready for even the faintest intimation of a moving object on that horizon. But while he stands like a statue, behind him are forms becoming every moment more and more defined. He hears them not, because their step is noiseless; he sees them not, because his eye and all his faculties are employed in an opposite direction. While he strains every sense to catch the first intimations of approaching danger, it is creeping stealthily behind him; and when at last his ear distinguishes the tramp of armed men, it is too late, for a hostile hand is already on his shoulder, and, if his life is spared, it is only to be overpowered and disarmed.'[1]

And when the enemy does appear, brethren, let there be no dallying with him. If we 'give place to the devil,' granting him room to stand with us and negotiate, we are in the utmost peril. On many subjects, second thoughts are best; but in matters of moral duty, the first thoughts of a person whose conscience is reasonably enlightened are almost always true thoughts. If second thoughts be waited for, they often bring in worldly considerations, and tend towards a compromise. When Satan finds that the first clear instinctive 'Nay' of the conscience is the utterance of a strong will, which holds to its words, he knows well that his efforts are vain with that soul; for it is God's Spirit that has made the will strong. If promptly,

[1] Joseph Addison Alexander.

prayerfully, watchfully, we 'resist the devil,' he '*will flee from us.*' Though this world is still practically so under Satan as its god and prince, as that he 'blinds the minds of them which believe not,' and 'leads them captive at his will,' yet in truth Jesus has vanquished him, 'spoiling' him, and 'triumphing over him;' and wherever gospel truth is received and welcomed in any soul, there 'the prince of this world is cast out,' and thus that soul is 'delivered from the power of darkness.' Every struggle against Satan's vengeful assaults to recover his position, if earnestly maintained in the strength of Christ, will certainly be successful,—'for the mouth of the Lord hath spoken it.' Satan is too shrewd to go on persistently wasting his energies, when he sees distinctly that, through strong faith, almightiness is enlisted against him. The grand old dreamer says that the fight between Christian and Apollyon in the Valley of Humiliation 'was the dreadfullest fight that ever he saw;' but that, in the end, after Christian had made at him again and again with the sword of the Spirit, 'Apollyon spread forth his dragon's wings and sped him away, that Christian saw him no more.' He may come back and repeat his assaults many times, in hope of finding unguarded moments, seasons of faithlessness and consequent feebleness. To the Lord Himself he applied temptation after temptation in the wilderness; and even at the close of that effort departed from Him only 'for a season,' to return with bitter fury in Gethsemane. But every assault well repelled confirms the believer's spiritual strength; and the assurance holds good universally, 'Resist the devil, and he will flee from you.'

The apostle continues: '*Draw nigh to God, and He will draw nigh to you.*' If we consider the military figure to be still retained, then, taking this injunction in connection with the previous, which we have examined, the picture perhaps is that of two hosts facing each other on the eve of battle—the host of God and the host of Satan, with each king present among his troops. Some who have hitherto been in the ranks of Satan, now convinced that he is a vile and cruel usurper, and that the battle must end in the destruction of all who adhere to him, forsake their station and move toward the side of God. Their old king and his myrmidons observe their movement, and strive to prevent them; but they 'resist' stoutly, and steadily 'draw nigh to' Him whom they now recognise as their only true and rightful Lord. Of this '*drawing nigh to God*' the most prominent element is prayer, the special manifestation of longings for Him; but the expression exhibits generally a movement of the whole soul—all the thoughts and affections, and consequently also their issues in the outward life—towards Him. The prodigal in the 'far country,' musing on his folly and wickedness, says, 'I will arise and go to my Father;' and he does arise and go to his Father.

But how will he be received? Will his Father's righteous anger find utterance, and nought else? The gospel has been given to us to answer this question, and it tells us that the King will '*draw nigh to us.*' The Father saw His returning prodigal 'when he was yet a great way off, and had compassion, and ran, and fell on his neck, and kissed him.' Nay, the very willingness of the prodigal to return to his Father's house—the willingness of those who have been in Satan's ranks to draw nigh to God—springs from His willingness to draw nigh to them. It is He that puts the longing for Himself into our souls, through His Spirit. It is 'in the day of Messiah's power' that 'His people are willing.' 'No man can come unto Me,' said Jesus, 'except the Father who hath sent Me draw him.' 'Of His own will begat He us with the word of truth, that we should be a kind of first-fruits of His creatures:' that is the genesis of all true religion. Let no fears, then, dear friends, keep us back from God. Our God is 'very pitiful and of tender mercy.' 'He that spared not His own Son, but delivered Him up for us all,' may surely claim our fullest confidence, when He tells us that 'He waiteth to be gracious.'

'But observe,' the apostle continues, 'that if this approach to God is to give Him glory or bring you profit, it must be not formal merely, but real; not partial only, but of the whole nature. Prayer for God's forgiveness and for the help of His Spirit is proved to be sincere by earnest effort after conformity of character to His will, and this as regards both heart and outward life. *Cleanse your hands, ye sinners; and purify your hearts, ye double-minded.*' It is important to notice that what is here enjoined is not set forth as something antecedent to 'drawing nigh to God,' but involved in it as an essential element. Fleshly wisdom says, 'Reform, and then you may approach God with some reasonable hope of acceptance.' The teaching of the gospel is, that the spiritual life which is needed for any true moral activity is to be obtained only in nearness to God through Jesus Christ, and that the duty of every hearer of the gospel, whatever the measure of his defilement be, when the glad tidings come to him, is to believe that '*now* is the accepted time.' But it was 'our iniquities' that 'separated between us and God;' and therefore all real drawing near to Him involves hatred of those iniquities, and earnest endeavour to shun them.

In the Old Testament usage, which here, as very often, our apostle follows in his mode of employing words and phrases, the term 'sinner' has mainly reference to *manifest* wickedness; and the 'hands' are very frequently, and most naturally, taken to represent all the instrumentalities by which the soul acts upon the outer world. Accordingly, pointing by the name '*sinners*' to the many outward violations of the law of God of which his readers had been guilty, James calls upon them to '*cleanse their hands.*' Very similarly, Paul, in writing to Timothy, says, 'I will that men pray everywhere, lifting up holy hands' (1 Tim. ii. 8). The visible moral deformities, however, revealed a lamentable perversity of *heart*. The 'sinners' were '*double-minded.*' Their souls were perhaps not altogether destitute of love to God and trust in Him, but were certainly also occupied to a lamentable degree by love to the world and confidence in it. It became them, therefore, if they indeed desired to have their 'Maker as their Husband,' and to 'draw near to Him,' to recognise the folly and guilt of being 'adulterous,' as in the 4th verse the apostle has declared them to be, and to '*purify*' (or 'make chaste') '*their hearts.*' The truth exhibited by James in his double precept here, that approaches to God are sincere and successful only when they include true and earnest longings and endeavours after purity and beauty of spirit and of life, is one of vast practical moment, and which accordingly meets us everywhere in the Bible. 'Blessed are the pure in heart, for they shall see God.' 'If I regard iniquity in my heart, the Lord will not hear me.' 'I will wash mine hands in innocency; so will I compass Thine altar, O Lord.' 'Who shall ascend into the hill of the Lord, or who shall stand in His holy place? He that hath *clean hands and a pure heart.*'

The apostle proceeds now to remind his readers, that the very first evidence of true desire to 'draw nigh to God' is deep penitential sorrow for sin. The needfulness of this sorrow, and also of energetic thought regarding it, in order to resist our natural tendency to frivolity, is shown in the copiousness of the language. Word is piled upon word—expressions of 'lamentation and mourning and woe,'—that the most inconsiderate reader may have brought distinctly and impressively before him, how necessary is the night of repentant weeping, if there is to come a morning of spiritual joy. The Christian life, brethren, is a life of happiness—of 'peace which passeth all understanding,' 'joy unspeakable and full of glory.' Believers know indeed the seriousness of life, and thus their happiness is tinged with gravity; but for that very reason it is deep, and broad, and lasting. In a world like this, where death is the one great certainty, any joy which is not tempered with seriousness must be like the crackling of a fire of thorns, where speedily again all is cold and dark. But after seasons of backsliding and spiritual torpor, this characteristic seriousness of the Christian must deepen into sorrow, the intensely bitter sorrow of self-upbraiding for unthankfulness and disloyalty to our gracious King and Father. And, considering the energy with which the 'law of sin in the members' wages its war with 'the law of the mind,' the professing Christian whose history has given him no experience of this sorrow has reason to fear that his immunity is due rather to blindness and hardness of heart than to uninterrupted growth in grace. '*Be afflicted*, then,' says James to those professing servants of God who had been beguiled by the seductions of the world ('Have a feeling of distress,' instead of the thoughtlessness and baseless mirth which arise out of the 'friendship of the world'), '*and mourn, and weep; let your laughter*' (the 'laughter of the fool,' who, in the midst of great everlasting realities, looks only at shadows) '*be turned to mourning, and your joy to heaviness.*' 'Dejection'—the sorrowful casting down of those eyes which aforetime sent greedy and arrogant glances out to the vanities of the world,—this is the exact representative of the original term here rendered '*heaviness.*' The type of the penitent is the publican who, 'standing afar off, would not lift up so much as his eyes unto heaven, but smote upon his breast, saying, God be merciful to me, a sinner.'

In the 10th verse James closes the paragraph by summing up the teaching of the whole : '*Humble yourselves in the sight of the Lord.*' This is substantially a repetition of the theme or fundamental injunction which began the paragraph : 'Submit yourselves to God.' Since 'God resisteth the proud, but giveth grace unto the humble,' the obvious demand of true wisdom is that all who have permitted the proud self-reliance which shows itself in 'friendship with this world' to gain power over them, should at once '*humble themselves.*' And this '*in the sight of the Lord.*' The sense of His presence whose 'eyes are as a flame of fire,' will secure what, in a work so repulsive to the carnal mind, nothing else will — genuine sincerity. It is in the measure of the distinctness with which through faith we see God, too, that the soul perceives the grounds of humility, recognising in the light of the divine character its own defilement and deformity. 'I have heard of Thee by the hearing of the ear; but now mine eye seeth Thee : wherefore I abhor myself, and repent in dust and ashes.'

With the mercy and tenderness characteristic of the divine word, even in its stern passages, the injunction 'Humble yourselves' has appended to it a gracious promise; so that the paragraph which has been so searching and scathing lays firm hold of the heart at its close with 'bands of love.' 'Humble yourselves in the sight of the Lord,' as in the light of His ineffable excellence you see your ignorance, and sin, and weakness,—'*and He shall lift you up*' to true though as yet imperfect knowledge, and holiness, and strength here,—and yonder to the 'open vision' of the 'Altogether Lovely,' to absolute spiritual beauty, to strength which will enable you to 'serve Him day and night in His temple' and to bear the 'exceeding and eternal weight of glory.'

XXIII.

EVIL SPEAKING AND JUDGING.

'Speak not evil one of another, brethren. He that speaketh evil of his brother, and judgeth his brother, speaketh evil of the law, and judgeth the law: but if thou judge the law, thou art not a doer of the law, but a judge. 12 There is one lawgiver, who is able to save and to destroy: who art thou that judgest another?'—JAMES iv. 11, 12.

THE substance of the paragraph immediately preceding these words was, that, however little worldly persons may think it, yet, when we look closely into the matter, we find the spirit of worldliness to be an arrogant assumption of being independent of God, and that the only radical cure for it—the only course to be pursued by those who have been aroused to a conviction of its influence over them—is to 'submit themselves to God,' to 'humble themselves' sincerely and fully before Him. James proceeds now to give one or two illustrations of forms which worldliness often takes, and had in fact taken among many of his first readers,—showing how in these a want of reverence for God is involved, and that consequently true submission to Him will exhibit itself in a careful avoidance of such conduct.

We have first a command to abstain from detraction and calumny: '*Speak not evil one of another, brethren.*' You will remember that the apostle has spoken already on sins of the tongue at considerable length, in the 3rd chapter. His exhortation here, however, is not a mere repetition of anything said there, but has a distinctive character. In the observations made in the 3rd chapter, he had main if not exclusive reference, as is plain on a careful study, to the various vices of speech which spring out of bigotry and contention in religious and ecclesiastical matters,—the first injunction of the chapter, 'My brethren, be not many masters' ('teachers'), being a kind of key-word to the whole. Here, on the other hand, as we see, his precept forms part of an address on worldliness, and thus bears primarily on the ordinary intercourse of life— common talk on common matters. Even professedly Christian society in the apostle's days, it seems, needed the exhortation to avoid evil-speaking; and we have no reason to doubt that in every age of the church this fault has been a prevalent one. Certainly our own age is not free from it.

The motives by which people are led to evil-speaking are various. *Definite malignity and vindictiveness* sometimes, no doubt. On the ground of some real or fancied wrong done him, a man hates another; and the simplest, readiest, and most efficient way of taking revenge is to circulate a story to the other's discredit. In other cases *envy* is the impelling influence. A man prospers and enjoys repute among his fellows more than we do; and what the 'evil eye' has seen, really or in imagination, the venomous tongue tells, that this fair repute may be tarnished. There are persons in the world —probably most of us have met individuals of the kind—of so mean and wretched a spirit, that any success of others is felt by them as if it were a wrong to themselves; and thus their discourse is ever full of slander and detraction. With envy, sometimes *direct self-seeking* is connected. Suspicions against a man are thrown out, or a false or exaggerated story is put into circulation, in the hope that certain advantages in the way of business, for example, may thus be taken away from the object of the calumny, and come to his detractor. Cases of surrender to the influence of such motives as these, however, are rare, one may reasonably hope, among professing Christians, and even among the higher class of mere men of the world.

But one motive operating often in all classes of society is *vanity*—the desire for a little prominence in company,—which scandal is found to give most easily. It is an unhappy fact, patent enough to all who think on the subject, that the average tone of conversation among us is low. Through a want of spirituality or of general intelligence, or of both, neither religious subjects nor really important secular subjects find much welcome in general social talk. They are either not introduced at all, or, if they are, the conversation soon languishes. But everything which tells against the personal character of an absent acquaintance, or which tends to exhibit him in a ridiculous light, is generally received with much favour, and felt to impart a pleasant piquancy to a conversation perhaps otherwise dull. Thus it happens, that for a man who loves a temporary prominence, and is not scrupulous with regard to his means, no way of gaining it is better suited than evil-speaking; the more particularly as there is no kind of subject on which it is so easy to seem smart as in the discussion of personal character, where, falling on the ears of listeners somewhat sympathetic, severe remarks and exaggerated sketches pass for clever, which on any other subject would be seen to be simply stupid. There can be no doubt, therefore, that vanity is a very common cause of evil-speaking. However destitute a person may be of respectable intellectual resources for shining in society, he can at least calumniate or deride his neighbour. But probably, after all, most of the ordinary calumnious gossip of society is to be ascribed to the *mere desire to talk*, even when all innocent materials for talk are wanting.

People are brought together who seem to have no objects of common interest, or what they have are soon exhausted; still the fire of conversation must be maintained, and, as other fuel does not present itself, personal character is thrown in. This, beyond question, is the true origin of much calumnious discourse,—which yet in such a case is not the less really a sin, that there is no conscious malevolence. There ought to be moral energy to act on the principle that silence, or innocent dulness, is immeasurably better and nobler than the propagation of what may injure, and cannot by possibility do good.

The sin of evil-speaking exhibits itself mainly in these forms: the propagation of what is known to be a calumnious lie,—the exaggeration or distortion of truth,—the hasty passing on of what may or may not be truth, but certainly has not been inquired into,—and the needless telling of what is known to be truth.

The first of these is simply diabolical. To Satan—who 'when he speaketh a lie, speaketh of his own, for he is a liar, and the father of it'—no work is more congenial than wilful calumny. In Eden he dared to whisper into the ear of Eve insinuations of insincerity even against God; and he has diligently tried (ah, how successfully!) to persuade her children that their Divine King has the spirit of 'an austere man, taking up that He laid not down, and reaping that He did not sow.' His hatred to man, too, has no manifestation more distinctly indicating his bitterness and his alienation from all good, than when he acts as 'the accuser of the brethren.' No characteristic of our spiritual adversary is more prominent than his love of calumny; and, indeed, his very name 'devil' means 'the calumniator.' In no way, then, can a man more distinctly prove himself a 'child of the devil,' who bears his father's image, than by inventing and propagating slanderous lies. It is difficult to suppose that any person who, by the utmost energy of self-deception, can fancy himself a Christian, could be guilty of this form of evil-speaking.

But the other forms of the sin are certainly not unknown in the church of Christ: it is to be feared, indeed, that in various degrees of heinousness, they are far from uncommon. And the debasing influence of this sin cannot be overstated. You all know—for you have all met men of the kind—the ineffable meanness of the habitual detractor. His whole moral nature is enervated, and everything like manliness and healthy tone taken away. In immediate connection with *praise* he insinuates his depreciatory hints, as poison may be given in perfume. All of us know the 'but' for which his commendations are meant to prepare the way. He loves vague generalities too, uttered in such a connection that suggestions of evil will certainly be taken as pointing in a particular direction; whilst yet refutation can hardly be given, nor the charge of personal calumny brought home.

Into exaggeration and distortion of truth all of us are extremely apt to be drawn, often unconsciously. There are very few things more difficult than to tell the exact truth on any matter of complexity and delicacy. Misconception, prejudice, and excited feeling frequently colour and distort to our minds what has been told to us or observed by us; and therefore thoughtfulness, self-control, and knowledge of the force of words are all required, in a high degree, in order to the accurate relation of anything which has to do with personal character. Any one of us would probably be astonished, and often deeply pained, if a story bearing on character which he had himself told, were heard by him again, after it had been passed on two or three times,—each propagator contributing his quota of unconscious distortion. Consideration of this hazard of unintentional misrepresentation might well deter men of a truthful spirit from speaking on matters in which such misrepresentation would do harm. But even supposing that we knew with absolute certainty some evil regarding a brother, and were sure that we could tell it without swerving a hair's-breadth from the narrow path of truthful representation, yet another question would enter: Is there need for telling it? The spirit of Christianity very plainly interposes a prohibition, unless there is need; and what constitutes need must be decided by the Christian judgement for itself, with regard to each case as it arises. The principles taught by the gospel of love on this whole subject may perhaps be reduced to these: that we should never believe evil of another, until we cannot help it; that we should never say anything against another, unless we are sure that duty obliges us; and that if we feel sure that duty obliges us so to speak, then we should tell of the evil in a spirit of love and of sorrow.

The apostle's exhortation here has primary reference to the conduct of Christians to each other; and the argument enforcing it, which is involved in the word of address, 'brethren,' he sets forth fully and impressively by the repetition of this designation: 'He that speaketh evil of *his brother*, and judgeth *his brother*, speaketh evil of the law.' By the use of this word he calls on them to bethink themselves how grossly inconsistent it is to say in their prayers, 'Our Father which art in heaven,' and yet calumniate a member of the brotherhood,—to profess love to 'Him which begat,' and show hatred to 'him that is begotten of Him.'

The expressed prohibition in the 11th verse is of evil-speaking; but in the argument which follows there is obviously implied also a prohibition of 'judging:' 'He that speaketh evil of his brother, and *judgeth his brother*, speaketh evil of the law, and judgeth the law.' The apostle assumes that in those to whom he writes—rational beings, who profess to feel themselves responsible to God for their views, and feelings, and conduct—a 'judgement' by the mind must be the basis on which any expressed opinion regarding character rests. As a matter of fact, would it not be flattery often to talk of a 'judgement' of any kind preceding the utterance of calumny? Is not detraction in many cases the merest parrot-prattle, dishonouring to us as reasonable creatures, as well as hurtful to our brethren and dishonouring to the law of God? The reference to 'judging' is introduced partly to lead into the course of argument which the apostle has in view, but partly also to suggest that 'judgement' is wrong in itself, whether it induce evil-speaking or not. This latter object is more distinctly shown when—in accordance with the reading of the Greek text found in the oldest manuscripts, and received by the modern critical editors—we substitute 'or' for 'and' in the beginning of the second clause of the 11th verse: 'He that speaketh evil of his brother, *or* judgeth his brother.'

The force of the statement that it is wrong to 'judge another' is plainly limited,—the context showing, and the good sense of every reader at once perceiving, that here, as often in Scripture, by the simple 'judgement' is meant *unfavourable* judgement. In the apostle's precept, moreover, as in that of Jesus in the Sermon on the Mount, which is clearly in his mind, 'Judge not, that ye be not judged,' there is no prohibition of our coming to conclusions regarding the character of men from their avowed principles and visible conduct. 'That would have been the enjoining of a kind of physical impossibility. You might as well forbid me to have an unfavourable opinion of a fox and a wolf, as characters to be detested and avoided, as of some men whom I know personally, and many of whom I have sure information.'[1] Indeed, to 'judge' according to avowed principles and visible conduct is a *duty:* 'Beware of false prophets, which come to you in sheep's clothing, but inwardly they are ravening wolves: *ye shall know them by their fruits.*' But to 'judge' of motives and character without tangible and most convincing evidence is a sin. It is sinful to do it, *even if the judgement be kept to ourselves.* The effect on our own souls is evil—narrowing, chilling, withering. Evil is wrought, too, against him whom we judge, at least if he and we stand at all in close relations,—because he is denied the benefit of a love and fellowship which, it may be, God brought us near to him specially that we might have the opportunity of giving for his help, whereas we 'pass by on the other side.'

In support of his prohibition of evil-speaking and judging, James had many lines of argument open to him. In that which has been chosen, he sets forth two grounds for his counsel. The first is, that the conduct which he forbids *involves a condemnation of God's law:* 'He that speaketh evil of his brother, and judgeth his brother, *speaketh evil of the law, and judgeth the law.*' By some commentators it has been thought that James is here speaking with reference mainly to a particular class of uncharitable judgements and utterances, —namely, such as were founded on differences of opinion regarding the obligation of Christians to retain the ceremonial observances of Judaism; and that the argument employed has this meaning: 'Because those who blame their brethren for giving up the old ritualism, thereby condemn *the distinctive law of the New Economy,* which does not require it.' This view lies under these fatal objections, that it gives an altogether exceptional application to the term 'law,' and that there is

[1] Dr. William Anderson, of Glasgow.

nothing in the context, or in the whole Epistle, to suggest in the slightest degree that limitation of the precept here supposed.[1] James's use of the word 'law' elsewhere gives us every reason to believe that here he means by it the grand code of moral obligation written on man's heart at the beginning,—taught in all Scripture, the oracles of the Old Covenant as well as those of the New, but most fully exhibited in the teaching and example of the Lord Jesus. The apostle lifts up the thoughts of his readers to the relation in which their conduct stands to this great law. 'Judging a brother, when Christ has expressly said to you, Judge not, is practically judging and condemning His precept, and the great code to which it belongs,—declaring the divine law to be undeserving of your obedience.' Very similarly one might say, 'To insult your neighbour is to insult God's law, and therefore to insult God;' and other series of the same kind will readily suggest themselves. It is obviously true, not of uncharitable judgement merely, but of every sin, that the man who commits it practically judges and condemns God's law; but, as obviously, the remark comes in with a point and power in the present connection which would be lacking

---

[1] Alford explains 'judgeth the law' thus—'viz., by setting himself up over that law,—as pronouncing upon its observance or non-observance by another;' his meaning being further exhibited by a note on the next clause: 'Seeing that he who judges, judges not only the man before him, but the law also; for he pronounces not only on the fact, but on that fact being or not being a breach of the law.' That is to say, apparently, a man who 'judges *what the law is*' 'judges the law.' But clearly this is not the natural meaning of 'judging the law,' in the connection in which the words occur here. The sense must be, 'judging *what the law should be*,' 'judging whether the law is a right law or a wrong,'—it being distinctly implied, too, according to the context, that the judgement is a condemnatory one. Every right-minded man is continually for himself judging what the law is, and yet surely is very far from 'judging the law' in the sense in which James employs the expression.

elsewhere. With regard to such offences as evil-speaking and harsh judgements, moreover, it is peculiarly needful to bring in the truth that they fall fully under the sweep of divine law. The men of the world—and in many cases Christians also, through the influence of worldly society—are apt to think of such conduct as belonging to a kind of moral neutral ground; so that, whilst certainly not right, it is yet not decidedly wrong. Now, as was shown in the beginning of the lecture, James's purpose in this section of the Epistle is to exhibit the spirit of worldliness as being essentially arrogance towards God, insubmissiveness to the Divine King. In accordance with this purpose, he tells his readers here that the practice of detraction, which they considered a mere trifle or peccadillo, was really a breach of the King's law, and thus a 'judging' and a defiance of it and of Him.

The apostle's second argument in support of the prohibition he has given, is that the conduct forbidden *involves the assumption of a position which belongs to God alone:* '*But if thou judge the law, thou art not a doer of the law, but a judge. There is One Lawgiver, who is able to save and to destroy: who art thou that judgest another?*' More exactly rendered, and with the translation introduced of words contained in the oldest manuscripts, the last part of the sentence runs thus: 'One is the Lawgiver and Judge, He who is able to save and to destroy; but thou—who art thou that judgest thy neighbour?' According to the course of thought, the contrast in the first part appears not to be between 'a doer of the law' and 'a judge (of the law),' but between 'a doer of the law' (that is, a subject, one under law, whose office with regard to it is simply to do what it enjoins) and 'a judge,' taken in the most general sense—one belonging to an entirely different category from 'doers'—one whose office is not to obey laws, but to judge men and laws. The connection shows that 'a judge' pure and simple is thought of, controlled by no authority, above even the law. The words of the 12th verse must be felt by every reader to come in with singular power,—to be most solemn, and striking, and silencing. *One is the Lawgiver and Judge:*' One, not many neighbours, with varying standards of right: One, to whom should converge the thoughts, the reverence, the obedience of all, seeing that with Him we all 'have to do:' One who, being *'Lawgiver'* as well as *'Judge,'* knows His own law perfectly, and can therefore administer it with perfect wisdom and justice,—and whose decisions carry power with them at every point and for ever, seeing that *'He is able to save and to destroy.'* Then comes the withering contrast, *'But thou'*—a creature with no wisdom, no holiness, no power,—*'thou,'* ignorant in great measure alike of the law and of men's hearts and circumstances, thyself every day a transgressor of the law, and unable, even when most favourably placed, to make thy decisions effective beyond a narrow sphere and a little time—*'who art thou that judgest thy neighbour?'*

XXIV.

VAIN CONFIDENCE REGARDING THE FUTURE.

'Go to now, ye that say, To-day, or to-morrow, we will go into such a city, and continue there a year, and buy and sell, and get gain; 14 Whereas ye know not what shall be on the morrow. For what is your life? It is even a vapour, that appeareth for a little time, and then vanisheth away. 15 For that ye ought to say, If the Lord will, we shall live, and do this, or that. 16 But now ye rejoice in your boastings: all such rejoicing is evil. 17 Therefore to him that knoweth to do good, and doeth it not, to him it is sin.'—JAMES iv. 13-17.

IN this paragraph the apostle brings forward another example illustrating the truth which is the central thought of this chapter,—namely, that the root of all worldliness is pride, arrogance of heart towards God, and that consequently the only effectual remedy for it—the plain and instant duty of every Christian who has in any degree allowed a worldly spirit to gain power over him—is to 'submit himself to God,' to 'humble himself in the sight of the Lord.' The form of worldliness of which he here speaks is presumptuous confidence with respect to the future, calculating on time to come without reference to God's providence; as if the future and all which it brings with it were in our hands.

The expression rendered '*Go to now,*' which occurs in the New Testament only here and in the 1st verse of the next chapter, is a phrase of a rousing character, calling attention to some exhortation to follow, like the shaking of a sleeper to wake him that he may hear tidings of moment. In the present instance the exhortation is not expressed, but implied, particularly in the last three verses of the paragraph. As in the 1st chapter of Isaiah God's appeal of love is introduced by 'Come and let us reason together,' so here, somewhat similarly, the apostle says in substance, 'Look now and bethink yourselves regarding your religious position; bring up your conduct before the tribunal of reason and conscience, and there as in God's sight pronounce judgement, while still repentance and hope are open to you.' The persons here addressed are merchants of a kind who have in all ages been found in great numbers in the East. In Dothan, the sons of Jacob 'lifted up their eyes and looked, and behold a company of Ishmaelites came from Gilead, with their camels, bearing spicery, and balm, and myrrh, going to carry it down to Egypt.' So still the business of a respectable and intelligent class of merchants is to convey the products of one region to some distant city, where they remain until they have sold their goods, and bought others suitable for another distant market; and thus the operation is repeated, until perhaps after a considerable number of years the trader is enabled to return prosperously to his home. Such evidently are the traders here. The reading 'to-day *and* to-morrow,' which has better manuscript authority than that given in the Authorized Version, sets forth with peculiar liveliness the completeness of the vain confidence described—the definiteness of the arrangements which these merchants make for the future, without any thought of God. '*We will journey to-day and to-morrow to such a city*' (to Antioch, or Damascus, or Alexandria), '*and will spend there a year, and will trade and get gain.*' An observant reader will see a peculiar force in the '*ands,*' accumulating one presumptuous expectation on another.

VER. 14.] *Vain Confidence regarding the Future.*

'*Whereas ye know not what shall be on the morrow.*' 'You form plans with confident security for a long time to come. What certainty have you that your trafficking in that city will be gainful? What certainty have you that you will remain alive in that city a year; or that, if you do, you will be in health to buy and sell? What certainty have you that you will ever reach that city? You say, To-day and to-morrow we will go; but the wise king said long ago, "Boast not thyself of to-morrow, for thou knowest not what a day may bring forth." You may go from your homes healthy and hopeful, with your servants and your train of camels; and, ere another day dawn, robbery or hurricane, sickness or accident, any one of innumerable circumstances, may have blighted your prospects utterly. Nay, you yourselves may have gone away for ever from all buying and selling and getting gain, to meet God; *for what is your life*—of what character or quality? Altogether untrustworthy in duration, you know well, *for it is a vapour*' (or, still more pointedly and strikingly, according to what is probably the original reading, '*ye* are a vapour') '*that appeareth for a little time, and then vanisheth away.* From the moist ground the vapour rises at the first touch of the morning sun, and glides gracefully up the mountain-side, softening the rugged outlines of the cliffs with a robe of beauty. But the very beams which called it forth, scatter it when they gain strength. At noon you look for it, but it is gone, and the place which knew it knows it no more. Such is your life; and yet on this transitory mist you, in foolish self-dependence, build great towers of hope, as if it were enduring as the everlasting hills. Have you never heard what the Saviour said of a man whose ground brought forth plentifully, and who promised his soul much goods for many years: "Thou fool, this night thy soul shall be required of thee"?'

Treating the 14th verse as parenthetical, the apostle makes the 15th in form a continuation of the sentence begun in the 13th, thus: 'Go to now, ye that say, To-day and to-morrow we will go to such a city, and continue there a year, and buy and sell, and get gain; *for that ye ought to say* (more exactly, 'instead of saying'), *If the Lord will, we shall live, and do this, or that.*' This is not to be regarded as a command that, whenever we have occasion to speak of purposes or expectations, we should utter these words, or words of similar import. Beyond doubt, the constant use of such language with respect to trifling affairs would, in creatures such as we are, and situated as we are, have a tendency to rub off reverence for God and His holy name. Thus the practice might very easily degenerate into an act of mere superstitious reliance on a form, when the feeling which had been the life of the form was gone. Taking the commentary of apostolic usage, we find that the same inspired writer who says to the Corinthians, 'I will come to you shortly, if the Lord will' (1 Cor. iv. 19), and again, 'I trust to tarry a while with you, if the Lord permit' (1 Cor. xvi. 7), says also to them in another place simply, 'I will come unto you when I shall pass through Macedonia, for I do pass through Macedonia' (1 Cor. xvi. 5); and to the Romans, 'When I have performed this, I will come by you into Spain' (Rom. xv. 28). The meaning of our apostle's injunction is plainly this, that at all times, in reference to everything, when looking forward, we should remember reverentially, thankfully, lovingly, God's providential government of the world, and our absolute dependence on His will for continued life and health, and for the accomplishment of any purpose or expectation; and that it will be well both for ourselves and for others, if we often, on such occasions as the Christian judgement—or rather, perhaps, the delicate Christian instinct—suggests, express this conviction of dependence by some such phrase as 'If the Lord will.'

'*But now ye rejoice in your boastings: all such rejoicing is evil.*' 'But, as things really are, instead of thus humbly and gratefully acknowledging your dependence on God, in your vainglorious dreams you exult and boast, speaking high swelling words of confidence regarding the future and your doings in it, your buying and selling and getting gain. All such arrogant exultation is evil.'[1] There is an exultation, a rejoicing, a glorying, which is good. 'My soul shall make her *boast* in the Lord,' David sings, leading the universal choir of believing hearts; and Paul '*gloried*,' as every true believer glories with him, 'in the cross of Christ.' But all such glorying as we have here, boasting in self and not in God, through proud presumption of secure life, and health, and success,—this is *evil;* it dishonours God, it saps everything of spirituality which may be in us, and it exerts a baneful influence around.

Now, brethren, what James wrote to the merchants among the Jewish Christians of his day, is nowise less applicable in our time. The forms of human life vary; the texture takes different shapes and hues in different ages and countries; but

---

[1] In connection with καυχᾶσθαι, ἐν may express the *ground* of the 'glorying,' as in i. 9, 10. If such be the force of ἐν here, then the meaning is, that these men 'exult' in the fact of their being daring enough to speak so loftily and independently regarding their future. This, however, brings in a somewhat remote thought, which, from the πᾶσα καύχησις τοιαύτη following, appears to take the principal place. Now the whole context indicates that it is not merely glorying regarding their arrogant confidence as to the future against which the exhortation of the apostle is directed, but this arrogant confidence itself, and the utterances which spring from it. It appears probable, therefore, that καυχᾶσθαι simply designates such proud speeches as have been quoted in ver. 13, such speeches themselves being in truth the expression of exultation in fancied independence. In this case we must hold ἐν as used to exhibit the state or sphere. So Huther and others.

the spirit is substantially the same, the hazards for the soul the same, the refuge for the soul the same. In an age like ours, when natural science is every day so greatly increasing the means of money-making, when trade has so many ramifications, and, connected with it, so much that is exciting, there is very great peril of a man's losing the thought of God, and, amid the whir of commercial machinery, failing to hear that 'still small voice' which reminds us that 'life, and breath, and all things' are at His disposal. For our time, therefore, the apostle's words have, if possible, even greater force than they had for his own. And the teaching is not for merchants only. All kinds of anticipations of the future in which worldly desires of any sort come into play, involve the same danger. 'The mother of Sisera looked out at a window, and cried through the lattice, Why is his chariot so long in coming? why tarry the wheels of his chariots? Her wise ladies answered her, yea, she returned answer to herself, Have they not sped? have they not divided the prey? to Sisera a prey of divers colours, a prey of divers colours of needlework, of divers colours of needlework on both sides, meet for the necks of them that take the spoil?' Nothing but worldly hope, worldly confidence—no thought of God or His providence; but meanwhile the enemy of the Lord has perished.

'All such rejoicing'—all arrogant forecasting in any sphere and on any subject—'is evil.' But to the energetic prosecution of all the activities of life, to sagacious forecast and vigorous exertion founded thereon, all maintained in a spirit of reverential remembrance of God, the words of James are in no measure hostile. The Bible is eminently stimulative to industry. Its principle is, that 'if any man will not work, neither should he eat;' and every intelligent and faithful holder of Bible truth is 'diligent in his business.' Now in many departments this cannot be done without looking forward, perhaps far forward—without deciding to 'go to such a city, and continue there' a week, or a month, or a year, 'and buy and sell.' On all such resolutions of honest, God-fearing men, formed and carried out in the humble spirit of those who always say in their hearts, if not with their lips, 'If the Lord will,' He does not frown. The thought of divine providence, of his heavenly Father's watchful care, cheers the Christian in all his work; and the remembrance that our life is but 'a vapour, that appeareth for a little time, and then vanisheth away'—the taking in of death into his calculations—does not unnerve, but stimulates. 'Whatsoever his hand findeth to do, he does it with his might;' bearing in mind that 'there is no work, nor device, nor knowledge, nor wisdom, in the grave, whither he goeth.'

But, brethren, is not that fact on which the apostle's appeal is founded a very strange one,—that our ignorance of the future, and our knowledge of the brevity and uncertainty of life, exert so little influence on the views and conduct of vast multitudes? For reasons of infinite wisdom, having reference both to our good and to His own glory—some of which we can perceive even now—God has hidden our earthly future from us. Prophecy sheds light on the great principles and outlines of God's administration,—but with regard to the future history even of the church we know almost nothing in detail; and respecting our own personal earthly future absolutely nothing. We may conjecture, but we have no knowledge; and few things are more calculated to bring with liveliness before us the contrast between our littleness and God's greatness, than the consideration that 'we know not what a day may bring forth.' We speculate, and reason, and guess; we grapple with the future, tearing at the veil, sometimes, as if we defied omnipotence to keep it there; and yet we know nothing, whilst

'He knoweth the end from the beginning.' Eternity is to Him one great present, which in all its length and breadth, with all its events and all their relations to each other, He surveys at a glance, without movement or effort.

We are ignorant of what will befall us even if we continue to live,—and we may die. Ere another day dawn, 'the silver cord may be loosed, and the golden bowl broken, and the pitcher broken at the fountain, and the wheel broken at the cistern.' We know this,—that we certainly shall die one day, and that that may be to-day. No man or woman in the world doubts it; nothing is a more utter commonplace than that our life is 'as a shadow,' 'as a flower of the grass,' 'as a vapour.' Yet what vast numbers act as if they were to live for ever, as if all men were mortal except themselves! The very familiarity of the truth, the fact that we know it so well and hold it so certain, deadens it to us. As Coleridge finely says, 'Truths of all others the most awful and interesting, are too often considered as so true that they lose all the power of truth, and lie bedridden in the dormitory of the soul, side by side with the most despised and exploded errors.'[1]

The words of the 17th verse, looked at by themselves, set forth a general principle regarding sin,—that knowledge and responsibility go together. If, with reference to any point of morals, neither conscience, however candidly interrogated, nor revelation, however honestly and carefully studied, yielded any light, sin could not have place at all; and the clearer the light on God's law, the deeper is the sinfulness of those who break it, whether by committing what God forbids or neglecting what He enjoins. In their connection, however, which is clearly with the immediately preceding paragraph,—not, as has been supposed by some, with all the previous part of the Epistle,—

[1] *Aids to Reflection:* Introductory Aphorism i.

the words seem intended specially to press home to the consciences of the readers the responsibility resting on them all, from the fact that the truths of which the apostle has been speaking are so familiar to all. 'It is the tritest of all commonplaces,' he says, 'that life is a vapour, and that for its continuance, and everything which rests on its continuance, we depend absolutely on the will of God. Knowing this so well, then, bear in mind your responsibility; repent of your proud and foolish speeches, and of the spirit which gave them utterance; humble yourselves in the sight of the Lord, and resolve in His strength henceforth to cherish ever a child-like sense of dependence on Him. *To him that knoweth to do good, and doeth it not, to him it is sin.*'

XXV.

WOES OF THE WICKED RICH.

'Go to now, ye rich men, weep and howl for your miseries that shall come upon you. 2 Your riches are corrupted, and your garments are moth-eaten. 3 Your gold and silver is cankered; and the rust of them shall be a witness against you, and shall eat your flesh as it were fire. Ye have heaped treasure together for the last days. 4 Behold, the hire of the labourers which have reaped down your fields, which is of you kept back by fraud, crieth: and the cries of them which have reaped are entered into the ears of the Lord of sabaoth. 5 Ye have lived in pleasure on the earth, and been wanton; ye have nourished your hearts, as in a day of slaughter. 6 Ye have condemned and killed the just; and he doth not resist you.'—JAMES v. 1-6.

THROUGHOUT the previous chapter the apostle has been occupied with the subject of worldliness, and the enervating and debasing influence on the character of professing Christians of sympathy in any degree with the longings and efforts of persons who seek their portion on the earth. Dwelling on the fact that the root of worldliness is pride, arrogant self-assertion against God, he has illustrated this by an examination of two of the innumerable forms in which the worldly spirit shows itself—depreciation of others for self-advancement, and confidence in the duration of life and of prosperity. Having closed his remarks on these examples, the apostle at this point, in very natural accordance with that elevated strain of solemn appeal which has pervaded the 4th chapter, turns aside for a moment to address those avowed enemies of Christianity, the wealthy unbelieving Jews, through free intercourse with whom it was that many of the professed followers of Jesus had been led far astray. That by the words '*Ye rich men*,' in the 1st verse, are intended not wealthy Christians (probably a very small class), but wealthy unbelievers, those same 'rich men' who were spoken of in the 6th and 7th verses of the 2nd chapter as oppressors of the Christians and blasphemers of the 'worthy name' of Jesus, is plain from the tone of the whole passage. And that the unbelievers who were in the apostle's mind were mainly, if not exclusively, Jews, may reasonably be inferred from the nationality and circumstances of those Christians to whom the letter was addressed. Confirmation of this view is afforded by the use in the 4th verse of the distinctively Israelitish name for God, 'The Lord of sabaoth;' and also by the nature of the doom denounced, which seems to point in the first instance to the calamities that came upon the Jews throughout the world at the time of the destruction of Jerusalem.

To the wealthy unbelieving Jews, then, James proclaims their sin and their coming miseries, in words which sound exactly like an utterance of one of the old prophets. The paragraph contains the 'burden' of Israel's wicked rich, and we seem to hear again almost literally Amos's outpouring of holy indignation : ' Hear this, O ye that swallow up the needy, even to make the poor of the land to fail,—saying, When will the new moon be gone, that we may sell corn? and the Sabbath, that we may set forth wheat, making the ephah small, and the shekel great, and falsifying the balances by deceit? that we may buy the poor for silver, and the needy for a pair of shoes; yea, and sell the refuse of the wheat? The Lord hath sworn by the excellency of Jacob, Surely I will never forget any of their works. Shall not the land tremble for this, and every one mourn that dwelleth therein? And it shall rise up wholly as a flood; and it shall be cast out and drowned, as by the flood of Egypt. And it shall come to pass in that day, saith the Lord God, that I will cause the sun to go down at noon, and I will darken the earth in the clear day: and I will turn your feasts into mourning, and all your songs into lamentation; and I will bring up sackcloth upon all loins, and baldness upon every head; and I will make it as the mourning of an only son, and the end thereof as a bitter day' (Amos viii. 4–10).

The apostle's language in the verses before us was well fitted to arouse and alarm those Christians who, forgetting that 'friendship with the world is enmity with God,' had been drawn away to some extent into sympathy with the views and likings of these worldlings, and into imitation of their practices. It seems highly probable, however, that we are not to regard the paragraph as a mere rhetorical apostrophe, addressed only in *form* to the enemies of the church, whilst intended really to influence none but Christian readers. There was much in the writings of our Lord's apostles to interest all thoughtful persons, whether believers in Him or not— particularly to interest Jews, whose philosophy and literature were solely religious; and no Epistle was more likely to attract the attention of the unconverted Jews than one addressed specially to the Christians of their nation by James, a man whose character, as we know, commanded the utmost respect from all classes in Jerusalem. We may well suppose, therefore, that wherever copies of this letter went, its contents became known in one way or another to many beyond the church. It would seem, indeed, to be hinted at the beginning of the letter by the generality of the address, 'To the twelve tribes which are in the Dispersion,' that a wider circle of readers than the

Christian converts was not altogether absent from James's thoughts. His 'heart's desire and prayer to God for Israel' was, like Paul's, 'that they might be saved;' and the paragraph before us is an arrow, shot indeed at a venture, but with the devout hope that somewhere a joint might be found in the harness of the hitherto stiff-necked and rebellious among his people, by which it might enter, and wound, and bring the soul to 'the Lord that healeth us.'

The apostle begins by calling on the wicked rich men to *'weep and howl for their miseries that were coming on.'* The *command* has obviously, according to a familiar usage of the Hebrew prophets, the force of 'you well may.' 'You may well wail with the bitterest lamentation in anticipation of your coming woes, for the most intense distress will be justified by their awfulness.'

Throughout the whole paragraph the strain is one of simple denunciation of doom. But we know that the great mission of God's servants and of His word is one of grace,—that 'whatever things were written aforetime were written' to this intent mainly, that men 'through comfort of the Scriptures might have *hope*.' This is true of the utterances of righteous indignation in Scripture, as well as of its tender pleadings. The Saviour's 'Woe unto you, scribes and Pharisees, hypocrites,' was as really a word of love as His 'Come unto Me, all ye that labour and are heavy laden, and I will give you rest.' The most definite denunciations have all an undertone of yearning appeal to repent, and of gracious promise if only men will repent and turn to the Lord. Jonah by divine command proclaimed, 'Yet forty days, and Nineveh shall be overthrown;' and yet, as the sequel of the narrative tells us, when 'God saw their works, that they turned from their evil way, God repented of the evil that He had said that He would do unto them, and He did it not.' So the apostle's utterance of doom to the wicked rich, in the paragraph before us, was a call of grace, if only they would hear and be wise.

It seems likely, as has been already said, that James's prediction of '*miseries that should come upon*' these men points in the first instance to the destruction of Jerusalem, which occurred forty years after our Lord's ascension; and therefore, from any date to which the writing of this Epistle can reasonably be referred, could not be very far off, at most from twenty to twenty-five years. The solemn emphasis with which our Lord dwells on that terrible event, as a manifestation of God's wrath for Israel's iniquities, renders it in every way probable, when we consider the nature of this paragraph, that the woes of that time are here included. 'There shall be great tribulation,' our Lord foretold, 'such as was not since the beginning of the world to this time, no, nor ever shall be;' and the narrative of the overthrow written by Josephus the contemporary historian reads, on this as on all the particulars of the Lord's predictions on this subject, almost like a designed commentary to describe their minute fulfilment. About the same time as the overrunning of Palestine, and the siege and destruction of its capital, by the Roman legions, there were throughout the whole world, wherever Jews were found, outbreaks of hostility and cruelty against them on the part of those among whom they lived. Thus 'the twelve tribes that were in the Dispersion' suffered 'miseries' similar to those which befell their brethren in the Holy City. Both at Jerusalem and elsewhere, too (as in all cases of the kind, the highest trees having always to endure the fiercest violence of the tempest), the cruelties fell with special frequency and severity on the richer and more influential classes of society. As the wealthy Jews had taken the lead in sin, so through

God's providence they were made to take the lead in suffering.

But the destruction of Jerusalem, and all the miseries connected with it, were, like every other visitation of God for judgement during the course of human history, representative of the great judgement at the close. In the Lord's prophecy regarding the overthrow of the city, given in the 24th chapter of Matthew, this representative character of the catastrophe, as shadowing forth one immeasurably more awful yet to come on all the finally impenitent of the human race, is distinctly exhibited to the mind of every thoughtful reader. To that great day our apostle also would plainly carry forward the thoughts of his readers,—a day when there shall come 'indignation and wrath, tribulation and anguish, upon every soul of man that doeth evil, of the Jew first, and also of the Gentile.'

The statements which follow regarding the 'riches,' 'garments,' and 'gold and silver,' may be understood in two ways,— as *a figurative description of the imminence and nature of the doom*, or as *a literal description of the evidence of the sin* for which God was about to inflict the doom. According to the former view, the meaning may be thus paraphrased: 'That wealth in which you have such pride, and on which you build such lofty and far-reaching hopes, is about to be taken from you utterly; and if you would open your eyes to look at it in the light shed by the predictions of the Lord Jesus and by His doings in providence, you would read upon it on all sides God's writing of doom,—you would see your wealth corrupted, your piles of rich raiment moth-eaten, your gold and silver rusted through.' On the latter view, the sense is: 'Your store-rooms, your coffers, your wardrobes, reveal your wickedness. With the poor always around you, whom God has sent to you to receive a share of what He, the Proprietor of all, has given to your stewardship, you have yet wealth of every kind mouldering from want of use. God's children—your own brethren—are shivering at your gate, whilst you have piles of raiment which the moths have been permitted to possess. God's poor are houseless and hungry, whilst your gold and silver, which He gave you to *occupy*, that, like the steward in the parable, you might "make unto yourselves friends," but, unlike him, prove yourselves thereby faithful to your Lord,—this gold and silver lies wholly unused, and covered with rust, in your treasure-chests.' Either of these meanings comes naturally out of the words employed by the apostle, and is pertinent to his object. Considering this, and remembering how often Scripture illustrates the natural connection between sin and death, by showing that sin generates its own punishment,—the eye wilfully closed becoming judicially blinded, the heart wilfully obdurate becoming judicially hardened,—it seems reasonable to suppose that both thoughts, the thought of sin and the thought of doom, were in James's mind. This view best answers all exegetical requirements; for whilst, on the one hand, the idea of *punishment* seems to be the prominent one in the first part of the passage, seeing that otherwise we should not have anywhere that statement of the 'miseries' coming upon these wicked rich men, which the words of the 1st verse lead us to look for,— on the other hand, the most satisfactory sense of the statement, 'The rust of them shall eat your flesh as it were fire,' is afforded by the supposition that here rust as an evidence of niggardliness was in the apostle's thoughts.

By '*riches*' some interpreters hold 'hoarded stores of grain,' or other produce of the ground, to be specially intended, because thus the verb 'are corrupted,' or 'rotten,' has its exact primary significance. The word so rendered, however, is occasionally used somewhat loosely, like our own 'corrupt;' and it is perhaps better to regard the 'corruption of the riches' as a general expression, of which the statements that follow regarding the garments and the precious metals are examples. The mention of *'garments'* in this connection strikes a European reader as a little strange, particularly if, as seems probable, the idea of doom be here the prominent one. But in the East—in all ages, we have reason to think—it has been not uncommon for wealthy men to invest a considerable portion of their riches in 'changes of raiment.' Given as presents, these are esteemed conspicuous marks of honour and affection;[1] and among the great men who frequent courts, the highest distinction is deemed to belong to those who are able to show themselves in a succession of different sumptuous robes. The all but immobility of the fashion of attire in the East, moreover, makes a store of garments useful for a very long time, possibly for generations.

It is well known that gold and silver are not liable to *'rust'* in the strict sense of the word. Some interpreters have therefore supposed that James employs this term loosely, as including the tarnishing to which the precious metals are exposed. But in the declaration, 'The rust of them shall eat your flesh as it were fire,' there is manifest reference to corrosion by rust proper. The true explanation of the little difficulty, no doubt, is that the general idea in the writer's mind was that of destruction of property in the modes caused by want of use,—of which that naturally suggesting itself when *metals* are specially mentioned is rust. This, accordingly, he names, though not strictly applicable to gold and silver. 'The stern and vivid

---

[1] Illustrations in the history of Joseph and Naaman will occur to every reader.

depiction of prophetic denunciation does not take such trifles into account.'[1]

Regarding the 'rust' the apostle goes on to declare to the wicked rich, that it '*should be a witness against them, and should eat their flesh as it were fire.*' The rust is manifestly looked at as a 'crying' evidence of sinful hoarding. Of palaces built with the fruits of oppression Habakkuk says: 'The stone shall cry out of the wall, and the beam out of the timber shall answer it' (ii. 11). Similarly here: 'When the Lord comes to judgement, the rust on that hoarded wealth, which should have been feeding the hungry and clothing the naked, will bear loud testimony before Him to your narrowness and obduracy of heart, and bring down His stern condemnation; and, your consciences waking up into terrible activity, remorse for your ungodliness and inhumanity will torture you,—the rust, so to speak, passing over from your wealth to prey on your flesh, and causing you anguish like that produced by fire.' Thus, as Manton says, the rust 'is not only *witness*, but *executioner.*' The paraphrase just given sets forth the meaning of the words according to our Authorized Version. In this clause, at least, our translators evidently held the apostle to be looking on the rust as an *evidence of sin*. But we have seen reason to consider its primary reference, when first mentioned, to be rather to *doom;* and this may be spoken of here also. The original words rendered '*shall be a witness against you*,' may mean, and perhaps more naturally do mean, 'shall be a witness *to* you.' With this rendering, the sense of the clause might be: 'The destruction which impends on your property will testify to you of that which will come upon yourselves, and through the conviction thus produced will torture you.' But '*to eat the flesh as fire*' is an expression which seems

[1] Alford.

most naturally to suggest the work of a remorseful conscience,—the very word 'remorse' indicating, according to its etymology, a *gnawing* or *corrosion* like that of rust. The thought of *evidence of sin* and that of *doom* being both in the apostle's mind throughout the passage, the former, I apprehend, here assumes prominence.

In the closing statement of the 3rd verse, '*Ye have heaped treasure together for* (more accurately 'in') *the last days*,' we see still both thoughts present. 'In an age when prophecy and providence indicate so clearly to all who are willing to discern the signs of the times, that a great crisis is at hand,—an age when everything which can appeal to your religious feeling, your patriotism, your highest self-interest, is calling on you with peculiar distinctness to hold earthly property as of but minor moment, to set your affections on the things which are above, and to strive to lead back your misguided nation to the God whom they have forsaken,—*in these last days* you have been greedily heaping up treasure for yourselves.' James's words, if we turn them to purposes of exhortation, are thus parallel to Paul's—spoken, like these, with reference to the impending destruction of Jerusalem, and also more generally to the fact that since the advent of Christ we are in the last age of the world, and have a far clearer revelation of the solemnity and momentousness of death and of the Lord's second advent for judgement than those who lived under the earlier Economies: 'This I say, brethren, the time is short: it remaineth, that both they that have wives be as though they had none; and they that weep, as though they wept not; and they that rejoice, as though they rejoiced not; and they that buy, as though they possessed not; and they that use this world, as not abusing it: for the fashion of this world passeth away' (1 Cor. vii. 29–31). But again, *doom* also is before the apostle's mind. 'Ye have heaped up treasures, and in your arrogance and wilful ignorance ye are saying, To-morrow shall be as this day, and much more abundant; but in truth ye are *in the last days*, and the desolating flood of divine judgement is about to sweep away everything in which ye have trusted and delighted. The men of Sodom did eat, they drank, they bought, they sold, they planted, they builded; but the same day that Lot went out of Sodom it rained fire and brimstone from heaven, and destroyed them all. Even thus, said the Lord Jesus, shall it be in the day when the Son of man is revealed.'

You will observe that in the verses we have been examining we have one of those manifest reminiscences and echoes of the Sermon on the Mount, which abound in this Epistle. The apostle has evidently before his mind the Lord's exhortation: 'Lay not up for yourselves treasures upon earth, where moth and rust doth corrupt, and where thieves break through and steal; but lay up for yourselves treasures in heaven, where neither moth nor rust doth corrupt, and where thieves do not break through nor steal: for where your treasure is, there will your heart be also' (Matt. vi. 19–21).

Thus far we have had a denunciation of judgement, with an indication given also, in the form of the utterance, of the nature of one great sin of those wicked rich men whom the apostle is addressing,—hoarding money in the midst of the hungry and the naked, and this at a time when God was with special distinctness calling on them to hold worldly possessions loosely. James proceeds now to a formal arraignment, setting forth further charges of sin in detail, and calling attention to these by his introductory '*Behold*.' He accuses them first of *injustice*, specially in the way of defrauding their servants: '*The hire of the labourers who have reaped down your fields,* which is of you kept back by fraud, crieth[1] : and the cries of them which have reaped are entered into the ears of the Lord of sabaoth.' As the voice of Abel's blood 'cried' unto God from the ground, —as 'the cry of Sodom and Gomorrah was great,'—so, from the coffers of these wicked men, the money which should have been given to their servants as wages, but had been fraudulently withheld, was ever making a loud appeal to heaven. They starved the poor to enrich themselves. Their stately mansions, their sumptuous fare, their gay clothing and gold rings, were maintained at the cost of servants' unremunerated toil. Is this voice of which the apostle speaks silent in our day? Ah, brethren, if we remember how wide of range the reference of James's charge is, — that in the eyes of God substantially the same sin here spoken of is committed by those who, though there be no breach of positive contract, yet take advantage of the necessities of the poor in an overcrowded country, by making them work for wages which bear no reasonable proportion to the profits of the employer; who distress poor tradespeople by long and needless delay in payment of money due ; or who in other similar ways diminish the income of those that at the best can but barely keep the

---

[1] Huther (followed by Alford) takes ἀφ' ὑμῶν with κράζει, 'crieth from you,' that is, from your coffers, where it ought not to be ; and refers to Gen. iv. 10 and Ex. ii. 23. The use of the personal pronoun, however, when not the men themselves but only their purses or coffers are meant, is harsh, and altogether unsupported by the passages mentioned, where in the one place the LXX. have ἐκ τῆς γῆς, and in the other ἀπὸ τῶν ἔργων. It seems better, therefore, to adhere to the old construction, connecting ἀφ' ὑμῶν with ἀπεστερημένος (or ἀφυστερημένος); and if we suppose the fact to have been present to the apostle's mind, that the great landowners of whom he is speaking in most cases negotiated with their labourers not immediately, but through stewards, the use of ἀπό instead of ὑπό need cause no difficulty. The fraud, whilst committed immediately 'by' the subordinates, was 'from' the rich proprietors themselves, being in accordance with their spirit and general instructions.

wolf of starvation from the door;—is there not reason to fear that not merely from much of the wealth of our nation a loud 'cry' is going up to God, but even from the riches of many members of the church of Christ, who taught us to 'give unto our servants that which is just and equal, knowing that we also have a Master in heaven,' and to 'bear one another's burdens, and so fulfil His law'?[1] Our apostle speaks particularly of the defrauding of farm labourers '*which reaped*,' evidently because those employers whom he had immediately before his mind were in many cases wealthy landowners; and not improbably also because hard-heartedness is peculiarly glaring when, amid the joys of 'harvest-home,' men can defraud their reapers, and, while their barns are full of corn, can let the children of their servants pine for want of bread.

Not merely do the wages fraudulently withheld 'cry' to heaven, but the cries of the reapers themselves also '*are entered into the ears of the Lord of sabaoth*' (that is, 'of hosts,'

[1] It would be ungrateful to God not to acknowledge that during the last fifty years there has been in our country, in some important departments of labour at least, a great improvement in the condition of the employed. Even so recently as 1843, the miners in our coal-pits were treated in great measure as slaves, and feeble women had to toil like beasts of burden; and in the factories little children from five years of age were kept at work for thirteen hours a day, so that all energy and hope were crushed out of them, and disease and depravity took firm hold.

> 'How long, they say, how long, O cruel nation,
>   Will you stand, to move the world, on a child's heart,—
> Stifle down with a mailed heel its palpitation,
>   And tread onward to your throne amid the mart?
> Our blood splashes upward, O gold-heaper,
>   And your purple shows your path!
> But the child's sob in the silence curses deeper
>   Than the strong man in his wrath.'
>   MRS. BROWNING'S *Cry of the Children.*

Now, through the influence of wisdom and Christian principle on our legislation, these things are only memories.

the Hebrew word being employed here by James, as sometimes in the Greek version of the Old Testament, which was familiar to his readers). '*One* hears the wail of the poor whom ye oppress,' says James to the rich men, 'though ye are deaf,—One whose "hosts" can overthrow in a moment all your puny power, and overwhelm you with utter destruction.'

The next charge is that of *lavish self-indulgence*: '*Ye have lived in pleasure on the earth and been wanton; ye have nourished your hearts as in a day of slaughter.*' The apostle seems to be carried forward in thought by the energy of his spirit to the great day of final account, and as from the midst of its dread solemnities comes forth his stern accusation of the wicked rich standing near. This point of view is suggested by the form of the verbs in the original,—the exact rendering being not 'ye have lived in pleasure,' but the simple past, 'ye lived in pleasure,' and so with the other verbs. You cannot fail to see that, supposing the utterance to be as from beside the 'great white throne,' a peculiar force and pertinence are given to the expression '*on the earth:*' for though the judgement will be held in this world, yet 'the earth,' as the scene of the old forms of human life, will appear to men to be far away.

The rich men have been spoken of in the first verses of the paragraph as simply hoarding their money. Here we have them described as expending it profusely. These two charges are not inconsistent with each other; and in the lives of very many of those who count it the chief end of man to glorify and enjoy himself both sins manifestly co-exist. A man of large income lays up money by closing his eyes to the claims of benevolence,—whilst at the same time on his own self-gratification he spends without stint. Such saving and such spending are both alike utterly opposed to the principles of stewardship for God. The man has forgotten entirely that 'the silver and the gold are God's,' and this no less when men have them in their keeping than when they are yet in the mine. '*Ye lived in pleasure on the earth*,' says James, 'and earth alone was in your thoughts; not heaven, where God was listening to the cry of those whom ye oppressed; not hell, where many a man who when on the earth had like you been clothed in purple and fine linen, and fared sumptuously every day, and like you had disregarded the appeal of God's poor, was in torment. Ye lived in pleasure, *and were wanton*, squandering in wild revelry what had been wrung from the poor by tyranny and fraud.'

It has been thought by some interpreters, that in the last words of the 5th verse there is a reference to the abundance and festivity found in the house of a Jew on a day when he had presented a sacrifice to God,—a large part of the animal offered being, according to the law, returned by the priest, and a feast held. There are several allusions in Scripture to such feasts, somewhat similar to that supposed to be made here. But all the oldest manuscripts of the New Testament omit the particle of comparison '*as;*' and on the removal of it from the text, this reference becomes untenable. There can be little doubt that the apostle, having before his mind the impending 'day of the Lord's vengeance,' and the rich men's mad revelries and utter brute-like disregard of the future, likens them here to oxen, who graze as quietly and find in their rich pastures as much satisfaction on the very day when they are to be killed as on any other day. 'As if ye were natural brute beasts, made to be taken and destroyed (2 Pet. ii. 12), *ye nourished your hearts*—pampered all your likings—on the eve of your destruction, when many indications of providence might have told you that you had come to your very *slaughter-day*.'

Woes of the Wicked Rich.

The last accusation which James brings against these men is that of *high-handed cruelty*: '*Ye have condemned and killed the just, and he doth not resist you.*' By many '*the just* (or righteous) man' here is regarded as practically equivalent to 'just men,' an individual being taken to represent the class who were the objects of the rich men's persecution.[1] This is a mode of expression not uncommon in Scripture, particularly in the Old Testament; but in a passage like this, which is in form a definite historical statement, it seems hardly natural to give the words a general meaning. It is difficult, too, on this view, to account for the sudden transition in the last clause from the historical form, '*Ye condemned*, ye *killed* the just one,' to the present, '*he doth* not resist you.' Besides, it can hardly be doubted that in the apostolic age 'The Just One' was a common designation of the Lord Jesus, especially in the discourse of Jewish Christians to each other (such as we have in this Epistle),—so that the first thought in the minds of James's readers, regarding the words which he here uses, would almost certainly be that he referred to the Saviour. To the people of Jerusalem, assembled in Solomon's Porch, Peter said, 'Ye denied the Holy One and the Just' (Acts iii. 14). Stephen said to the Sanhedrin, 'Your fathers have slain them which showed before of the coming of the Just One, of whom

---

[1] On this view of the meaning, an interesting parallel to the apostle's words is found in the Apocrypha (Wisd. ii. 10–20). The exact accordance of the verse with the circumstances of James's own death, too, as related by Hegesippus, is very striking. 'The scribes and Pharisees,' says the historian, 'threw down the Just from the pinnacle of the temple, and said, Let us stone James the Just, and they began to stone him; for he had not been killed by the fall, but, turning round, knelt and said, I beseech Thee, Lord God and Father, forgive them, for they know not what they do. But whilst they were thus stoning him, one of the fullers took the club with which he used to beat the clothes, and struck the head of the Just. Thus he suffered martyrdom.'

ye have been now the betrayers and murderers' (Acts vii. 52). To Paul, Ananias spoke thus: 'The God of our fathers hath chosen thee, that thou shouldest know His will, and see that (strictly, as here, 'the') Just One' (Acts xxii. 14). It seems to me, therefore, decidedly more probable that by 'the just one,' in the verse before us, James means the Lord Jesus.

Perhaps comparatively few of those who were the arrogant and cruel persecutors of Christ's church, at the time when this Epistle was written, had personally taken part in the judicial murder of the Lord—so perfectly described, you observe, by the apostle's words, 'Ye condemned—ye killed.' But it is the rich Jewish unbelievers as a *class* whom he addresses, and it was mainly to their class that that maddest, wickedest deed in the history of the world was due. In the Gospels we see proof everywhere that it was the chief priests and rulers who had a bitter, murderous hatred to Jesus; and even when the common people took an active part in the proceedings connected with the judicial murder—as, for example, in calling for Barabbas—it was because 'the chief priests and elders persuaded' them to do this (Matt. xxvii. 20). To this prominence of the wealthy and influential men of the nation in the sin, Peter adverts in his address to the people in Solomon's Porch, 'And now, brethren, I wot that through ignorance ye did it, as did also your rulers' (Acts iii. 17); Paul also, in writing to the Corinthians, 'We speak the wisdom of God in a mystery; which (wisdom) none of the princes of this world knew,—for had they known it, they would not have crucified the Lord of glory' (1 Cor. ii. 7, 8). The rich men spoken of by James here, who persecuted Christians, exhibited exactly the same spirit, and therefore in the eyes of God were guilty of the same sin, as those who had murdered the Lord; for it is Christ in His people that the world hates. 'Saul, Saul, why persecutest thou *Me?*' The wickedness of the *class* of wealthy unbelieving Jews, then—as indeed the wickedness of the human race, but of these immediately and most manifestly—had culminated in the crucifixion of the Lord; and, according to the teaching of several of His parables, expressly for this, as the decisive act of renunciation of loyalty to God, came the utter overthrow of the city and commonwealth. Because the husbandmen said, ' This is the Heir, come let us kill Him,' and cast Him out of the vineyard, and slew Him,—the Lord of the vineyard miserably destroyed those wicked men.

From the historical form of expression, as of an utterance on the Judgement Day, 'Ye condemned—ye killed—the Just One,' James suddenly returns to the present, '*He doth not resist you.*' There is in these words a conjunction of tender and earnest appeal with solemn warning, to which the suddenness of the transition gives extraordinary force, and which fittingly closes this striking paragraph. '*He doth not resist you* —did not then, for He was led as a lamb to the slaughter, and as a sheep before her shearers is dumb, so He opened not His mouth,—does not now, while ye are serving yourselves heirs to the iniquity of your fathers, by condemning and killing His people. Still He bears with you,—He who wields all power in heaven and in earth : will He not win you by this marvellous long-suffering? But oh, bethink you, if your murderous opposition to Him continue, what certainly must the end be? The quiet is not, cannot be, for ever. How terrible will be His vengeance for your accumulated guilt ! *He doth not resist you*,—and in the very silence there is that which should fill His foes with terror. It is the dead calm before the earthquake.'

XXVI.

PATIENCE THROUGH THE BLESSED HOPE.

'Be patient therefore, brethren, unto the coming of the Lord. Behold, the husbandman waiteth for the precious fruit of the earth, and hath long patience for it, until he receive the early and latter rain. 8 Be ye also patient; stablish your hearts: for the coming of the Lord draweth nigh.'—JAMES v. 7, 8.

FROM his solemn warning, by way of apostrophe, to the bigoted and cruel oppressors of the church, the apostle comes back at this point to resume the ordinary course of his Epistle,—the word '*brethren*' intimating that his address is again directly to Christians. He exhorts them to bear their sufferings with patience. The connection of thought, while in a general way with the whole announcement in the preceding paragraph, seems to be more particularly with the ideas suggested by the solemn 'doth not resist you,' the last words of the paragraph. Those same objects of expectation which were calculated to fill the persecutors with dread were fitted to animate and sustain believers; for the Lord when He comes, whether personally at the great consummation of this world's history, or in those striking acts of providence which the wise recognise as His visitations — lively proofs of His presence, precursors of His final advent,—comes not to punish and crush His foes only, but to bless His people.

The Jewish Christians to whom James wrote were, many of them, as we have seen, in sore trouble through the oppression of the enemies of the truth, particularly their own unbelieving countrymen. The Saviour had given them warning that it would be so,—that if the world hated and persecuted Him, it would also hate and persecute those who honoured His name and strove to walk in His ways. Still, no doubt, times of almost faithless wonderment would come, and flashes of sinful impatience dart across their souls; and even in their hours of devoutest and most child-like feeling the cry would go up, 'How long, O Lord, how long?' In all ages when the world's hostility to vital religion was permitted by God to show itself in virulent and lengthened persecution,—when prisons were crowded with God's saints, when lips which had taught and comforted many were silenced by death on a scaffold, when smoke went curling up towards heaven from fires that were torturing and destroying the excellent of the earth,—and yet the heaven was silent, and no bolt of divine vengeance came forth to consume the enemies of the Lord in a moment,—this must have proved a most severe trial of that quietness and restfulness of heart in God to which believers are called.

Few things, if any, in the life of faith are more difficult than to accept cordially the divine forbearance with arrogant and oppressive sin—the sublime long-suffering which permits great moral problems to be worked out fully by the experience of generations, through centuries and millenniums, for God's glory and the good of His angelic and human children everlastingly. It is the way of God to move slowly. Though immediately on the commission of the first sin a promise of grace was given, yet thousands of years had to elapse before the right time came, the fulness of time, when the Son of God was manifested in flesh for our redemption. When He did come, thirty years of His life passed over before His claims to be from God were made known beyond the very narrowest circle. Since His ascension to glory, when all power was given to Him in heaven and in earth, to quicken whom He would, well-nigh two thousand years have gone, and still by far the larger part of our world is in heathen, Mohammedan, or Antichristian darkness; whilst even in lands of gospel light genuine piety seems to rule but a small proportion of the people. It accords with all this that God should be long silent while His people are oppressed. Look at the view given us of this from the side of heaven: 'And when He had opened the fifth seal, I saw under the altar the souls of them that were slain for the word of God, and for the testimony which they held: and they cried with a loud voice, saying, How long, O Lord, holy and true, dost thou not judge and avenge our blood on them that dwell on the earth? And white robes were given unto every one of them; and it was said unto them, that they should rest yet for a little season, until their fellow-servants also and their brethren, that should be killed as they were, should be fulfilled' (Rev. vi. 9–11). How wonderful is this divine calm above — 'It was said unto them that they should rest' — in contrast with the turmoil, and weary waiting, and anxious appeals below!

The apostle exhorts his readers to '*be patient*' under the oppression of their enemies — to seek oneness of will with God, and wait His time with child-like hearts. This is true Christian patience. It has no Stoical affectation of indifference to suffering, — it acknowledges that trouble in itself is 'not joyous, but grievous;' but it recognises God's hand even in afflictions which immediately come from the selfishness and malignity of evil men; in God's hand it sees that of a Father who will never chasten longer or more severely than is really needful; and thus it waits His time for deliverance. That time certainly will come. Commonly His providence enriches His people with many comforts here —periods, long periods often, of health, and peace, and prosperity (for 'godliness hath the promise of this life' as well as of the future). But however many or however gloomy the days be during which He afflicts us, and the years in which we see evil, yet assuredly one day He will make us glad. 'Weeping may endure for a night,' and the night may seem very long and very dark; 'but joy cometh in the morning.'

To that blessed morning, as dawning on the whole church of God, now for the first time without any sorrowing member —to the day of the Lord's personal coming, to clothe His people with the garments of everlasting glory and beauty—is undoubtedly the grand if not the exclusive reference of the apostle's words here, in speaking of the limit beyond which patience, waiting in any form or measure, will not be needed, —'*unto the coming of the Lord.*' The paragraph before this, describing the miseries about to come on the rich oppressors of the church, probably points forward in the first instance, as we have seen, to the calamities connected with the destruction of Jerusalem, but plainly also points beyond these to the 'tribulation and anguish' of Christ's enemies at the Judgement Day. Now the expression used in the passage before us, 'the coming of the Lord,' is beyond question employed sometimes in the New Testament of the destruction of the wicked capital and apostate commonwealth of Israel, as similar language is employed in the Old Testament of similar providential judgements. To it, therefore, James may be supposed to have still some reference in the exhortation before us; if at all, however, only very slightly, as it appears to me. The whole tone of the passage suggests a completeness and grandeur of deliverance,—and this not from the oppression of evil men merely, but from all the troubles of every kind which necessitate patience, — such as plainly to indicate that the Saviour's personal advent was fully before the writer's mind, His advent to raise the dead and judge the world, to visit His enemies with 'everlasting destruction from His presence and from the glory of His power,' and to introduce His friends into the fulness of salvation.

This grand event, the consummation of the divine probationary dealings with this world, is always exhibited in Scripture as for every wise soul the supremely influential fact of the future, and the object of the most ardent longings of the Christian heart. The great spur to energetic service of God is the thought that 'when Christ, who is our life, shall appear, then we also shall appear with Him in glory.' The great support in trouble is the consideration that, 'when His glory shall be revealed, we shall be glad also with exceeding joy.' Conversion is 'turning to God, to serve Him, and to wait for His Son from heaven;' and thus it seems a natural description of Christians, that they are persons who 'love the appearing of the Lord.' This loving expectation of the second coming stands in vital connection with a loving apprehension of the objects of the first coming. Enjoying now precious first-fruits from the advent to sow, we anticipate the glorious fulness of harvest at the advent to reap. We 'look' with brightness of spirit 'for that blessed hope, even His glorious appearing,' because we are filled with thankfulness and love by the remembrance that 'He gave Himself for us, to redeem us from all iniquity.' Believing as a historical fact, most clearly demonstrated, that 'Christ was once offered to bear the sins of many,' we see here ample evidence leading us to accept the sweet assurance, that 'to them that look for Him shall He appear the second time, without sin, unto salvation.' Thus we 'show forth the

VER. 7.] *Patience through the Blessed Hope.* 369

Lord's death till He come;' and 'the contemplations and affections of the believer, travelling between His abasement and His exaltation, find in Jesus under both aspects together a complete salvation.'[1]

By any one who considers the subject, it can hardly be doubted that the second coming of the Lord holds a far less prominent position in the thoughts of most Christians of our day than it did in those of the apostles, and, as is evident from the tone of their writings, they desired that it should do in those of their readers. Is this because we have a less lively love to the Saviour, and longing to be with Him,—because knowing about Jesus does not so fully bring us to know Jesus as our divine Friend and Brother? Whatever the reason, the fact, I think, is certain. The death of the individual has to a great extent taken in the mind of the modern church, as exhibited in the discourses of the pulpit and in religious literature, that place which in the church of the first days was occupied by the Lord's personal advent. Now, however much it may seem to us that this is practically the same thing, and however influential the thought of death will assuredly be on all who look it fairly in the face, yet is it not reasonable to suppose that our religious life must suffer as really, though not to the same degree, by altering the relative prominence given to the articles of our faith in Scripture as by believing positive error? No truth can exert on the mind and heart exactly the same influence as another. Now it seems plain that the Divine Spirit would have Christians to keep before their souls that day with which for them no ideas can be connected but those of blessedness,—the day when the Redeemer shall appear in glory, and all His redeemed ones, gathered together, shall be

[1] Principal David Brown, of Aberdeen, in his singularly able and satisfying work on *The Second Advent.*

2 A

perfectly, publicly, and simultaneously glorified with Him. The substitution for this, then, the putting in its appointed place of prominence in each believer's mind, of the time of his own death—a time, considered simply in itself, not attractive, but repulsive, round which, even for those who fully know that the sting has been taken away, some gloom will hang, and which introduces into a blessedness, ineffable indeed, yet but preparatory to that which remains to be revealed,—this substitution cannot but have in various ways an injurious effect. Its influence strengthens the tendency, of which it seems to be itself in some measure an expression, to gather in the soul's thoughts and yearnings round herself, instead of sending them out fully, joyously, lovingly, to the Saviour. It can hardly be questioned, I think, that the doctrines of pre-millennialism—seriously erroneous doctrines, as it appears to me—have obtained that wide acceptance which they have in our day mainly through a natural and extreme reaction, in the minds of Christians of an ardent and affectionate temperament, from that tone of thinking and feeling which has put the Lord's glorious appearing so far out of view. The best thing one can desire, with regard to the controversy which the pre-millennialists have stirred up, is that it may lead to the giving to that grand event its primitive and proper place in the contemplations and hopes of the church generally.

Having exhorted the suffering Christians to 'be patient till the coming of the Lord,' the apostle, according to his wont, elucidates and enforces his advice by an illustration: '*Behold, the husbandman waiteth for the precious fruit of the earth, and hath long patience for it, until he receive the early and latter rain. Be ye also patient ; stablish your hearts.*' The grain is '*precious*' to the farmer, an object of very high value, because not merely

VER. 8.] *Patience through the Blessed Hope.* 371

his own worldly prosperity, but the comfort and very life of others, depend on the ingathering by himself and his fellow-farmers of an abundant harvest; and yet he waits for it with '*long patience.*' Eager as he is to have his harvest, still he waits for it quietly, knowing from experience that, according to the arrangements of God, months must intervene between the sowing and the reaping, and that nothing he can do can materially accelerate the processes of nature. Sprouting and growing, blade, and ear, and full corn in the ear, must be waited for, and all the various agencies by which God brings the plant from stage to stage. Early rains to aid the seed in bursting and sprouting, late rains to fill the ear, week after week of varied weather influence,—he has long patience for them, '*until he*' (or rather, perhaps, his corn) '*receive*' them all. 'As he is patient for his harvest, the precious fruit of the earth; so, brethren' (thus the apostle applies his illustration), '*be ye patient* for the infinitely more precious fruit that ye look for from the spiritual field in which ye have sown. He that soweth to the Spirit shall of the Spirit reap life everlasting—ineffable and unending beauty and joy for the whole nature; but let us be patient: it is *in due season* that we shall reap, if we faint not. In the sphere of the Spirit, as in that of outward nature, a time must intervene, according to the divine appointment, between the sowing and the harvest: let us wait, then, all the needful stages. And to this end *stablish your hearts.*' Ah, brethren, what need there is for this! While the experienced farmer waits long, the child grows impatient because the seed he put into his little garden bed yesterday is not yielding him fruit, or at least putting forth leaves, to-day; and in the spiritual sphere we are all apt to be like children, not in trustfulness, but in ignorance and weakness. 'Stablish your hearts,' then,—have them firm, strong, manly. And for nothing does the heart so much need to be stablished, well sustained, as for patience. Less strength of soul will suffice to work vigorously than is needed to accept quietly an intimation from God that we must not work, but only endure. Less manliness will carry a soldier valiantly through the battle than is needed to bear the pain and weariness of months in the hospital afterwards. But we shall be enabled to stablish our hearts by planting our feet on the one 'sure foundation,' and laying firm hold on that which is enduring. The promises of God are all unchanging, as being His utterances, 'with whom is no variableness;' they 'are all yea and amen in Christ Jesus.' 'Heaven and earth shall pass away,' but of these divine declarations 'not one jot or tittle.' By a lively faith, with a child-like, prayerful heart, let us appropriate these promises, realizing their truthfulness and their sweetness: thus, thus only, thus certainly, we shall be strong to bear no less than strong to labour.

'Bear, then' (the apostle says to his readers tried by the difficulties of the world), 'bear patiently and manfully; for your patience will not be vain: *the coming of the Lord draweth nigh.*' It would be a great thing to say, 'Your harvest is *certain.*' The farmer, even after his 'long patience,' may find that the fields yield him 'no meat,' because 'God's judgements are in the earth, that the inhabitants of the world may learn righteousness.' But no heavens as brass, nor earth as iron, no locust nor cankerworm, can come between him who 'soweth to the Spirit' and a glorious harvest of blessedness and holy beauty,—for 'the mouth of the Lord hath spoken it.' 'For if when we were enemies we were reconciled to God by the death of His Son, much more, being reconciled, we shall be saved by His life.' 'And in that day shall He send His angels, and gather together His elect from the four winds, from the uttermost part of the earth unto the uttermost part of heaven,' and 'a crown of righteousness shall the Lord, the righteous Judge, give to all them that love His appearing.'

The harvest, however, is not merely certain, but *near:* 'the coming of the Lord *draweth nigh.*' 'The Lord is at hand,' says Paul to the Philippians. ' Behold, I come quickly,' is the promise of the Saviour Himself. At first sight, declarations like these from the Lord and His apostles startle us, through their apparent inconsistency with what we know to have subsequently happened. Eighteen centuries have gone by. The world has continued 'buying and selling, planting and building, marrying and giving in marriage.' The 'sign of the Son of man' has not yet appeared in the sky. Scoffers say, 'Where is the promise of His coming? for since the fathers fell asleep all things continue as they were from the beginning of the creation.' How, then, could the Saviour's second advent be predicted in those old days as then near? Because thus the eye of God sees it. The Apostle Peter, you remember, answers the question in this way, telling us that when 'some men count the Lord slack concerning His promise,' they leave out of their computation this element, that with Him 'a thousand years are as one day.' God's 'soons' and 'quicklies' are not to be estimated by our impatient arithmetic. ' Ethiopia shall soon stretch forth her hands unto God,' comes sounding to us over the distance of three thousand years, and how very partially is it yet fulfilled ! 'Near' and 'distant' are relative terms. For the little child, whose limbs soon grow weary, the friend's house is far away, which for his father is but a step from home. So to the child, reckoning by his life, an event seems long past, far away in a hoary antiquity, which to the man on whom have come the snows of many winters, and who reckons by *his* life, seems to have occurred but yesterday. Now faith, in the measure of its vigour, enables us to see things in the light of God, giving us oneness of view with Him. Thus when our apostle says, 'The coming of the Lord draweth nigh,' he speaks as one who has been taught to reckon according to the years of the lifetime of the Most High—unbeginning, unending. On the same principle, Paul estimates the Christian's affliction—affliction spread perhaps over threescore years and ten—as 'but for a moment,' because the standard by which he computed was the 'eternal' duration of the 'weight of glory' that was to follow.

That such is the correct explanation of these 'nighs,' 'soons,' and 'quicklies,' is shown by the fact that our Lord and His apostles in other places tell us of various things, of a kind requiring what men call a long time, which are to happen before His coming. Paul, too, finding that the Thessalonians had misconceived the principle of the reckoning, expressly cautions them against this error as a dangerous one. 'Now we beseech you, brethren, by the coming of our Lord Jesus Christ, and by our gathering together unto Him, that ye be not soon shaken in mind, or be troubled, neither by spirit, nor by word, nor by letter as from us, as that the day of Christ is at hand. Let no man deceive you by any means' (2 Thess. ii. 1–3). Yet the church should always feel her Lord's coming to be near; and when her faith is lively, and her love glowing, she does. As under the clear Eastern sky a range of lofty mountains, which is yet many days' journey distant, seems almost at hand; so in the pellucid atmosphere of faith, the great towering event of the future, dwarfing all else, seems close above us. In seasons of elevated spirituality we feel the advent to be near. Chronologically, many years, as men reckon, may yet be to elapse, but faith sees Him coming 'like to a roe or a young hart leaping on the mountains of spices.' And when the grand event has happened, brethren, and we look back upon it from the eternity of blessedness and glory, we shall see ever more clearly—for we shall understand the reckoning ever more perfectly—how exactly the Lord fulfilled His promise, 'Behold, I come *quickly*.'

Well might the suffering Christians of James's day 'be patient' and 'stablish their hearts;' well may *we* in every trouble and alarm be patient and stablish our hearts,—'for the coming of the Lord draweth nigh.'

XXVII.

MURMURING AGAINST BRETHREN.

'Grudge not one against another, brethren, lest ye be condemned : behold, the Judge standeth before the door. 10 Take, my brethren, the prophets, who have spoken in the name of the Lord, for an example of suffering affliction and of patience. 11 Behold, we count them happy which endure. Ye have heard of the patience of Job, and have seen the end of the Lord ; that the Lord is very pitiful, and of tender mercy.'—JAMES v. 9-11.

THESE verses continue that instruction and exhortation on the subject of patience which was begun in the 7th verse. Here, in the 9th, the apostle, skilled through divine teaching in the ways of the human heart, cautions his readers against impatience *with each other.* They were liable, he tells them, to murmur not merely against their enemies, and against the long-suffering of God, but against their fellow-believers. ' *Grudge not one against another, brethren.*' The word '*grudge*' was used in the older English in a somewhat more general sense than now, being quite equivalent to 'murmur' or 'grumble.' The exact meaning of the original term here translated ' grudge ' is ' groan ' or ' sigh heavily,'—the reference in this place manifestly being to the groaning or sighing not of simple sorrow, but of vexation and ill-humour. The apostle's warning goes deep, you see. Even though there be no word or act of ill-will to brethren,—though the feeling remain buried in the heart, or have only the inarticulate utterance of a sigh,—

yet exercises of the soul of this kind are grievously hurtful to the soul itself. They corrode and enfeeble; they sully the tender bloom of the beauty of holiness.

The injunction, like so many of the apostle's, is thrown into a very general form, and should be accepted by us and pondered as of universal validity. Yet there can be no doubt, looking at the context, that the apostle has special reference to the peculiar spiritual perils of this kind belonging to a time of *trouble*, such as that in which his first readers found themselves. Suffering of any sort, particularly if severe and long continued, is apt to develop an irritability which, unless there be a very lively faith and constant vigilance, will lead to fretfulness. Even where the soul is so governed by Christian principle, that there is no murmuring against God, or against the human authors of the trouble if it be immediately from men,—yet the irritability may show itself towards friends around, and under the provocation of very trifling sources of annoyance. When confronted with a *great* trouble, the new man in Christ girds up his loins to resist temptation, and stand in the evil day; but in the reaction from this strain, ungirded, he falls by the stroke of what is in itself comparatively a very small temptation. All who have had much experience in sick-rooms, either as patients or as nurses, know something of this. Murmuring against one another, then, is a sin to which the members of a persecuted church are peculiarly exposed: circumstances fitted to fret will occur in their intercourse every day,—and against this danger the apostle faithfully warns his suffering brethren.

His affectionate word of address, '*Brethren*,' has a special force here. It is not unworthy of notice, by the way, that we find him employing this term with unusual frequency in this part of his letter—four times within six verses—as if he were influenced by the feeling that one of the principal supports of patience is to be found in remembering, and heartily entering into, the close relationship of believers in Christ to each other. In the passage before us, the 'brethren' is obviously fitted to show in a very lively way the incongruity of grudging against each other with their Christian profession. Christians are in a peculiar sense the family of God. From the far country of darkness and death, into which we had wandered, His grace has brought us home; and now, not merely through the fact of our being His moral creatures, but by the new spiritual birth, we are 'sons and daughters of the Lord Almighty.' Now, as we 'love Him that begat,' so we cannot but love with brotherly affection 'them also that are begotten of Him,' discerning in them somewhat of those excellences which, as they appear in infinite perfection in the character of our common Father, have won for Him our supreme love. This 'brotherly kindness' is often set forth, as you remember, by our Lord and His apostles as one great evidence of genuine piety. 'By this shall all men know that ye are My disciples, if ye have love one to another.' 'We know that we have passed from death unto life, because we love the brethren: he that loveth not his brother, abideth in death.' You see, then, what a power, what a wealth of argument for every true Christian heart, there is in the form of the apostle's warning here: '*Brethren*, grudge not one against another.'

He proceeds to enforce the warning, bringing in a very solemn thought: '*lest ye be condemned*.' According to what has been found to be the best supported reading, the form of the thought is slightly different, though its substance is the same,— 'that ye be not judged.' We have here one of the many unmistakeable references in this Epistle to the Sermon on the Mount; and, following out the reference (Matt. vii. 1), we

VER. 9.]   *Murmuring against Brethren.*   379

discern an intimation implied, that the essence of the sin against which the apostle's present exhortation is directed is violating the Saviour's precept, '*Judge not.*' It is evident from this and other places in the Epistle, that abstinence from 'judging' was counted by the apostle, under the guidance of the Spirit, one of the grand subdivisions of the fundamental law of human society, 'Thou shalt love thy neighbour as thyself,'—a subdivision under which he instinctively classed many forms of duty. That violating the command 'Judge not' is the essence of the sin of which he is here speaking, will be plain on a little consideration. Try to bring up before your minds the position of these oppressed Jewish Christians. Suppose one of them summoned by some bigoted enemy of the cross among his countrymen before a tribunal, on some paltry pretext, but really, as the accused and all around well know, because he loves and honours Jesus. If it be in one of the cities where the Jews are allowed by the Romans to settle disputes on minor matters in courts of their own, the result can hardly be doubtful, the judges themselves having an intense hatred to the religion and followers of the Nazarene. Or if the cause be tried before a heathen judge, here also the probabilities are in favour of condemnation. A judge so sensible and honest as Gallio, who refused to decide a question of words and names and subtleties of a religion strange to him, and drave Paul's accusers from the judgement-seat, was rare in the Roman world; and many times, no doubt, the law was strained by corrupt magistrates for selfish ends, in the interest of wealthy enemies of Christ. The accused Christian, then, suffers in his person or his goods, or both. While the suffering is still fresh, his thoughts happen to turn to a brother believer, one in every way as prominent a member of the church as himself, and in all respects, so far as he knows, as likely as himself to bring down upon his head the vengeance of the unbelievers. Yet day passes after day, month after month, and no evil comes nigh this brother; he pursues his avocations and enjoys his religious privileges in peace. Or he too is accused, and tried,—but allowed to go free. If, spiritually, the sufferer be off his guard, 'grudging' enters and gains strength in his soul, withering its joys and energies. To some extent, in all likelihood—unconsciously perhaps to himself, but really—the murmuring is against divine providence, as if God were partial in His allotments. And as against the Christian neighbour, on what does the 'grudging' rest? Plainly on uncharitable judgements, unkind and, it may be, utterly baseless suspicions,—that his Christianity, after all, is not so pronounced and bright as it should be; that he is but a trimmer, who for his own ends contrives to keep on good terms with the enemies of Christ, as well as with His friends; that possibly he may have condescended to bribe his judge; or the like. You observe how decidedly here 'judging' is the essence of the sin; and in any other case of 'grudging' which might be supposed, an investigation would trace it to the same root. Thus you see how it is that the apostle gives his present warning the turn he does.

'*That ye be not judged.*' Nothing is more plainly taught in Scripture, my brethren,—and no truth is it more needful for Christians to have vividly before their minds,—than that likeness of character to God is one element, the grand element, in the salvation given through Christ. The believer is, by God's grace, through his faith translated 'out of darkness into marvellous light,' in which he sees the divine character to be infinitely lovely, and by the transforming power of love becomes himself a 'partaker of God's holiness.' Now 'God is love;' and thus the spirit of genuine Christianity is a spirit of love. Whatever gifts and excellences a man may have, if

this be wanting, he is thereby proved not to be a Christian.
'Though I speak with the tongues of men and of angels, and
have not love, I am become as sounding brass or a tinkling
cymbal. And though I have the gift of prophecy, and understand all mysteries, and all knowledge; and though I have all
faith, so that I could remove mountains, and have not love, I
am nothing. And though I bestow all my goods to feed the
poor, and though I give my body to be burned, and have not
love, it profiteth me nothing.' That a man should really with
the heart know God as a pardoning God, as the royal Creditor
who with a kingly heart forgave him freely 'all that debt,' and
yet be himself unloving, unforgiving to his fellow-servants,—this
is always set forth in Scripture as in the nature of things utterly
impossible, altogether monstrous. Here, then, you see, lies
the gist of the apostle's argument. 'Murmuring against your
neighbour implies uncharitable judgement of him; and uncharitable judgement is directly opposed to the spirit of true
Christianity. Consequently the man who habitually indulges
in such judgement has the very greatest reason to fear that he
is not a Christian,—that he has not been brought out into the
sphere of pardon, but is still in that of *judgement*, judgement
to condemnation. Grudge not, then, one against another,
brethren, that ye be not judged.'

'Bethink you, moreover,' thus he continues, 'that the time
of judgement is not far off: *behold, the Judge standeth before
the door.*' The apostle has already, in the 8th verse, encouraged
the believers to restfulness of spirit, by the assurance that 'the
coming of the Lord draweth nigh;' and now he brings in this
great fact again under a lively figure, to point and enforce his
solemn warning. The statement bears on both parts of the
previous exhortation. 'You judge your brethren,' he says: 'ah,
dear friends, this is very foolish work, and very needless, even

if it were lawful; for we cannot judge aright,—and One is very near us, even at our doors, who has a commission to judge, and all needed wisdom for the work. Even if there be real grounds of dissatisfaction among you, then, you may safely leave them all to His decision;[1] and remember that on the uncharitable judges among you His judgement will come down in sternest condemnation.'

The whole paragraph from the 7th verse to the 11th is, as we have seen, an exhortation to patience. Its sum is, 'Let patience have her work perfect, broken neither by discontent with God's dealings, nor by petulance with your fellow-men.' Of this, you observe, the 'grudge not' which we have been considering is a natural subdivision; and now, having spoken of that particular spiritual peril briefly, but with singular pointedness and force, the apostle goes on to support his *general* appeal, by a reference to a class of examples very familiar to the Jewish Christians, and justly carrying great weight with them,—those of the Old Testament prophets. These were men of high dignity in the service of God, His commissioned ambassadors, '*who spake in His name*,' as the apostle specially mentions. 'If God permitted trouble to befall *them*, it need be no matter of surprise to you that affliction has come upon *you*. Whether you can understand the reason for the divine procedure or not, it is plain that suffering is a part of the appointed experience of His people. And besides being instructed by looking at the simple fact that the prophets *had trouble*, it becomes you also to regard as well worthy of imitation the *conduct* which those eminent servants of God

---

[1] A very exact parallel is found in Phil. iv. 5: 'Let your moderation' ('your considerate and forbearing spirit,' 'your being possessed of the *gentleness* of heavenly wisdom:' compare James iii. 17 in the original) 'be known unto all men. The Lord is at hand.' The argument is precisely the same.

pursued under their trouble.' Both of these points are expressly presented by the apostle.

'*Take the prophets,*' he says, '*as an example of affliction.*'[1] A very natural thought to young believers is, that it is strange that afflictions should continue with us after conversion. 'Is not affliction an element of death, and have we not passed from death unto life? Being united to Christ, do we not occupy a higher position than Adam before his fall? Now Adam unfallen had no affliction.' Thinking of such difficulties as these, our apostle does not here, however, enter into the philosophy of the question. He has said somewhat on that head in the very beginning of his letter. Here he contents himself with pointing to the undoubted fact that God's most illustrious servants had suffered. 'No strange thing has happened to you,' he says, 'for the same afflictions have been accomplished in your brethren which have been in the world.' Moses had to struggle for many years with a stiff-necked and rebellious people. David was hunted by Saul 'like a partridge on the mountains,' and for years, like his Son and Lord, 'had not where to lay his head;' and in advanced life he had again to become a fugitive through the rebellion of the son he loved most dearly. Elijah's life was sought by the wicked rulers of Israel with vengeful fury. Jeremiah's life was one of continued persecution. Similar, more or less, were the experiences of all the holy men of old. 'Which of the prophets,' Stephen asks the Sanhedrin, 'have not your fathers persecuted?' To suffer in the same cause with men like these should surely be deemed an honour and a source of thankfulness. 'Take them also, then,' says the apostle, '*as an example of patience;*' 'look not merely at their sufferings, but at their spirit under it.' 'Moses was

---

[1] The word 'suffering,' which our translators have inserted here, is quite unneeded, and indeed obscures the meaning.

very meek,' the Scripture tells us, 'above all the men which were upon the face of the earth.' David in time of trouble says, 'I was dumb, I opened not my mouth, because Thou didst it;' 'I know, O Lord, that Thy judgements are right, and that Thou in faithfulness hast afflicted me.' Jeremiah says, 'Wherefore should a living man complain, a man for the punishment of his sins? Let us search and try our ways, and turn again to the Lord.' This is the spirit in which trouble ought to be borne,—this is the exercise of soul through which it will 'bear peaceable fruits of righteousness.' 'Take then, my brethren, the prophets, who have spoken in the name of the Lord, for an example of affliction and of patience.'

By his '*behold*' the apostle calls special attention to his next remark, as presenting something of particular weight, crowning his arguments for patience. '*We count them happy*'—call them blessed—'*which endure*' (or rather, according to the best supported reading, '*which endured*,'—the prophets and other suffering saints of old being still before him). We have here another reference to the Sermon on the Mount. Coming, as these words do, immediately after the allusion to the example of the prophets, we cannot doubt that the writer had before his mind the passage which closes the beatitudes: 'Blessed are they which are persecuted for righteousness' sake; for theirs is the kingdom of heaven. Blessed are ye when men shall revile you, and persecute you, and shall say all manner of evil against you falsely, for My sake. Rejoice, and be exceeding glad: for great is your reward in heaven; for so persecuted they the prophets which were before you.' 'Now,' says James, 'it is one of the great principles which have been taught us by the Lord, and of which as Christians we have professed our acceptance, that they who endure are blessed. Prove, then, by your conduct that you understand this truth, and really believe it. Being called in God's providence to suffer, see that you endure.' For '*endure*' here, as you see, is not, as we sometimes employ the word, 'to be in affliction' merely, but 'to bear affliction patiently,' the word in the original being indeed the verbal form of the noun in the next clause rendered 'patience.'

'Them which endure we *count happy*' or '*blessed*,' for various reasons. They are 'blessed' through the growth in spiritual beauty and strength which patient endurance gives them. 'I am the true Vine, and My Father is the Husbandman. Every branch in Me that beareth fruit, He purgeth it, *that it may bring forth more fruit ;*' and 'endurance' is the acceptance of the work of the pruning-knife. The waters of the fountain-head, the heart, being purified through penitence and faith, a pellucid stream of holiness must ultimately flow by every channel throughout the whole man. Now by affliction 'endured' God graciously quickens the work, deepening the channels and increasing their decline. 'They which endure' are 'blessed,' also, in the joy that they have through increasing knowledge of God. 'Tribulation worketh patience, and patience *experience*,' —an experience which deepens and broadens their happiness in fellowship with Him,—and from which, too, springs vivid '*hope*.' Knowing God better, they look forward with always fuller confidence to that future of glory which He has promised to them that love Him.

The general thought, 'Trouble patiently endured has a happy issue,' leads now to the mention of an illustration from Bible history in which this is very strikingly exemplified : '*Ye have heard of the patience of Job, and have seen the end of the Lord, that the Lord is very pitiful, and of tender mercy.*'

'*The end of the Lord*' is a somewhat singular expression. By some interpreters it has been supposed to mean 'the closing scene of the life of the Lord Jesus;' the arguments put forward in support of this view being,—that this sense comes naturally out of the words; that it would be strange if, when examples of patience are cited by an apostle, the grand example given by Jesus, when He 'endured the contradiction of sinners against Himself' in the judgement-hall and on the cross, were omitted; and that by the use of the words 'heard' and 'seen,' in the two clauses respectively, a reference seems to be intimated in the former case to an instance long past, known only by history, in the latter to one which some of the readers had themselves witnessed. This is ingenious; but the more closely we look at the passage, the more we shall be convinced that the view is wholly unnatural. The seeming equality on which the cases of Job and the Saviour would thus be put, is entirely alien from Scripture usage. The last clause of the verse, too, would have no very manifest pertinence or force in its connection. Further (and this alone might decide the question), we should, on this view of the meaning merely have additional examples of patience, not advancing the argument,—examples unnaturally separated from those already given by the first clause of the verse, and in no way specially illustrating it. The arguments in support of this interpretation are easily answered. If the explanation of the 6th verse which we have seen reason to adopt be the true one, then the patience of the Lord Jesus *has* been referred to with peculiar impressiveness. Whether this be so or not, however, it is certainly not our part to say dogmatically that a particular line of illustration *ought* to be taken in any part of Holy Scripture; and meek, conscientious study will always deepen our conviction, that what has been given is the best which could be given—the utterance of infinite wisdom and kindness. As for the use of 'heard' and 'seen,' these words fall in at least as naturally with a reference of the whole to Job: 'Ye have heard—in the readings of the synagogue and in religious addresses and conversations—of the patience of Job; and, in considering his history, have seen the close which God gave to his career.' This, no doubt, is the meaning: '*the Lord's conclusion,*' granted to the life in which patience was so signally shown,—'*the end given by the Lord ;*' just as, for example, 'perils of robbers,' as Paul uses the expression in Second Corinthians, are 'perils caused by robbers,' not 'perils encountered by them.'

This is the only place in the New Testament where Job is referred to. By it, as well as by the allusions in Ezekiel to that patriarch in conjunction with Noah and Daniel, the Divine Spirit teaches us that the book which tells us of him is, in its basis at least, a history, and not, as many have been disposed to think, an entirely fictitious poem.

'*Ye have seen the end of the Lord.*' 'The Lord,' as the sacred record tells us, 'turned the captivity of Job, and blessed his latter end more than his beginning.' Here is illustrated the justice of our reckoning when 'we count them happy which endure.' The happy issue (or rather its manifest beginning) may not come perhaps, as it did in Job's case, in this world; but certainly to all affliction endured with Christian patience there will come a happy issue.

The 'end' which the Lord gave to Job exemplified the truth '*that the Lord is very pitiful and of tender mercy,*'[1] that 'He doth not afflict willingly, nor grieve the children of men.' As we muse on his history, we feel the assurance brought home to

[1] The precise force of ὅτι here is somewhat uncertain. '*That,*' of the Authorised Version (amplified by the Revisers into '*how that*'), makes the clause a second object to ἴδετε, stating fully the truth respecting the divine character which was illustrated in 'the end given by the Lord' to Job's history. The sense of '*because*' or '*for,*' introducing a reflection of the

our hearts, which James has given us before, that 'Blessed is the man that endureth temptation; for when he is tried, he shall receive the crown of life which the Lord hath promised to them that love him.' However 'great' the 'tribulation' be which God allots us in His providence, yet all they that 'have washed their robes and made them white in the blood of the Lamb, *come out of it.*' Then 'are they before the throne of God, and serve Him day and night in His temple: and He that sitteth on the throne shall dwell among them. They shall hunger no more, neither thirst any more; neither shall the sun light on them, nor any heat. For the Lamb which is in the midst of the throne shall feed them, and shall lead them unto living fountains of waters; and God shall wipe away all tears from their eyes.'

apostle in connection with his reference to 'the end given by the Lord,' is also suitable enough. It has been preferred by many expositors and translators, the Vulgate, for example, Luther, and the English versions prior to the Authorized. Alford remarks that the repetition of 'the Lord' appears more natural on this view of the meaning of ὅτι than on the other.

XXVIII.

SWEARING.

'But above all things, my brethren, swear not, neither by heaven, neither by the earth, neither by any other oath: but let your yea be yea, and your nay, nay; lest ye fall into condemnation.'—JAMES v. 12.

THE apostle has now said nearly all that it was in his heart to say to his brethren in the letter. There still, however, remain a few things to which he desires to draw their attention, and these he gathers up in conclusion. In the exhortations which follow, then, we are not to look for that closeness of connection in thought which we have found to exist generally throughout the earlier part of the Epistle. In our own familiar letters, you know, when we are coming near the close, we consider whether there be any other things which we should wish to say to our friend; and if there be, we state them often in a very isolated way. Something of the same kind is found in almost all the apostolic letters; and this is one of the many evidences of that genuine human element in the Word of God, appealing to brotherly sympathy, which has somewhat to do with the winning power exercised by the sacred record over all candid hearts. These exhortations of James, however, do not seem to stand *altogether* unconnected; and the thought binding the precept in the 12th verse to what immediately precedes is evidently this, that impatience under trouble often leads to the use of wild, wicked language, dishonouring to God and hurtful to the soul.

'*But above all things, my brethren, swear not, neither by heaven, neither by the earth, neither by any other oath.*' Here again we have an unmistakeable reference to the Sermon on the Mount; and, indeed, James's words are simply a repetition, in a somewhat condensed form, of the injunction there given by Jesus: 'I say unto you, Swear not at all: neither by heaven, for it is God's throne: nor by the earth, for it is His footstool: neither by Jerusalem, for it is the city of the great King. Neither shalt thou swear by thy head, because thou canst not make one hair white or black. But let your communication be, Yea, yea; Nay, nay: for whatsoever is more than these cometh of evil' (Matt. v. 34–37). The terms of the injunction in both places are universal, 'Swear not,' 'Swear not at all.' Whether the universality is absolute or relative, however,—whether swearing under any circumstances is prohibited, or merely all oaths of a particular kind,—must be decided by an examination of the context, and the general teaching of Scripture. 'Thou shalt not kill,' is a precept universal in terms; yet ordinary good sense sees it to be perfectly compatible with that other, 'Whoso sheddeth man's blood, by man shall his blood be shed.' The act of a magistrate in inflicting capital punishment on a murderer, is felt not to come within the sweep of the universality; which therefore is relative, not absolute. The command regarding swearing is held, as you know, by the members of the Society of Friends, and some other small bodies of Christians, to be of absolute universality; so that they consider it wrong to take an oath in a court of justice, and are by our laws permitted to substitute a simple affirmation. By the church generally it has been held that the prohibition does not extend to all oaths. The grounds of this view are very strong; and, as the matter is one of considerable practical importance, I shall endeavour to set them before you somewhat fully.

It seems plain that an oath has nothing in its own nature immoral. It is an appeal to Him who knows the heart regarding the truth of testimony or the sincerity of promises. Now nothing is clearer than that it is our duty to have a sense of the presence of the Omniscient always with us as a governing power; and it can scarcely be wrong in itself for a person who, while making a declaration, is deeply influenced by the thought, 'Thou God seest me,' to say so. 'Thou shalt not take the name of the Lord thy God in vain,' is a precept of universal and perpetual obligation; but if, as has been generally held, the commandment has a special, though by no means exclusive, reference to oaths, the very mode of expression suggests that circumstances may occur in which, for the confirmation of testimony, we may and should 'take' that glorious name on our lips, if only we do this thoughtfully and solemnly. A reverential oath honours, not dishonours, God; though an oath on the lips of a man whose heart is heedless of God, whose state of soul is in no accordance with his words of solemn appeal, is a glaring insult to the divine majesty. It is true that, in the intercourse of perfect beings, there would be no oaths, because so entire would be their mutual confidence that oaths would be altogether needless. In a sense, therefore, though not exactly the sense in which the expression is used in the passage, 'whatsoever is more than Yea, yea, Nay, nay,' in *every* case 'cometh of evil,' for it would not have existed had there been no moral evil in the world. But, as a matter of fact, we are in a world of contention and broken confidence; and if in any case 'an oath for confirmation' is to be 'an end of all strife,' then we can hardly suppose its use at times inconsistent with the religion which aims at putting 'an end to all strife,' diffusing 'peace on earth.'

We find accordingly, that, under the Old Economy, to swear in certain circumstances by the name of the Lord was a matter of express and repeated divine command. 'Thou shalt fear the Lord thy God, and serve Him, and shalt swear by His name' (Deut. vi. 13). Again: 'Thou shalt fear the Lord thy God; Him shalt thou serve, and to Him shalt thou cleave, and swear by His name' (Deut. x. 20). In the judicial law particular cases were specified in which the decision between contending parties was to be by means of an oath. For example: 'If a man deliver unto his neighbour an ass, or an ox, or a sheep, or any beast, to keep; and it die, or be hurt, or driven away, no man seeing it: then shall an oath of the Lord be between them both, that he hath not put his hand unto his neighbour's goods; and the owner of it shall accept thereof, and he shall not make it good' (Ex. xxii. 10, 11). Apart from judicial procedure, we have mention made in Scripture of oaths sworn by eminent servants of God at times when they were plainly under the influence of the loftiest inspiration. For example: 'And Elijah the Tishbite, who was of the inhabitants of Gilead, said unto Ahab, As the Lord God of Israel liveth, before whom I stand, there shall not be dew nor rain these years, but according to my word' (1 Kings xvii. 1).

Supposing it, however, to be proved beyond controversy, that sincere and solemn oath-taking was permitted under the Old Dispensation, it may be held that this, like polygamy and slavery, was not approved by God, but only tolerated 'for the hardness of the people's hearts.' Isaiah has a passage strikingly contradictory of this view, where, speaking of the church of the latter days—the days of Messiah—he mentions it among the characteristic features of that time, that 'he who blesseth himself in the earth, shall bless himself in the God of truth; and he that sweareth in the earth, shall swear by the God of truth; because the former troubles are forgotten, and because they are hid from Mine eyes' (Isa. lxv. 16). Looking into the New Testament for illustration of the will of God on this matter, we find that our perfect example, the Lord Jesus, took an oath before a magistrate. 'The high priest answered and said unto Him, I adjure thee by the living God, that thou tell us whether thou be the Christ, the Son of God. Jesus saith unto him, Thou hast said' (Matt. xxvi. 63, 64). According to Jewish law, this was a declaration on oath, as fully as if the Lord had Himself employed words corresponding to those used by the high priest.[1] Express appeals to God for confirmation of testimony we have in such words of the Apostle Paul as these: 'Moreover, I call God for a record upon my soul, that to spare you I came not as yet unto Corinth' (2 Cor. i. 23); 'The God and Father of our Lord Jesus Christ, which is blessed for evermore, knoweth that I lie not' (2 Cor. xi. 31); 'The things which I write unto you, behold, before God, I lie not' (Gal. i. 20). Now it is true that Paul was not a perfect man, and none could be readier than he to confess daily sin; but it is one of 'the things most surely believed among us,' that in writing those letters which are contained in the New Testament he wrote 'as he was moved by the Holy Ghost,' and that thus all his words have divine sanction. In the Apocalypse an angel is represented as

[1] For evidence from rabbinical books that this was a mode of taking an oath deemed binding, see Robinson's *The Evangelists and the Mishna*, p. 152; or Tholuck's *Commentary on the Sermon on the Mount*, p. 254, note (Clark's Foreign Theological Library).

confirming his declaration by an oath: 'And the angel which I saw stand upon the sea and upon the earth lifted up his hand to heaven, and sware by Him that liveth for ever and ever, who created heaven and the things that therein are, and the earth and the things that therein are, and the sea and the things which are therein, that there should be time no longer' (Rev. x. 5, 6). Nay, God Himself is many times described in His Word as condescending to strengthen the feeble faith of men by thus confirming His declarations. Instances are so numerous in which He is said to have sworn by Himself ('As I live, saith the Lord'), that I need not quote any particular cases. We have no case of this indeed in the New Testament; but however God may have permitted among His ancient people conduct which for us, under gospel light, is sinful, His own actings at all times must be held to exemplify absolute holiness.

My argument, then, on this part of the subject is complete. The Israelites had a divine command to swear in certain circumstances; oaths were taken by illustrious servants of God under both Economies, at times when they were undoubtedly under the influence of inspiration; and even by God Himself, alike in the lowliness of humanity, assumed for our redemption, and in His glory. It is clear, then, that the injunction of the Apostle James in the verse under consideration, and that of the Saviour in the Sermon on the Mount, of which this is a repetition, have relation not absolutely to all oaths, but only to all of a particular kind.

An expression in the Sermon on the Mount enables us to put the demonstration in a very concise form. 'Let your communication be, Yea, yea; Nay, nay: for whatsoever is more than these cometh of evil.' These last words are plainly not restricted to time or dispensation: they teach that there is something essentially immoral in the excess—the 'more than these'—of which our Lord speaks. Now God, the absolutely Holy One, has many times given more than a simple 'Yea, yea, Nay, nay,' confirming His declarations of judgement or of mercy by an oath, 'that by two immutable things, in which it was impossible for God to lie,' sinners on the one hand might be roused to repentance, and, on the other, those 'might have a strong consolation, who have fled for refuge to lay hold upon the hope set before us.' It is manifest, then, that the 'more than these' has relation to a class of oaths only, not to all.[1]

An examination of the details in the form of the injunction, as given either in the Sermon on the Mount or by James, fully supports this conclusion. 'Swear not at all,' says the Lord,— 'neither by heaven, for it is God's throne: nor by the earth, for it is His footstool: neither by Jerusalem, for it is the city of the great King. Neither shalt thou swear by thy head, because thou canst not make one hair white or black.' Similarly His apostle: 'Swear not, neither by heaven, neither by the earth.' Among the ways in which the Pharisees had made void God's law by their traditions, was their introduction into the system of oaths of such subtleties as we have learned in modern times to call Jesuitical. The form of swearing enjoined by the law was *in the name of God:* 'As the Lord liveth.' Now, maintaining the awful solemnity and binding obligation of this oath, and of one or two others—such as, 'By the gold of the temple'—to which for some reason they attached a peculiar sacredness, the Pharisees taught also that most forms of oath were comparatively light, might be used

[1] The argument is exhibited pretty nearly as above by Dr. Wardlaw, to whose exposition of this verse (as also to Dr. Adam's) I have been much indebted.

freely in ordinary conversation, and need not be regarded as in any way specially obligatory. To this monstrous teaching, glaringly foolish as well as wicked, our Lord adverts at length in His great discourse on the iniquity of the scribes and Pharisees, spoken three days before His crucifixion : 'Woe unto you, ye blind guides, which say, Whosoever shall swear by the temple, it is nothing; but whosoever shall swear by the gold of the temple, he is a debtor! Ye fools and blind : for whether is greater, the gold, or the temple that sanctifieth the gold? And, Whosoever shall swear by the altar, it is nothing; but whosoever sweareth by the gift that is upon it, he is guilty. Ye fools and blind : for whether is greater, the gift, or the altar that sanctifieth the gift? Whoso therefore shall swear by the altar, sweareth by it, and by all things thereon. And whoso shall swear by the temple, sweareth by it, and by Him that dwelleth therein. And he that shall swear by heaven, sweareth by the throne of God, and by Him that sitteth thereon' (Matt. xxiii. 16–22). Now you observe that the forms of oath adduced both by Jesus in the Sermon on the Mount and by James, in illustration of the reference of their injunctions, are all *of the secondary kind*—oaths 'by heaven,' 'by the earth,' and the like; the Lord showing, in what He says of them, that if these forms had any meaning or force at all, this was derived from the thing named being conceived as in some close relation to God, and that consequently their light use involved irreverence to the divine majesty. The oath *by the name of God*, the appointed formula, is not alluded to either by the Lord or His apostle; and this omission of the great fundamental oath—the oath which must always have been foremost in the mind of a Jew, when there was any discourse on the subject of oaths generally—must be held, it appears to me, as intended to show that under the Christian dispensation also that grand oath may be taken, under the circumstances in which it was lawful under Judaism, whilst all others are absolutely forbidden. James's words, '*by any other oath*,' might be supposed to include the great oath, 'As the Lord liveth.' But comparing, by way of commentary, the more detailed illustrations in the Sermon on the Mount, of which, as we have seen, the verse in James is obviously a condensed repetition; and considering that, if the grand fundamental formula had been in the apostle's thoughts as included in his prohibition, it would certainly have been expressly mentioned, and not thrown in incidentally under a mere *et cetera*,—we cannot doubt that by 'any other oath' he means 'any other oath of the same kind'—such, namely, as were freely used in careless, trivial talk.

The sum of the matter, then, seems to be this, that, consistently with the law of Christ, an oath may be taken in a court of justice, or in great religious crises, such as those in which Elijah and Paul employed it,—times when men feel themselves with special vividness to be in the presence of the unseen divine Judge. Such crises, calling for express appeals to God by way of oath, must be determined by the individual Christian judgement; but they can occur but rarely, I should suppose, in any life, and in the quiet lives of most believers will never occur at all. The oath, too, is always to be a direct, express appeal to God, not any circuitous form; and the heart must be full of reverence and godly fear, accordant with the solemnity of the words.

The earnestness of our apostle's exhortation to avoid swearing under all other circumstances, to avoid all oaths of passion or thoughtlessness, is shown by his introductory words, '*Above all things*,'—the force of which, in their connection, is plainly, 'Guard yourselves with pre-eminent care against this sin.' The grounds of this 'above all things' are various. Thus, for example, the facility with which the sin is committed, and its consequent frightful commonness. From one point of view it seems strange that this vice should be common; for surely of all kinds of sin it is the most utterly gratuitous—the most absolutely unremunerative, even as regards the wretched sort of remuneration which sin ever gives. Covetousness, pride, falsehood, and even the lowest sensual vices, do or may bring some temporary advantage, enjoyment, or excitement; but profanity brings no gain. Indeed, even before fellow-men it brings nothing but loss. Besides exciting the disapproval and disgust of all good men, the person who habitually supports his assertions by an oath seems thereby to obtrude an acknowledgement that he considers his bare word unlikely, and indeed unworthy, to be believed,—and when a person thus puts his own moral worth low, men will naturally take him at his own valuation. Yet, as a matter of fact, this sin has always been a common one. Many instances of swearing recorded in the Old Testament show that even the great oath by the Lord was often used with much irreverence. The statements of our Lord, and of James in the text, show that in later days also, though the Pharisees had taught the people to abstain from taking the 'name' of the Lord in vain literally, yet oaths of some kind were constantly heard. A writer who has spent many years as a missionary in Syria says: 'This people are fearfully profane. Everybody curses and swears when in a passion. No people that I have ever known can compare with these Orientals for profaneness in the use of the names and attributes of God. The evil habit seems inveterate and universal. When Peter, therefore, began to curse and to swear on that dismal night of temptation, we are not to suppose that it was something foreign to his former habits. He merely relapsed, under high excitement, into what, as a sailor and a fisherman, he had been accustomed to all his life. The people now use the very same sort of oaths that are mentioned and condemned by our Lord. They swear by the head, by their life, by heaven, and by the temple, or, what is in its place, the church. The forms of cursing and swearing, however, are almost infinite, and fall on the pained ear all day long.'[1]

Among ourselves, too, as you know, this vice is lamentably common. One can hardly go a little way along a street without hearing some blasphemy, and, alas, very often from the lips of the young. It might well be doubted, brethren, whether there can be a more striking evidence of the existence and energy of human depravity, than the fact that our boys and girls so often count it a proof of their becoming men and women, and 'putting away childish things,' to blaspheme their Maker. And not oaths only, in the strict sense of the word, but also the most profane and unclean ribaldry, and the most horrible curses, pollute the air. Imprecations are flippantly tossed about, which would utterly shock the person who utters them, if even for a moment he thought of their meaning; and the names of the most solemn realities in the universe are thrown carelessly from the lips, as if they were but figments of a foolish imagination. Now all the sins of the tongue, swearing among them, need to be guarded against with particular care, from the facility with which they are committed; and the prevalence of any vice, and especially a sin of the tongue, in the community we live among, increases the temptation, and renders vigilance doubly needful. '*Above all things*,' then, 'swear not.'

[1] Dr. Thomson's *The Land and the Book*, pp. 190, 191 (Nelson s edition).

Another ground for the apostle's special earnestness in the present exhortation is, that this sin is peculiarly dishonouring to God, and deadening to the moral nature of him who practises it. Reverence for God is the basis of all that is truly beautiful and noble in God's moral creatures. The first petition of every wise man's prayer is, 'Hallowed be Thy name,' for in this is summed up all good. Now profane swearing is a direct defiance of God, or, at the least, involves vast irreverence; and the habit hardens the soul against that sentiment which alone can lift us into true happiness and spiritual beauty. The swearer systematically prepares his heart to be the highway of all wicked thoughts and affections.

Surely, then, in every aspect, this exhortation is one which it becomes a servant of God to deliver with all earnestness: 'Above all things, my brethren, swear not.'

'*But let your yea be yea; and your nay, nay.*' Taken by themselves, these words might signify, 'Let your statements be always true, your yes always meaning yes, and your no, no;' and this thought, I think, is included in or suggested by their force here. But in their present connection, and as illustrated by the parallel expression in the Sermon on the Mount, they plainly mean primarily, 'Let your assertions be free from all foolish and wicked expletives; let your Yes be simple Yes, and your No simple No.' A consistently truthful, candid character, such as the principles of the gospel will produce in a man, in the measure in which they are understood and believed, will give his simplest words weight. You observe that this injunction excludes from the Christian's vocabulary everything of the nature of minced oaths, as well as those more pronounced. Such expressions are foolish, and in utterly bad taste, and with any sensible hearer weaken rather than strengthen credit; and the use of them tends to enervate the soul, diminishing reverence for God and for naked truth.

'*Lest ye fall into condemnation*'—that condemnation which the Lord has expressly threatened: 'Thou shalt not take the name of the Lord thy God in vain; *for the Lord will not hold him guiltless that taketh His name in vain.*' This is a sin which with special directness and glaringness insults God: therefore certainly, 'however the breakers of this commandment may escape punishment from men, yet the Lord our God will not suffer them to escape His righteous judgement.' This is a truth surely eminently fitted to lead all who ponder it to 'swear not at all.'

XXIX.

PRAYER AND PRAISE.

'Is any among you afflicted? let him pray. Is any merry? let him sing psalms. 14 Is any sick among you? let him call for the elders of the church; and let them pray over him, anointing him with oil in the name of the Lord: 15 And the prayer of faith shall save the sick, and the Lord shall raise him up; and if he have committed sins, they shall be forgiven him.'—JAMES v. 13-15.

THE 13th verse appears to me to be closely attached to the 12th,—the apostle proceeding here to set forth with much terseness and liveliness the kind of language which becomes saints, in contrast with the swearing which he has forbidden. 'For every tone of feeling,' he says, 'that can ever rightly occupy the heart, in any condition in which Providence may place us, true religion has fitting modes of expression, honouring to God and helpful to ourselves and our brethren.' Circumstances of *trouble*, and the sorrowful heart of the sufferer, naturally come first before his mind, seeing that impatience under trouble, and its unhallowed utterances, have been the subject of his rebuke. '*Is any among you afflicted? let him pray.*' The lively *question*, 'Is any among you afflicted?' and afterwards, 'Is any merry?' 'Is any sick among you?'—instead of the simple, quiet, 'If any among you be afflicted, merry, sick,'—accords with that direct, stirring style of address which characterizes the whole Epistle. Similarly, you remember, we had in the 3rd chapter (ver. 13),

'Who is a wise man and endued with knowledge amongst you? let him show out of a good conversation his works with meekness of wisdom.' '*Is any among you afflicted*,' then—distressed, from whatever cause? How should the Christian life in him show itself? By *prayer*, certainly. The unbeliever, looking only at secondary causes and the 'course of nature,' as if affliction *did* 'come forth from the earth, and trouble spring out of the ground,' aims at a kind of torpid, pagan indifference. Or if he thinks of God as the Author of his troubles, he 'kicks against the pricks,' 'like a bullock unaccustomed to the yoke,' or 'as a wild bull in a net' he frets and rages, struggles and pulls, thereby only entangling himself the more, and making his position worse by discontent and passion. But the Christian—recognising his affliction as Fatherly chastisement, inflicted by the God who is love, and who, because He is love, chastens His children, that they may be made more childlike—will always feel, if his faith be intelligent and vigorous, that nothing is so becoming and needful under trial as earnest wrestling with his heavenly Father in prayer. He will ask for *comfort* through a sense of the divine presence and goodness: 'Hide not Thy face from Thy servant, for I am in trouble; from the end of the earth will I cry unto Thee when my heart is overwhelmed; lead me to the Rock that is higher than I.' He will ask for *wisdom* to grow in grace through the discipline: 'Teach me to do Thy will, for Thou art my God; Thy Spirit is good, lead me into the land of uprightness.' And he will pray for *deliverance* from the cause of his distress, as far and as speedily as God sees meet: 'O Lord, I pray Thee, turn the counsel of Ahithophel into foolishness; save me from all them that persecute me: heal me, for my bones are vexed.' Such is the exercise of soul which beseems an afflicted saint.

But religion, while very precious and sustaining in times of suffering, is not less really needful, and has as perfect adaptation, for seasons of prosperity and gladness. For the night when weeping endures it has its words of prayer, for the morning when joy comes it has its songs of praise. '*Is any merry? let him sing psalms.*' By '*merry*' is meant here, not, as often in modern English, 'full of boisterous gaiety,' but, generally, 'cheerful,' 'in good spirits.' Its meaning is well shown by the only other place in the New Testament in which the original word here used occurs, where Paul, before the shipwreck at Malta, exhorts his companions to 'be of good cheer,' because God had told him that their lives would not be lost. For him who 'is of good cheer,' then, the apostle's injunction is to '*sing praise.*' This seems to be the exact force of the original term, which our translators have somewhat unduly limited by using the word 'psalms.' I have no doubt that, the more a Christian knows of God, and of himself, and of the Book of Psalms, the more he will delight in those wonderful compositions, and feel their transcendent poetic beauty, and wealth of religious experience; but the apostle's words here are quite general, leaving room for any kind of sacred song.

The present is one of many passages both in the Old Testament and the New which set forth the dignity and usefulness of the service of praise. 'Praise is comely.' Hearty congregational singing is a favourable sign of the spiritual condition of the people,—particularly congregational singing in which, conjoined with that fulness of tone which proves general heartiness, there are also the grave sweet melody and pleasant blending of parts which evince diligent, conscientious study by persons desirous to lay their best on God's altar. In the ages when ceremonialism began to stifle vital religion, and true Christian catholicity became corrupted and narrowed into the apostasy of Roman Catholicism, there was no more striking symptom of the change from life to death than the departure of congregational praise. Sacred song was at once an utterance and a stimulus of independent thought and feeling, such as the usurping priesthood dared not leave to the people. So the chanting by hired choristers of hymns in a dead language, and often in honour of saints and angels, took the place of that hearty congregational praise of God which even a heathen writer of the first age speaks of as one of the prominent features of Christian service. But when at the Reformation, through the mercy of God, the Sun of Righteousness at last melted the frost of centuries, and the silver streams of the water of life, so long sealed up and silent, began once more to gush joyously over the world, then along their banks arose again the strains of Zion. Wherever spiritual life is found, it expresses itself, as all manifest revivals of religion distinctly attest, in hearty praise. The 'living in Jerusalem' say, 'The dead praise not the Lord, neither any that go down into silence; but *we* will bless the Lord from this time forth and for evermore.' The words of the apostle in the verse before us suggest that not merely in the sanctuary, but at home, in the family circle or in solitude, the singing of God's praise is pleasant and helpful for the soul. When God in His providence is bidding us 'be of good cheer'—when the truth is with liveliness borne in upon our hearts, that 'He crowneth us with loving-kindness and tender mercies'—the tones of sacred song are to the new man in Christ the most natural of all utterances. They are felt to be honouring to God, and sweet and stimulating to the heart. Individual and family happiness, individual and family piety, would, beyond question, be strengthened and beautified, if there were a more general following out of the apostle's rule, 'Is any man merry? let him sing praise.'

I need hardly observe that, though the apostle in this verse recommends to believers those religious exercises which are *specially* suitable in the contrasted conditions respectively,—prayer in trouble, and praise in prosperity,—yet in neither case does he put aside the other exercise as unsuitable. Often, as you know, praise passes into prayer, and prayer is pervaded by the spirit of praise. Indeed the spiritual man, in all circumstances in which he may be placed, should feel himself impelled both to prayer and praise. When he is 'of good cheer,' and praises the bounteous Giver of his enjoyments, he remembers at the same time how prone prosperity is to make a man 'turn again to folly;' and, 'lacking wisdom,' he '*asks* of God, who giveth to all men liberally, and upbraideth not.' In trouble, while praying earnestly, he finds that the 'patience' which God gives 'worketh experience' of the divine mercy and faithfulness, 'and experience hope,' and hope impels to praise. Ay, and through the praise the hope will often grow stronger and brighter; for now, as well as in Saul's days, the 'evil spirit' of despondency and fear will flee before the tones of David's harp. At midnight, in the inner prison, their feet fast in the stocks, and their backs raw with the stripes, 'Paul and Silas *prayed, and sang praises* unto God.'

The truth is, that prayer and praise are fundamentally one, the outgoing of the soul in love and trust to God. They are flowers growing on one stem. Thus we come to the general principle which underlies James's teaching here,— that a Christian, throughout his whole life, whatever its turnings be, however varied its conditions, should in them all, and with regard to them all, acknowledge God, with humility, and thankfulness, and love, communing with Him in holy fellowship. Such is beyond question the ideal of the Christian life,—'*praying* without ceasing,' 'blessing the Lord at all times, His *praise* continually in our mouths.' This implies oneness of will with God, the childlike acceptance of His will as ours: in prosperity thanking Him as the Giver, and devoting what He gives to His glory; in adversity, meekly bearing what He sends, and striving to gain the spiritual advantage which He intends for us in sending it. 'I have learned,' says Paul, 'in whatsoever state I am, therewith to be content;' and certainly, as a good woman said, who on a bed of weariness and pain, and in the depths of poverty, was praising God, it '*takes* learning' to do this. She spoke of the side she had experience of—'knowing how to suffer need;' but the other side, to bear prosperity without vain confidence, 'knowing how to abound,' perhaps takes even more learning. But 'all things are possible to him that believeth.'

The teaching of the apostle in this verse, however, has a bearing not merely on our exercise of soul in the reception of what God's providence allots us, but on our own choice of occupations and sources of enjoyment. A Christian, he tells us, is so to live, that in the midst of everything, and in connection with everything, in which he is engaged, he can sincerely and reasonably praise God, and ask God's blessing. In all honest labour, and in all innocent enjoyment, this may be done. Any occupation or source of excitement and pleasure in regard to which it would be felt to be unnatural to ask God's blessing or give God thanks, — with which it would be felt to be a gross incongruity to mingle prayer and praise, and thus formally sanctify it,—or (for this practically is the same thing) which has a manifest tendency to dissipate devotional feeling,—is not an occupation or enjoyment for a

Christian. This may to some appear 'an hard saying;' and certainly the principle thus laid down is one fitted to cause serious 'searchings of heart' in all of us, and which, if faithfully carried out, would most materially alter the mode of life of many professing Christians. But beyond question, as it seems to me, no one will candidly ponder and develop before his mind the teaching of the apostle in the verse under consideration—which is simply a forcible and condensed statement of teaching to be found everywhere in the Bible by the man who chooses to see it,—without coming to the conclusion that such *is* the principle laid down by God. A Christian is a consecrated person—a member of 'a peculiar people,' who are 'redeemed' by the blood of Christ 'from all iniquity,' to be 'zealous of good works' and 'shine as lights in the world.' Their whole life is a consecrated life. Thus all the occupations and enjoyments of such consecrated men and women, all the scenes in which they choose to mingle, should certainly be such as either actually are, or at least without obvious incongruity and absurdity might be, consecrated, 'sanctified by the word of God and prayer' (1 Tim. iv. 5).

In the 14th and 15th verses the apostle reverts to the subject of affliction; and having in the first clause of the 13th enjoined prayer on those who are in trouble, he now, with reference to a special form of affliction, bodily illness, illustrates the efficiency of prayer,—bringing here, however, into particular prominence the value of *intercessory* prayer for the sufferer, and giving directions on this head.

'*Is any sick among you? let him call for the elders of the church.*' There can be no doubt, judging from the ordinary use of the word in the New Testament, that by '*elders*' are meant here not generally the older people in the congregation, but specially the office-bearers so named; and the apostle's injunction is one of many passages on which, taken together so as to cast light on each other, we Presbyterians base our system of church polity. The words before us certainly suggest that in the primitive church each congregation had its spiritual interests watched over by a body of elders, somewhat such as with us constitute a kirk-session. The apostle intimates here that one duty of the elders—one which, unquestionably, all who had the welfare of their brethren warmly at heart would deem very important—was to visit the members of the church in time of illness, to minister comfort, and counsel, and help. Such being a duty of the elders, it was correspondingly the duty of a member when he was ill to send for the elders. It would be well in various ways, brethren,—it would prevent many weary and unsatisfied longings on the part of the sick, many serious and hurtful misconceptions on the part of their relatives, many painful regrets on the part of Christian office-bearers,—if this injunction of Scripture were uniformly acted on. Ministers and elders cannot know of cases of illness unless they are told; and the rule is surely very simple, straightforward, and reasonable: 'Is any sick among you? let him *call* for the elders of the church.' The apostle's mode of expression appears to imply that notice of illness was to be sent to the *body* of elders, and that in those early days of the church they visited their sick—for we may presume that James here merely suggests for general adoption what was already, under apostolic advice, a practice in many congregations— either as a body, or at least by a deputation of more than one member: 'Let him call for the *elders*, and let *them* pray over him.' It seems naturally suggested by the clause, at all events, that this was a part of Christian work in which *all* the elders were expected to share, not merely those of them who 'laboured in the word and doctrine'—the ministers, as we now call them; and certainly there are few modes, if any, in which elders can more efficiently aid the minister, or benefit the congregation, than by assiduous and affectionate visiting of the sick.

Summoned to the bedside of a sufferer, the elders are to '*pray over him*,' to wrestle with God for their afflicted brother. With this is, in the apostle's injunction, associated also another duty, that of '*anointing him with oil in the name of the Lord.*' Oil has always been extensively used and highly valued in the medical practice of the East; and many commentators have thought that the reference here is simply to such a medical application, accompanied with prayer for the divine blessing on these ordinary means of cure. Besides other objections which might be urged against this view, this fact alone seems to me sufficient to set it aside,—that the apostle, from the unlimited form of his question, 'Is any sick among you?' must be supposed to speak of *any* case of illness. Now we cannot imagine that oil would be deemed a fitting medical application in *every* kind of disease. The anointing of which James speaks had, no doubt, a symbolical, sacred character. That anointing with which the Jewish Christians to whom he wrote were familiar, in many parts of the ceremonial of the Old Economy, was well understood to be emblematic of divine influence. Him in whose name they trusted they called by pre-eminence the Messiah or Christ, 'the *Anointed* One,' as having the influences of the Spirit 'poured' on Him without measure. Thus in the anointing of the sick they would recognise a symbol of the gracious Spirit through whom answers to prayer come. 'If the Spirit of Him that raised up Jesus from the dead dwell in you, He that raised up Christ from the dead shall also quicken your mortal bodies by His

Spirit that dwelleth in you' (Rom. viii. 11[1]); and of this great final quickening by the Spirit, the supernatural cures in answer to prayer were prelusive. A statement made by the Evangelist Mark illustrates that before us. In speaking of the mission on which the Lord during His ministry sent the apostles, he says that 'they cast out many devils, and anointed with oil many that were sick, and healed them' (Mark vi. 13). The reference there is most manifestly to miraculous cures, and the use of oil was plainly not medicinal, any more than the applications of spittle, or clay moistened with spittle, mentioned in the accounts of our Lord's miraculous works: it was emblematic. The case before us appears to be precisely similar. The sacred character of the anointing spoken of by James is shown very clearly—and at the same time the ground of the hope of help—by the addition, '*in the name of the Lord.*' Our apostle often, indeed generally, uses the name '*Lord*' as representing the 'Jehovah' of the Old Testament (for example, in verses 10 and 11), and it might be so taken here; but the analogy of the mode of expression recorded as having been employed by apostles in working miracles leads us rather to take it in the common New Testament sense, 'The Lord Jesus.' Thus Peter, you remember, said to the lame man at the Beautiful Gate of the temple, 'In the name of Jesus Christ of Nazareth, rise up and walk' (Acts iii. 6).

The 15th verse describes the results which will follow from the procedure enjoined in the 14th: '*And the prayer of faith shall save the sick, and the Lord shall raise him up.*' The latter clause being manifestly parallel to and explanatory of the former, it is clear that '*save*' here designates bodily healing. This is a common use of the word in the New

---

[1] This verse is pertinent to my argument, whether the true reading be the genitive or the accusative after διά.

Testament. Thus, when Jairus, petitioning the Saviour on behalf of his little sick daughter, says, 'I pray Thee, come and lay Thy hands on her, that she may be healed' (Mark v. 23), the term there rendered 'healed' is the same as that employed here. One cannot sufficiently admire the fulness, and bless God for it, with which in this passage—a passage where otherwise priestly assumption and ceremonialism might have found plausible entrenchment—the true source of help is exhibited, and any shadow of support for trust in mere ritual prevented. It is on the '*prayer*,' you observe, that emphasis is laid as a means of bringing down blessing, the anointing passing quite into the background. It is the 'prayer *of faith*,' moreover, a prayer which springs from belief in God's promises, from hearty confidence in His power and love,—not a mere form of words, possessed, however carelessly they be pattered over, of some magical virtue. And when the prayer of faith has been offered, the work of help is done wholly by Him 'that heareth prayer,' and to Him alone is glory due: 'The *Lord* shall raise him up.'

A difficulty occurs to every mind, connected with the universal unconditional terms of the promise given here that the result of the prayer of faith, under the circumstances described, will be bodily healing. It is plain that the words had primary and peculiar relation to an age of miraculous powers; but we have no reason to believe that even the apostles healed or could heal all the sick in whom they were interested. We know, indeed, that it was not so. 'Trophimus,' Paul tells Timothy, he 'left at Miletus sick' (2 Tim. iv. 20). The same difficulty presents itself in the promise of Christ regarding the 'signs' which were to 'follow them that believe'— 'They shall lay hands on the sick, and they shall recover' (Mark xvi. 18); and in the yet wider promise, 'What things soever ye desire when ye pray, believe that ye receive them, and ye shall have them' (Mark xi. 24). The explanation of the difficulty is no doubt to be found in the fact that in all such promises the condition is implied, 'in so far as accords with God's will.' The Christian heart feels this, and therefore the condition need not always be expressed. Putting the same thing in a slightly different form, indeed, we may truly say that the 'prayer of faith' is *always* answered, either by the bestowal of the specific object asked for, or by the gift of something better. We have every reason to believe, therefore, that in the first age many sick persons were, in answer to prayer, restored to health, often in the way of obvious miracle. We have equal reason to believe that the same occurs now, as really by the gracious action of the Divine Hearer of prayer, though without that startling suddenness and absence of ordinary means which constituted a healing miraculous. All who have been 'taught of God' will have no doubt, moreover, that in every age of the church, whenever true prayer has been offered by the sick, either alone or in conjunction with 'the elders of the church' or other brethren, 'healing,' 'quickening,' has certainly been granted in answer, though it might not be for the body.

The apostle continues: '*And if he have committed sins, they shall be forgiven him.*' No truth is more plainly taught in Scripture, than that our race, universally, is by nature depraved: 'If we say that we have no sin, we deceive ourselves, and the truth is not in us.' The reference here, then, where the 'committing of sins' is put as a mere supposition, must be not to sin generally, but to special sins, through which the disease has been brought on. Bible doctrine in regard to affliction is, that whilst, had there been no sin in the world, there would have been no suffering—for suffering is an element in the curse,—yet God does not, in this world, so apportion suffering as that the greatest sufferer can be pronounced the greatest sinner. This latter truth, opposed to a very natural idea, which was particularly prevalent among the Jews, is taught with much fulness and clearness in the book of Job, and by our Lord in connection with the case of those Galileans 'whose blood Pilate mingled with their sacrifices,' and again with that of the man born blind. But it is also true, plainly taught in Scripture, and manifest every day in the world, that in many instances particular forms of sin draw after them particular forms of suffering. The drunkard and the licentious man or woman, for example, often suffer in the body for their iniquities. To something of this kind, in all likelihood, our Lord alludes in His words to the man who had been healed at Bethesda: 'Behold, thou art made whole; sin no more, lest a worse thing come unto thee.' Now, in all persons suffering consciously for special sins,—when the Spirit of the Lord deals savingly with them, longing for a sense of the pardon of those sins will mingle with and overtop the longing for mere bodily healing. It was so, we may suppose, with the paralytic who was let down through the roof before Jesus, and to whom, reading his longings, the gracious Saviour said, 'Son, thy sins are forgiven thee,' before He said, 'Arise, and take up thy bed, and go thy way into thine house.'

It is the unvaried teaching of the Bible on this subject, that sins are forgiven only when they are repented of: 'Repent and be converted, that your sins may be blotted out' (Acts iii. 19). In the statement of James under consideration, then, it is implied that in the sufferer of whom he speaks he presupposes genuine penitence of spirit, 'a broken and contrite heart.' True Christian longings, and no empty superstition, are supposed to have led him to 'call for the elders of the church,' and the 'prayer of faith' has, all through, been going up from his own soul. In answer comes a sense of pardon—pardon of which, in the first age, miraculous healing granted by God would often be evidence.

To the two sacraments ordained in the New Testament, Roman Catholicism, as you know, has added five. One of these is 'extreme unction'—the application by a priest to the body of a person believed to be near death, of oil which has received the blessing of a bishop. The sick person is anointed in the form of the cross, on the eyes, ears, mouth, and some other organs,—a formula of prayer being recited each time for pardon of the sins which had been committed through the instrumentality of the sight, hearing, and the rest. This rite is held to be an efficient means of grace to the departing soul, remitting sins not previously remitted. The only passage appealed to as scriptural authority for this sacrament is the statement contained in the 14th and 15th verses now before us; the Council of Trent declaring that, whilst 'promulgated' here, it had been 'instituted' by Christ. It is difficult to conceive of anything more impudent than the attempt to maintain this support of priestly power by the authority of the present passage,—the basing of a rite which is appointed to be administered only to those who are believed to be dying, and with a reference to their death, on a practice which was intended, as the words of the apostle plainly show, to obtain the restoration of the sufferer to health. With arguments like this in support of its peculiar tenets, it is certainly not to be wondered at that Popery discourages biblical study among its votaries.

The injunction—or rather, perhaps, accurately stated, the recommendation—of the apostle regarding anointing, had an obvious suitableness for the Christian communities gathered from among the Jews, to whom the symbolic meaning of the practice was so familiar and expressive. No hint of any such precept or advice is given in any of the apostolic letters to churches of Gentile Christians; and, all things considered, we have not the slightest reason to suppose that James's recommendation on this head was meant to be of universal or permanent force in the church.[1]

[1] How long and how widely symbolic anointing of the sick was retained as a Christian usage, we have not data sufficient to determine. Tertullian (*Ad Scapul.* § 4) tells of special favour shown by the Emperor Septimius Severus (who reigned A.D. 193–211) to a Christian named Proculus, *qui eum per oleum aliquando curaverat.* The language is a little vague, but, in its connection, it seems to refer to symbolic unction, and to speak of a cure which was deemed at least very remarkable.

In various quarters the practice has been revived in modern times. In the town of Woolwich and the neighbourhood, for example, there is a small sect bearing the name of 'The Peculiar People,' one of whose tenets is that only prayer and anointing with oil should be resorted to in illness. The newspapers occasionally mention severe remarks made at coroners' inquests with regard to their neglect of application for medical help.

XXX.

CONFESSION AND PRAYER.

'Confess your faults one to another, and pray one for another, that ye may be healed. The effectual fervent prayer of a righteous man availeth much. 17 Elias was a man subject to like passions as we are, and he prayed earnestly that it might not rain ; and it rained not on the earth by the space of three years and six months : 18 And he prayed again, and the heaven gave rain, and the earth brought forth her fruit.'—JAMES v. 16-18.

THE advice given in the previous verses naturally leads to the recommendation before us,—one calculated in a very high degree to promote the prosperity and happiness of the church. The connecting thought is this: 'I have said that Christians when they are sick should summon to their bedsides the elders of the church, and that their united believing prayer will bring down God's blessing in restored health and spiritual comfort. Not merely the official representatives of the church, however, but all the children of God, can help their brethren mightily. Wherefore, *Confess your faults one to another, and pray one for another, that ye may be healed.*'

Our view of the breadth of the reference of the apostle's precept must depend, at least to a certain extent, on the meaning which we attach to the clause, '*that ye may be healed.*' A reader's first thought naturally is, that the discourse is still of the sick,—and we cannot doubt that these are included. Considering, however, that we have clearly passed into a new section, and that the brethren are addressed in the most general way, and are called on to confess to each other, and to pray for each other, without any specification of the sick, it seems to me that we must hold the application of '*healed*' to be wider than merely to deliverance from bodily disease. The connection between sin and suffering has been already alluded to in the close of the previous paragraph. The view of sin too, as itself a spiritual disease, and of God—who, as you remember, had proclaimed Himself to Israel at Marah under the name, 'The Lord that healeth thee'—as the Physician of souls, was familiar to James's readers from Old Testament imagery; and the particular word here employed in the original is often used of spiritual healing. The apostle speaks here, then, I apprehend, of deliverance *both spiritual and bodily*—the cure of the malady of sin, and of bodily disease where this fruit and image of sin was present. Thus understood, the present section leads most naturally to the last statement in the Epistle, regarding the blessedness of him who 'converteth a sinner from the error of his way.'

'*Confess your faults one to another.*' Confession of sin *to God* is of the essence of true repentance; for a man who will not look up and acknowledge his iniquity manifestly does not clearly see or deeply feel its evil. Only through unreservedness of heart towards God can we enjoy peace with Him. 'If we confess our sins, He is faithful and just to forgive us our sins, and to cleanse us from all unrighteousness.' 'When I kept silence,' says David, 'my bones waxed old through my roaring all the day long: for day and night Thy hand was heavy upon me; my moisture is turned into the drought of summer. I acknowledged my sin unto Thee, and mine iniquity have I not hid: I said, I will confess my transgressions unto the Lord; and Thou forgavest the iniquity of my sin.' The injunction before us, however, relates to confession *to man*. Now there is nothing in the general teaching of Scripture, or in the present precept when interpreted reasonably, to assign to this duty anything like the same extent of reference as belongs to confession to God. To Him we are called upon to lay bare our souls *absolutely*—to make penitential acknowledgement of all the sins of which we are conscious, and then, sensible that none can fully 'understand his errors,' to pray, 'Cleanse Thou me from secret faults.' But there are very many sins which it is not needful, many which it would be positively wrong, to reveal to our fellow-men. To take but one instance,—sins of thought may but for a moment, and in a very vague form, have been permitted to occupy the mind. Now the effort to bring them out before our own minds with the clearness and definiteness needful for our stating them to another, would, in multitudes of cases, do us moral harm, without advantage of any kind. Again, it might often happen that much moral injury might be done to the person who received our confession, by the acknowledgements which we made, and this however carefully we might choose our confidant. Indeed, circumstances of various kinds, and connected with offences of all sorts, may often render it in the very highest degree undesirable, or actually sinful, to make them known to our fellow-men.

In considering, then, what classes of '*faults*' James has here before his mind, *injuries to men* first occur to us. To make a frank acknowledgement of having done wrong, when 'a brother hath aught against us,' is one of the plainest duties of the Christian code of morals. Our Lord tells us that a soul unwilling to do this is in a condition in which worship cannot be acceptable to God; and therefore, even if the gift be already before the altar, the man is to 'go his way, first be reconciled to his brother, and then come and offer his gift.' Cases may easily be conceived, too, in which, though an injured person is unconscious of the injury, and ample material reparation may be possible without the accompaniment of confession, yet this also is at the least very desirable. For example, suppose that of two Christian merchants who have business transactions with each other, the one gains an advantage over the other in a way which that other does not know, and can never know, —a way perhaps strictly legal, but which afterthought convinces him who pursued it to be inconsistent with the highest morality. He might easily in most cases, without saying anything on the subject, make up to his friend in some subsequent transaction all the loss; and sometimes anything more than this may not be needed. Yet I can well believe that a confession would often bring more completeness of comfort to the offender, and not a little spiritual benefit to both parties. If the injury which has been done to a brother has been of a kind to affect his reputation,—for instance, if it has consisted in the circulation, whether through carelessness or from some definitely bad motive, of a calumnious report,—it is evident that confession should in such a case not merely be made to the wronged person himself, but be published as widely, if possible, as the calumny. This may be very humbling to the offender, but the discipline is salutary, and without such wide confession honourable reparation for the wrong is not made.

But it seems reasonable to take the apostle's recommendation before us as having a wider reference than simply to cases of the kind which I have mentioned. There are few greater burdens than the burden of a guilty secret, and the heart that has such feels as if the spiritual weight would be lightened through confession,—the hearer helping to bear it, after a sort. This longing for confession is strikingly illustrated by a tradition which Hood has wrought into a poem of singular power,—that Eugene Aram, a murderer of the last century in England, a man of high cultivation, and a teacher by profession, sometimes told his scholars the story of his crime, with all circumstantial details, but under the guise of a dream. Apart, however, from extreme cases like this, there are, no doubt —it may be in the very quietest walks of Christian life—many people of a tender, sensitive temperament, who, yearning for sympathy and guidance, long to speak to a Christian friend of some of their weaknesses and sins. It is true that the only perfect and satisfying sympathy, and the only wholly trustworthy guidance, are those of the Divine Man who 'was made in all things like unto His brethren, that He might be merciful'—'tempted like as we are,' that He might be 'touched with the feeling of our infirmities;' yet at times, particularly times of bodily prostration, in hearts of the class which I have mentioned there comes a weary craving for a visible confidant and adviser. For such a feeling, being not in itself sinful, provision has been made by Christianity, through the brotherly relation of believers to each other. 'Confess your faults one to another, and'—here comes the corresponding injunction to the Christian friends of penitents—'pray one for another.' As Paul has it, 'Bear ye one another's burdens, and so fulfil the law of Christ.' Where such unburdening of the conscience is resorted to, not in the spirit of religious gossip, but seriously and devoutly, as a help graciously granted by the Saviour to our weakness, comfort and real spiritual benefit may often, in no small measure, be obtained through it. From the nature of the case, however, this can only be when confession to brethren is held as a somewhat exceptional procedure, to be adopted occasionally under special pressure of feeling. Whenever it becomes in any way methodized into a system, for periodical observance, then, as it seems to me, the desire for it is certainly a symptom of spiritual disease,—a disease which the supposed remedy will only aggravate. It is manifestly of the highest importance, too, if the present recommendation of our apostle is to be carried out with any real benefit to the penitent, that the burdened heart should select its confidant with very great care. A friend truly pious and affectionate, experienced and discreet, may be of much service; no other can reasonably be expected to be.

This injunction of the Apostle James is the passage of Scripture principally pleaded in support of the Roman Catholic system of private confession of sin to a priest,—which that Church enjoins to be performed periodically, and teaches to be necessary for salvation, and to secure salvation certainly through the absolution given by the priest after full confession. This abominable system is, beyond doubt, and has been all down the generations since it was introduced, more prolific of impurity and hardness of heart, and indeed moral evil of every kind, than anything else in the ecclesiastical arrangements of any religious sect,—perhaps indeed it would hardly be too strong to say, than any one agency of any kind existing in the world. The Reformers, who knew well the nature and effects of auricular confession, used to call the confessional 'the slaughter-house of consciences.' But it is the strongest of all the props of priestly domination over souls, and therefore among the very last things which Romanism would be willing to renounce. I need scarcely point out to you that this vile system has no shadow of support in the passage before us. Here again, as in examining the preceding paragraph, one cannot sufficiently admire and praise the divine wisdom and love which have so fenced in the inspired words from the possibility of being even plausibly misinterpreted by any one who looks at them with ordinary intelligence and candour. You observe that, by a clearly marked transition, the apostle has passed from his reference to the office-bearers of the church, to the *brethren generally*,—including the office-bearers, no doubt, on occasion, as hearers of such confession as he has alluded to, but certainly not speaking of them alone. Again, the confession enjoined is *mutual;* so that, even if it were incumbent on me to confess to a priest, it would be equally incumbent on him to confess to me. And of any view to the obtaining of *authoritative absolution*, in the confession here spoken of, there is not the remotest hint. Thus priestly assumption has no standing-ground on this text.

The apostle proceeds: '*and pray one for another.*' This recommendation, in its position here, points out especially, as I have already said, the duty of such believers as have confession of faults made to them by brethren. They can counsel them, and comfort them; but the chief help they can render is to pray for them. The breadth in the mode of expression, however, naturally leads us to find in James's words, besides the immediate reference, also a general precept to cultivate prayer for our fellow-Christians. Intercessory prayer is one of the sweetest and most profitable of all our religious duties and privileges. Springing from love, it exercises, widens, and strengthens love. It brings down blessing on others, and it quickens the spirituality of the intercessor. 'I exhort,' says Paul to Timothy, 'that, first of all, supplications, prayers, intercessions, and giving of thanks, be made *for all men.*' The believer recognises the brotherhood of universal humanity, and by prayer 'for all men' exerts a positive beneficent influence on behalf of all; whilst any other mode of exhibiting the spirit of brotherhood has its range necessarily confined to a very narrow circle. But whilst honouring and praying for all men, he feels himself bound by a peculiarly close and tender tie to his brethren in Christ. For them his love is not of benevolence merely, but of complacency, sympathy, delight. Accordingly he is urged by the impulses of the new life to 'watch unto prayer with all perseverance and supplication *for all saints*.' These words of the Apostle Paul stand in immediate and most suggestive connection with the magnificent passage, so familiar to us all, regarding the Christian's warfare and armour. As a Christian soldier, a Vicars or a Havelock, in entering on an ordinary earthly battle, would pray not for himself alone, but for all his fellow-soldiers, feeling that they form one army, and that the success of one is the success of all; so in the grand spiritual warfare every believer is constrained to pray for every other. The high priest of the Old Economy had in his breastplate, resting on his heart, when he went in before the Lord to pray, the names of the twelve tribes of Israel,—a fact beautifully symbolizing the tender love and constant care with which our great Divine High Priest continually intercedes for His people, none of them forgotten, none of them even for a moment put aside. We, too, who in Him are 'priests unto God,' should—and in the measure of the liveliness and intelligence of our faith we do—cast each of us by intercessory prayer his little grain of incense into the Divine High Priest's censer. The fact is not without deep significance, my brethren, that in our repetition of the prayer which Jesus taught His disciples, we never say 'I' or 'mine,' but always with our own wants join those of all everywhere who through the common Saviour trust in '*Our* Father who is in heaven.' Illustrations of the power of intercessory prayer abound in the Word of God. One instance, striking in itself, and closely illustrative of the case particularly alluded to by our apostle, that of prayer for fellow-believers who have fallen into sin, is exhibited to us in God's statement to Job's friends: 'My servant Job shall pray for you, for him will I accept; lest I deal with you after your folly, in that ye have not spoken of Me the thing which is right, like My servant Job.'

The apostle's recommendation to his readers to 'pray one for another,' he proceeds to enforce by a statement of the great power of prayer, illustrated by an example. Prayer, he says, '*availeth much*,'—a truth most precious to the believing heart. Whilst there are some points connected with it which we cannot understand, as there are connected with everything in the relations between the Infinite One and His moral creatures; yet nothing is more plainly revealed in Scripture, than that prayer is a most efficient means of obtaining blessing. The praying soul is through the very exercise refreshed, purified, and elevated, feeling itself in the presence-chamber of the Divine King and Father. But besides this reflex influence of the spiritual act, God *answers* prayer in the strictest and most definite sense. 'Ask, and it shall be given you,' is the command, with the promise. It is evidently of this direct power that the apostle is mainly thinking here, the injunction to intercede with God for blessings on brethren having led him to make the statement; and it is the direct power which the example adduced by him sets with liveliness before us.

The prayer which he declares to 'avail much' is that of '*a righteous man*,' by which, comparing his own teaching in this Epistle with the ordinary use of the expression in Scripture, we know him to mean a man genuinely pious—one who has a faith which reveals its vitality by originating and sustaining a godly life. Such a man, being a child of God, has freedom of access to his Father, and will not be 'sent empty away.' 'The

Lord will fulfil the desire of them that fear Him.' 'The prayer of the upright is His delight.' But 'if I regard iniquity in my heart, the Lord will not hear me.' For successful prayer, oneness of will with God is needful. If two harps be strung to the same key, but not otherwise, then let one be struck, and the other will give a responsive sound. Now 'God is love,' and the substance of 'righteousness' is love, for 'love is the fulfilling of the law.'

But James mentions another condition of success. Not merely must the prayer be that of 'a righteous man,' but it must be '*effectual fervent*.' This part of the sentence is a somewhat remarkable exception to the usual admirable felicity of the renderings of our translators. These two words are employed to represent one of the original; and not merely is there this cumbrousness, but one of the terms chosen plainly introduces tautology into the statement, seeing that 'an effectual prayer availeth much' is not greatly different from 'an effectual prayer is effectual.' The exact force of the original word is not quite clear. On the whole, it seems to me that '*fervent*,' or '*having energy*,' is the idea intended by the apostle.[1] By

---

[1] Ἐνεργουμένη has been very variously understood. Three views only appear to be grammatically defensible. (1) The form may be regarded as passive, meaning 'inwrought (by the Holy Spirit).' This view of the sense brings out a most important truth, and one perfectly relevant to the point in hand; and the fact that the passive of ἐνεργεῖν does not occur elsewhere in N. T. (2 Cor. i. 6, iv. 12, where forms of the verb have by some been regarded as passive, being more naturally explained on the supposition that they are middle) would not of itself weigh much against it. But the apostle, if it had been his intention to bring in this new and important thought, would certainly not have left it to be doubtfully suggested by the use of one ambiguous word, but would have filled up the expression. (2) Taking the form as middle, we may render the participle 'working,' that is, 'by its working' or (so Revised Version) 'in its working.' This view lies under the objection of making the word utterly weak, adding really nothing to the thought of the sentence; for in what way conceivable could any prayer 'avail' except 'by its

his specifying this we are reminded of the melancholy truth that even 'righteous men,' the true children of God, are prone to fall into spiritual torpor, so that their very exercises of devotion lack energy of heart. Alas, what Christian does not remember times when his praying seemed to be little more than mechanical,—when, though perhaps the words were glowing, the soul was cold? There can be no power in such prayer. To 'avail much,' the 'righteous man's' cry to God must be not from the lip merely, but clearly and fully from the heart—and from the heart with its longings gathered up and concentrated on the object of supplication. This is a 'prayer having energy.' For all time the symbol of effectual supplication is Jacob's 'wrestling' with the Angel; and God's people approve themselves to be indeed the spiritual 'Israel,' 'princes who have power with God, and prevail,' only when, like Jacob, they cling to God, saying, 'I will not let Thee go, except Thou bless me.'

The example of the power of prayer which James introduces is from the history of the illustrious prophet Elijah. At the outset he obviates an objection which might naturally be raised

working'? To use the word thus is altogether unlike the vigorous, trenchant style of James. (3) Guided by the emphasis which the word has from its position, we may suppose that James employs the verb with something of a special intensity of signification, as equivalent to ἐνεργὴς εἶναι, 'to be operative, full of energy' (comp. 1 Cor. xvi. 9; Philem. 6; Heb. iv. 12, especially the last). This view, which is supported by the very high authority of Dean Scott, appears entirely satisfactory. To give the participle a purely adjectival force—as in A. V.—is hardly sustained by analogy. 'When full of force or energy' would bring out the thought precisely; but seeing that in fact fervour is the 'energy' of prayer, it is perhaps best to retain the familiar word, translating therefore, 'when fervent.' The very curious double rendering of our translators, 'effectual fervent,' is possibly due to a compromise between conflicting opinions in the committee of translators, or, more probably, to a clerical confusion in the notation of the result of their deliberations. It is wholly their own, for the earlier versions have simply 'fervent,' with the exception of Wycliffe's and the Rhemish, which have 'continual,' from the Vulgate, '*assidua*.'

to the applicability of the case. He feels that the grandeur of Elijah's character, the stupendousness of his miracles, the glory of the mode of his departure from earth, and the peculiar dignity with which Jewish superstition invested him as specially the guardian of Israel, might almost place him, in the feelings of the Jewish Christians, in a class of beings distinct from the human race, so that from the power of his prayers no conclusion regarding ours could fairly be drawn. This possible and probable difficulty the apostle removes at once by his introductory remark, that '*Elias was a man subject to like passions as we are*'—a man, not an angel—and a man of a nature like other men, with all the weaknesses which belong to humanity as we now find it in the world. Similarly Peter, when Cornelius fell down at his feet and worshipped him, said, 'Stand up; I myself also am a man;' and Paul and Barnabas said to the people of Lystra, who were about to sacrifice to them, 'Sirs, why do ye these things? We also are *men of like passions with you*,'—exactly the expression here used by James of Elijah. An interesting evidence that by our apostle the Lord Jesus was held to possess an ineffable dignity of nature, is afforded by comparing this description of Elijah, a man certainly in every point of view one of the very noblest of our race, with the name applied to the Saviour in Chap. ii. 1, 'our Lord Jesus Christ, the Lord of glory.'

In the history of this 'righteous man' Elijah the power of 'fervent prayer' was signally shown. '*He prayed earnestly*' (observe the prominence given to the 'fervent' character of the entreaty) '*that it might not rain, and it rained not on the earth*' (rather, probably, 'on the land' of Canaan,—a frequent use of the original term in Scripture) '*by the space of three years and six months; and he prayed again, and the heaven gave rain, and the earth brought forth her fruit.*' The immediate echo-like answer which comes to such prayer as Elijah's is vividly set forth by the language employed, 'He prayed earnestly that it might not rain, *and it rained not.*' This recalls to us at once the sublime 'Let there be light, and there was light,' and thus suggests the almightiness of the prayer which lays hold of the almightiness of God. The potency of the prayer is further indicated by the mention of the great length of time during which the drought that had been asked for continued, and, in the account of the effects of the second petition, by the detailed statement that all the elements and powers of nature yielded loyally to the imperial power of prayer: 'The heaven gave rain, and the earth brought forth her fruit.'

The statement made in this passage, and also in our Lord's address to the people of Nazareth, as recorded by Luke (iv. 25), regarding the duration of the drought, appears on first sight to be at variance with that given in the Old Testament narrative, where we are told that 'the word of the Lord came unto Elijah *in the third year*, saying, Go, show thyself unto Ahab; and I will send rain upon the earth' (1 Kings xviii. 1). A satisfactory solution of the difficulty, however, is afforded by the supposition, which is in every way probable, that in the specification of time in the passage in First Kings the reckoning is made not from the beginning of the drought, but from the period when the prophet left the brook Cherith and went to live with the widow at Zarephath.

The fact that Elijah prayed to God to withhold rain is not mentioned in the Old Testament, but was no doubt preserved by Jewish tradition, which is here accepted and authenticated by the inspired apostle; just as, for example, the names of the magicians of Pharaoh,—the fact that at Mount Sinai, amid the awful splendours of the manifestation of God, Moses said, 'I exceedingly fear and quake,'—and the prophecy of Enoch regarding the Lord's coming to judgement,—are known to us only through the New Testament.[1] In the narrative of the incidents preceding the return of rain there is no express mention of the offering up of prayer by the prophet; but every reader feels that, when 'he cast himself down upon the earth, and put his face between his knees,' he was pleading with God with intense fervour, and that here indeed lies the very life of that portion of the history.

Before Elijah left Zarephath, he had been told by God, in words quoted a little above, that rain was about to be given to the thirsty earth; and accordingly his petition on Carmel must have been that *now* Jehovah would fulfil His promise. Substantially, this is the sum of all prayer. The longing, 'Thy will be done,' is of the essence of all acceptable supplication; and hence no petition can be offered by any intelligent believer absolutely, without reservations, except such as is matter of definite promise. When a wrestling soul would 'bring forth its strong reasons' before the 'King of Jacob,' it turns instinctively to His own declarations of grace. Prayer answers promise, as fulfilment answers prayer. 'Surely I come quickly;' 'Amen, even so, come, Lord Jesus.' In regard to the first of Elijah's prayers which James mentions, that for the withholding of rain, it is reasonable to suppose, from the peculiar nature of the petition, that it had been made known to the prophet by revelation that a judgement of this kind would be tributary to the glory of the God of Israel, through the spiritual profiting of His people. Thus he was fully authorized to present His prayer. One may safely say, that without such special revelation of the divine will there can scarcely occur circumstances in which it would be right or wise—in which it would not be signally unwise and wrong—to offer such a petition. To all

[1] See 2 Tim. iii. 8; Heb. xii. 21; Jude 14.

who, without the peculiar commission and direction of Elias are disposed, in fancied zeal for the Lord God of hosts, to invoke drought, or to 'command fire to come down from heaven and consume the adversaries, even as Elias did,' Jesus says, 'Ye know not what manner of spirit ye are of.' Such a disposition has a much closer connection with arrogance and bigotry, with the 'wrath of man,' which 'worketh not the righteousness of God,' than with 'the wisdom that is from above, peaceable, gentle, full of mercy and good fruits.'

Both of the apostle's references to the history of Elijah obviously illustrate very strikingly his declaration, that 'the fervent prayer of a righteous man availeth much.' The second of them has a special suitableness and force in the connection in which it is introduced. He has been enjoining on his readers to 'pray one for another, that they might be healed,' particularly of spiritual torpor and disease. How cheering, then, the thought that, if the energy of Elijah's prayer brought rain to refresh the parched earth and revive a people ready to perish, as certainly the prayer of faith can bring down not merely on the petitioning heart, but on many souls besides, the genial showers of the Spirit's gracious influences!—for God has promised, saying, 'I will be as the dew unto Israel: he shall grow as the lily, and cast forth his roots as Lebanon. I will pour water upon him that is thirsty, and floods upon the dry ground: I will pour My Spirit upon thy seed, and My blessing upon thine offspring; and they shall spring up as among the grass, as willows by the water-courses.'

XXXI.

ERROR AND CONVERSION.

'Brethren, if any of you do err from the truth, and one convert him; 20 Let him know, that he which converteth the sinner from the error of his way shall save a soul from death, and shall hide a multitude of sins.'—JAMES V. 19, 20.

THE connection of these words with what precedes is not far to seek. The apostle has recommended to the brethren mutual confession of sin, and that they should ask for each other in prayer forgiveness of sin and spiritual strength. Sin, and desire for the deliverance of others as well as ourselves from sin, being thus the subjects occupying his mind, he very naturally passes on next to impress on his readers how great a thing it is to be the instrument in God's hand of bringing back a sinner to his heavenly Father. With this he fittingly closes his letter. His own aim, throughout all that he has written, has most obviously and directly been to stimulate Christians to higher attainments in godliness, and to arouse to sincere repentance those who only had 'a name to live.' Nothing, then, can be more meet than that he should conclude with an appeal to all God's children whom his words might reach, to do similar work in their various spheres, and by the various means which God might put in their power.

The form of this concluding exhortation is a little peculiar, —the peculiarity, as you will see on a moment's consideration, being advantageous to its effect. In the first part, contained in the 19th verse, James continues that style of direct address to his readers which has prevailed throughout the Epistle, thus securing that his statement or appeal will have for their consciences and hearts the special force always belonging to what is distinctly intended for ourselves. Then the second part is in form altogether general. The erring professing Christian, the 'any of you' of the 19th verse, is in the 20th classed under the far wider term 'sinner;' and the expressing of the subject, 'he which converteth,' makes this part a sentence quite complete in itself. Thus we have a truth of the greatest importance condensed into a shape striking and easily remembered: 'He which converteth a sinner from the error of his way shall save a soul from death, and shall hide a multitude of sins.' There are in the New Testament many of these summaries of truth, so expressed as to be complete in themselves, and thus carrying with them their full significance, or at least a very ample significance, even when quoted apart from the context in which they occur. In these we see an evidence of the watchful care of God, providing for all the wants of His children. Even we in these latter days, though we have Bibles in abundance, find very great advantage in these condensed statements—in such 'little gospels,' for example, as, 'God so loved the world, that He gave His only begotten Son, that whosoever believeth in Him should not perish, but have everlasting life.' It is plain, then, that they must have been vastly more required in the first ages of the church, when copies of even a single Gospel or Epistle could be possessed by only a few persons, and, in the case of the great majority of believers, the bread of life for daily sustenance must have been simply the truth borne in memory from public reading and exposition. In circumstances like these, it must manifestly have been of immeasurable benefit to have such portable statements of truth as that before us. Those given in Scripture, and others provided for the necessities of the time by the inspired teachers, constituted in all likelihood the class known by the special name of 'faithful sayings,' of which Paul in the Pastoral Epistles quotes several, obviously as precious commonplaces of the church's faith, 'familiar in their mouths as household words.'

One other remark on the form of the passage it seems desirable to make. I have spoken of it as an appeal or exhortation. Strictly speaking, it is an exhibition of the grounds of satisfaction and thankfulness possessed by the Christian who *has* reclaimed an erring brother: 'If any of you do err from the truth, and one convert him, let him (him who has thus gained his brother) know.' But this is, in effect, plainly an incitement to all Christians, by the setting forth of the most powerful motives, to labour for the conversion of sinners.

When we proceed to consider the passage in detail, the first thing which strikes us is the importance obviously ascribed by the apostle to apprehending and cleaving to '*the truth*.' You observe that '*to err* (or wander) *from the truth*' is employed by him clearly as having much the same force as 'to wander away from Christianity, as an agency for producing moral elevation and true happiness;' and '*the error* (or wandering—from the truth, obviously, in the connection) *of a man's way*' is that which constitutes him '*a sinner*.' The sense of the passage shows clearly enough (and, if confirmation be needed, it is afforded by the apostle's use of the expression elsewhere in the Epistle [1]) that by '*the truth*' he means not 'truthfulness' merely, but either 'the body of revealed truth,' or 'the kind of character, in all its length and breadth, which religious truth, received in the love of it, naturally forms.' The expression is used fre-

---

[1] See iii. 14.

quently, as you will remember, in the writings of the other apostles also in one or other of these senses. Indeed it was evidently the ordinary, or at least a very familiar, phrase in the primitive church to designate 'the gospel,' either looked at simply by itself, or as influencing men's hearts and moulding their lives.

In our day, the opponents of evangelical religion very often take up the ground that it is a matter almost of indifference what our views of truth are, — of little consequence what we believe, or whether we believe anything, provided our life is honourable. This principle pervades much of the teaching regarding religion in our popular literature. It is often avowed, for example, in defence of the freedom given in the Church of England for the teaching of almost all varieties of doctrine. 'A national religious association,' the defenders of the present state of things say, 'should comprise holders of all shades of belief; for its purpose is not to inculcate particular doctrinal tenets, but simply to secure throughout the country the presence of educated gentlemen, all teaching the people to live sober and respectable lives, to be upright and industrious, kind to their neighbours, and obedient to their rulers.' Among another and spiritually higher class than those who entertain such defective views of the nature and purposes of the church of Christ, positions of this kind are very popular,— that religion is but little a matter of the understanding, and almost solely of the heart; that doctrines have been the seeds of all the controversies and heartburnings which have disfigured the history of the church, whereas charity is the essence of Christianity, for 'God is love;' that Jesus said, 'I am the truth,' and those therefore who have Him in their hearts have the truth. All of you who have any acquaintance with the literature of what calls itself the 'Broad School' of religious thinkers are familiar with writing of this kind. Now such words contain much that is true and important; and just here, in the truth and preciousness of many of the statements, when understood in their proper relation to Bible teaching generally, lies their great power to mislead when distorted from that relation. When put forward to depreciate the importance of knowing and cherishing doctrinal truth, propositions of the kind I have quoted rest on a false assumption,— this, namely, that apart from the perception and belief of truth by the mind, the heart can become pure, and loving, and holy before God. Now, according to the plain teaching of such passages of Scripture as that before us—according to the whole tenor of Scripture indeed, as well as the declarations of experience—the knowledge and belief of certain grand truths are absolutely needful to produce holy affections. The man who has Jesus in his heart has 'the truth;' but Jesus enters the seat of the affections through the mind—through the intelligent belief of such truth regarding Him as dispels that atmosphere of falsehood which by nature fills the whole soul. 'If ye continue in My word,' said Jesus, 'then are ye My disciples indeed; and ye shall know the truth, and *the truth shall make you free.*' It is plainly implied that nothing else can.

Round truth controversy gathers, and controversy is often painful. But it by no means follows that true Christian happiness or true Christian love can rest better on the basis of a mere vague and dreamy sentiment than on truth believed,— or indeed can rest on any such basis at all. Jesus, the incarnate Love, the Prince of peace, spent very much of His public life in controversy. His apostles, too, lived much in controversy. John, to whom of all the followers of the Lord we should, from what we know of his character, look first for the manifestation of a true and beautiful charity, says in one of his letters, 'Whosoever transgresseth and abideth not

VER. 19.] *Error and Conversion.* 437

in the doctrine of Christ, hath not God;' and proceeds to charge thus the friends to whom he writes, regarding the heretical teachers who abounded at the time : 'If there come any unto you, and bring not this doctrine' (the 'doctrine of Christ,' just mentioned), 'receive him not into your house, neither bid him God speed; for he that biddeth him God speed is partaker of his evil deeds.' Controversy in which sentiments like these are propounded with intense earnestness by one of so loving a character, certainly proceeds on the supposition that some truths are of essential moment, vitally important for the peace and joy of the soul, for the existence and growth of godliness and spiritual beauty. As I have been led to refer to John's eminently clear and instructive testimony on this question, let him speak to us further as to what are these cardinal truths. Such as these : 'If we say that we have no sin, we deceive ourselves, and the truth is not in us :' 'In the beginning was the Word, and the Word was with God, and the Word was God :' 'And the Word was made flesh, and dwelt among us, full of grace and truth :' 'And He is the propitiation for our sins, and not for ours only, but also for the sins of the whole world :' 'If we confess our sins, God is faithful and just to forgive us our sins, and to cleanse us from all unrighteousness,' seeing that 'we have an Advocate with the Father, Jesus Christ the Righteous :' 'And he that keepeth God's commandments dwelleth in Him, and He in him; and hereby we know that He abideth in us, by the Spirit which He hath given us.' Such truths as these, in their connection and ramifications, as fully exhibited in Scripture, constitute the 'doctrine of Christ,' which it is of transcendent importance that a man know, and believe, and abide in, seeing that he who abides therein 'hath both the Father and the Son' (2 John 9).

From its nature, this truth, when believed, exercises supreme influence over the affections of the heart and in the regulation of the life, producing love to God and devotion to His will. But obviously it can do this only when *believed*. Till then, however fully known, it cannot hold sway. It is not truth *to me*—it remains a thing external to me—until I believe it. And in proportion to the intelligence and the realizing liveliness of our faith, will be the measure of power exerted over us by the truth believed. '*Error*,' then, in one who has professed himself a Christian (and to this class James specially refers in the passage before us: 'If any *of you* do err from the truth'), may show itself in two ways. There may be definite *disbelief*, definite acceptance of falsehood, such as that of Hymenæus and Philetus in Paul's days, who, as the apostle tells Timothy, 'concerning the truth have erred, saying that the resurrection is past already, and overthrow the faith of some' (2 Tim. ii. 18). Through the prevalent intellectual restlessness of our time, illustrations abound of this kind of error, in the most varied directions. The young Christian, in particular, is in much peril of being led seriously astray; and it becomes us all very earnestly, by candid and diligent study of the word of God, to 'build ourselves up on our most holy faith,—praying in the Holy Ghost.' But again, even whilst the creed continues sound, at least even where a man has no consciousness of intellectual deviation, there may be real and most serious 'wandering' from 'the truth,' through worldliness and torpor of spirit, rendering the creed practically a dead thing. The Apostle John, you remember, tells us that his great delight was to hear that his spiritual children '*walked* in truth' (3 John 4, and 2 John 4),—having it, that is, as an atmosphere, in which they lived and moved, and by which they were every moment sustained. In so far as this is not the case with us, in so far as in feeling or practice we are not pervaded and governed by 'the truth,' and thus approve ourselves 'children of light,' we are in 'error,' wanderers from 'the truth,' as really as if we definitely disbelieved it. There is something of this in all Christians; the best of us 'come short of the glory of God.' And alas, my brethren, there are lamentably many bearing the Christian name, and believing themselves to hold Christian truth, whose lives seem rather those of 'children of darkness.' In all — whether calling themselves Christians or not—who do not sincerely love God, the whole course of life is necessarily one of 'error.' 'Cain went out from the presence of the Lord, and dwelt in the land of *Wandering*,' and all other enemies of God do likewise. They stray in devious paths after shadows, 'seeking rest and finding none,' until, unless divine grace check them in their folly, 'their feet stumble on the dark mountains.' Let us then cleave to 'the truth,' dear brethren, in faith and in practice. We rejoice to believe in the certain perseverance of the saints in a state of grace, but we know that this is a perseverance in childlike submission to the enlightening and sanctifying power of the truth. Let us therefore 'watch and pray, lest we enter into temptation,' remembering that no doom is so terrible as that of the apostate professor of religion, 'who hath trodden under foot the Son of God, and done despite unto the Spirit of grace.'

Our apostle directs the attention of his readers to the blessed results of '*converting a sinner from the error of his way*.' It is evident that he has before his mind error of the most serious kind, whether of creed or conduct, or both. To '*convert a sinner*' is God's work, for no arm but that of the Almighty can arrest him, and turn him from his 'error' to 'the truth.' But He graciously employs human agency in the work, to exhibit and enforce the truth to mind and heart. The Spirit of God alone is the power that quickens the vines; but the Divine Husbandman employs His children in the culture, saying to every one of them, 'Son, go work to-day in My vineyard.' He permits us—and this is surely the highest conceivable honour for His moral creatures—to be 'labourers together with Him;' and to all earnest workers He gives no stinted praise, speaking often of the work that was done only in and through Himself as their work. To Paul, Jesus said, that He sent him to the Gentiles 'to open their eyes, and to turn them ('convert' them—the same word as here) from darkness to light, and from the power of Satan unto God' (Acts xxvi. 18). Similarly of John the Baptist it was predicted by the angel to Zacharias: 'He shall be filled with the Holy Ghost even from his mother's womb, and many of the children of Israel shall he turn (convert) to the Lord their God' (Luke i. 15, 16).

'Let believers, then,' says James, 'for their incitement to earnestness and perseverance in the work of God, consider this, that whosoever is instrumental in converting a sinner from the error of his ways, *shall save a soul from death.*' By nature, as you know, brethren, we are all spiritually dead. God made man 'a living soul;' and in Eden all the elements of his being sounded forth, in grand, rich, unbroken harmony, an anthem to the praise of his Father in heaven. He served God perfectly, and in the service had perfect joy. That was *life*. But

> 'Disproportioned sin
> Jarred against nature's chime, and with harsh din
> Broke the fair music that all creatures made
> To their great Lord, whose love their motion swayed
> In perfect diapason, whilst they stood
> In first obedience, and their state of good.'

For moral creatures such discord is *death;* and thus we are all now, by nature, 'dead in trespasses and sins.' From this death conversion delivers at once: for the Saviour's declaration was, 'Verily, verily, I say unto you, He that believeth on Me *hath* everlasting life' (John vi. 47). The apostle, however, seems to have mainly before his mind that intensity of debasement and misery in the world to come, to which by fair natural development this spiritual death of earth leads,—that unutterably awful condition which the Lord, 'the Faithful Witness,' describes as 'outer darkness, where shall be weeping and gnashing of teeth, where their worm dieth not, and the fire is not quenched,' and which His servant John calls 'the second death.' A person who rescues a fellow-creature from imminent danger of physical death, has justly very high satisfaction in the remembrance; yet this is but deliverance for the body—but the prolongation for, at the furthest, a few years, of a life in which there will be much weariness, and care, and sorrow. How rich must be the blessedness, then, of him who, by 'converting a sinner,' 'saves his *soul* from death,'—rescuing, and that for ever, not the body merely, but the 'glory' of man, as the Psalmist has it, the rational spirit on which God imprinted His own likeness, from the horrors of the place of woe!

'*And shall hide a multitude of sins.*' These words are employed, with a different application, by the Apostle Peter (1 Pet. iv. 8); and we may reasonably suppose, therefore, that the phrase—founded, as Peter's use of it in particular plainly enough indicates, on Prov. x. 12, 'Love covereth all sins'— was a familiar one among religious Jews. The language, as employed in any of the places, may, when taken apart from its connection, be referred to with some plausibility, and as a matter of fact very often is referred to, as intimating what the arrogance of the carnal mind would delight to find in the

Bible,—that salvation is through man's works, and not of God's free grace. The 'sins' are, on this view, regarded as those of the person in whom the 'love' or 'charity' reigns, or, in the present passage, who shows his love by 'converting' a brother. Supposing this to be the reference, the words are parallel to our Lord's statement, 'If ye forgive men their trespasses, your heavenly Father will also forgive you' (Matt. vi. 14). Candidly interpreted in the light of general New Testament teaching, the statement speaks of love not at all as being a meritorious ground of salvation, but simply as an evidence of true fruit-bearing faith. There is good reason, however, to question whether, in any of the three places where the passage before us occurs, the word 'sins' has that reference of which I have been speaking. In the place in Proverbs there cannot be a moment's doubt, when the context is looked at, that it is the sins of those *for* whom the love is entertained which are covered. In Peter also this seems considerably the more probable exposition; and, in the connection in which James makes the quotation, one can say the same even more decidedly. The natural and obvious interpretation of the clause as used by him is to take it as bringing out more explicitly the force of the preceding, 'shall save a soul from death.'

'Blessed,' says David, 'is he whose transgression is forgiven, whose *sin* is *covered*.' This is the '*covering*,' or '*hiding*,' spoken of by James. Manifestly, therefore, it is God's act; and in James's statement, that the Christian who 'converts a sinner' 'shall hide' that sinner's sins, 'hide' is employed, in accordance with the apostle's general liveliness of expression, for 'bringing about the hiding.' By leading the sinner to repentance he brings him within the sphere of God's covenant mercy, which 'hides his sins,' so that God looks upon them no more. In the ancient 'Holy of holies,' gospel grace was typified by the fact that the tables of the law, placed in the ark, were 'covered' by the blood-besprinkled mercy-seat, above which shone the Shekinah, the special symbol of the divine presence. So, in looking upon all who, through the work of His Spirit, have believed in Jesus, God sees not their wickedness calling for punishment, but the Saviour's perfect righteousness, which 'hides' their sins.

In every case these sins are '*a multitude.*' However morally correct the outward conduct of an unregenerate man may be, however noble in some respects his aspirations, yet love to God does not hold sway in his heart, and thus he is constantly disobedient to the 'first and great commandment.' The regenerate man, too, though the love of God is supreme in his heart, is yet guilty of many shortcomings and slips in his Father's service : 'In many things we offend all.' And the more fully that He 'who commanded the light to shine out of darkness, hath shined in our hearts, to give the light of the knowledge of the glory of God in the face of Jesus Christ,' ever the more clearly, in that 'marvellous light,' do we see the intensity of that darkness from which God's grace has brought us out, and 'the multitude' and abominableness of the sins committed under it, and also the greatness of the darkness which we still permit to remain in the corners and crannies of our souls and lives. 'Job answered the Lord, and said, I have heard of Thee by the hearing of the ear, but now mine eye seeth Thee; wherefore I abhor myself, and repent in dust and ashes.'

But however many or however heinous our sins may be, the mercy of God in Christ can 'hide' them all, and will do this for every one who believes the gospel. 'The blood of Jesus Christ, God's Son, cleanseth from *all* sin.' Beyond all question, then, 'he which converteth a sinner from the error of his way, shall save a soul from death, and shall hide a multitude of sins.'

You cannot but feel how efficient a stimulus there is in these words to earnest, persevering, prayerful effort for the spiritual good of those around us. If we saw our neighbour carefully cultivating a tree in his garden which he took for a good apple tree, but we knew to bear fruit that was deadly poison,—or if we saw, and he did not, that his house was on fire, and, if active measures were not immediately taken, would be burned down,—we should certainly think it the dictate of common humanity to warn him. Believing, then, that sin's fruit is bitter here, and will be unutterably and unendingly bitter hereafter; believing that sinners are every day fanning a fire which, if they continue impenitent, must devour for ever, and 'burn unto the lowest hell,'—can we, standing by, remain calm and silent? Is it Christian to say, or to act as if we said, 'Am I my brother's keeper?' Certainly, my brethren, in so far as we have the 'Spirit of Christ,' we shall, as God gives us opportunity, show to the 'dead in trespasses and sins' Him who is 'the Resurrection and the Life,' feeling it to be of all delights the most exquisite 'to save a soul from death.' 'They that be wise shall shine as the brightness of the firmament, and they that turn many to righteousness as the stars for ever and ever.' Wherefore 'Let him that heareth say, Come.'

THE END.

Geneva